SPORTS in the MOVIES

by

Ronald Bergan

Proteus Books
London and New York

PROTEUS BOOKS is an imprint of
The Proteus Publishing Group

United States
PROTEUS PUBLISHING CO., INC.
733 Third Avenue
New York, N.Y. 10017
distributed by:
THE SCRIBNER BOOK COMPANIES, INC.
597 Fifth Avenue
New York, N.Y. 10017

United Kingdom
PROTEUS (PUBLISHING) LIMITED
Bremar House,
Sale Place,
London, W2 1PT.

ISBN 0 86276 031 3 (hardback)
ISBN 0 86276 017 8 (paperback)

First published in U.S. 1982
First published in U.K. 1982

Editor   Christopher Goodwin
Typeset and Designed by   AGP Typesetting Ltd.
Printed in the UK by   The Anchor Press Ltd.
Photo Credits   The Kobal Collection
                  National Film Archive/Stills Library
                  The Periodical Library (p. 35).
Photo Research   Martin Hitchcock

CONTENTS

INTRODUCTION

I see them walk by in a dream / Dempsey and Cobb and Ruth, Tunney and Sande and Jones / Johnson and Matty and Young / Alex and Tilden and Thorpe / was there a flash of youth / That gave us a list like this, when our first tributes were sung.

Grantland Rice

Sports have always been part of the American entertainment industry and their presentation is very much allied to the razzle-dazzle of show business, so it is not strange that the movies are drawn to sports as easily as Esther Williams to water. Film, more than any other art form, has used sports as its subject matter because of their visual and dramatic properties as well as their popularism. Sports create myths and heroes, the very life-force of Hollywood. These myths and heroes, unlike those of the western, are contemporary and relevant to most people's experience.

Both sports and the movies are the supreme escapist entertainments, appealing generally to the same group of people. For millions of youngsters, Saturday afternoons mean watching or playing a game, and Saturday nights mean the movies. No wonder the nostalgic charm of sports and the movies is so strong. Sports represent childhood, youth, prowess and power; and the middle-aged spectator recaptures lost time as he sits on the stands remembering the days when his body did almost everything he wanted it to do. There is no other occupation where the gap between desire and performance is so noticeable as people age. Men pride themselves on the continuation of sexual activity into old age and even boast of it, but, on the whole, sex is a private affair behind closed doors. Sports, on the other hand, are practiced in public places with people looking on. If a man wants to prove he is still youthful, this is the area in which to do it. The active life of a pro-sportsman (excluding those in less strenuous sports such as golf, bowling etc) is in human terms parallel to the life of a butterfly. No sooner is man out of the cocoon of childhood, than he is fluttering awkwardly into middle-age. This tragi-comic situation has been allayed in the movies where anything is possible in the Never-Never-land of Hollywood. The outsider, the long shot, the weakling, the underdog all have their day and ageing Peter Pans continue in athletic postures. The poignancy is not always ignored and films such as *The Set-Up* (RKO 1949), *The Swimmer* (Col. 1968), *Number One* (UA 1969), *Fat City* (Col. 1972) and *Big Wednesday* (WB 1978) have all shown the insidious creeping up of age. In two classic American plays, *Death of a Salesman* and *Cat on a Hot Tin Roof*, college football symbolises the unfulfilled hopes of youth.

Big Daddy: ...But if you still got sports in your blood, go back to sports announcin' an...

Brick: Sit in a glass box watchin' games I can't play. Describin' what I can't do while players do it? Sweatin' out their disgust and confusion in contests I'm not fit for? Drinkin' a coke, half bourbon, so I can stand it? That's no damn good anymore — time just outran me, Big Daddy — got there first.

Tennessee Williams — *Cat on a Hot Tin Roof*

Just as children play at being doctors, teachers or parents, so adults play at being children. The stadium and the movie theater are two acceptable places to do it. The average baseball or basketball game lasts as long as a movie program and for those two hours or so, the world outside is kept at bay. In the Great Depression both sports and the movies prospered. Bread-lines and circuses, you might say. Two artificial and idealized worlds with their own rules and rituals, in which, unlike real life, there is some order and meaning. The adulation that sports personalities and movie stars receive is partly due to the fact that they have succeeded within a circumscribed territory where issues are clearer and more easily grasped than in the confusion of world politics and everyday life. Spectators at a game, like the audience at a movie, are a crowd of Walter Mitties projecting themselves into the catbird seat. How many would not sell their souls to play in a major-league or be up there on the screen? In *Damn Yankees* (WB 1958), a modern-day Faust trades his soul for a chance to play ball for the Washington Senators; and many an actor or actress has done the same to reach stardom.

Sports and the movies are the two great democratic institutions in American life, and neither is really concerned with the so-called serious pursuits of existence: politics, philosophy, religion and the Arts. They are linked by an anti-intellectualism. It is only fairly recently that intellectuals began to give any earnest consideration to Hollywood at all. Basically, Hollywood has always been synonymous with mindless, crass, and meretricious mass entertainment. When the studios did treat important subjects, they managed, on the whole, to drain them of any depth, presenting the most simplistic and basic reactions to them. Both sports and the movies have been a kind of antidote to solemnity and 'high art', which is why any sociological or philosophic approach to them is generally greeted with deep suspicion. Both are the realms of the philistine. Film psychiatrists are pompous gurus or of the crazy Viennese variety, mixing up their metaphors as much as their patients. Sociologists are treated as busybodies or as bespectacled, frigid women. (Frigidity, male or female, is popularly equated with intellectualism). In the last reel they have been taught by the more laid-back characters to loosen up, take off their glasses, let down their hair and trousers. Hollywood liked uncomplicated, straight male heroes, (Clark Gable, Gary Cooper etc) which is how most Americans want to see their sportsmen and Presidents. When there were intelligent, sensitive male stars, such as Ronald Coleman, Leslie Howard or Robert Donat, they were acceptable only because they had English accents. The arts have also suffered in Hollywood's hands, making them seem hopelessly boring, stuffed-shirt, or worse, morally uplifting. Gary Cooper in *Mr Deeds Goes to Town* (1936) wins the audience's support by kicking out of his house a parasite who wishes the newly-rich Deeds to help subsidize the opera. The Marx Brothers disrupt a performance of *Il Travatore* in *A Night at the Opera* (1935), by turning the Met into Yankee stadium. Groucho sells peanuts while Harpo and Chico toss a baseball to each other over the heads of the orchestra, which breaks into 'Take me out to the Ballgame'.

The dichotomy between sports and the more refined pursuits was much enjoyed in Hollywood. This is well characterized in *Designing Woman* (MGM 1957) in which sportswriter Gregory Peck marries sophisticated fashion-designer Lauren Bacall. Similarly, the milieu of horse-racing and boxing is opposed to that of *haute couture* in *The Champ* (MGM 1979) with a child in the middle of this tug-of-war. William Holden in *Golden Boy* (Col. 1937) is the violinist who is forced to become a boxer; while in *The Leather Saint* (Par. 1955) John Derek is the priest who has to do the same. The juxtaposition in the title *The Prizefighter and the Lady* (MGM 1933) says it all. In a few of Woody Allen's favorite things in *Manhattan* (1979), he includes Mozart with Willy Mays and a version of Cole Porter's 'You're the tops', featured in *Anything Goes* (1956), has the rhyme, 'You're a Met soprano, you're Marciano'.

Given the kinship between sports and movies, how have sports been treated on screen? Do sports movies work? Film critic Andrew Sarris thinks not. For him 'Sports are now. Movies are then. Sports are news. Movies are fables.' It is true that sports, by their very nature, set themselves up against any dramatization imposed upon them. The main attraction is their unscripted topicality and the thrill of the unexpected. Sports in a movie have the air of 'a fix'. Live sports on television or in the stadium have an unwritten screenplay of greater drama and tension than many a written one, which in part makes them so attractive to people for whom art is anathema. By the same token, war, sex or a journey is more exciting and unexpected in real life than in the movies. Not to see this is to misunderstand the nature of film. One does not enter a stadium with the same expectations with which one enters a movie theater. In a live transmission on TV, the camera is an objective eye through which people 'feel' a game in different ways, depending on which side they are backing. In story-features, however, the director, if successful, can make the audience react in the same manner to what they are witnessing, thus transmuting news into fable. In any case, sports are often only one element in a movie or, as we shall see, a symbol for the human condition. Generally, sports movies are neither better nor worse than other film genres, each with their own collection of clichés.

In sports, as in most Hollywood movies, identification is primary, and it is rare to come across a spectator who views it purely objectively or esthetically. Samuel Beckett, the writer, claims that when watching cricket, of which he is a fan, he is less interested in the score than in the flight of the ball; but we of the vociferous majority feel the need to put our emotional weight behind one contestant or team. This almost physical identification with the participants goes much deeper than mere team support, it is at the very heart of the need to belong to someone, a neighborhood, a town, a city, a nation. It is even stronger when you know the players personally. The closer you are, the more involved you become. Films force an identification with the protagonists by filling in their backgrounds. We see their home life, their training, their struggles, the blood, sweat and tears; whereas their opponents are impersonal machines, or the bad guys to be defeated, or an obstacle to be overcome on the road to self-esteem. When the big fight, big game or big race ends the movie, we have been so conditioned to the winning ethic that we are like the coach on the bench willing his team on. The emotion is similar to that which you experience in the stands, although, if the film abides by most of the conventions films invariably abide by, the outcome is seldom in doubt. Nevertheless, this foreknowledge does not diminish the tension, just as we know that Errol Flynn will run Basil Rathbone through with his sword or that James Bond will outwit his current archenemy. The hero in a sports movie does not always win, because his defeat is often part of the character-building process that sports are supposed to be about. *Winning* is, of course, the name of the game and also the name of a movie in which Paul Newman is a racing driver who 'just wants to win, he doesn't

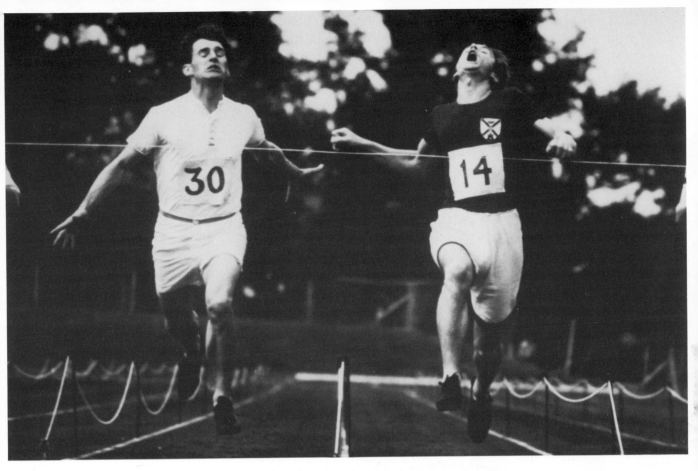

Eric Liddell (Ian Charleson) just beats Harold Abrahams (Ben Cross) (left) in *Chariots of Fire*

care what the stakes are', sacrificing his wife to that ideal. Sports are the perfect symbol for the competetive society where, to quote football coach Vince Lombardi, 'Winning isn't the most important thing — it's the only thing'. Sports are the survival of the fittest in the truest sense. Mrs Loman may plead that 'attention must be paid' to her husband Willie in *Death of a Salesman*, but there is no room in the American Dream for the loser. John Huston's explanation for the relative box-office failure of his *Fat City*, was that 'people don't care much about the spiritual processes of the defeated — but that's what it was about'. *The Bad News Bears* (1976) was a refreshing parable against the winning ethic and a good demonstration of Pierre de Coubertin's maxim, 'It's not winning that matters, it's taking part.'

Film seems to be the perfect medium for sports stories, although there have been few original screenplays. Most have been adapted from novels, short stories, plays and even poems. This is a field ploughed mainly by American writers. Mark Twain, Thomas Wolfe, Ernest Hemingway, Damon Runyon, Clifford Odets, Budd Schulberg, Paul Gallico, James Thurber, Norman Mailer, Phillip Roth and John Updike have all written extensively about sports. Despite this consecration of sports into the realms of 'literature', the movies, on the whole, have preferred to take their inspiration from the moralistic boys' novels of Horatio Alger or from the 'Muscular Christianity' school of Victorian England. There is nothing like sports in these novels for bringing out and developing the masculine virtues. Tom Brown proves to be a 'plucky youngster' on his first day at school by throwing himself into a game of football in *Tom Brown's Schooldays*. In 19th century novels, the virtuous boy triumphs over the bully by means of gentlemanly fisticuffs. Games are won by character and virtue alone and not, as in real life, by superior physical

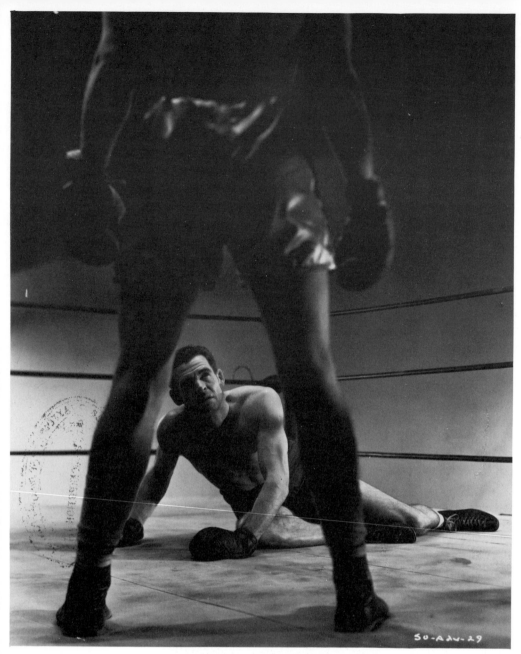

Robert Ryan in *The Set-Up*

stamina and technique. This strain runs through most sports movies, even the so-called 'hard-boiled' school. Spencer Tracy, the priest who runs *Boys' Town* (MGM 1938), thinks that most conflicts can be solved in the boxing-ring, and Pat O'Brien, the priest in *Angels with Dirty Faces* (WB 1938), feels that basketball may be the answer to street crime. Boxers refuse to take dives, jockeys will not pull a horse even at the risk of their lives.

Sports are an ideal metaphor. They are simple. Someone wins and someone loses. Most people understand that, even if the only race they take part in is the rat race. In *Chariots of Fire* (TCF 1981), Harold Abrahams (Ben Cross) had the rage to win his race at the 1924 Olympics and to beat the system, because he was an outsider, a Jew. Anti-Semitism helped push him towards the finishing line. But there is also the moral stand that comes from the refusal to play along with a system whose values are questionable, by not winning or participating. Tom Courtenay in *The Loneliness of the Long Distance Runner* (Br. Lion 1962), holds back from victory so as not to please the reform school governor, standing the moral exhortation 'Play up and play the game' on its head, while

8

Monty Clift in *From Here to Eternity* (Col. 1953) will not box for the platoon, no matter how great a pressure he is put under, for a principle.

Hollywood has not always made the distinction between the American Dream and American reality. The idea that democracy in America provides equal opportunities for all and that sports are the best demonstration of this, is embedded in the American consciousness. From the earliest silent movies to *Rocky* (UA 1976), screenplays have paid lip-service to this ideal. 'At a baseball game, we encounter real democracy of spirit,' said the Reverend Roland D. Sawyer in the thirties. The World Series and the Super Bowl may be the institutions that display all that is best in the full-blooded American male, but it is boxing that has been raised to emblematic status by the movie-makers. On one hand, it is an exemplification of America as the land of opportunity, where, if you have the athletic ability, you can fight your way out of the ghetto. (The existence of the ghetto is seldom questioned.) On the other hand, it is the American Dream gone awry. The boxers' battered faces are like the features of the All-American boy as seen in a distorting mirror. Boxing has been shown as a microcosm of a dog-eat-dog society, a symptom of capitalism or as the individual trying to survive in an iniquitous system. It is not for nothing that Brecht set his singspiel *The Rise and Fall of the City of Mahogonny* in and around a boxing ring. Mahogonny is a decadent city and the chorus sings 'First, remember, comes your belly, then the whoring act, and don't forget there's boxing and guzzling per contract.' There are few pro pro-boxing pictures and almost all of the dramas could end in the same way as *The Harder They Fall* (Col. 1965) with the sentence 'Professional boxing should be banned even if it takes an Act of Congress to do it.'

Allied to the worship of the concepts of Youth and Success in American life, is the idealization of the He-man. In the movies, sports are revealed as a reinforcement of the theory that it's a man's world where men are men and women are...nowhere. In the innumerable college movies of the twenties and thirties, football seems to be the main pursuit of the male students, while the females spend their time as cheerleaders or falling for or resisting the quarterback. Women are invariably seen in reaction shots to men's actions. Boxing being 'the last gladiatorial sport', has many a damsel clutching her bodice in distress at the ring-side at Madison Square Garden. Matches have been won or lost because of her presence or absence. An empty seat in the second row has done more damage to screen boxers than any right cross. Good women inspire men to physical triumph, floozies destroy them. To be strictly kosher, beefcake and cheesecake don't mix. In sports movies, if women did not exist, there would be no need to invent them. They foul up relationships. They come between a boxer and his manager in *Kid Galahad* (1937 and 1962), between a man and his horse in *Maryland* (1940), and between a man and his car in *Grand Prix* (MGM 1966), to give only a few examples. Two women, however, cannot be excluded from a study of sports in the movies. They are Sonja Henie, queen of the ice, and Esther Williams, prima ballerina of the water.

There are occasions when women enter the male ranks and severely bruise macho pride. Unfortunately, any attempt at a criticism of gender superiority is mitigated by the end. Barbra Streisand literally throws in the towel in *The Main Event* (WB 1979), and in *Pat and Mike* (1952), Katharine Hepburn, who saved Spencer Tracy from two hoodlums, pretends to need his male protection in order to keep him. Esther

Williams takes over a baseball team in *Take me out to the Ball Game* (MGM 1949), and she can't even hold a bat. Gene Kelly is only too pleased to show her. The same Gene Kelly is slighted by Cyd Charisse when she takes 'the male initiative' in *It's Always Fair Weather* (MGM 1955). She can also recite the names of all the heavyweight champs since John L. Sullivan, which shows that 'she's afraid to be a woman'. Mind you, Tatum O'Neal proves she's as good or as bad as any boy ball-player in *The Bad News Bears* (1976). When Paul Newman discovers that the owner of his ice-hockey team in *Slap-Shot* (1977) is a woman, he advises her to get herself a man otherwise her son will grow up a 'faggot'. There is only one thing worse than being a woman in the jock world and that is being a 'fag'. The only sport poor John Kerr plays at school in *Tea and Sympathy* (MGM 1956) is tennis, but he beats his opponents, not by superior strength or fitness, but by putting a spin on the ball, thus proving to his father (Edward Andrews) that he's a 'sissy'. In *The One and Only* (1978), a wrestling promoter bemoans 'My son, talk about fruits. I bought him a football and he decorated it.' However, Jack Cole, the dance director, playing a modern ballet-dancer in *Designing Woman*, after getting some pretty suspicious looks from Gregory Peck and his sporting cronies, turns out to be a hard nut rather than a fruit by knocking out tough gangsters with some nifty high kicks.

Contained within the machismo ethos is a basis of violence. Sports are often reckoned as a yardstick of general behavior. As violence in the streets increases, so coactively does violence in sports and in the movies. Of course football has always had built-in violence, which is believed to be its particular attraction, but in Britain sports such as soccer, rugby and even cricket have become more dangerous. Audiences have now come to expect the same violence in films, which accounts for the tremendous popularity of the Kung Fu 'chop socky' movies over the last decade starring Bruce Lee and clones. Violence to an unprecedented degree is found in films like *Slap-Shot, The Longest Yard* (Par. 1974), *Death Race 2000* (New World 1975) and *Raging Bull* (UA 1980), in which players speak dirty and play dirty. The inherent violence in sports has only recently been explored on the screen, although boxing has always been presented as a gruelling sport. Football injuries (there are over 15 deaths a year in the USA) were mostly treated rather lightly or comically, e.g. *The Freshman* (Pathe 1925), *Horse Feathers* (Par. 1932), *That's My Boy* (Par. 1951). *Rollerball* (UA 1975) demonstrates the ultimate in contact sport. The final game has no rules and no time limit. One plays to kill. It is science fiction, but as in all the best science fiction, it is a logical conclusion to trends noticeable in contemporary life. What did this new violence on the screen matter in the seventies, when the most violent game of all was being played in Vietnam? Will the very last sports picture-show star Ronald Reagan?

Sportsmen are usually so unsmiling in praise of the manly virtues that sports have always provided comedy with a theme as a general reaction against machismo and violence. Comics are not generally known for their physical prowess and Chaplin, Lloyd and Keaton were rather puny individuals. By placing a weedy figure in a sports situation, one creates comic incongruity. If one aspect of humor is the disparity between human aspiration and performance, then sports would seem to offer a rich vein of comedy. However, the reverse is generally true of the best comedies, when the comedian far outstrips in performance any aspiration he may have had. Chaplin makes sure he gets a crack at the title in *The Champion*

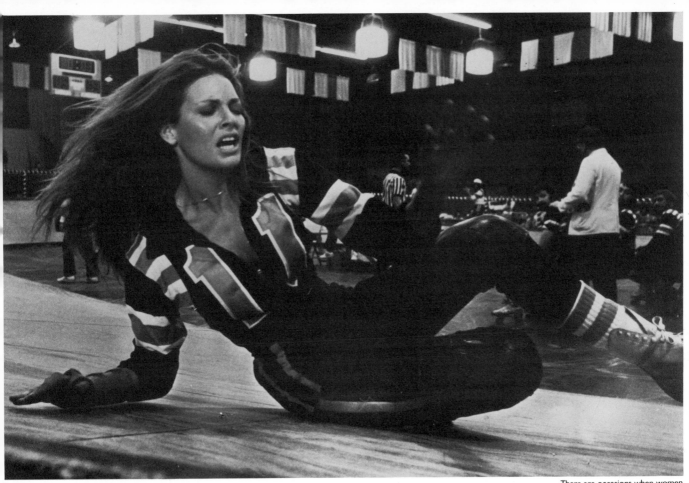

(1915) by putting a horse-shoe in one of his gloves. Buster Keaton unwittingly breaks every track record in *College* (UA 1927) in an attempt to get to his girl-friend in a hurry. Danny Kaye's milksop milkman becomes world middleweight champion in *The Kid from Brooklyn* (Goldwyn 1946) mainly through being able to duck more quickly than anyone else. Others such as The Marx Brothers, Lou Costello and Jerry Lewis, have won matches and races by means of a series of unbelievable incidents that make nonsense of the theory that in sports you need guts, strength, fitness, dedication and skill. The comic is the classic coward and weakling with none of the attributes required of a champion. All he needs is luck or ingenuity or, like Christy Mahon in Synge's play *The Playboy of the Western World*, to be convinced that he is the hero people imagine him to be.

It is not only in zany comedies that authenticity takes a tumble. If outsiders won as much as they do on the screen, most bookies would be bankrupt. It's a sure bet that in any race the underdog (or horse) will win. This is epitomized in *National Velvet* (MGM 1944) where Elizabeth Taylor as an inexperienced twelve-year-old girl wins the most arduous race in the world on an equally inexperienced horse. In *Breaking Away* (TCF 1979) a depleted and bruised cycle team from the wrong side of the tracks trounce their superbly fit WASP rivals. In this fantasy world, unknown stumblebums like Rocky can fight a draw with the world heavyweight boxing champion, and Dean Paul Martin is in the Wimbledon final against Guilermo Vilas in *Players* (Par. 1979).

Alfred Hitchcock defined drama as 'life with the boring bits left out'. Sports in the movies are handled like that. Every moment is the Big One. A match or contest is a series of climaxes. There is no room for the

11

niceties of the sport. Every round must have a knockdown, every inning a homer. The sound of a boxing glove meeting stubbly chin has to be amplified ten fold. Boxers rise from blows to flatten Superman and dance around again after catching sight of their girl rooting for them. Dirty tricks, like rubbing resin in the opponent's eyes, so obvious to every spectator, are not seen by a vigilant ref. In horse racing, jockeys use the whip unscrupulously on rivals or pull a horse so blatantly that any disciplinary committee would be wearing blinkers not to see it. An auto-car race would not be a race without the cremation of a driver. Football and baseball games are only won in the last seconds. Watching sports in the movies is similar to listening only to the *fortissimo* passages from a symphony or, if you prefer, having sex with orgasm alone and no foreplay.

The biographical pictures of sports stars are not much more factual than their fictional counterparts. Life imitating art is usually more convincing than art imitating life. In sports biopics, we are at least spared the inane anachronisms and crass philistinism we find in those of historical figures or great artists. (Don Ameche as Alexander Graham Bell, Greer Garson as Madame Curie, Charleton Heston as Michelangelo etc.) But how much truth remains in the filmed lives of Babe Ruth (William Bendix), Lou Gehrig (Gary Cooper), Jim Thorpe (Burt Lancaster), Rocky Graziano (Paul Newman), Knute Rockne (Pat O'Brien), Annette Kellerman (Esther Williams), Jake La Motta (Robert De Niro) or George Gipp and G.C. Alexander (both played by the incumbent President of the USA)? How many actors can carry out even an approximation of what made the great masters of sports? It is like a non-ballet dancer attempting the role of Pavlova. As a rule, with a lot of help from their friends in the cutting room and from stuntmen, most actors do passable imitations of sportsmen. Many received expert coaching from the champions themselves. The Babe was on hand for many baseball sagas and Jake La Motta is said to have done 1,000 rounds of sparring with Robert De Niro. Inevitably, a number of stars have shone at sports. Paul Newman (*Winning* 1969) and Steve McQueen (*Le Mans* Cinema Center 1971) were both experienced race drivers; Errol Flynn and Robert Ryan could handle themselves in the ring; and Johnny Weissmuller and Esther Williams were champion swimmers. Nevertheless, despite some attempts at veracity, film makers have concentrated more on the nineteenth hole, the *aprés ski*, the second half-time. The subjects for bios have inveterately been chosen, not for the talents that made them into sporting heroes, but for some deficiency or disability that put a blight on their careers. The drama inherent in the sporting event itself is not enough for the screenplay, thus the conflict on the field or in the ring must reflect another conflict outside it. In *The Pride of the Yankees* (RKO 1942), Lou Gehrig's Big C seems not to stand for the Cardinals or the catcher; Monty Stratton (James Stewart) in *The Stratton Story* (MGM 1949) continues to play in the big leagues after having a leg amputated; Jim Piersall (Anthony Perkins) goes insane in *Fear Strikes Out* (Par. 1956); Ben Hogan (Glenn Ford) in *Follow the Sun* (TCF 1951) struggles against car crash injuries; and Ronald 'Where's the rest of me?' Reagan suffers from double vision and epilepsy as G.C. Alexander in *The Winning Team* (WB 1952). It is difficult to imagine biopics of, say, Gene Tunney, Sugar 'Ray' Robinson, Ted Williams, Jim Brown or Bill Russell, unless they have some skeletons in their lockers.

Many of the more candidly fictionalized accounts of the lives of sportspersons, such as *North Dallas 40* (Par. 1979), *Bang the Drum Slowly* (Par. 1973) and *The Set-Up*, get nearer to the specific gravity of the sport than those disguised as truth. The biopictorial method of *Dawn* (1975), an Australian film based on the life of Olympic swimming champion Dawn Fraser, seems to have come closest to an actual life lived. The semi-documentary, *The Greatest* (1977) with a portly Muhammad Ali playing himself in the title role and a young actor (Phillip 'Chip' McAllister) as Cassius Clay, made the fight game look less exciting and far less dangerous than a game of tiddliwinks. Sports reach their apotheosis on the screen in two great documentaries on the Olympic Games, Leni Riefenstahl's *Olympia* (1938) and Kon Ichikawa's *Tokyo Olympiad* 1964. There is little here of the sports most of us experience as a weekend diversion or even of the sports we have come to recognize from the movies.

American sports such as football and baseball have become known throughout the world because of the movies, but as games they have been virtually unexportable. Does cricket say something about the British or bull-fighting about the Spanish? We see each sport emerging with its own image from a study of the way it has been treated on film. The image makers have partly created the image and partly reflected it. Sports as an integral element of social life, illuminate much of the character of a people. Their depiction in the movies, aside from purely entertainment value, provides insights into the psychology of a nation.

BOXING

More films have been made about boxing than any other sport. It is plainly the moviemaker's favorite and, presumably, the public's as well. What are the reasons for the screen's continual fascination with the fight game? Why has the subject attracted directors of the stature of Alfred Hitchcock, Rouben Mamoulian, King Vidor, Robert Wise, Mark Robson, John Huston, Luchino Visconti and Martin Scorsese? Why have writers from George Bernard Shaw to Norman Mailer written about it with such feeling? What possible satisfaction can anyone get from the unedifying spectacle of two men attempting to bash each other's brains out? Is it a requisite blood-letting rite to appease the savage god within us?

In purely cinematic terms, it is easier to frame two people in conflict on the screen than to encompass the sometimes complex pattern of a team game, or a race where what is happening behind the leader can be equally significant. Boxing provides a clear-cut one-to-one dramatic situation. The issues are well-defined, the iconography easy to read. Man is seen at his most elemental, stripped bare, literally and figuratively, with only his fists to defend himself against an equally unarmed opponent. He is the naked ape at his most vulnerable, hemmed in by that strange oxymoron the 'square ring'. There is no room to hide within that well-lit space. If you box badly, you pay for it with your blood. Fear hovers over the ring as much as cigar-smoke. Before the bell rings, the fighters seek out fear in the other's eyes. Former world light-heavyweight champion, Archie Moore, said 'Show me a fighter who's not afraid, and I'll show you a fighter that's easy to beat.' Around the ring is the mob baying for blood. They have not come to see the Noble Art of Self-Defence. They have come to see the knockout, the most unequivocal result in all

THE CHAMPION:
> This is the land of opportunity. Everybody's got a chance to win.

THE PROMOTER:
> It's very American.

THE CHAMPION:
> It's very smart.

Rocky
(UA 1976)

sports.

Boxing is a drama played out under strict rules as ritualised as the final shootout in a western. The boxer is as much of a loner as Gary Cooper in *High Noon* (1952) or Alan Ladd in *Shane* (1953), facing the enemy on behalf of the townsfolk or homesteaders. Boxers are our own modern-day surrogate avengers and we are the townsfolk clustered around the ring, willing him on but refusing to help. Sometimes he takes on the aspirations of a whole race such as Joe Louis, Muhammad Ali, or Jack Johnson as portrayed in *The Great White Hope* (TCF 1970), John Garfield as the Jewish boxer in *Body and Soul* (UA 1947) or Rocky Graziano (Paul Newman) in *Somebody Up There Likes Me* (MGM 1956) who has all the little people from the lower East Side pinning their hopes on him. From slave ship or immigration ship to championship.

There are easier ways of getting rich than boxing, but for

some it is the only way out of the ghetto. It was either the ring or the stage. When Rocky's girl-friend (Talia Shire) in *Rocky* asks Rocky (Sylvester Stallone) why he wants to fight, he replies, 'Because I can't sing or dance.' In *Somebody Up There Likes Me*, little Sal Mineo, on the run from the police, asks his now famous and respectable boyhood pal, Rocky Graziano (Paul Newman), 'We ain't got a chance, guys like us, do we?' The answer to his question is supposed to lie in Graziano's positive example, but Mineo cannot fight, nor sing nor dance, therefore nobody up there likes him.

Because everybody loves the story of Cinderella, the dream factory has been in the rags-to-riches trade since its beginnings. Unfortunately, for every Cinderella that marries the prince, there are thousands that end up with the impoverished woodcutter, and for every boxer who gets into the big time, there are thousands who end up without

a cent. The fairy story is an effective sop thrown to the have-nots to passify their discontent. That this dream of glory and riches is an illusory one, is well expressed in movies such as *The Set-Up* (RKO 1949), *The Harder They Fall* (Col. 1956), and *Fat City* (Col. 1972). It is easy to make the analogy between prize-fighting and prostitution. Whereas most other sports are generally done for love, pro-boxing is done for money. The manager is a pimp, the gym the brothel, the crowd the clients and so on. Is it a coincidence that George Bernard Shaw's novel on prizefighting *Cashel Byron's Profession* (1886) should have a similar title to his play on prostitution called *Mrs Warren's Profession*? In 1901 in his preface to the novel, Shaw wrote, 'The intelligent prize-fighter is not a knight-errant: he is a disillusioned man of business trying to make money at a certain weight and at certain risks, not of bodily injury but of pecuniary loss. The unintelligent prizefighter is often the helpless tool of a gang or gamblers, backers and showmen, who set him on to fight as they might set on a dog.'

Money, money, money is what makes the boxing world go round. The boxer is a round peg in a square ring, manipulated by others for profit. Toro (Mike Lane), the gentle giant in *The Harder They Fall* is left with 49 dollars and 7 cents out of a million-dollar gate. The prize-fighter does the fighting and the manager gains the prize. Boxers were the property of their managers as much as many of the actors playing them were the property of the studio bosses.

Money is the *leitmotif* of *Body and Soul* in which John Garfield is 'not just a kid who can fight. He's money.' In *The Magic Christian* (Commonwealth United 1970), Peter Sellers as trillionaire Guy Grand, creates havoc as he goes around the USA proving that everybody will do any-

14

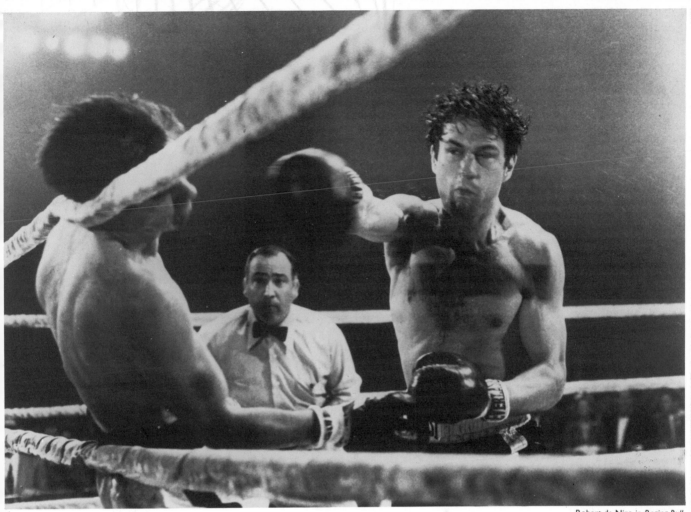

thing for money. He gets the heavyweight champion of the world and his challenger to prance around the ring in an effeminate manner during a bout. After mincing out of their corners and slapping each other with flapping wrists, the Champ succumbs to a feeble flurry from the challenger and lies sobbing on the canvas. It is, in fact, the money involved in professional boxing linking it with crime that gives it a sordid fascination. There is hardly a boxing picture which doesn't include a crook or two in the cast. Whatever the reality, the gangster in the movies is never far away from the fight-game. He is the third man in the fighter's corner. It is also the easiest game to fix, although the majority of heroes in boxing dramas are inclined to put pride before a fall and would rather suffer the consequences, like having their hands broken, than permit themselves to take a dive.

No matter how alluring boxing has been to film-makers as a subject of great dramatic potential and tragic dimensions or as a symbol which provides insights into society, its essential violence cannot be ignored. The attraction of violence and the abhorrence of it are two sides of the same coin, and the duality of sex and violence goes some way to explaining the ambivalent emotions that many people have towards the sport. 'The ring like all romantic institutions has a natural attraction for hysterical people,' wrote George Bernard Shaw and eighty years later, Martin Scorsese was to say about his *Raging Bull* (UA 1980), 'The ring is a kind of madness, and it seems to me that the man (Jake La Motta) had to go back through his mother's womb again in order to achieve some kind of sanity. My picture's really about that process, not boxing.' Whatever one's doubts about this statement and the demonstration of it in the film, it does reveal something about the link between sexuality and violence of which boxing is one 'acceptable' manifestation. Jake La Motta (Robert De Niro) is a paranoic as exhibited by his jealous ravings towards his wife (Cathy Moriarty) whom he loves neither wisely nor too well. The deficiency he feels in himself is further revealed when he claims to have 'girl's hands' and bemoans the fact that, as a middleweight, he can never fight the heavyweight champ, Joe Louis. La Motta works up a rage against opponent Tony Janiro, because he's convinced his wife finds the young fighter attractive. Asked how he feels about the fight, La Motta replies that Janiro is so good-looking he doesn't know whether to fuck him or fight him. Thus the opponent in the ring is not only the rival but the lover. After the brutal fight, De Niro's La Motta struts around the ring with arms raised and boasts to his wife, 'He ain't pretty no more.' The real Jake La Motta once commented to Norman Mailer that Mailer would never make a boxer as he wasn't queer enough. Whatever interpretation one puts on the word, whether it has sexual undertones or whether it just means odd or insane, it gave Scorsese a clue as to how to make the picture in which psychological rather than social questions are posed. Both *Raging Bull* and *Champion* (UA 1949), which tells of a ruthless and over-ambitious prize-fighter (Kirk Douglas), say more about the leading protagonists than about the fight-game.

Allied to Scorsese's comment above, is Wilhelm Reich's view that the fantasies that a man can have in sexual intercourse of a 'return to the mother's womb' are pathological and that repressed sexuality turns into aggression or anxiety. Aggression takes on some of the overtones of sexuality it replaces and hence we have sadism. Reich goes on to 'prove' that aggression is caused by sexual deprivation by referring to the common assumption that, because it gratifies aggressive instincts, professional athletes should not have sexual intercourse before competing as it diminishes athletic powers. There is an amusing scene in *The Main Event* (WB 1979) when Barbra Streisand tries to get Ryan O'Neil to have sex with her on the night before a big fight. 'What about the ills of sex before a fight?' he asks. 'You don't believe that crap, do you?' she replies. (In *Rocky*, our hero steers well clear of his girl-friend while training for the championship thus benefitting from his storage of strength.)

For Jake La Motta, the ring does not seem to provide an outlet for violence, but a continuation of the violence outside it. In *The Iron Man* (UI 1951), Jeff Chandler literally wishes to kill his opponents, but away from boxing he's a regular guy. For Paul Newman in *Somebody Up There Likes Me*, the ring is a fine place in which to vent his spleen. He's told by the army coach, 'You've got what a lot of fighters don't have. Hate. Let your hate do some good for you.' The same Paul Newman gives a display of excessive masochism in *Cool Hand Luke* (WB 1967) when faced with the massive George Kennedy in a boxing match in a prison camp. Kennedy's gloves keep coming at him, but Newman will not give in. The fight goes on and on, as Newman goes down again and again only to rise once more. The fight ends with neither of them being able to raise their gloves above their waists. Masochism is here interpreted as the invincible spirit of Luke.

In the movies, women are generally shown as having a restraining influence on men's violence. Audrey Totter in *The Set-Up* leaves Robert Ryan, because she cannot stand the mental and physical battering he takes. Pier Angeli in *Somebody Up There Likes Me* sees the fight-game as full of 'meanness, blood and ignorance'. The three women in *Body and Soul* react in different ways to John Garfield's career. Good girl Lilli Palmer leaves him when she sees the corrupting influence on him; bad girl Hazel Brooks shouts for Garfield to kill his opponent, and his Jewish mother (Anne Revere) says 'Prize-fighting? That's a sport?' Boxing movies may describe the world of men and male values, but it is the women in the background that give them meaning.

Understandably, the movies have gone for the more sensational aspects of boxing. Dramatic sluggers who take a lot of punishment but retain the ability to land a knockout blow have been highlighted as opposed to men who are quite spectacular in the art of defending themselves and building

up a points lead with skill and technique. Rarely is boxing seen as the Noble Art it can so often be. *Gentleman Jim* (WB 1942) is one of the few exceptions. Most of the time it has been treated not as a sport, but as a racket. Boxing has provided material for slapstick comedies, gangster movies, *films noirs*, musicals and social conscience pictures. Whichever way one looks at it, boxing has attained a mystique that Hollywood has helped to perpetuate.

The general public was able to witness a prize-fight on screen for the very first time only four years after Edison had introduced his Kinetograph to the world. It was the 1897 Jim Corbett-Bob Fitzsimmons fight which, according to one film historian 'was to bring the odium of pugilism upon the screen all across Puritan America.' (This fight is well recreated in *City of Badmen* — TCF 1953.) Prizefighting on film brought further opprobrium from the establishment in 1910 when Jack Johnson beat James J. Jeffries for the heavyweight championship of the world. A Federal law was passed that barred 'any film or other pictorial representation of any prizefight' intended for showing to the public. This might have had something to do with the fact that Johnson was the first black fighter to beat a white one for the championship. The church and the community thought the film could lead to racial conflict. (Some of this atmosphere is caught in *The Great White Hope* — TCF 1970.)

Boxing may have been a serious business, but in the silent era it was often used as a comic set-piece. *The Knockout* (Keystone 1914) is a hilarious Mack Sennett two-reeler in which Charlie Chaplin plays a referee in a fight between Fatty Arbuckle and Edgar Kennedy. Charlie is a frightened little fellow caught between two giants in a farcical ballet. Chaplin returned to boxing in *The Champion* (Essanay 1915), this time as a would-be pugilist. He takes it up because he is hungry and has a pug dog to support. Charlie immediately becomes challenger for the title held by Young Hippo. In the silent comedies, nobody seemed to bother about enormous weight differences. Flyweights regularly took on

heavyweights without a murmur. Part of the pleasure derived from comic boxing is the enjoyment of seeing the little man (most of us) defeat the big bruiser in an anti-Charles Atlas fantasy. Charlie, obviously a flyweight, trains for the championship on beer. The atmosphere of the big fight is well captured as the animated spectators surround a small ring. Charlie proves wily enough to escape Young Hippo, kicking him when his huge opponent's back is turned. Each time one of them scores a knockdown, he bows and parades to the crowd. Hippo holds Charlie steady with one hand so he can hit him with the other, but Charlie's dog saves him by ringing the bell. Finally, when Charlie looks like losing, his dog rushes into the ring, gets his teeth into the seat of Hippo's pants and pulls him down. Both boxers are out for the count, but Charlie is first to stagger to his feet and is declared the new champion. Lloyd Bacon (later to direct *42nd Street* etc) plays the trainer and Edna Purviance, his daughter. So successful was this bout that Chaplin decided to use many of the same gags 16 years later in *City Lights*.

The other great silent film comedian, Buster Keaton, also put on boxing gloves in *Battling Butler* (Schenk 1924). Keaton often claimed it to be his favorite film and it is interesting to try to understand why. Buster plays a soft, little rich boy who goes camping in the mountains with his valet ('Snitz' Edwards) and all modern conveniences. He meets a beautiful mountain girl whom he wishes to marry, but her father and brother greet the proposal with derision. 'That jelly fish couldn't take care of himself — let alone a wife. We don't want any weaklings in our family.' In order to help the situation, the valet boasts that Buster is really the world lightweight contender who just happens to have the same name, Alfred Butler. Buster is forced to play along although the only gloves he's ever worn are kid gloves. Preparing for his fight against the Alabama Murderer at a training camp, Buster gets himself hopelessly entwined in the ropes, and tries to protect himself from his sparring partner only in the places where he has just been hit. This is Keaton at his best with those

spaniel eyes expressing innocence and bewilderment. He doesn't have to fight the Alabama Murderer after all. Unbeknown to Buster, who is waiting nervously in the dressing-room, his name-sake is in the ring with the Murderer. It is when 'Battling' Butler returns to the dressing-room triumphant that things turn nasty. The sadistic champion, who suspects Buster has been making eyes at his wife, begins to punch him. This would have wiped the smile off his face if Keaton ever smiled. But Buster, due to anger and love for his girl, suddenly finds untapped strength. The fight becomes serious and breaks the film's comic surface. The blows are real and painful. The subjective camera brings the spectator into the fight. Buster delivers a left to the jaw and a right to the stomach and then a right to the jaw which lays the champion out. In a frenzy, Buster continues to strike the unconscious man until he has to be pulled off. This scene leaves a bitter taste in the mouth which is hardly dispelled by the charming ending. Wearing a top hat, frock coat and swinging a cane, Buster leads his girl through the city streets. The camera pulls back to reveal that he is still wearing his boxing trunks. The brutal and prolonged locker-room fight that precedes this ending is certainly disorienting in such a genial context. It is as if Keaton, conscious of his small stature, wanted to prove that he could beat a bigger man in a fight in all seriousness, and he could only demonstrate this by dropping his comic mask.

Warner Bros. starred Monte Blue in *Hogan's Alley* (1925) and *One-Round Hogan* (1927) the first of many boxing dramas they were to issue. The first had the hero refusing to use his fist on the villain as he might injure his hand for the forthcoming championship, and the second had Hogan holding back in the ring, because a friend of his had been killed in a fight. Needless to say, he lets himself go in the final round of the movie. The silent comedies and dramas set the pattern for all the boxing films to come.

The Ring (British International Pictures 1927) was considered by one critic at the time as 'the most magnificent British film ever made'. As it

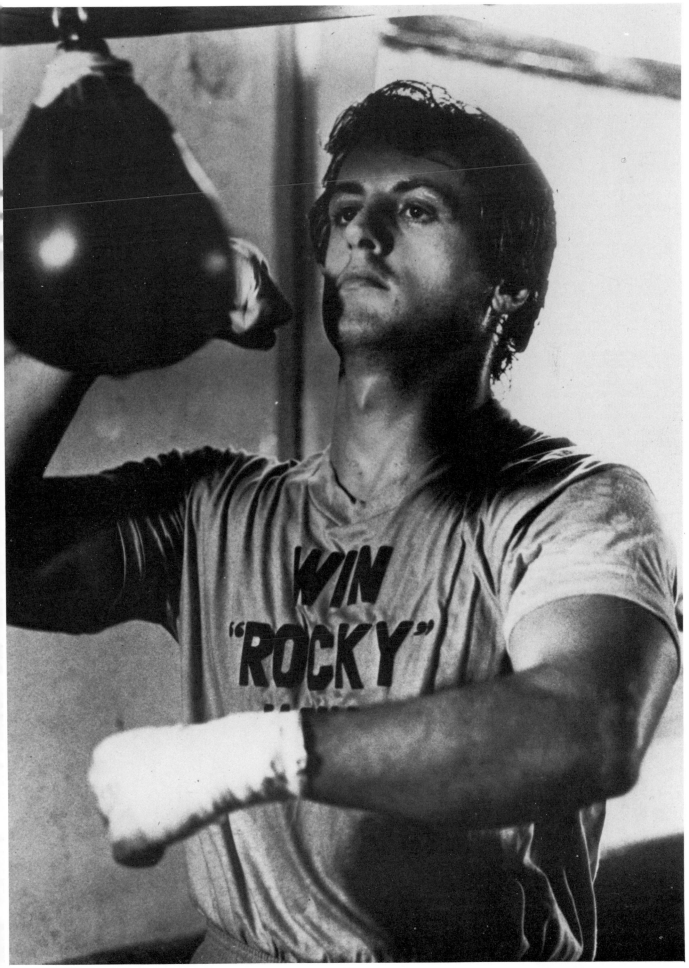

was directed by Alfred Hitchcock this is not surprising. The story concerns a fighter (Carl Brisson) who is discovered in a side-show by the reigning champ (Ian Hunter). When he starts to earn good money in the professional ranks, he is able to marry his girl-friend from the fun fair, although she rather fancies the champion. The champion has given her a snake-bracelet which she continues to wear. As the wedding ring is put on her finger, the bracelet falls down over her wrist from where it had been hidden under her sleeve. The film is full of obvious visual symbols of this kind. The title refers to the boxing ring, the wedding ring and the bracelet. The wife goes out with the champion and the husband's jealousy is aroused. The final fight uses the boxing ring as a place where the husband's honor can be satisfied as he faces his rival. The plot (an original screenplay by Hitchcock and Eliot Stannard) may be melodramatic, but the background against which it is set is full of delightful details and movement. There is an almost documentary approach to the fairground and fight scenes. Hitchcock often used to go to the Albert Hall for the big fights, where he noticed the habit of pouring a bottle of champagne over a fighter to revive him, an incident which he used in the film.

Charlie Chaplin managed to ignore the coming of sound in 1927 and continued to make silent films (with sound effects and music) until 1940. By refurbishing material from *The Knockout* and *The Champion*, he created one of the great comic boxing scenes in *City Lights* (UA 1931). In order to provide money for the blind flower girl (Virginia Cherrill), Charlie accepts a fight to make some easy money. All he has to do is lie down after a couple of rounds. Unfortunately, his opponent with whom he had made this arrangement is replaced at the last moment by a massive fellow who challenges Charlie on a winner-take-all basis. Before the fight, Charlie tries to make friends with his opponent in the dressing room. He smiles and moves his head from side to side coyly, grasping his knee in his hands like a pin-up girl. These rather effeminate overtures of friendship shock the tough boxers around him. His opponent retreats behind a curtain to

change into his boxing trunks. The gag is executed so brilliantly that even without understanding the homosexual implications, its very innocence provides laughter. In the ring, Charlie realises that he must keep away from his adversary at all costs. He does this by keeping the ref between himself and the pugilist and by dancing around the ring. The whole fight is choreographed at great speed, but finally his opponent catches up with him and Charlie is knocked out, and so must find other means of helping the blind girl. The boxing match provides a marvellous counterpoint to the rather over-sentimental tale that contains it.

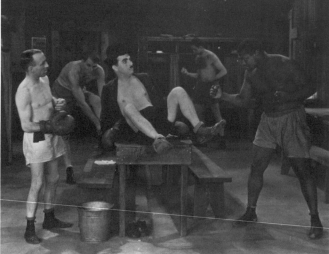

Charlie Chaplin in *City Lights*

The Iron Man (U 1931 — Remade in 1951) was one of the first boxing talkies. Directed by Tod Browning, it concerned a swollen-headed boxer (Lew Ayres) married to gold-digger Jean Harlow. By being ko'd in his last bout, he gains a sense of proportion, but loses Harlow, who didn't really love him anyway. Jean Harlow, who had a small part in *City Lights*, was being given a big publicity buildup in 1931 and appeared in no less than six films that year. Made between *Dracula* and *Freaks*, it seemed just a chore for Browning, although the fights did generate some excitement.

MGM entered the pugilistic stakes with *The Champ* (1931 — Remade in 1979), a maudlin tale of an ex-prizefighter (Wallace Beery) and his small son (Jackie Cooper) trying to scrape a living in Tijuana, Mexico. Beery is addicted to gambling and drink but, because of the faith of his son in him, he

decides to get himself back into shape for a comeback. His wife (Irene Rich) left him some years before but now decides to rescue her child from what she considers to be an unsuitable upbringing. He wins his comeback fight by knocking out a Mexican, but the terrible beating he has taken in the process, causes him to collapse and die in the dressing room in his son's arms. The best parts of the film (directed by King Vidor) are those involving the colorful world of the racetrack, boxing arenas and bars around which 'The Champ' and his little boy drift. Less good is the tension between the bourgeois wife and the vagabond father. Wallace Beery emerg-

ed in the movie from his previous roles as a heavy into the good-bad ugly guy. He won an Oscar for his warm-hearted performance.

A year before Max Baer became world heavyweight champion, he took the lead in *The Prizefighter and the Lady*

(MGM 1933 — *Every Woman's Man* GB). Baer, who was always considered a clown in the ring, turned out to be a natural. Former world champs, Jess Willard, Jim Jeffries and Jack Dempsey also make appearances, proving that there is something of the actor in all pugilists (and sometimes vice versa). The plot involves Baer falling for high-class gangster's moll, Myrna Loy, and ends with a match between Baer and the actual world champion at the time, Primo Carnera. Baer and Carnera were to meet in a real championship seven months later. In the film they fight a draw, but in reality Max gave Carnera a beating, clowning as always. Carnera was knocked down eleven times in eleven rounds before being stopped. The mock fight is the most interesting section of the film and a real curiosity for fight fans.

Palooka (UA 1934 — *The Great Schnozzle* GB) was inspired by Ham Fisher's comic book creation, Joe Palooka. Joe (Stuart Erwin) falls for vamp (Lupe Velez), who changes her lovers depending on their success in the ring. Without any prelims, Palooka is matched with the world champ through the finagling of his crooked manager, Jimmy Durante. He manages to win the championship because his opponent (played by James Cagney's brother, William) is

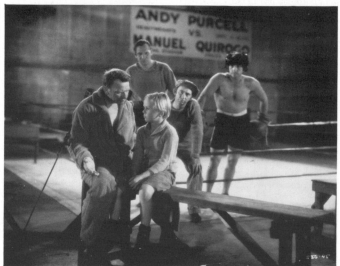

Above: Wallace Beery and Jackie Cooper in *The Champ* (1932)

Carl Brisson (center) in *The Ring*

Overleaf: Jon Voight and Ricky Schroder in *The Champ* (1979)

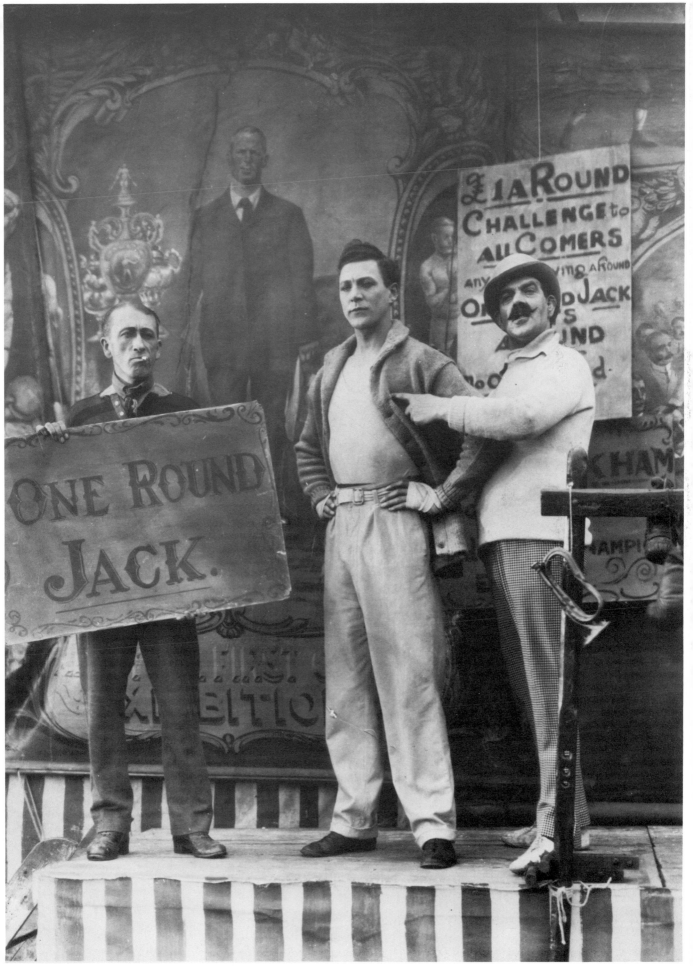

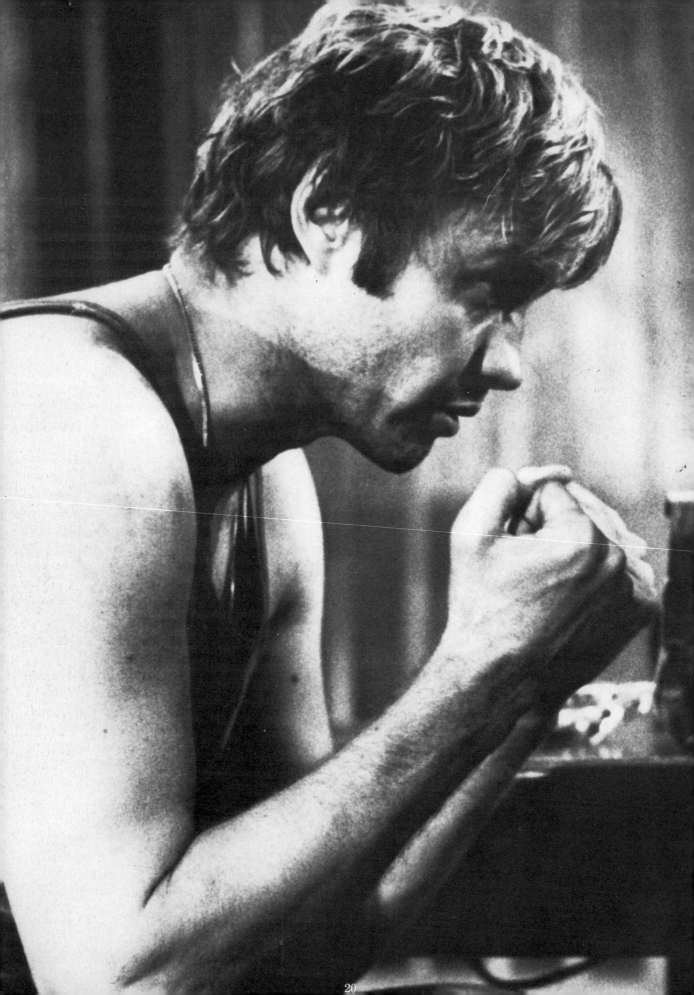

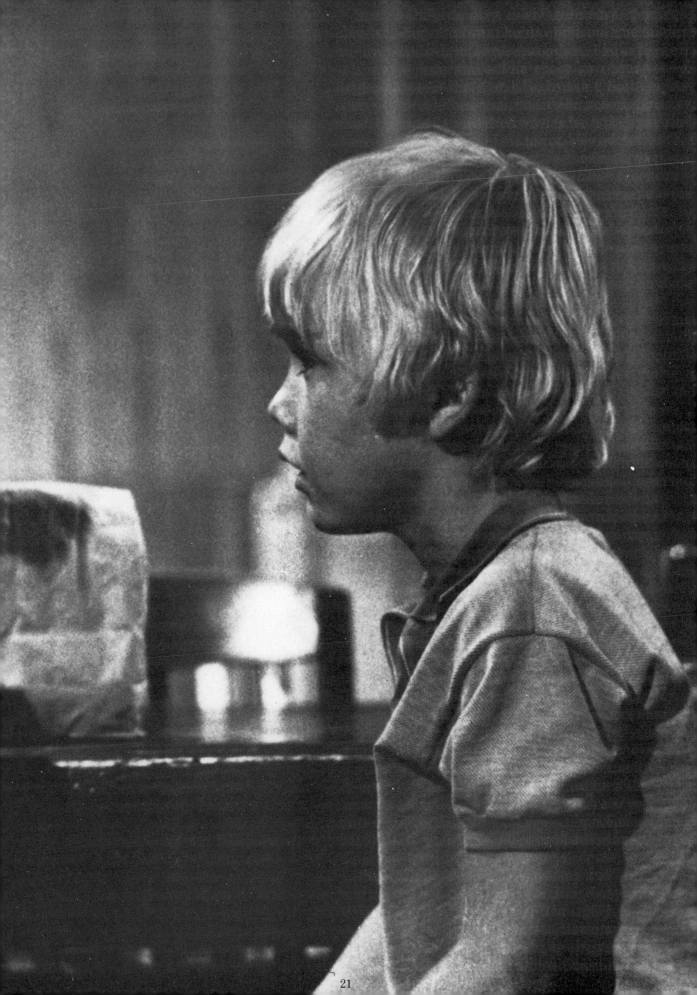

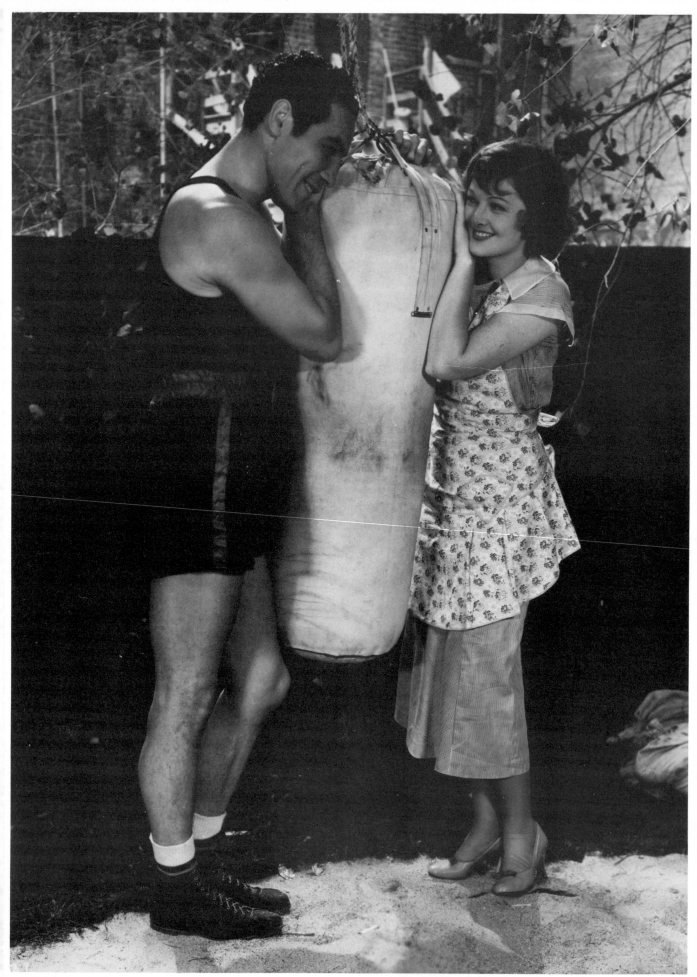

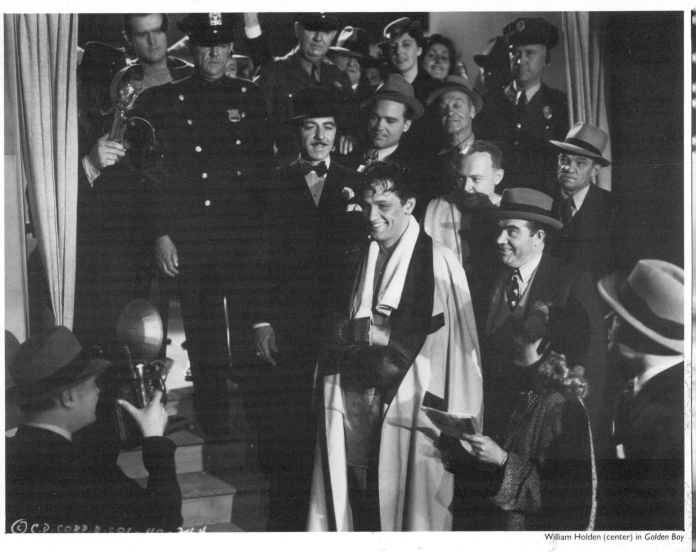

William Holden (center) in *Golden Boy*

too drunk to stand up when hit. 'It's a neclipse!' cries Schnozzle.

A drunken fighter also appeared in *The Irish in Us* (WB 1935), when fight promoter James Cagney has to step into the ring because one of his boxers has been ko'd by booze. Both Cagney and his brother and trainer Pat O'Brien are in love with the same girl (Olivia de Havilland). In the final fight lasting 15 minutes of screen time, Cagney is taking a beating until Pat whispers during rounds that it is Cagney that Olivia really loves. This love and the Irish in him seems to produce extra hate for his opponent and he wins by a KO and gets the girl. Surprise! Surprise! Lloyd Bacon directed.

One of the first musicals to feature boxing was the all dancing, all singing, all punching *Cain and Mabel* (WB 1936) starring Clark Gable and Marion Davis. He is heavyweight champion of the world (what else?) and she is a musical com-

edy star seeking publicity. Of course Gable and Davis fall for each other. At the end, to illustrate what pests women can be to boxers, Gable is making mincemeat of his opponent when he hears Davis calling him. He turns at the sound of her voice and is knocked out. 'Gee, Mabel, I lost every penny I had in the world.' 'Never mind. I bet on the other guy and I've enough for both of us.' Quite a punch-line to end a pleasant musical-comedy. Gable weighed in at 187 lbs according to the publicity. Lloyd Bacon pops up again as director. His down-to-earth and economical approach made him the ideal Warner Bros. director of the thirties.

Harold Lloyd's transition to sound movies was not difficult, although his best work was done in the twenties. In *The Milky Way* (Par. 1936), he plays a milkman who unwittingly becomes a prizefighter. He learns to box in waltz time with a one-two-boom-boom, but he's really good at ducking. Harold's glasses were his

trade-mark and he never removes them even when in the ring and one can't hit a man with glasses. The hero is not a superman but rather a mild-mannered Clark Kent. One memorable exchange: 'How'd you get that black eye?' asks Harold's sister, not knowing of his pugilistic pursuits. 'Er, I was shadow boxing and the shadow won.' Directed by Leo McCarey, it was one of Lloyd's funniest sound films, but unfortunately the original was destroyed when Sam Goldwyn's remake *The Kid from Brooklyn* (1946) came out. There are, however, several extant copies.

Although boxing pictures were quite numerous in the thirties, boxing was never really treated seriously until the end of the decade. Warner Bros. especially relished the seamy background of the fight game and its link with organized crime, producing several boxing movies, usually with the word kid in the title. They 'kidded' the public with *The Personality Kid* (1934), *The*

Kid Comes Back (1938), *The Kid from Kokomo* (1939), and *Kid Nightingale* (1939). By far the best was *Kid Galahad* (1937) (remade as a circus drama, *The Wagons Roll at Night* — WB 1941 and as an Elvis Presley vehicle in 1962). The director Michael Curtiz handled the boxing world with more realism than in previous movies on the subject. The picture had the pace and economy that one expected from Warners. Wayne Morris, whose brawny good-looks cast him as a boxer many times, plays Ward Guisenberry, a hick as his name implies, who now works as a bellhop in the big city. Edward G. Robinson is the fight manager who, persuaded by his girl Fluff (Bette Davis), makes him into a champ. The contrast between the chivalrous, clean-living Kid Galahad (as he is dubbed) and the crooked world in which he finds himself, is well delineated. The plot gets slightly bogged down when Morris falls for Robinson's virginal sister (Jane Bryan) which works Robinson

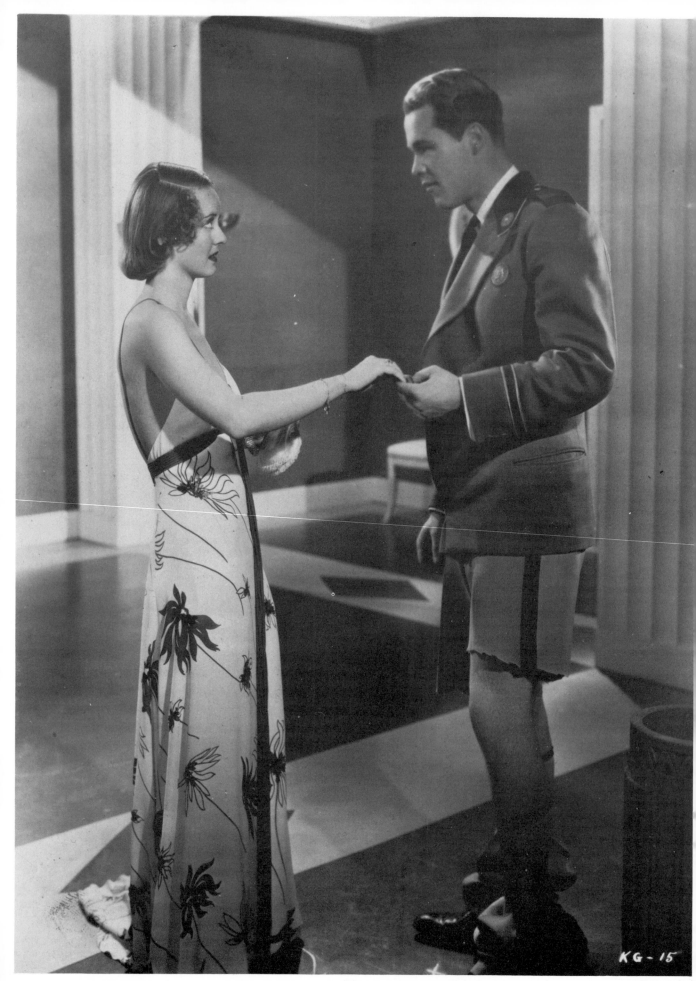

KG-15

up into an almost incestuous jealousy. The manager, out of revenge, matches the Kid with someone he knows to be too good for him. In a violent bout, which would set the pattern for many later screen brawls, the Kid finally comes out on top by keeping away from his slugging opponent, boxing him instead of carrying the fight. In the eleventh round he catches him with a right hand and the fight is over. The film ends with a shootout in the dressing-room between old rivals Robinson and racketeer Humphrey Bogart in which both are killed.

Clifford Odets' 1937 play about a slum boy who has to give up the violin and become a boxer to earn money, ruining his hands in the process, was given a compromisingly happy ending in *Golden Boy* (Col. 1939). The main point of Odets' proletarian allegory was that poverty destroys a man and allows no room for beauty. In the film, his girl (Barbara Stanwyck) assures him that his broken hands will mend and he will play the violin again. Twenty-one-year-old William Holden made his debut as Joe Bonaparte, who is really too sensitive to become a great prizefighter and too poor to be a great violinist. *Golden Boy* was one of the archetypal boxing melos that Stanley Donen so beautifully parodied in his *Dynamite Fists*, the first part of *Movie, Movie* (WB 1978). The director Rouben Mamoulian was happiest in the action scenes. The fight in which Holden, with hate in his eyes for the sport and the people who exploit it, kills his black opponent, is shot almost entirely in close-up, back and forth from the boxers to the frenzied spectators, never letting us observe the scene objectively. The fight was a gain for the picture over the play, adding a realism it did not have. Much of the best dialogue, snappily delivered by Stanwyck and Adolph Menjou (as Joe's manager) was a departure from the original text. Unfortunately, Lee J. Cobb's Italian paterfamilias still remained to sob things like 'Money, money! We gotta souls. We gotta take care of 'em.' A little more liniment and less shmaltz would have made it a better movie.

The actor who played Joe Bonaparte on stage in *Golden Boy* for the radical New York Group Theater was John Gar-

Left: Bette Davis and Wayne Morris, the bell-hop who becomes a fighter in *Kid Galahad* (1937)

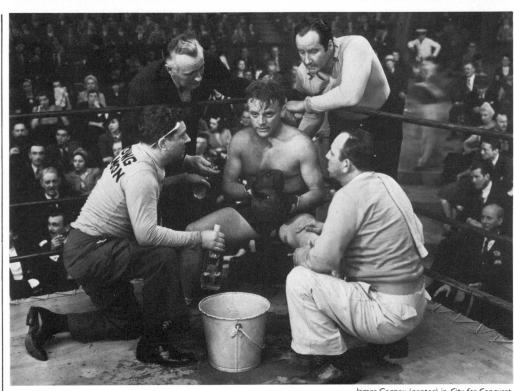

James Cagney (center) in *City for Conquest*

field and on the strength of his performance was offered a Warner Bros. contract. He was about to play the lead in a Broadway revival in 1952 when he died of a heart attack. In *They Made Me a Criminal* (WB 1939), he portrays a southpaw champion who gets framed in a murder rap. In the opening scene he is speaking to reporters in the dressing room after successfully defending his title. We and they are led to believe that he lives a clean life and the only woman he loves is his mother. Cut to Garfield with a drink in his hands and a broad in his arms. A reporter discovers the dissolute life he leads (he doesn't even possess a mother), and threatens to expose him. Garfield's manager kills the reporter and skips town with the broad, leaving Garfield to face the music. Garfield runs away, changes his name and finds himself way out in Arizona working on a reform-school farm where the only inmates happen to be the Dead End Kids. He decides to box again in order to earn enough money to save the farm from ruin. Meanwhile, Claude Rains as a perceptive, misunderstood and miscast detective continues his search for the missing champ. He's an educated cop who believes that the way a man stands, walks and moves will always give him away. In a ludicrous coincidence, Rains sees a photo of Garfield in a local Arizona

paper. He travels down to see the fight and Garfield spots him buying a ticket. He decides to change from southpaw to orthodox so that Rains won't recognize him. This assumes that the detective could only identify him by his boxing stance. Strange as it seems, Garfield loses the bout because of the switch in styles, but stays enough rounds to win money and save the ranch. (There is similar switch-hitting for a different reason in *Rocky II* – UA 1980.) The film contains the usual ambiguous notion of hero-worship among the Dead End Kids who were always being saved from a criminal future by an adult exemplar. It was directed in a sober, intelligent and enjoyable manner by, rather surprisingly, Busby Berkeley, bringing out John Garfield's humane tough-guy qualities.

James Cagney boxed again in *City for Conquest* (WB 1940). New York was the city well captured by director Anatole Litvak. Cagney is a truck driver who becomes a fighter to help pay for his younger brother's music lessons. Arthur Kennedy (in his film debut) plays the would-be composer. Kennedy's music (courtesy of Max Steiner) is what keeps Cagney going, especially one banal theme which he asks his brother to play on the piano *ad nauseam*. Cagney is blinded during a match, not by a punch, but by

having resin rubbed into his eyes by an unscrupulous opponent. All he can do after that is get a job selling newspapers, but he can still listen to the first performance of his brother's New York symphony on the radio at his news-stand. By his sacrifice, the fruits of brutish boxing have gone to nourish beauty. Even James Cagney's marvellous performance cannot save the mawkish ending. Anthony Quinn and Elia Kazan appear as heavies.

After the grimness of movies such as *Golden Boy* and *City for Conquest*, a touch of fantasy and comedy was welcomed by the boxing fraternity. It was provided by *Here Comes Mr Jordan* (Col. 1941). (In the remake entitled *Heaven Can Wait* (Par. 1978), boxing was changed to football.) Robert Montgomery plays a prizefighter who is killed in an airplane crash fifty years before he is due to die because of the bungling of heavenly messenger Edward Everett Horton. He is recorded in the celestial register as the next heavyweight champion of the world. As his body has been cremated, Montgomery has to return to earth in another man's body and try to win the championship. It was reasonably amusing whimsy which seemed to be saying in the dark days of 1941 that 'God is in his heaven and all is right in the world (championship).'

25

In 1942 Warner Bros. produced one of the very best sporting biopics with *Gentleman Jim*. James J. Corbett was the first world heavyweight champion to win under the Marquis of Queensbury Rules by knocking out John L. Sullivan in the 21st round at the Olympic Club in New Orleans on September 7 1892. Errol Flynn was perfect casting as Corbett. Like Corbett, Flynn was 6ft 1in, and weighed 180 lbs. Ward Bond, a former USC tackle, played the boozing John L. Sullivan. The film charts the rise of Jim from bank clerk to national hero in a sport that was once outlawed and into which he brought finesse. As Jim's reputation increases so does his conceit, but at the party to celebrate his championship win, Sullivan arrives and hands over his belt to the new champion. Jim is touched and pays tribute to Sullivan, saying there will never be another John L. The director Raoul Walsh, whose movies rarely omit a fist fight, made it into an enjoyable naughty-nineties period piece, and the brain vs brawn finale is well staged. It is one of Flynn's best performances, although one critic thought his feet were more mobile than his features.

John L. Sullivan had his own biopic in *The Great John L.* (UA 1945 — *A Man Called Sullivan* — GB). Greg McClure starred in his first film as 'The Boston Strong Boy.' It tells of the rise and fall of the man who claimed he could 'lick any son-fabitch in the house' and who trained on black velvet (a mixture of champagne and stout.) The story moves through the locales of London, Paris and New York. We see Sullivan giving an exhibition bout with the Prince of Wales at Buckingham Palace and in a fight, the best moment of the film, with a French savate boxer. (In *Boxe Francaise*, kicking above the belt is permitted.) The Frenchman kicks him in the jaw, throws flowers to his admirers and pirouettes around the ring. Although Sullivan falls for musical-comedy star Linda Darnell, he really loves his childhood sweetheart Barbara Britton. After he loses his title to Corbett, it is pretty heavy going as drink and women lead to his downfall. Greg McClure did not have the star personality to carry the picture and ended up playing Joe Palooka.

Danny Kaye, following in Harold Lloyd's footwork, entered the ring in Samuel Goldwyn's *The Kid from Brooklyn* (1946), a successful remake of *The Milky Way* with the added attraction of songs and Technicolor. Kaye went through many of the same routines as Lloyd, bringing to them his own manic personality. His main quality as the milkman turned boxer is his uncanny ability to duck like lightning. Thus the cream puff milkman is transformed into 'The Tiger' and he begins to believe in his own bogus persona by imitating 'the action of a tiger'. Danny's comic mask is that of the coward finding himself in a situation requiring courage. In *Up in Arms* (1944), the hypochondriac becomes a war hero, and in *The Kid from Brooklyn* he becomes middleweight champion of the world and wins beautiful Virginia Mayo. It could have been another episode in *The Secret Life of Walter Mitty* (1947).

The term *Film Noir* was used in France after the war when Hollywood thrillers of the forties were seen for the first time in French movie houses. It is used to describe a dark suspenseful drama using the shadowy city streets, bars and nightclubs in a world of corruption and crime. The three most notable boxing *films noirs* were *Body and Soul* (UA 1947), *The Set-Up* (RKO 1949), and *Champion* (UA 1949). *The Killers* (UI 1946), although not a boxing drama, opens with a vicious fight in which Burt Lancaster is beaten. Based on a laconic Hemingway story, it set the tone for the three important boxing *films noirs* to follow.

The atmosphere is immediately established at the opening of *Body and Soul* by James Wong Howe's photography. A deserted training ring at night. The camera tracks to a shack where we discover John Garfield lying on a bed in the shadows. Garfield's voice begins the tough forties-style narration as the film goes into flashback. It is New York's East Side when times are bad. Garfield, an unemployed Jewish lad, spends his time in pool-rooms and on the sidewalks. After winning an amateur boxing contest, he meets Lilli Palmer, an artist. She is the unobtainable feminine ideal for a guy like him. When his mother (Anne Revere) becomes widowed, Garfield turns pro to save her from poverty. She wants him to get an education and not become a prizefighter. 'Fight for something, not for money,' she urges. Garfield rises quickly in the fight game as others fall to his devastating right. There is a montage of his fights, each ending with a spectacular knockout, although he seems incredibly vulnerable in the ring. 21 fights, 19 KO's. But he is not satisfied and wants to get into the big money. His voracity leads him to get involved with a crooked promoter. Another wicked influence to taint the hero even further is a showgirl Alice (Hazel Brooks). While he is training, we see her legs come into his vision as he punches the bag. By now he is almost totally corrupted by money. He neglects his mother (always the worst sign of a nogoodnik) and takes up with Alice. Now he is just a pawn in the world of capital, owned body and soul as the title song keeps reminding us. Finally, he has the chance of making a large sum and getting out of the sport, if he takes a dive. He is prepared to do this, but predictably various moral issues come into play to test his conscience. Firstly, a Jewish delivery boy is brought in especially to say, 'Over in Europe, people are killing people like us just because of our religion.' The Jews of the neighborhood are putting their money on him because of what he represents to them. When his friend and trainer (Canada Lee) dies, we realise there is no way Garfield is going to throw the fight. But he does not decide until the final round. A close-up of his eyes reveals that he has changed his mind and as he comes out of his corner the commentator says 'I've never seen anything like it in my life. A silence has descended. He's like a tiger stalking his prey.' Needless to say he knocks out his opponent in the last moments. After the fight, he turns his back on Alice and falls into Lilli Palmer's arms. He now deserves the good girl, because he has rejected the false values imposed upon him by an unjust society. However, the open ending is a cop out. We are left with the impression that the gangsters are going to let him get away with his betrayal of them as if his new morality somehow conferred on him a defence against them. Like *Golden Boy*, the obligatory happy ending avoids the very real social issues raised. A great deal of the film is powerful despite the over-insistent direction and script. This is due mainly to the camera work and the expressive bullish performance by Garfield, touching ones from Canada Lee and Anne Revere as a restrained (*sic*) Jewish mother. In the same year as its release Rober Rossen (the director) Abraham Polonsky (script writer) and John Garfield were all brought before the HUAC anti-communist hearings in 1947, marking them for life.

The Set-Up has a simpler and less conventional story line than *Body and Soul*. *Body and Soul* is social criticism disguised as *film noir*, whereas *The Set-Up* is a metaphysical contemplation better suited to the *angst* of the genre. It is staged entirely at night and takes place between 9.10 p.m. and 10.22 p.m., exactly the 72 minutes running time of the film. *The Set-Up* is far removed from the high life of the boxers whose names hit the headlines, concentrating on dingy hotels, out-of-town boxing halls and over-crowded dressing rooms. The world of the small-time, third-rate boxers who take regular beatings for a paltry sum. One of these boxers is 35-year-old Stoker Thompson (Robert Ryan) who still feels the heavyweight championship is 'one punch away'. We see his life before, during and after his last fight. His wife (Audrey Totter) has walked out on him as she can not stand the punishment he keeps taking. His manager (George Tobias) has sold him for 50 dollars to throw the fight against an up-and-coming young boxer. Not wanting to split the dough and knowing that Stoker would never consider anything crooked, the manager doesn't tell his fighter about the fix because he thinks he will lose anyway. Stoker is alone waiting for his fight. He has no wife, no child no family and no friend. Around him is the debris of the fight game; a punch-drunk bruiser turned imbecile, the old prizefighter selling programs and other losers like himself. There are also the young fighters who cannot see their own future in the human wreckage around them. At the center of everything is the brilliantly lit ring surrounded by a sadistic mob chewing pop-corn.

Right: Errol Flynn in *Gentleman Jim*

Overleaf: Lionel Stander (right) and Danny Kaye as *The Kid from Brooklyn*

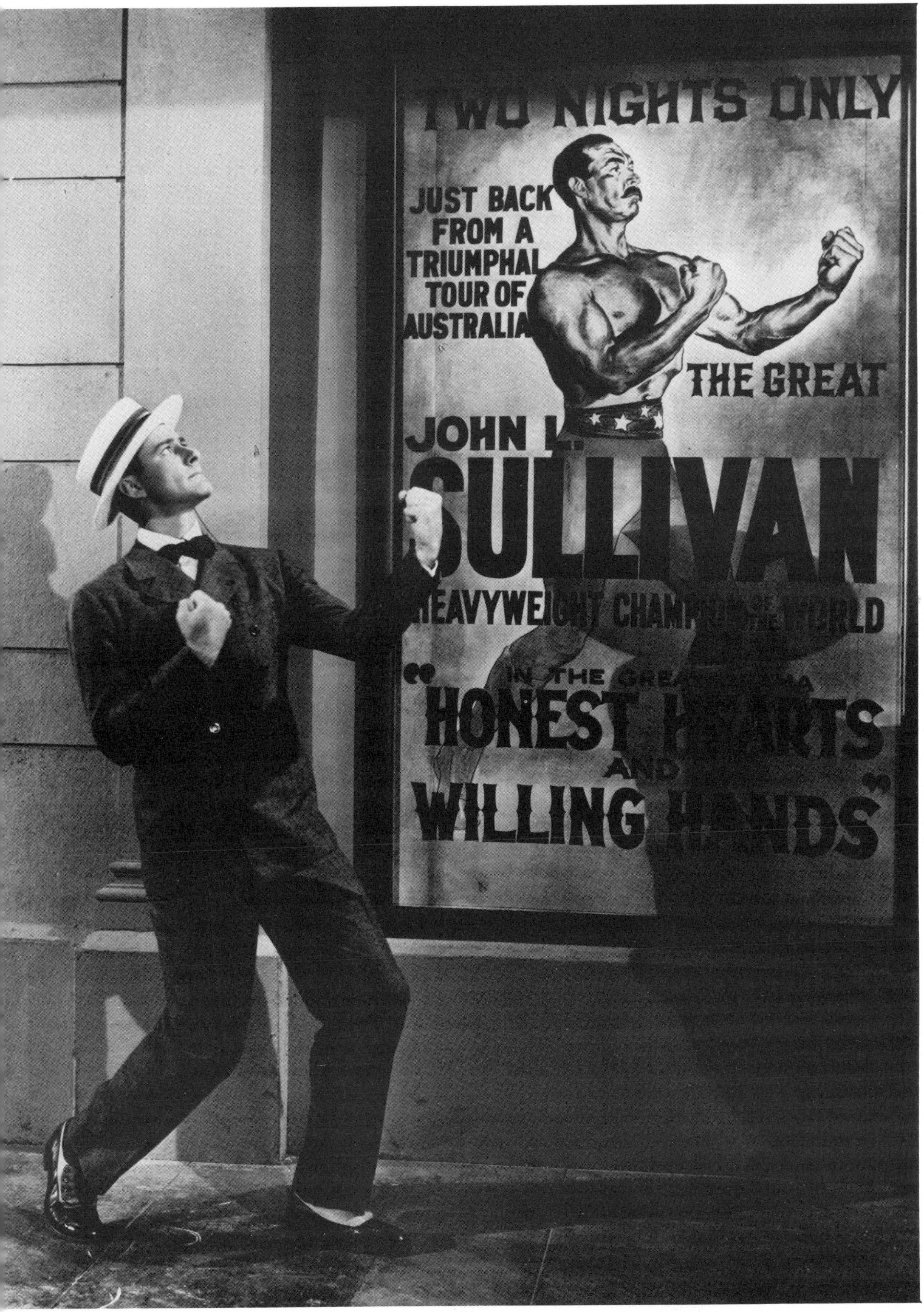
TWO NIGHTS ONLY
JUST BACK
FROM A
TRIUMPHAL
TOUR OF
AUSTRALIA
THE GREAT
JOHN L.
SULLIVAN
IN THE
HONEST
AND
WILLING

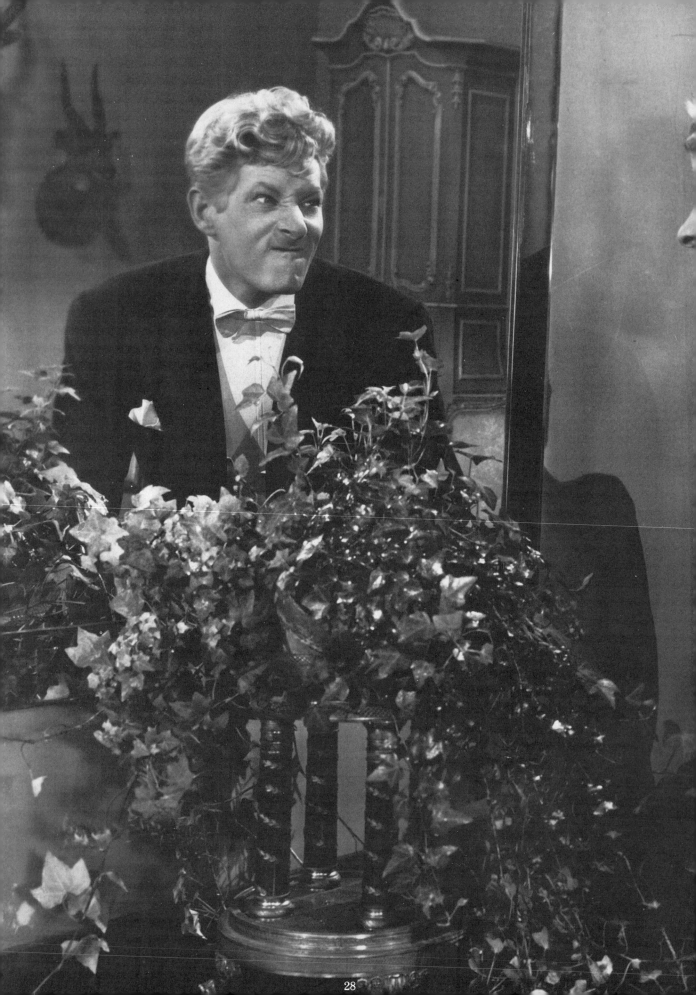

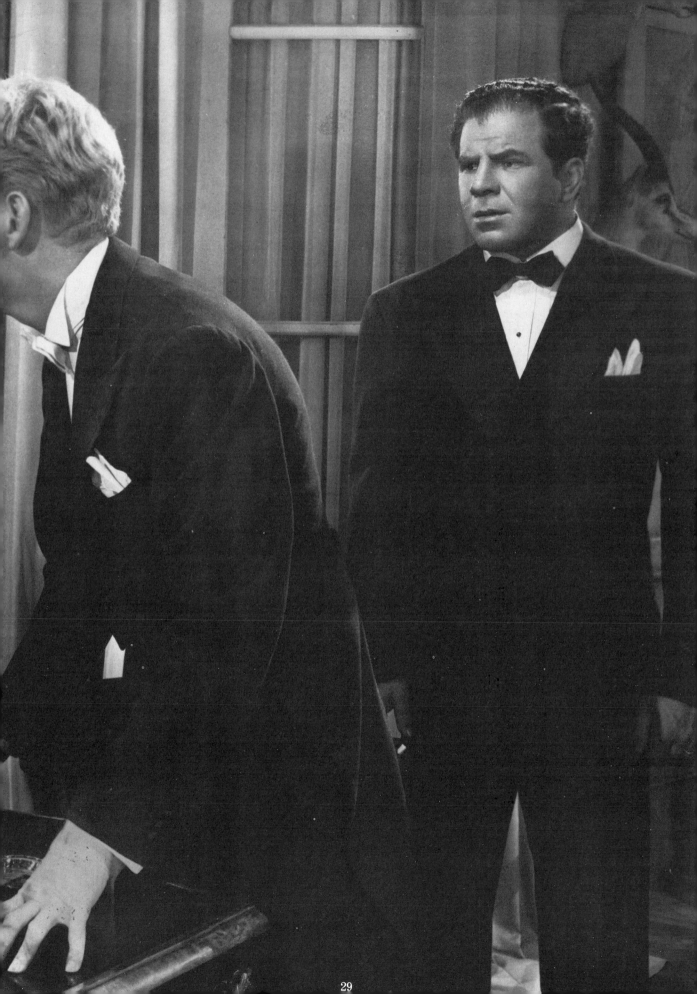

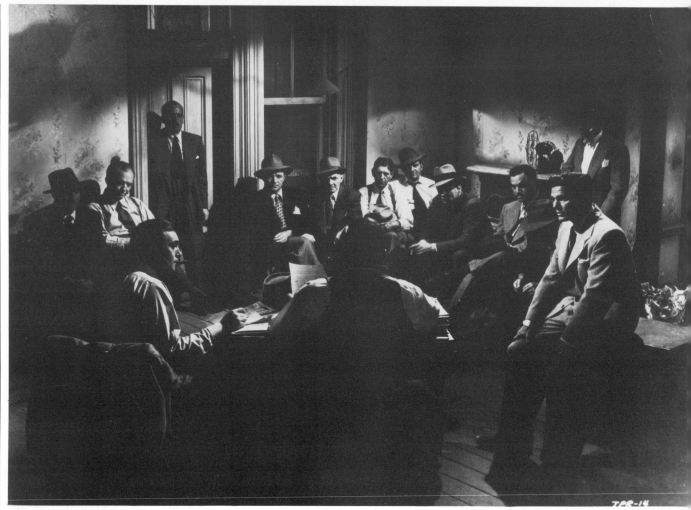

and spitting at the losers, and a blind man listening to the sounds of pain. Stoker fights the battle of his life to justify himself in his wife's eyes. Four savage rounds are fought with a rate of punching that would certainly startle the customers at Madison Square Garden. After his victory he waits in the empty boxing-hall for the hoodlums to come and beat him up. Out of this desolation comes the sense of futile pride that is the essence of boxing as a movie myth. In a society which is based on the supremacy of the individual, the individual learns to take on all responsibility for failure. The film seems to hint that the American Dream might be a great 'con', but in America even the loser has his day. The theme is returned to in John Huston's *Fat City* (Col. 1972). Director Robert Wise has excellently evoked the steaming hot night in the shabby arena and environs. Former boxer Robert Ryan, mostly forced to play chilling villains in his career, gives perhaps his most compelling performance.

Robert Wise worked with Mark Robson on the cutting of *Citizen Kane* (RKO 1941) and their careers have charted, more or less, similar waters, each directing two important boxing dramas. Mark Robson's *Champion* was released in the same month as *The Set-Up* and suffered by comparison. A study in ruthless ambition, it tells the story of Midge Kelly (Kirk Douglas) who alienates his friends and family, deceives women and double-crosses the manager who helped him. He finally goes mad and dies in the dressing room after a defeat. Midge may be a heel, but he doesn't really deserve the punishment meted out to him. In fact, he has a finer side. He sends money to his mom and helps his crippled brother Connie (Arthur Kennedy). Compared with the character in Ring Lardner's short story (from which Carl Foreman adapted the film), he's an angel.

The picture opens with Midge and his brother on the road and looking for work. They get a job in a wayside cafe, but Midge soon finds he can make more dough by fighting. The gymnastic progress of a raw recruit to a pro ready for his debut is described in an excellent sequence in which music and movement achieve an almost balletic effect. He soon rises to the top, leaving his wife (Ruth Roman) for blonde nightclub singer Marilyn Maxwell and then moves on to Lola Albright. In his fights everybody except Midge leads with their chins which he obligingly hits. In his last fight, Kirk Douglas with his prominent jaw stuck out seems to have caught the habit. In an excessively brutal travesty of prizefighting, he gets his upper-cut comeuppances. The graphic depiction of the gyms, the ring-side and big city life is dispelled by the over-dramatized fights and the sentimental approach to the subject. As an exposé of the boxing business it is weak, because Midge, like Jake La Motta in *Raging Bull*, is basically such a nasty character that he would have been the same had he been in hairdressing.

Jeff Chandler played a heavyweight champion in *The Iron Man* (UI 1951 — a remake of the 1931 Tod Browning version) who advances on his opponents with his jaw fully exposed, but when hit on it goes berserk. He is very unpopular with the crowds because he has the killer instinct. This is very curious as this type of boxer sells tickets. When his friend Speed (Rock Hudson) challenges him, he loses his title not his temper, gaining the respect of the crowd for the first time.

There have been a number of world-class boxers who were deaf-mutes and Tony Curtis plays one in the pretentiously titled *The Flesh and The Fury* (UI 1952).Curtis only grunts for most of the film, but gives a touching performance. He has an operation which restores his hearing in one ear and he learns to speak like Tony Curtis. However, he is warned that if he fights again, he risks losing his hearing. Hearing Jan Sterling sing in a night-club, he decides to fight for the world championship. During the fight the sound-track starts getting fuzzy and we realise that he may never hear Mona Freeman nag him after they're

BARCODE: 33220002309602
DUE DATE: 11-03-10 02:56PM

Art Center College of Design
RECEIPT
Patron: Larin-Baranda, Alejandro
11-03-2010 2:25PM

INVOICE #: 82480
STATUS: * RENEWED
DESCRIPTION: Screen tests, portraits, nu
AMOUNT OWED: $1.40
AMOUNT PAID: $1.40
BALANCE: $0.00

INVOICE #: 82481
STATUS: * RENEWED
DESCRIPTION: Indian circus / Mary Ellen
AMOUNT OWED: $1.40
AMOUNT PAID: $1.40
BALANCE: $0.00

Total Paid: $2.80

#100 11-03-2010 2:25PM
Item(s) checked out to Larin-Baranda, Al

TITLE: Sports in the movies
BARCODE: 33220000284575
DUE DATE: 11-24-10

TITLE: Nightmare USA : the untold story
BARCODE: 33220002470859
DUE DATE: 11-24-10

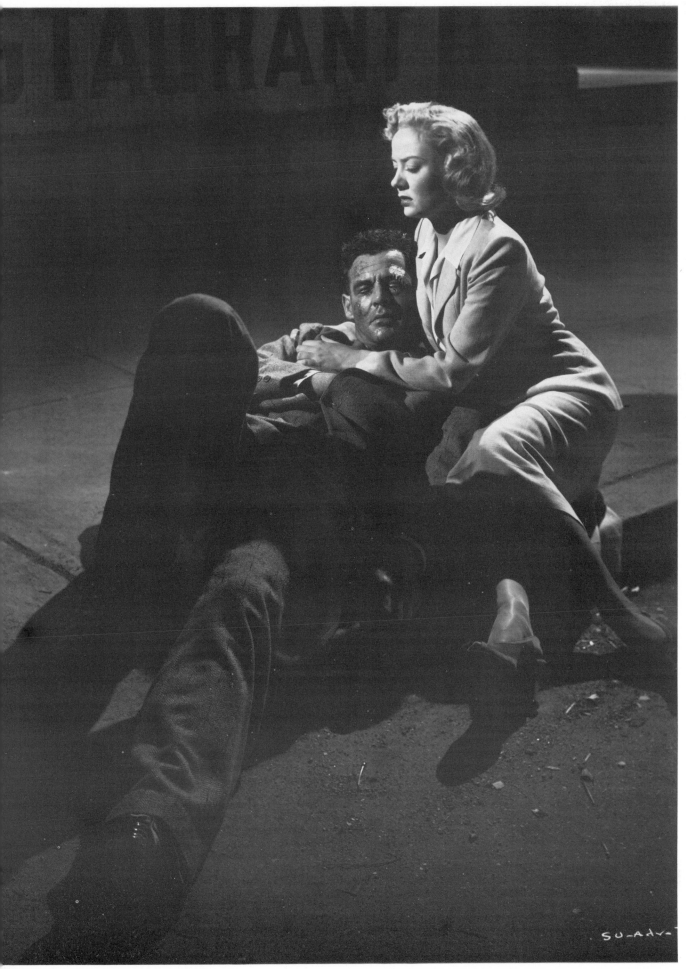

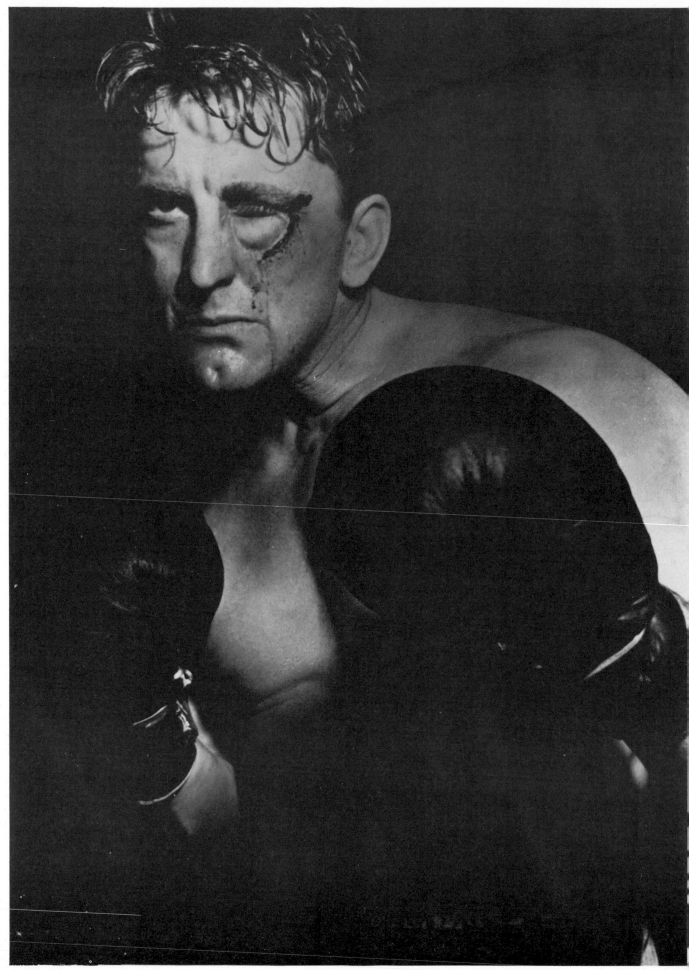

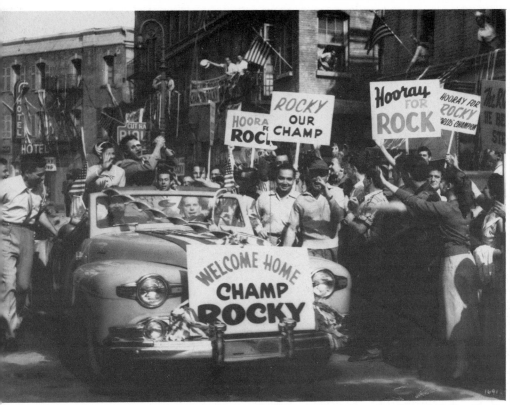

Pier Angeli and Paul Newman in the final scene from *Somebody Up There Likes Me*

married. But after the fight, walking arm in arm with Mona, he slowly begins to hear the newsboys shouting his victory.

Three outstanding movies of the fifties had boxers as heroes, although they were not about boxing at all. In *The Quiet Man* (Republic 1952), John Wayne is an ex-boxer who returns to his native Ireland for a peaceful life. He's soon being challenged to fight by bellicose squire Victor McLaglen. Wayne does not rise to the challenge and in flashback we see why. He killed a man in the ring and will no longer raise his hand to anyone. Needless to say, he finally forgets his scruples and gives McLaglen the beating he deserves. Because Prewitt (Montgomery Clift) once blinded a friend in a bout, he refuses to box for the platoon in *From Here to Eternity* (Col. 1953), and is therefore beaten and humiliated. Boxing would have given him the chance to be part of the system in which there is little room for ethics and by resisting he is crushed by it. One of Marlon Brando's most famous roles was as the washed-up boxer Terry Malloy in *On the Waterfront* (Col. 1954) in which he speaks the poignant lines (quoted in *Raging Bull*) to his brother (Rod Steiger) in the back of a taxi: 'I

coulda had class. I coulda been somebody. I coulda been a contender instead of a bum, which is what I am.'

Tony Curtis as a grocery clerk, whose father (Jim Backus) is hitting the bottle, enters *The Square Jungle* (UI 1955) in order to pay his old man's debts. He becomes champ, but as his erudite trainer (Ernest Borgnine) says, quoting the Bard, 'Uneasy is the head that wears the crown.' A boxing tragedy might still be adapted from one of Shakespeare's History plays, but *The Square Jungle* ain't it.

Audie Murphy is welterweight champion who was 'born in the dumps and educated in an alley' in *The World in My Corner* (UI 1955). In this cliché-ridden rags to riches yarn, Murphy lusts for money and poor little rich girl, Barbara Rush. That the acquisition of money through boxing is corruptive is a perennial theme of the movies. It never occurred to the film studios that they acquired money by the same means.

A fighting milkman, violinist, bellhop and operatic tenor (John Payne in *Kid Night-*

ingale) preceded John Derek as a fighting priest in *The Leather Saint* (Par. 1955). Whatever happened to turning the other cheek? He doesn't get much chance as he hits his opponents with only one punch that puts them to sleep quicker than any of his sermons. The boxing fraternity don't know he's a priest, although they call his right cross a 'Sunday punch' without realizing how witty they are. Why is he a prizefighter? Well, it's to buy an iron lung and other medical necessities for the parish hospital. What about love interest? Well, he's a high Episcopalian who has taken a vow of celibacy for one year, which considering the record of screen boxers' involvement with women is a damn (sorry!) good thing. He marries Jody Lawrence in the end. Not to be confused with the same year's *The Left Hand of God*.

One of the best numbers in the MGM musical *It's Always Fair Weather* (1955) takes place in Stillman's gym. Gene Kelly manages a fighter ('I won the kid in a crap game. I couldn't hock him, so I thought I'd do something with him.') and invites Cyd Charisse to meet him at the gym. As she enters, all the boxers immediately stop training and give her wolf whistles. They gather round breaking into a pastiche of a college anthem. 'Like the ivy covered walls of Harvard, our alma mater is Stillman's gym. Stillman's rah! rah!' Stillman's on 7th Avenue is rather like a college and has become part of boxing mythology. As the boxers try to remember the heavyweight

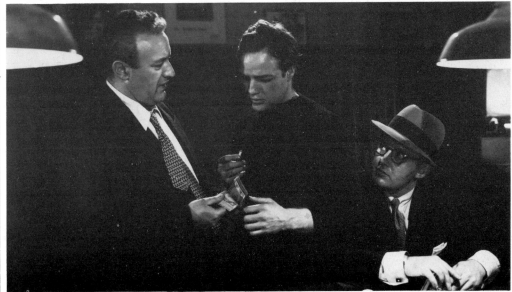

Marlon Brando in *On the Waterfront*

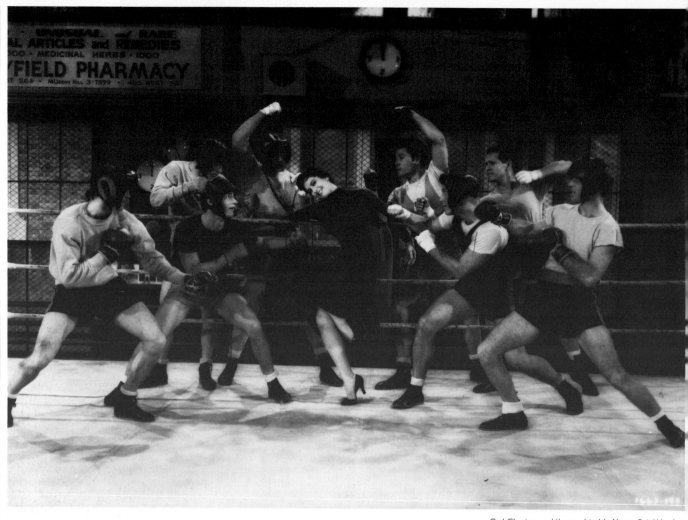

champs from the Great John L., Charisse recites them all. The boxers then go into a number praising her with 'Baby, you knock me out. What a dame! You belong in the Hall of Fame.' Charisse shows some nifty footwork in a dance in the ring with erotic implications as she sings 'You've got me hanging on the ropes.' Chaplin had made his fight in *City Limits* almost a ballet, but here at last is a full-blown musical number in a boxing ring, with dancers looking convincing as boxers.

In 1955, two movies were released that saw the fight game from completely different viewpoints. They were *Somebody Up There Likes Me* (MGM) and *The Harder They Fall* (Col.). Obviously the more positive view came from MGM, the studio which more than any other cosily reinforced middle-class values. In *Somebody Up There Likes Me*, almost everything is lovely in The Garden, whereas in *The Harder They Fall*, almost nothing is.

Robert Wise, who had directed the powerful *The Set-Up*

for RKO had MGM's glossier movie machine behind him on this biopic of Rocky Graziano, world middleweight champion in 1947. Despite this, it is directed in an energetic and entertaining manner with enough atmosphere to conjure up New York's East Side in the studio. There are some early scenes which foreshadow *West Side Story* (UA 1961). One of the main joys of the movie is Paul Newman's electric and likeable performance in a role that was originally meant for James Dean. The problem lies in Ernest Lehman's script which makes every utterance sound like part of a thesis to prove that a man can fight his way out of the ghetto to share in the American Dream. The film opens with a testimonial from the real Rocky Graziano which reads 'This is the way I remember it — definitely', while over the credits croons the bland voice of Perry Como with the title song. Nothing bland about the first images where a little boy is being punched sadistically by his father

(Harold J. Stone) ostensibly teaching him to box. The father is a bitter, failed boxer and he makes his son suffer for it. Rocky grows up hating his father and all father figures. He drifts into petty crime, finding himself first in reform school and then at a penitentiary. When he comes out he is offered a contract by a minor fight manager (Everett Sloane). He doesn't quite understand that he can make money fighting. 'All my life I've been fighting and all my life I've got into trouble from it.' As a fighter he begins to gain self-respect, the respect of others and the love of a good woman (Pier Angeli). She hates the fight game, but realizes that it's the only way a guy like Rocky can be someone. 'I didn't marry a man, did I? I married a middleweight.' The ring is considered such a meaningful alternative to a hard life that the script significantly prevents us from seeing the hero ever beaten. The first Tony Zale-Graziano bout which Rocky lost by KO is only heard on the radio. The second en-

counter in which Rocky becomes world champion is vividly recreated. Paul Newman captures exactly Graziano's crouching style and facing him is a dead ringer for Tony Zale. During the fight, there is a shot of a deserted (rather stagey) East Side street with radios blaring from every window. In various locales almost everybody who played a part in Graziano's life is listening in. The army boxing coach, the soda-jerk philosopher, the father who now faces the truth about himself, and his friend (Sal Mineo) who comprehends that a life of crime is not the only way. The crowd at the fight, instead of the cannibals seen in *Golden Boy* or *The Set-Up*, look like Ivy Leaguers. The ending with Graziano receiving a ticker tape reception on the East Side and looking up at the heavens, is a spurious celebration of professional boxing as an essential part of the American Dream and a justification of the sermonising that has preceded it.

The movies either condemn pro-boxing as a vicious racket

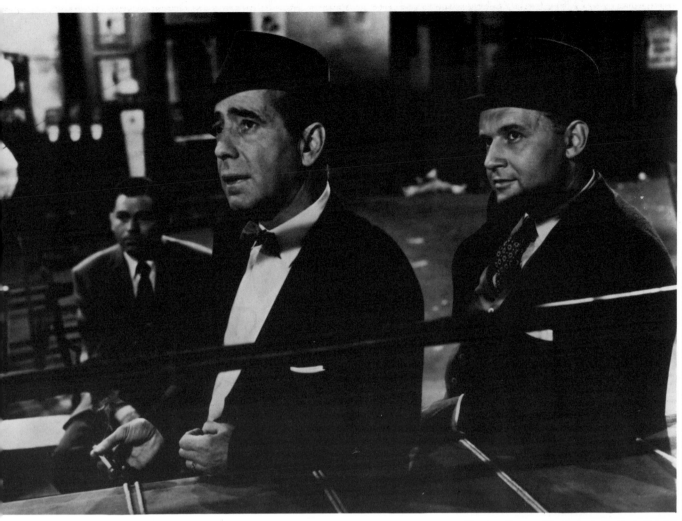

Humphrey Bogart and Rod Steiger in *The Harder They Fall*

that exploits the boxer or praise it as a means for the underprivileged to better themselves, but they hardly ever question the social conditions that help produce this phenomenon. *The Harder They Fall*, adapted by Philip Yordan from the Budd Schulberg novel, is a most powerful condemnation of prizefighting, despite its sophistry. It is still remembered with a certain bitterness by the apologists for the fight game. In *Ring Magazine*, boxing's bible, E.J. Gary wrote in February 1981: Remember when kids, afraid of the dark, would conjure up nasty things in their mind — bogie men, hobgoblins, and witches of every variety? Many of those kids grew up to become investigative reporters. And, as such, they still see nasty things in the dark. Only now, they put them into print believing boxing to be as "corrupt as it ever was" — going back to the scenes made famous in *The Harder They Fall*. The only problem is that while boxing welcomes good investigative reporting — nay,

even needs it! — it doesn't need an exposé based on sensationalism and sensationalism alone.' The boxing world was not kind to *The Harder They Fall* when it came out 25 years ago, treating it in the same terms as the above. Humphrey Bogart, in his last screen role, plays a sports columnist who, after reluctantly working for a crooked syndicate, decides to write an article which begins with the words 'Professional boxing should be banned even if it takes an Act of Congress to do it.'

The story is loosely based on the life of Primo Carnera although it was close enough for Carnera to sue Columbia for over 10,000 dollars. Mike Lane, a former circus strong man at 6ft 10ins and 275 lbs, played Toro 'The Wild Bull of the Andes'. In fact, he is muscle-bound, has a glass jaw and can't fight his way out of a wet paper-bag, but racketeer Nick Benko (Rod Steiger) gets him to a world championship by merely buying off every fighter along the way and creating a vast phony publicity

campaign. Toro is unaware that the succession of opponents he has knocked out were not seeing stars but dollar signs. When one of them dies from a brain hemorrhage from injuries received in a previous fight, Toro is distraught. Bogart, who has helped spread the lies about him, has a *crise de conscience* and decides to tell the boxer everything. Toro doesn't believe him, so Bogart gets trainer 'Jersey' Joe Walcott to prove it. In two seconds Toro is felled, but the truth hits him even harder. The world championship is coming up against Brannen (Max Baer), and Steiger knowing the champ can't be bought, throws Toro to the wolves. Toro fights courageously, getting up after each knockdown. His eyes are cut, his nose broken and his jaw fractured before he is finally counted out and taken to hospital. Toro has earned 49 dollars and 7 cents. The picture conveys the cynical message that anyone connected with the fight game has his price. Fair enough, but its demon-

stration smacks of special pleading and leaves too many questions unanswered. Are there no honest people at all in the business? Would a boxer as transparently talentless as Toro ever get to a world championship? Would millions of fight fans be taken in by so many fraudulent matches? Is it possible to get 28 boxers in a row knocked out in fake fights? Would a manager really give only 49 dollars and 7 cents to a heavyweight challenger out of a million dollar gate? To be honest, the film is so gripping and well-acted that these questions don't arise until one has emerged into the light. Incidentally, the sounds of the KOs were produced by hitting a side of ham near a sensitive mike. Pounded by Walcott and Baer, it must be one of the rare occasions when a real ham stood in for actors. (Rocky in *Rocky I*, trains by using a side of beef as a punch bag, giving new meaning to the phrase 'beating one's meat.')

In the lively comedy, *Designing Woman* (MGM 1957), Gregory Peck is a sportswriter married to sophisticated fashion designer Lauren Bacall, the woman of the punnish title. She attempts to participate in her husband's life, but when she goes to a prizefight she faints away at the first sign of blood. While Peck tries to play poker with his sporting cronies, Bacall entertains her arty friends in the next room. Being directed by the very decor-conscious Vincente Minnelli, art seems to triumph over sport in the end, due to the efforts of a ballet dancer (Jack Cole) who shows in a fight that he's pretty handy with his feet. Peck is on the run from boxing racketeers and his bodyguard is called Maxie (Micky O'Shaunessy), a punchy pug who sleeps with his eyes open. He is willing to protect Peck with his life even if anyone so much as looks at him 'crosseyed'. When Peck wants him to go into action, he is only to say 'Crosseyed Maxie!' and Maxie goes into his ring routine. The punch-drunk boxer has always been a figure of fun, but punch-drunkeness i.e. brain damage is no laughing matter, nevertheless O'Shaunessy's performance makes it seem amusing.

In 1960, Luchino Visconti's *Rocco and his Brothers* (Titanus Films) ran into trouble with the censors. This epic three-hour neo-realist drama, tells of a mother (Katerina Paxinou) and her four sons, who go north to Milan to find jobs to escape the poverty of the south. The streets are not exactly lined with gold, and they struggle to make ends meet in an unfeeling metropolis. For one of the brothers (Renato Salvatori), the ring offers an opportunity to get easy money, flashy clothes and beautiful women. He gets involved with a homosexual fight promoter (Roger Hanin), gets into debt and starts to lose. To save the family, his younger brother Rocco (Alain Delon), a kind of 'wise fool', enters the game although he wouldn't harm a flyweight. He detests boxing but succeeds in it. Delon is not to blame if the saintly character he plays is rather unconvincing. No boxer could be so gentle and yet so successful.

Former world heavyweight champion Joe Frazier sang with a pop group and made a record. Elvis Presley beat him to it by playing a singing boxer in *Kid Galahad* (Par. 1962). At 27, Elvis was already putting on a bit around the waist, and

although he would keep appearing in swimming trunks in movies such as *Fun in Acapulco* (Par. 1963), as a boxer he appeared rather too paunchy to be a successful welterweight. The story differed considerably from the 1937 version, but the essential idea still remained. Just out of the army and broke Presley finds himself at a training camp owned by Gig Young. Elvis is offered a job as sparring partner to one of Young's hopes. At first he takes a lot of punishment as the boxer hits him with a barrage of punches. (This is sparring?) Then, all at once, Elvis spots an opening, lets fly with a right and knocks his opponent out. Following a series of sensational knockouts, Elvis proposes to Gig Young's sister (Joan Blackman). He wants to give up boxing and buy an auto-repair shop. Young, who opposes the marriage, perversely makes a match for Elvis with the vastly more experienced 'Sugar Boy' Romero (i.e. in a fight not marriage). All the townsfolk are there to cheer Elvis on. His face, looking more like a podgy Linda Darnell than ever, is punched in close-up for 5 rounds until he suddenly and passionlessly lands a knockout blow. Presley is no longer the sullen rebel of previous movies, but a credit to the community, full of moral virtue. 'And you sing, too?'

someone asks. He does. He sings 7 songs between bouts.

Requiem for a Heavyweight (Col. 1962 — *Blood Money* — GB) starred Anthony Quinn as an ageing prizefighter called Mountain Rivera. The picture opens with Rivera taking a savage beating until being knocked cold in the 7th round. The bout is shot subjectively showing the KO'd boxer's viewpoint. (A blank screen for five minutes would have been nearer the truth.) Unknown to him, his manager (James Gleason) has assured a gambling syndicate that he wouldn't last beyond the 2nd. Ma Greevy (Madame Spivy), boss of the syndicate, sets her thugs onto the manager demanding he pay her losses within 3 weeks. The onus is on the boxer to pay. The ring doctor tells Rivera that he may go blind if he fights again, so he begins to look for work accompanied by his faithful trainer Army (Mickey Rooney). However, 17 years of being hit around the head is not much qualification for a job. Like Primo Carnera and other former champions, he gets a chance to earn money as a clownish wrestler dressed in a Red Indian costume.

Quinn gives yet another of his 'noble savage' performances, whimpering for the audience's sympathy. Adapted from Rod Serling's powerful TV play, the movie, as directed

by Ralph Nelson, is too hamfisted and the degradation piled on too relentlessly to be touching. The drama is played out against a suitably tacky New York backdrop.

When *The Great White Hope* (TCF 1970) was released, Variety warned its black readers that 'such pix feature blacks in a losing light.' It was ten years since the Civil Rights movement began and America's twenty million black citizens wanted a more positive image of themselves in the media. Movies directed by black directors such as Ossie Davis *(Cotton Comes to Harlem)*, Sidney Poitier *(Uptown Saturday Night)* and Gordon Parks *(Shaft)* were much more appealing to black audiences where they were not seen from a white perspective. *The Great White Hope* appeared six years before the flash champ Apollo Creed in *Rocky I*. Hollywood, as a microcosm of prevalent views in the USA, gave blacks a raw deal. Racial discrimination forced them into playing stereotypes. The first sound movie, *The Jazz Singer* (WB 1927), featured the white man in black face, so offensive to blacks. It was not much better in sport. Since Jack Johnson, the first black heavyweight champion of the world, lost his title in 1915, black heavyweights were barred from the

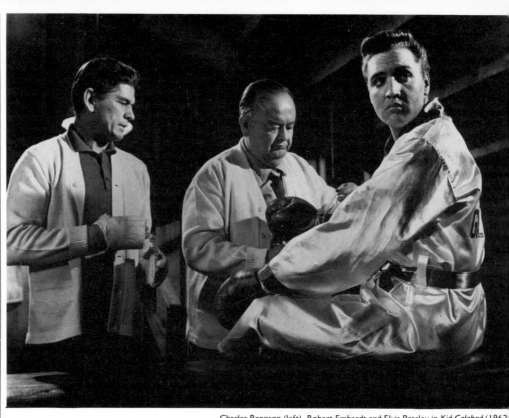

Charles Bronson (left), Robert Emhardt and Elvis Presley in *Kid Galahad* (1962

world championship for more than 20 years. They were not even allowed to challenge. It wasn't until Joe Louis came along in the '30s that the color bar was smashed. A group of racists are attempting to find the great white hope in order to topple the black champion, Jack Jefferson (James Earl Jones). Howard Sackler, who wrote the Broadway play and adapted it for the screen, based the story on the life of Jack Johnson. Jefferson is barely tolerated as champion, but the limit is reached when he takes a white mistress (Jane Alexander). By contravening the segregation laws, he is forced into exile in Europe. Because he wishes the case against him dropped so he can return home, Jefferson eventually decides to play the white man's game. He agrees to take a dive against the latest white hope, because nobody good enough to beat him squarely can be found. The final fight is rather too artificially staged in the movie. Jefferson allows himself to take a beating in front of the white crowd. Among them on this hot afternoon is a little black fan-seller, unhappy for his hero. As if spurred on by this image, Jefferson makes a fight of it and the little boy becomes animated at the change. Finally the black champion realizes he must lie

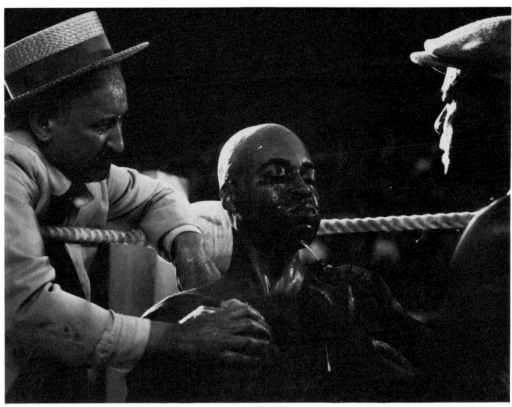

James Earl Jones in *The Great White Hope*

down and swallow his racial pride. He is knocked out in slow motion as the whole crowd counts to the fatal ten. There is still a controversy regarding the Jack Johnson-Jess Willard fight. Some people consider Johnson's claim that he took a dive was merely an excuse for

losing because he was so out of condition from his drinking and lack of fights during his exile; while others point to the famous photo of Johnson lying on the canvas seemingly shielding his eyes from the sun. The director, Martin Ritt, does not use this image. Ritt is a par-

ticularly sensitive director, especially with racial themes such as *Sounder* and *Conrack*. Here Ritt is a little too restricted by the stage original, but there are some effective moments. Blacks being barred from seeing Jefferson fight, gather outside the stadium to pray and sing. The camera rises high away from them and over the stands towards the ring. The fight, which he wins, is not seen except for close-ups of Earl Jones laughing and punching. The public expect him to smile. James Earl Jones, who played the part on Broadway, gives a fine resonant performance in a role that Paul Robeson would have relished had he been given the chance.

'Yesterday is dead and gone and tomorrow is out of sight and it's bad to be alone — Help me make it through the night', thus went Marvin Hamlisch's dirge as sung by Kris Kristofferson over the titles of *Fat City* (Col. 1972). (A better title for the song would have been 'Help me make it through the fight'.) Contemplation of the fight-game seems to inspire a melancholy view of life and *Fat City* is no exception. Adapted by Leonard Gardner from his own novel, it tells of Billy Tully (Stacy Keach) who is attempting a comeback on the small-time boxing circuit at the age of 29. While training in the gym, he meets Ernie (Jeff Bridges), a

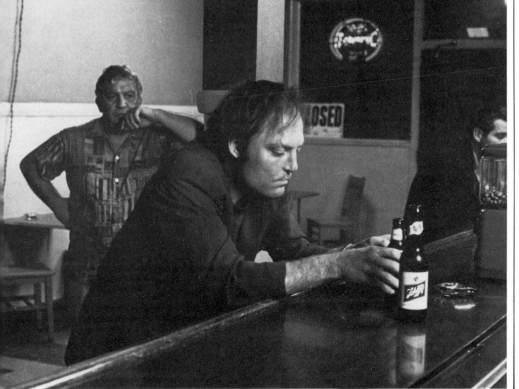

Stacy Keach in *Fat City*

young amateur, and persuades him to turn pro. The film traces their friendship, (there is a real fraternity among boxers), Tully's decline and the younger boxer's minor success. It takes place mainly in the small town of Stockton in the San Joaquin valley, North California, around the flop-houses, the dingy bars and half-empty boxing halls. Nobody does anything very noble. Nobody arranges a fix, nor is there any dramatic gesture of male pride. Boxing is just a tough way of making enough money to keep oneself in booze and broads. In an area of high unemployment, picking walnuts is the only alternative. Set in the late 40s, it could have been set in the 70s. There is something of the *Weltschmerz* of the Vietnam vet in Tully and of the rookie in Ernie. 'Don't waste your green years. Before you know it, your life's slipped away down the drain,' says Tully, not yet 30, to his young companion. Tully and Ernie go to a diner where they see a very old, feeble-minded Chinese dishwasher. 'How would you like to be him in the future?' Tully asks. 'Maybe he's happy,' answers Ernie. 'Maybe we're all happy' replies Tully dolefully, and turning around he sees life freeze for a moment. Muhammad Ali was reputed to have told director John Huston after a screening, 'Man, that's for real — that's me talking up there.' This seems a surprising comment from one of the most successful boxers ever about a film which depicts the no-hopers in the world of fifth-rate boxing, but the screenplay is so full of generalizations on the human condition that even Ali could identify with a loser in one way or another. If it is as Huston says 'about the spiritual process of the defeated and the futility and indestructibility of hope', the film itself is defeatist as it offers not a glimmer of hope nor any possibility for change. Most of the light is the artificial light in bars and above the ring. However, Huston knew the territory he explored. When he was 16, he saw the Dempsey-Firpo fight and thought it terrific theater. He was himself amateur lightweight champion of California before entering on a short pro career. Featured in the film are former champs, Curtis Cokes, Art Aragon and Reuben Navarro.

Jon Voight is *The All-*

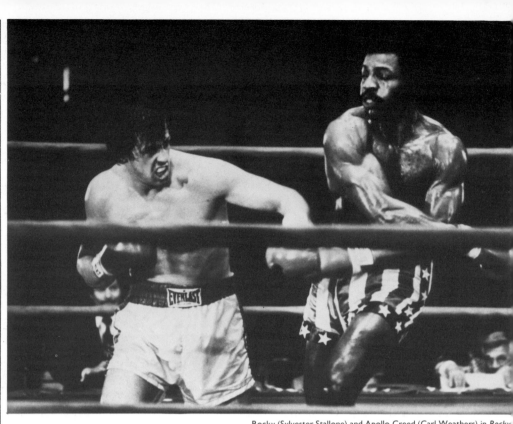

Rocky (Sylvester Stallone) and Apollo Creed (Carl Weathers) in *Rocky*

American Boy (WB 1973), a promising amateur boxer, hopeful of a place in the Olympics. But he doesn't want to assume the burden of anyone else's ambitions except his own. He wants to be his own man. 'A middle-class white sonofabitch,' says the team manager and the girl-friend he gets pregnant is also rather stinting in her praises. 'You're the most pathetic person I've ever met. Because you could be so much and you won't be anything.' It has to be said that no matter how much one may sympathize with his rebellion, the character becomes a pain in the ass. In one long scene in a gym, empty at first, then slowly filling with fighters doing exercises, the sounds of the gym mingle with the sounds of a Gregorian chant. You may find this deeply moving or you may throw up depending on which way your sensibilities lie. Charles Eastman wrote and directed.

In these violent times, the brutality that can exist within the confines of a boxing ring under the Queensbury rules is not enough for some people. For those who find boxing gloves an unnecessary protection used only by sissies, a number of movies featuring bare-knuckle fights are available. In *Hard Times* (1975 — *The Streetfighter* — GB), Charles Bronson gets involved

in illegal bare-knuckle bouts in the New Orleans of the depression era. The fights are arranged by gamblers on the docks and in the warehouses. Bronson (53 years old) enters the fights somewhat reluctantly. There is pain in his lived-in face, but he can handle himself. He knocks out a young giant who dares mock him by calling out, 'Hey, Pop, you're a little too old for this, ain't you?' He also beats the local champ in a bloody battle to satisfy the most demanding savage. Walter Hill directs his first film in a labored manner, trying too hard for mythic qualities against a background cluttered with period detail, but Bronson, as the archetypal movie loner, is pleasing even if one finds the subject antipathetic.

After the Sidney Poitier-Bill Cosby smash hit *Uptown Saturday Night* (WB 1974), it was inevitable they should say *Let's Do It Again* (WB 1975). The duo play members of the Sons and Daughters of Shaka Lodge who need to collect enough money to put up a new meeting hall. Being an amateur hypnotist, Poitier gets the idea of using his powers to make a puny pugilist into a champ. So successful is the hypnotized fighter (Jimmy Walker very funny), that Cosby dreams of one day matching Ali with a psyched-up

Sammy Davis Jr. Most of the punches and gags are telegraphed well in advance, but it is a likeable black Runyonesque yarn. George Foreman, ex-heavyweight champ makes an appearance.

Rocky (UA 1976) was the biggest boxing box-office hit for 20 years and a personal success story for Sylvester Stallone, who claims to have written the script in 3½ days. It won Oscars for Best Picture, Best Director (John G. Avildsen) and Best Editing (Richard Halsey). Rocky (Stallone) is a routine boxer living in the tough lower South Side of Philadelphia. Mickey (Burgess Meredith), the manager of his gym tells him, 'You fight like an ape. You'll never amount to anything.' On TV Rocky sees an interview given by Apollo Creed (Carl Weathers), a former Oakland raiders lineback), Heavyweight Champion of the World, who talks about his forthcoming Bicentennial Championship fight to be held in Philadelphia. Later in the week, Creed learns his opponent has been injured and the other contenders refuse to fight at such short notice, so the champ and promoters decide to give a local unknown the chance to prove that America is still the land of opportunity. Creed selects from a list a southpaw nicknamed 'The Italian Stallion' (Stallone in Italian

– an 'in' joke), for the obvious ethnic appeal of the contest. Who discovered America? An Italian.' Rocky gets his big break just as Ruby Keeler did in *42nd Street* when the star was unable to go on. ('You're going out an oldster, but you've got to come back a champ' could have been said to 30-year-old Rocky.) Mickey begs Rocky for a chance to get him into shape for the fight 5 weeks away. The training sequences are so real one can smell the sweat. There is an exuberant, popular feel to Avildsen's direction of these sequences, helped by the disco music of Bill Conti. The first time Rocky runs up the library stairs he gets a stitch. After a few weeks training he almost flies up the stairs and leaps into the air with exhileration. The film builds towards the climactic fight. All Rocky wants to do is go the distance to prove he isn't just another bum. The preparations in the dressing room are meticulously observed and then the entry into the ring. The black champion enters on a float dressed as George Washington and then strips to his starred-and-striped vest and trunks. Uncle Tom has become Uncle Sam. The fight itself is excitingly photographed, with occasional high shots of the ring. (Stallone is credited with the 'Boxing choreography'.) At first Rocky is outclassed, but suddenly he lands a terrific uppercut to the jaw and Creed takes an eight-count. By the end, both men are battered and bruised and the fight is declared a draw. There was no way there could not be a return in a sequel.

Stallone trained for six months before filming. He was under the eye of former fighter-trainer Jimmy Gambina, who was also technical director on the film; and he watched film of Rocky Marciano and Ezzard Charles. 'I had to teach myself to be a flat-footed steam engine who took 10 punches to give one.' Stallone's own story of how he came from nowhere to become champion of the Motion Picture Academy, parallels the story of *Rocky*. This Hollywood dream come true, somehow takes the sting out of the critics who say that the idea of Rocky getting a crack at the title is preposterous, although it is difficult to believe a champion would reach so low down for a challenger. The clichés of a poor boy's road to fame in the

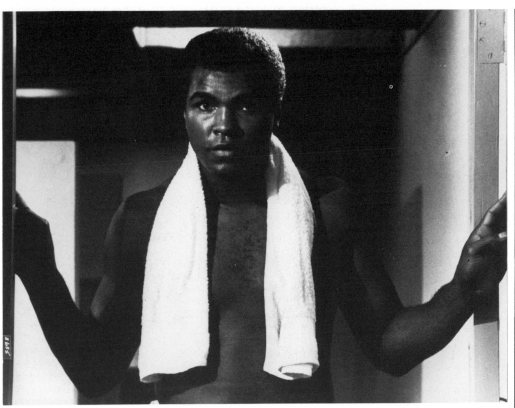

Muhammed Ali in *The Greatest*

golden land of opportunity are all there, but with enough tongue-in-the-cheek to make it palatable. It is in the tradition of *Somebody Up There Likes Me*, but it's more street wise than Robert Wise. The climax with Rocky and his girl-friend (Talia Shire) crying in each other's arms above the roar of the crowd is irresistible in its old-fashioned way and proves they do make movies like they used to. Audiences obviously want to believe in a happy ending where tomorrow doesn't exist. *Rocky* is another example of the American Dream as an opiate, lulling people away from responsibility and change into a Panglossian garden.

A real life champion, Muhammad Ali, was seen as himself in a movie about himself called *The Greatest* (Col. 1977). The movie directed by Tom Gries is rather like an

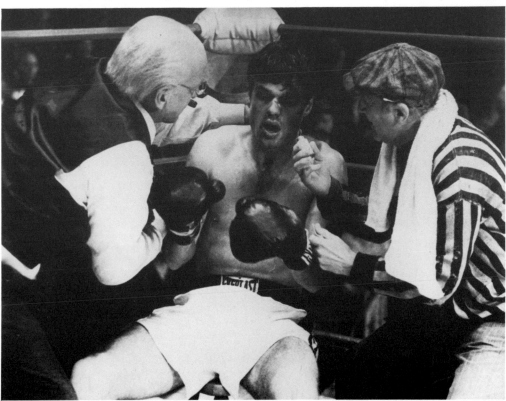

Corner action in *Movie Movie*

extended commercial advertizing a renowned and well-loved product. The message is clear. Cassius Clay is leading a wicked life. One night he's accosted by some Black Muslims as he's entering a hotel with a white whore. He's taken to a meeting to hear Malcolm X (James Earl Jones), is converted to Islam and becomes Muhammad Ali. Ali, who to nobody's surprise proves he can act, is more restrained, less amusing and exciting than he is in the flesh. The reconstructions of the Liston and Foreman fights are disappointing. The memory of the real thing is too fresh in the minds of fight fans. We do have the 35-year-old Ali playing the 22-year-old Cassius Clay shouting at Liston 'All right, you big ugly bear. This town ain't big enough for two fast hands. One of us has gotta leave.' There is the Foreman bout in Zaire with Ali pretending to be out on his feet and tiring Foreman out in the tropical heat. Nevertheless, it's all so tame and Ali and the actors impersonating Liston and Foreman hardly work up a sweat. But, although most of the film is an innocuous PR job, Ring Lardner Jnr's screenplay still has the courage to include Malcolm X's 'A white man is a blue-eyed devil' and Ali's protest against the Vietnam war saying 'No Vietcong ever called me nigger.' Super-star Muhammad Ali is always fascinating to watch even though his personality is slightly filtered through the camera lens.

Joey Popchick (Harry Hamlin) is a poor law student, who, in order to finance a trip to Vienna for his sister (Kathleen Beller) to save her eye-sight, abandons his studies for the fast money of the boxing ring. He is on the way to getting a crack at the title, when a crooked promoter (Eli Wallach) orders him to throw a vital fight. Joey refuses and his stubborness costs the life of his faithful trainer (George C. Scott). To avenge the death of his friend, Joey quickly completes his law studies so that he can personally prosecute the promoter in court. Told straight, this resumé could well be a fight picture of the thirties or forties, but it is, in fact, Stanley Donen's spoof *Dynamite Hands*, the first half of *Movie, Movie* (WB 1978) shot in black and white. Larry Gelbart and Sheldon Keller's dialogue is witty and the cast ad-

mirably straight-faced in delivering it. They have a nice line in mixed metaphors and *non sequiturs*. When someone attacks Joey's decision to give up his studies because of his sister, he retorts, 'My sister's eyes are below the belt.' 'These hands are for reading books,' says the boxer. 'I've taped more hands than you have in your head,' says the trainer, 'Gloves' Malloy (Scott). It is always assumed that parodies only work when one is familiar with the original, but in *Dynamite Hands* even if one has never seen a boxing melo, one can guess what it was like and enjoy it.

Presumably Franco Zeffirelli was not making a parody when he made *The Champ* (MGM 1979). This is even more of a tear-jerker than the 1931 version. In fact, there is not a dry eye on the screen. Jon Voight, giving a good imitation of Brando in *On the Waterfront*, works at a race-track. He drinks and is a bit soft in the head from all the punches he took when he was a boxer. But his little golden-haired blue-eyed gap-toothed 8-year-old son (Ricky Shroder) looks up to him and calls him 'The Champ'. When his ex-wife (Faye Dunnaway), a successful fashion designer, comes to claim the boy, Voight is distraught. He takes on a fight to justify his son's confidence in him, but we know that he is doomed. In the fight, in which both boxers would have been knocked out in the first minute in reality, Voight takes a lot of punishment but wins. As Wallace Beery did all those years ago, he dies in his son's arms in the dressing room. The son will be brought up in the most respectable middle-class way by a now loving mother and her husband. The color photography throughout is soft, the acting mostly loud. It's a pity Zeffirelli didn't go the whole hog and set it all to the music of Puccini.

The Main Event (WB 1979) is more about the battle of the sexes than bruisers. The posters had Barbra Streisand posing in boxing gear, supposedly to create a gender-reversal frisson, although with a nose like hers she makes an unrealistic boxer. The screenplay gets a lot of fun out of a woman finding herself in a macho environment. Streisand plays a perfume manufacturer, (she has the 'nose' for it), who goes bankrupt and finds that

her only asset is a boxer's contract. She has inherited 'Kid Natural' (Ryan O'Neil). He seems to have given up fighting and runs the Knockout Driving Academy, a driving school in the shape of a boxing glove. ('The thumb leaks a little') Barbra tries to get him back into the ring in order to earn some money for her. He objects. 'Do you want my body on your head for the rest of your life?' She finally persuades him to make a comeback and begins to promote him like perfume. 'You're treating me like an object. You think I'm a girl?' She handles herself well in a man's world even sleeping in a dorm with trainers and sparring partners. Unfortunately, she soon finds out that her protegé can do everything except box. 'Hands weren't meant for hitting' he explains. In the final fight, he suddenly and unconvincingly becomes a good boxer. If he wins, their partnership is over, so abandoning its previous feminist tone, she, like the film, throws in the towel while he's on top. A fatuous ending to a likeable screwball comedy that could've been a Gable-Lombard vehicle except for the explicit language and the bed-sharing.

Rocky II (UA 1980) continues exactly from where *Rocky* left off. (I suppose the world needed another *Rocky* like a punch in the head.) Once you've seen *Rocky One*, you've seen them both. Structurally the films are very much alike. Rocky preparing for his fight with the champion Apollo Creed. At first he gives up fighting for his wife's sake, and because he might lose the sight of one eye. He works for a while in his brother-in-law's meat shop, but when he is laid off, he finds he's not qualified to do anything. 'It's all I know,' he says. It's not that Rocky is punchy, he has a 'relaxed brain'. He finally decides to return to the ring against the will of his shrinking-violet wife. 'I don't ask you to stop being a woman. Don't ask me to stop being a man.' In the championship, he has to switch from south-paw to orthodox to protect his eye. Not an easy thing to do as most boxers will testify, but even with this handicap he wins the Championship of the World. Sylvester Stallone this time directs as well as stars and writes. His creation of the good-hearted pug is still very

funny. A cross between Lee J. Cobb and Robert Mitchum, his self-mocking performance helps one swallow the simple emotions and situations represented.

Jake La Motta won the world middleweight championship in June 1949 when Marcel Cerdan retired hurt with a torn shoulder muscle. He lost the title to 'Sugar' Ray Robinson on a technical knockout in February 1951. Born on New York's Lower East Side and raised in the Bronx, he was convicted of attempted burglary, was married five times, was imprisoned on a moral charge involving a 14-year-old prostitute at his Miami night club, became penniless, had a career as a stand-up comedian and became the subject of Martin Scorsese's *Raging Bull* (US 1980). La Motta told Scorsese after it was released, 'You have made me champ again.' Conversely, the movie can only discredit the man even further. Bob Waters in *Ring Magazine* writes, 'Because of his incredible record, Jake La Motta is a candidate for Boxing's Hall of Fame...The Hall of Fame doesn't judge men by their demeanor out of the ring. It judges them on what they did in the ring...When La Motta agreed to throw the fight with Billy Fox, he also agreed to forego consideration by posterity.' His demeanor outside the ring is the main concern of the movie, the boxing is almost incidental. Virtually no idea is given of the progression of his career or of any of his bouts. The fights are treated as an excuse for a series of powerful and beautifully photographed black and white images. At times slow motion is used aptly, at others meaninglessly. Robinson's final rapid fire blows being reduced to slow motion is a mere aesthetic conceit. The director builds up La Motta's championship shot at Cerdan with a long triumphal tracking shot following him into the ring. By jumping from round to round and giving no explanation of how or why La Motta wins, the excitement is dissipated. What emerges is not the director's dislike of boxing, but his complete indifference to it. He makes no attempt to understand it, but overlays it with a histrionic approach and pretentious images such as blood dripping from a rope. He also tries to counterbalance the violence of the man with the cloying music of

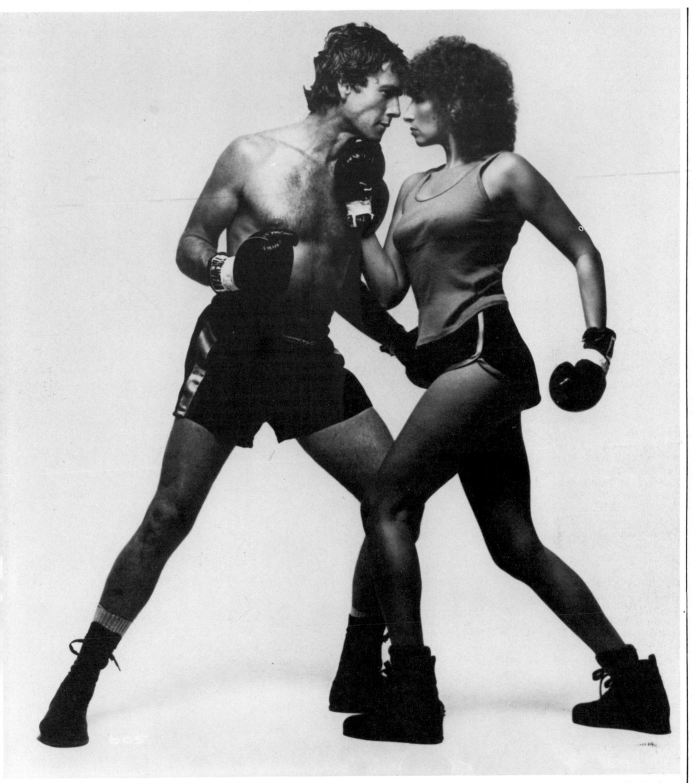

Ryan O'Neal and Barbra Streisand in *The Main Event*

Mascagni and by ending the film with a quote from the St John Gospel, 'One thing I know that, whereas I was blind, now I see.' Nothing that precedes it justifies this, unless it is the picture of La Motta in prison beating his hands against the wall. La Motta neither changes (except physically) nor develops. The structure of the film parallels the monotony of the character, because of the consistent alternation between professional fights and domestic ones. Virtually an anti-biopic, it tells us nothing of his past, nor is there much interest in conventional narrative techniques. It does tell us a little of the close-knit Italian American community that produced La Motta, Scorsese and Robert De Niro with the underlying rigid and sentimental codes of masculinity. It presents the male animal's primitive emotions, but there is no way that Scorsese or even De Niro can make such a completely unattractive protagonist into Samson Agonistes. The background to the picture would make a good movie in itself. The effect it had on La Motta's life, throwing him once more into the limelight, and Robert De Niro's preparation for the rôle. De Niro gained a horrifying 60 lbs in 4 months and then had to take it all off again in the following 4 months. There is madness in this method acting. The actor's art is that of illusion, but there are those who think this self-inflicted punishment was vindicated by De Niro's extraordinary Oscar-winning performance.

Overleaf: Robert De Niro as Jake La Motta in *Raging Bull*

41

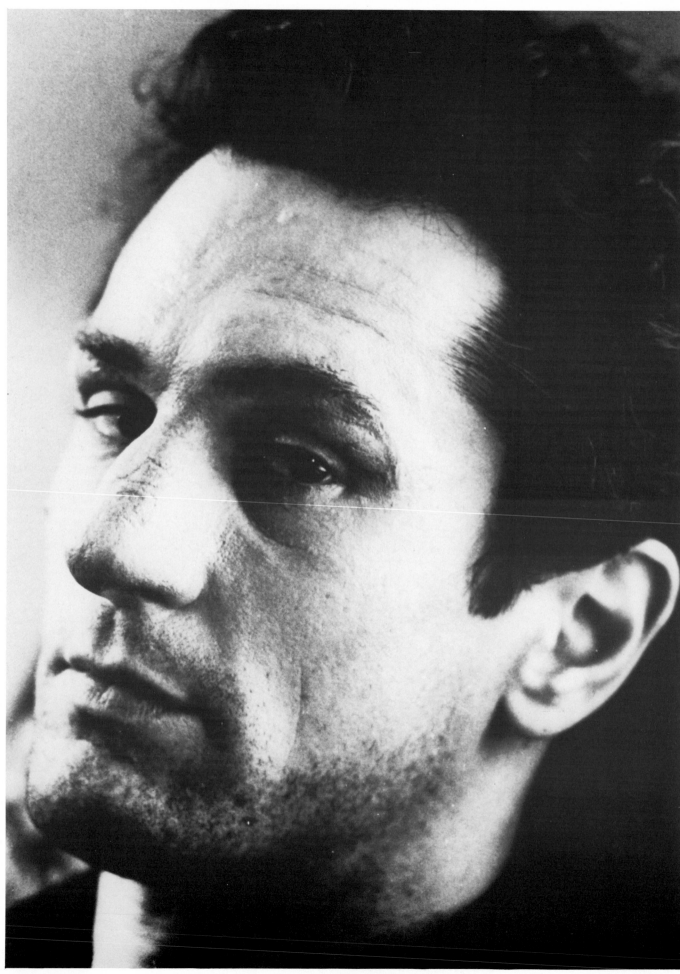

OTHER BOXING MOVIES

Hold Everything *WB 1930* was one of many movies in which Joe E. Brown found himself in a sporting context. It also starred former light-heavy champ, George Carpentier.

Dumbbells in Ermine *WB 1930* was an entertaining comedy about a young girl (Barbara Kent) in love with prizefighter, Robert Armstrong. James Gleason played his trainer.

Winner Take All *WB 1932* had James Cagney in his first incarnation as a prizefighter. Cagney trained hard to look the part in this mediocre drama.

The Life of Jimmy Dolan *WB 1933* (**The Kid's Last Fight** — GB) was remade in 1939 as the far superior **They Made Me a Criminal**. Douglas Fairbanks Jr is the lightweight (in more senses than one) champ wrongly accused of murder. On the lam, he finds himself at a home for crippled children and in order to help pay the mortgage on the home, takes on heavyweight King Cobra.

The Personality Kid *WB 1934* was prizefighter Pat O'Brien whose marriage and career are on the rocks, until his wife announces she's going to have a baby. Suddenly, he has something to fight for. O'Brien had been a boxer in his college days.

Conflict *UI. 1936* starred John Wayne as a lumberjack involved in fake prizefights. When he meets Jean Rogers, he decides to fight fair. Based on Jack London's 'The Abysmal Brute'.

The Perfect Specimen *WB 1937* was a tame comedy in which Errol Flynn proved he could handle himself with his fists as well as he had previously with swords. Flynn had reputedly done some amateur boxing in Australia which stood him in good stead for this and the later **Gentleman Jim**.

When's Your Birthday? *Renown 1937* was the vital question asked by boxer Joe E. Brown, because he can only win if the horoscopes of the fighters are favorable. Amusing nonsense.

Spirit of Youth *Grand National Films 1938* featured reigning Heavyweight Champion of the world, Joe Louis in a story of how a boxer is saved from a K.O. by the appearance of his home-town sweetheart at the ringside. The New York critic in 1938 said, 'It's an all-color picture; members of the so-called ruling white race enter it only to be knocked flat.'

The Kid Comes Back *WB 1938* actually starred secondary role heavy, Barton MacLane, which gives one some idea of this cheapie boxing melodrama. Wayne 'Kid Galahad' Morris and Maxie Rosenbloom featured.

The Kid from Kokomo *WB 1938* starred Pat O'Brien as a fighter who believed that he and Whistler had the same mother. The movie goes to show that writers and directors can be as brainless as fighters.

The Crowd Roars *MGM 1938* when Robert Taylor wins by a K.O., despite the threats of underworld boss Edward Arnold. Maureen O'Sullivan backs him up.

Kid Nightingale *WB 1939* was a pathetic comedy in which John Payne played an operatic tenor who prefered the ring to 'The Ring.'

Golden Gloves *Par. 1940* introduced Robert Ryan to the screen in a small role. Ryan had been heavyweight champion of Dartmouth College, and he is matched here with Richard Denning in the climax of this tale of corruption in 'amateur' boxing. This was one of the first of a run of second features directed by Edward Dmytryk, who went on to bigger things.

The Leather Pushers *UI 1940* had a ludicrous finale in which boxer Richard Arlen has to give his blood to save the life of his stabbed pal Andy Devine, not long before a fight. Andy spurs Arlen on through a loudspeaker hooked up from the dressing room to the ringside.

Sunday Punch *MGM 1942* told the crazy story of how William Lundigan has to decide between continuing as a head-puncher or becoming a head-shrinker.

Footlight Serenade *TCF 1942* was a particularly inane Betty Grable musical in which Victor Mature played a boxer who switches the ring for the stage. They star in a revue called 'Down and Out' (an inappropriate title for something supposed to be light and uplifting) which has a big boxing number as its climax. Most of Mature's famous roles were played bare-chested, prompting Groucho Marx to comment that he avoided movies with Mature in them, because the hero's bust was always bigger than the heroine's.

The Navy Way *Par. 1944* preached that it is not winning that counts in life, but the methods used. Prizefighter Johnny Jersey (Robert Lowery), whose call-up robbed him of a chance at the championship, wins by fighting dirty thus shocking all the decent, clean-living tars watching. Johnny learns to be just like them, thanks to pretty W.A.V.E. Jean Parker

Joe Palooka, Champ *Monogram 1946* was ideal kiddie-matinee fodder with Joe Kirkwood Jr. in the title role and Leon Errol as his manager. Joe Louis and Henry Armstrong appear briefly.

Killer McCoy *MGM 1947* was notable for being Mickey Rooney's first grown-up role. (He was 27 years old). To the background music of **Liebenstraum**, he becomes lightweight champion of the world in order to keep his father out of debt. Rooney gets mixed up with gangsters, but emerges with his integrity intact to win the heart of insipid college girl, Ann Blyth.

The Big Punch *WB 1948* starred Gordon MacRae and Wayne Morris. MacRae is a boxer framed for murder after refusing to throw a fight, and Morris leaves the ring in order to enter the church. The sort of movie that gives both boxing and religion a bad name.

Whiplash *WB 1949* told of a struggling artist (Dane Clark) who becomes a prizefighter. Alexis Smith is the woman who goades him on and Zachary Scott is her mad, bad, crippled ex-fighter husband. Confucius say: 'Man cannot paint with boxing-gloves on, nor can he box with a paint-brush.'

Right Cross *MGM 1950* gently lifted the lid on the boxing world. Ricardo Montalban is the Mexican fighter who feels everyone is against him because of his race. Dick Powell (sports writer), Lionel Barrymore (manager) and June Allyson were also cast. Marilyn Monroe slinks by.

The Golden Gloves Story *Eagle Lion 1950* wasn't really worth telling. Dewey Martin and Kevin O'Morison are two middleweight rivals for the championship and a girl (Gregg Sherwood). Ex-middleweight champ Tony Zale appeared in it.

Sailor Beware *Par. 1951* was a navy farce starring Dean Martin and Jerry Lewis as the cad and the cretin. The one bright spot in the movie was Jerry Lewis taking on a battling sailor in the ring.

Abbott and Costello Meet The Invisible Man *UI 1951* in the boxing milieu. Bud and Lou are private eyes helping to clear the name of a prizefighter charged with beating his manager to death. The fighter swallows a serum that makes him invisible. Lou, posing as a boxer, sees his opponents knocked flat by the invisible man. Not many gags are visible or risible.

The Ring *UA 1952* was a serious attempt to look at racial discrimination against Mexican-Americans in LA and a young boxer's efforts to win greater freedom and prestige for his people. Against the conventions of the genre, he doesn't become champion. He is knocked out by top lightweight Art Aragon (playing himself). The boxing scenes have pace and plausibility, while the acting from Lalo Rios, Rita Moreno and Gerald Mohr is effective, even if there is a thin line between histrionics and hysterics.

The Fighter *UA 1952* was adapted from Jack London's story 'The Mexican'. It told of Filipe Rivera's efforts to make enough money in 1910 to buy guns for the Mexican Revolution. He takes on a first-rate contender in the ring on a winner-takes-all deal. Typically, he takes a terrible beating until, seeing the figures of his murdered family before his half-blinded eyes, he knocks out his over-confident opponent. Richard Conte played Filipe. Well-photographed Mexican corn.

Off-Limits *Par. 1953* (**Military Policeman** — GB) teamed Bob Hope with Mickey Rooney in the army. A prizefighter manager in civilian life, Hope agrees to train Rooney. Rooney is Hope's last small white hope. Rooney cannot win a bout without Hope's instructions in the corner. He loses when Hope gets seasick while watching his protegé battling on a battleship. When Rooney is challenging for the championship, Hope is kept away from the fight by racketeers. By watching it on TV, he is able to give Rooney advice through a walkie-talkie.

City of Badmen *TCF 1953* was Carson City. In this Technicolor western, thieves try to steal the takings of the Bob Fitzsimmons-Jim Corbett world title fight on March 17 1897. Veteran stuntman, Gil Perkins was Fitzsimmons and John Day played Corbett. They trained for a month to fight old-style and the ring was the authentic 8-poster instead of the current 4-poster. Dale Robertson starred.

The Joe Louis Story *UA 1953* covered two decades of 'The Brown Bomber's' life starting in Detroit in 1932 and ending with his defeat by Rocky Marciano in 1951. Coley Wallace had the difficult task of convincing as Joe Louis, possibly the finest heavyweight champion of all time. Wallace stood 6ft 2ins and weighed 200 lbs about the same weight as Joe. He had an impressive pro record and was one of the few boxers to have defeated Marciano as an amateur. His acting and Robert Gordon's direction left a lot to be desired. The best moments were the newsreel clips of Joe's actual fights. The producer Sterling Silliphant lost money and backers, because the picture wouldn't play in the South. Perhaps they couldn't bear to watch Joe Louis demolishing Max Schmeling and the Aryan supremacy theory at the same time.

Carmen Jones *TCF 1954* was Oscar Hammerstein II's version of Bizet's 'Carmen', which converted the bullfighter Escamillo into the prizefighter Husky Miller. His famous theme song was sung from an open car and went: 'Stand up and fight until you hear the bell — Stand toe to toe — Give blow for blow.' Well, that's show-bizetness!

Tennessee Champ *MGM 1954* had religion rearing its haloed head again in the shape of Dewey Martin, a pious youth, who becomes champion, because he believes God is in his corner. He finds himself facing the man he thought he had killed and promptly begins to demolish him again. It was a sprightly comedy thanks to the presence of Shelley Winters, Keenan Wynn and Charles Buchinsky (later Bronson).

A Heart As Big As That (**Un Coeur Gros Comme Ca**) *Films de la Pleiade 1961* was the story of a young boxer from Senegal discovering Paris. It is not exactly a documentary nor a work of fiction. The director Francois Reichenbach filmed the boxer, Abdoulaye Faye, preparing for and losing fights. Reichenbach edited several fights into one and also 20 hours of tape of Faye talking with wonderful simplicity. The cast were 'unknown boxers and fans.'

Walkover *Film Polski-Syrena Films 1965* was directed by Jerzy Skolimowski and is one of the few films about amateur boxing. In **Walkover** Skolimowski, himself an amateur boxer, played a rootless 30-year-old who decides to return to boxing. It is not only his hobby, it is his obsession. Rather an equivocal film, it creates a feeling for the industrial locale and poses various questions about competition, the problems of youth and ageing. Skolimowski's first feature was a documentary called **Boxing** (1961).

The Adventures of Bullwhip Griffin *Walt Disney 1967* is no more than an over-extended bar brawl set during the California gold rush. Roddy McDowall earns the nickname of 'Bullwhip' when he K.O.'s Mountain Ox (Mike Mazurki) with a lucky punch. In the return fight, he is revived by the kiss of Suzanne Pleshette after almost being knocked out.

The Legendary Champs *Turn of the Century Fights Inc. 1967* was a fascinating documentary including film of almost every world heavyweight title fight from 1882 to 1929 i.e. from John L to Gene T. There is Jack Johnson seemingly shading his eyes in the hot Havana sun while on the canvas, and Dempsey and Charlie Chaplin having a mock fight.

A.K.A. Cassius Clay *1970*, Muhammad Ali discusses how he would have defeated Johnson, Dempsey, Louis and Marciano. There is also film of his bouts, his being accepted into the Black Muslims, and an appearance by Stepin Fetchitt, the wonderful black comedian from the movies when blacks were expected to do exactly what his name implied.

Jack Johnson *1971* was a cunningly edited documentary of the life of the great champion, using stills and old newsreels. It is narrated by Brock Peters with a jazz score by Miles Davis. A good corrective to **The Great White Hope**.

Penitentiary *Eagle Films 1981* is an almost exclusively black prison where a prisoner has to fight for survival every day. Leon Isaac Kennedy is the unjustly imprisoned hero who tries to 'keep his ass clean' by taking on all comers in and out of the boxing ring. The boxing, screwing, language and violence are pretty realistic, but underneath it's a corny old Cagney-Raft prison movie. Jamaa Fanaka (producer, director and writer) has the skill to make a less exploitive movie.

FOOTBALL

Football has been called 'the fighting spirit of America itself'. A game of strength, courage and speed, it is a combination of power and grace — the power is constant as two machines collide, the grace comes intermittently like sparks off the wheels of a giant locomotive. A terrible beauty is born in a Bowl, which is shattered by permanent injury or death. Football is good, bad, ugly, sagacious, stupid and explicitly violent. It is, according to Dave Meggyesy, former St Louis Cardinals' pro, 'one of the most dehumanizing experiences a person can face'. The players may be 'the custodians of the concepts of democracy' but they themselves are bondsmen under a dictatorship run by moguls and implemented by martinets whose voices make those of drill sergeants sound sweet to the ear. Football is a Big Business in which players are only cogs in the wheeling and dealing. Football players are commonly seen as ten-ton trucks with crew-cuts, as broad as they are thick and yet a player (Red Grange) could lead Damon Runyon to write. 'He is melody and symphony. He is crashing sound.' Melody is harmony, war is discord and football is a war game full of military terms such as blitz, bomb, platoon, squad and attack. In Vietnam 'end run' was used to describe outflanking operations. It is the sport favored by Presidents Eisenhower, Kennedy, Nixon and Ford. Football is presumed to build initiative, self-confidence, discipline and teamwork, qualities needed for survival in a highly competitive society. Football may be tough, but the world outside the stadium is infinitely tougher. Sporting glory, like youth, fades fast. Biff Loman in *Death of a Salesman*, encouraged by his father Willie, neglects his studies for football. Years later, Willie still visualizes his 34-year-old no-hoper son as he once was.

God...remember that Eb-

Sometimes, Rock, when the team's up against it, when things are wrong and the breaks are beating the boys, tell them to go in there with all they've got and win just one for the Gipper...

PAT O'BRIEN as **Knute Rockne, All-American**
(WB 1940)

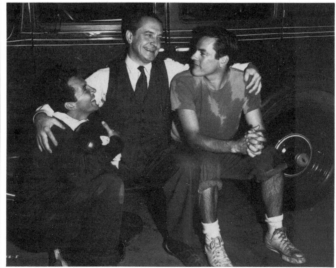

Cameron Mitchell (left), Frederic March (center) and Kevin McCarthy as Biff in *Death of a Salesman*

bet's Field game? The championship of the city? When that team came out...he was the tallest, remember? Like a young god. Hercules...something like that. And the sun, the sun all around him...Remember how he waved to me? Right up from the field, with the

representatives of three colleges standing by? And the buyers I brought, and the cheers when he came out — Loman, Loman, Loman! God Almighty, he'll be great yet. A star like that, magnificent, can never really fade away!

But both Willie and his son

have to wake up from the pipe dream engendered by his high-school football triumphs.

Biff: I'm not bringing home any prizes anymore and you're going to stop waiting for me to bring them home.

One can imagine many of the football heroes of those carefree college movies becoming like Biff Loman in a post happy-ending existence. Nevertheless the dream continued aided by the Dream Factory, despite dissension creeping in with pictures such as *M*A*S*H* (TCF 1970), *The Longest Yard* (Par. 1974) and *North Dallas 40* (Par. 1974). It is no surprise to find that *Flash Gordon* (1980 model) is New York Jets quarterback. He demonstrates his gridiron skill by quarterbacking through evil Ming's minions in order to save Dale from a fate worse than death. Flash is the apotheosis of the All-American, the Aryan clean-cut guy who would make any coach proud to have on his team. Dr Zarkov is the coach, Dale, the pretty co-ed and Ming, the pinko attempting to destroy the sport and therefore the American way of life. 'Football is more than a game. It is an American Institution.' How then has that other great American Institution, Hollywood, portrayed this seasonal ritual test of he-manhood? Do the movies contain the truths, half-truths, received ideas and images of the sport as described above?

There are three basic types of football movie. The first is of the rah-rah college variety of which there was an abundance in the 1920's and 1930's. The second is the inspirational drama where football symbolizes character-building and sometimes the nation. The third type is the Post-Vietnam movie, which took a more abrasive and raunchier view of the 'football mentality', a mentality which seemed to be allied with that which got the US involved in Vietnam.

The only plot of the college

movie concerns the handsome quarterback who, neglecting the sweet co-ed who dotes on him, falls for the indispensable college widow, and as a consequence finds his football game suffering. He comes to his senses two minutes before the final whistle of the big game with his team losing. Suddenly realizing he loves the sweet co-ed after all, he scores the winning touchdown. As Groucho says in *Horse Feathers* (Par. 1932), 'A college widow stood for something in those days. In fact, she stood for plenty.' Every fall, in the 20s and 30s, thousands of Americans who had never been near a college, rooted for college teams like the best of alumni. For over 50 years, football was almost exclusively a university affair and it's ironic that the sport with the most anti-intellectual image should be linked with places of learning. Even today, attendance at college is virtually a prerequisite for the playing of football. In *Breaking Away* (TCF 1979) the high-school football star, son of a stone-cutter, has trouble adjusting to life off the playing fields and he takes his frustration out on the more privileged college students. In the earlier pictures no such social comment was made. The world outside college hardly existed. How clean and white all the students were! If a young girl wandered accidentally into a dressing room, she would not have heard a single obscenity nor seen any male nudity. Football was the *raison d'être* of the college where the goal of every male student was 2 upright posts and a cross-bar, and the only book he saw was the playbook. It would seem that the Groves of Academe had been cut down to make room for football fields.

The more dramatic formula was generally one of boy meets ball, boy loses ball, boy gets ball — co-existing with the usual boy meets girl theme. Football provided a means of exorcising character deficiencies and pointing the way for young people. *Knute Rockne, All-American* is the archetypal inspirational hagio-pic in this category. Sometimes the perennial argument of when is an amateur an amateur was raised, but anything that ruffled the system was soon ironed out by the end. However, in the 1960s, when student protests, awakened by the Vietnam war and racial injustice, swept the campuses, issues were not so simple. Nixon saw an analogy between military action in Vietnam and football. 'It's like football. You run a play and it fails. Then you turn around and call the same play again, because they aren't expecting it.' It was the calling into question of this 'football mentality' that forced the football movie to grow up.

In the same year as Red Grange was recruited to pro-

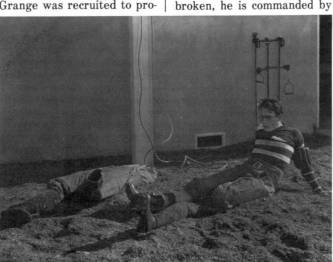

Harold Lloyd and the tackling dummy in *The Freshman*

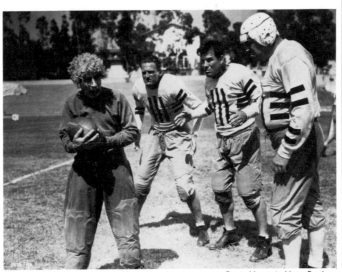

Brave Harpo in *Horse Feathers*.

University of Illinois, Harold Lloyd scored the winning touchdown for Tate College in *The Freshman* (Pathe 1925). Coming in on the wave of the college craze, *The Freshman* was a gentle spoof on college life and the sport around which it seemed to revolve. Harold 'Speedy' Lamb has arrived at college full of pre-conceived ideas of what makes a college man. He introduces himself to his fellow students in the same manner as a movie hero he had

fessional football from the once seen. 'I'm just a regular fellow — Step right up and call me Speedy,' finishing with a little jig. He is determined to become the most popular man on the campus which means joining the football team. Harold, still wearing his glasses, turns out on the first day of training much to the scorn of the strapping guys on the team. He waits his turn at the tackling dummy. When it is broken, he is commanded by place. He good-heartedly accepts and allows himself to be tackled mercilessly until he finally collapses at the coach's feet. It is a cruel and unfunny episode in an otherwise hilarious film. The coach was not unlike coaches who were known for their iron discipline and scant regard for injuries. Injuries, however, do not seem to have much physical reality in football movies of this period. They are rather like those that Tom suffers at the

the sadistic coach to take its paws of Jerry. He might literally be flattened by a steam-roller one minute, but he's his own cat-shape the next. By the last reel, Harold thinks he has been selected for the big game, but he's really only the water boy. You see, men don't throw passes to guys who wear glasses. Waiting on the bench to be called, he watches anxiously as Tate College is losing and the number of injured players mounts until there is no one else to send in. Although he is only the water boy, Harold argues passionately with the coach to be sent in. The coach, with an air of what-the-hell pessimism, gives Harold the chance to prove himself. On he goes and finds himself at the bottom of every pile up, but suddenly he has the ball in his grasp. First strolling, which confuses the opposing team, he then makes a wild dash and is across the goal line as the final whistle blows. Harold naturally becomes a hero and everyone now imitates his little jig. Mainly because of a wonderful set-piece at the college dance, this is one of Harold Lloyd's funniest comedies, so it is perhaps carping to question the whole philosophy of conformity. Harold, by proving himself at football, is in the end accepted by the loathsome under-graduates.

From Harold Lloyd's strivings towards bespectacled respectability, we come to the apple-cart upsetting antics of the Marx Brothers in *Horse Feathers* (Par. 1932). The anarchic tone is set by Groucho singing 'Whatever it is, I'm against it.' Under the guise of respectability, as a doctor, lawyer, hotel-manager or, as in *Horse Feathers*, the dean of a college, Groucho punctures social conventions from within with his irreverant jibes. Beneath every stuffed shirt, is a Groucho bursting to get out. What better place to create havoc than within the conservative Ivy-covered walls of a college. As Professor Wagstaff, dean of Huxley college founded in 1888, (the year they won their last football match,) Groucho is forced to do something about improving the team. Knowing of the illegal practise of buying pro football players to play for a college, Groucho's son, Zeppo, tells him he can buy two of the greatest players in the country. They hang out at a speakeasy downtown where the password is 'Swordfish'. They can buy them in time for the big game against Darwin college. (Is it possible there is an academic joke here? Huxley vs Darwin.) Chico and Harpo get the players, but the brothers are kidnapped on the day of the game. Meanwhile Groucho, who has the football signals, is being seduced by the college widow (Thelma Holt) because she is really a spy for Darwin. To cut a long pair of pants short, Chico and Harpo are prisoners in their underwear. They manage to escape, arriving onto the field by horse-cart like Ben Hur in his chariot. The first half is over and Huxley are down 12–0 to Darwin. They rush to the bench and start playing pinochle. Now it is eleven players from Darwin faced with Huxley players and 3 Marx brothers. (3½ if you count Zeppo.) Groucho, who is busy flirting in the stands, suddenly gets up and tackles a Darwin player heading for a touchdown. 'That'll teach him to pass a lady without tipping his hat.' He then joins the backfield. Chico and Harpo rush into a huddle. When the huddle breaks, they're playing pinochle. At the scrimmage, Chico signals, 'Uno, due, tre vendi-this-a-time, we go left en-di.' Harpo attaches a rubber band to the ball. He throws to Chico and as the Darwin team head for the pass receiver, Harpo scores again by scattering banana skins behind him as he runs for the goal-line. Huxley win by a vast score, thanks to the Marx Brothers total disregard for the rules, something they did on almost every occasion. Football survived this subversive comic attack on it. However, the knockabout humor of the finale to all their films, is not nearly as telling or as amusing as Groucho's verbal felicities, Chico's verbal infelicities, and Harpo's non-verbal felicities. Their next movie was *Duck Soup* (Par. 1933) which took the logical step from satirizing college football to satirizing war.

The Marx Brothers' first two pictures for MGM, *A Night at the Opera* (1935) and *A Day at the Races* (1937), were directed by Sam Wood, who injected an element of sentimentality into their films completely absent from the Marx Brothers' earlier work for Paramount. There was no shortage of sentimentality in his direction of *Navy Blue and*

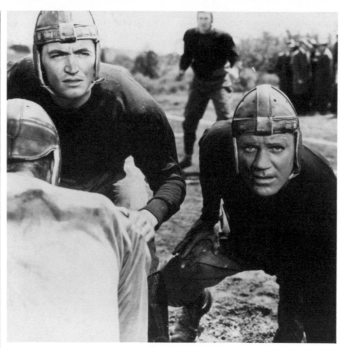

Pat O'Brien (right) as *Knute Rockne — All American*

Gold (MGM 1937). Annapolis is the setting for this tale of 3 young men (Robert Young, James Stewart, Tom Brown) from different backgrounds who are coached for the Navy football team. Their ultimate ambition is to play in the big game against the Army. However, before this can be realized, they and the audience have to suffer various trials and tribulations. Finally, all three play against the Army. The Navy wins and the coach sheds tears of joy when he hears the news on his sickbed. The life of the cadets is well portrayed and there is a genuine atmosphere of youthful high spirits, but the dramatic part of the story is sentimental hokum.

The problem of professionalism in college football is tackled in a modest way in *Saturday's Heroes* (RKO 1937). Val Webster (Van Heflin), the star of Calton University's football team, is caught selling complimentary tickets and is asked to resign. Val leaves warning he'll 'blow the whole football set-up wide open.' He is appointed assistant coach at Weston college, a small school whose next game is against Calton. Val persuades the President of Weston to subsidize players openly and not in secret and to refuse to meet any college team that isn't equally open. College players today are really pros, but pretend to be amateurs, he tells them. Weston defeats Calton for the first time in 12 years (in the last minute natch!), the

Presidents come to an agreement to pay its players openly and Val is vindicated. All very noble, except that the way in which Val helps Weston to win, not only smacks of smart practise but is unconvincing. With a minute to play, one of the players, pretending to be walking off the field in a rage, has the ball passed to him and he sprints to a touchdown before the astonished Calton team can start after him.

Football has had few more legendary figures than *Knute Rockne, All-American* (WB 1940 – *A Modern Hero* GB) and Pat O'Brien few better roles. His melodramatic delivery of the famous locker-room pep-talk speech 'Win just one for the Gipper' became his party piece which he performed everywhere. It is not strange that the Irish-American actor who specialized in soft-spoken but tough cops and priests should play the part of the Norwegian-American football coach. 'The Rock' did combine the qualities of cop and priest that made him one of the most revered of all college coaches. Lloyd Bacon directed this heady Frank Merriwell stuff in an unashamedly sentimental way. If at the time it inspired young men to do-or-die heroics, it is difficult to imagine even the most dedicated young jock today being no more than amused. (The Gipper speech is often parodied. In *Airplane* (Par. 1980), the doctor tries to inspire the pilot of a runaway plane by referring to his pal

who died in Vietnam. 'Win one for Zipper,' he says. Burt Reynolds gives his own version in *The Longest Yard*.) The story, based on the private papers of Mrs Rockne and reports by friends and associates, starts with the Rockne family arriving in America in 1892 and settling in Chicago where cute Knute, aged 7, learns to play football. Years pass and Knute has earned enough money to get a place at the then unknown University of Notre Dame, where he shares a room with Gus Dorais (Owen Davis Jr.). In the fall of 1913, Notre Dame beats The Army decisively, thanks to the Dorais to Rockne forward pass. The game launched the traditional series between Notre Dame and The Army. After Rockne graduates with honors in chemistry, he becomes coach to his old team and makes The Fighting Irish of Notre Dame into a household name. His leadership inspires them to new heights. But not everything goes smoothly. There is a bad defeat by The Army, Rockne is attacked by sports writers, he is stricken by illness, he is hauled before an investigating committee to defend the sport he loves, and of course George Gipp dies at the age of 23. In 1931, while on vacation with his family in Miami, he is called to California on urgent business. He decides to take a plane, much against his wife's wishes (wives are always prescient after the event), because he wants to hurry back to his family. But the plane crashes, Knute Rockne is killed and the whole nation mourns with the help of the Moreau Choir of Notre Dame. The movie has something to interest everyone. It is a must for all alumni of Notre Dame. The football freak won't be disappointed either. We are shown the development of Rockne's famous backfield shift, presented as an historically important event. (At least as important as James Stewart in *The Glenn Miller Story* (1954) discovering the unique sound of the band. Both Rockne and Miller were killed in plane crashes.) For the movie buff there is the chance to see Pat O'Brien at his ghastly best and for cliché collectors, there is enough to stuff a linebacker's helmet. For the politically-minded there is 29-year-old Ronald Reagan as the dying Gipper, rehearsing for his last and most important role.

Even with Mickey Mouse courses and special 'brain coaches', a large percentage of student-athletes leave college after 4 years without a degree. The campus jock with the stone-age IQ has long been a figure for jest. In *Rise and Shine* (TCF 1941), based on James Thurber's 'My Life and Hard Times', Clayton College is fortunate to have among its students the greatest halfback that ever lived. That he is also as great a half-wit as he is a halfback, causes a few problems. Jack Oakie plays this dumbbell, rather broadly, which is dictated by the general style of the film. For example, Milton Berle is cast as Seabiscuit, a man who thinks he's a horse and who ends up pulling a cart in order to get Oakie to the big game in time. He has been kidnapped by racketeers on the night before the game against Notre Dame, but is rescued by George Murphy just in time to get back for the last quarter. Oakie, who is always terrified of the dam bursting, is told by Murphy that the dam has bust. The terrified Oakie, who has the ball, runs 95 yards for a touchdown and out of the stadium seeking high ground.

Another halfback appeared in *Easy Living* (RKO 1949) directed by Jacques Tourneur, master of the macabre, which starred Victor Mature of whom the director might have said 'I worked with a Zombie.' Star player Mature has hopes of being named coach at Illinois State, only to find himself eliminated in favor of best friend, Sonny Tufts, because the college authorities feel that his selfish wife (Lizabeth Scott) won't fit into the new environment. Poor Mature is also turned down for insurance because a medical examination reveals a heart condition which threatens his playing career. He takes his troubles to a bar and club secretary, Lucille Ball. (She's the only ball it's safe to handle.) On the eve of the championship playoff, Tufts injures a knee and Mature is offered a big bonus to substitute. Just before the game, Lucille urges him not to endanger his life. He does not play and is miserable again. When Lizabeth hears of his ailment, she rushes to his side and they begin a new life at a small college where he finds a coaching berth. The picture is a victory of style over content. Adapted from Irwin Shaw's 'Education of the Heart',

Charles Schnee's script is wordy but civilized. Tourneur underplays the game itself with the exception of a few dramatically necessary training sequences and concentrates on the interaction of characters. The lighting creates a fine contrast between the brightness of the football field and the dimly-lit team work rooms.

Jim Thorpe is still considered to be the greatest all-round athlete that America has ever produced. The stature of the movie *Jim Thorpe, All-American* (WB 1951 *Man of Bronze* — GB) looms less large

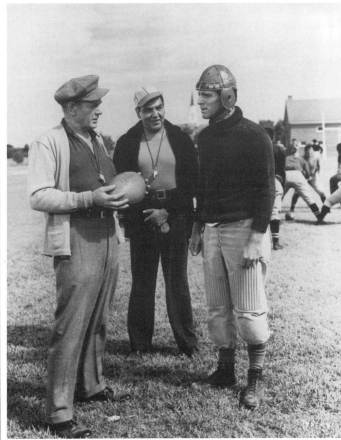

Charles Bickford (left) and Burt Lancaster (right) in *Jim Thorpe — All American*

than its subject. Directed by Michael Curtiz, it's quite enjoyable when running and jumping, but no so good when standing still. Burt Lancaster, suitably athletic and bronzed, is excellent as Jim Thorpe, the American-Indian brought up on an Oklahoma reservation. The film while raising the racial issue, plays it down. 1951 was still too early in Hollywood's evolutionary terms to have expected more than a tentative finger to be pointed at the sporting establishment for their treatment of Thorpe after the 1912 Olympics, and although the screenplay attempts to set forth Thorpe's

triumphs and set-backs sensitively, the impression that remains is of the stereotyped Indian's fatal attraction to drink. Aside from the more sympathetic westerns such as *Broken Arrow* (1950), *Apache* (1954 with Lancaster) and *Little Big Man* (1970), films on the Indian in modern society have been few and far between. There was *The Outsider* (1961) and *Flap* (1970 — a flop). The movie begins with the young Indian boy running like a gazelle in the wild country rather than going to school. Later, knowing his mother wants him to make a success out of his life, he enters Carlisle Indian School. He finds study difficult and is happiest when running. He meets and falls in love with Margaret Miller (Phyllis Thaxter). In order to impress her further, Thorpe takes up football and is immediately a force to be reckoned with. The real Thorpe, only suggested by Lancaster on the field, was 'absolutely fearless smashing through a line or ripping into a rival runner or making a savage block with cruel recklessness'. The famous Carlisle-Pennsylvania football classic is recreated when Thorpe and Penn's Ashenbrunner, both All-Americans, clashed. After

the Olympic Games in 1912, he marries Margaret and joins the pro football ranks. When his small son dies, he turns to drink and the movie turns to melodrama. It ends, however, on an up-beat, when his own coach from Carlisle, Pop Warner (gruff stalwart Charles Bickford) tells him that the State of Oklahoma is putting up a monument to one of its most famous sons — Jim Thorpe, the greatest athlete of them all.

The dubious notion of the weakling suddenly inspired to great feats of sporting endeavor, because of fraternal and paternal faith in him, is described in a poker-faced manner at the climax of *That's My Boy* (Par. 1951), an above-average Dean Martin-Jerry Lewis vehicle. 'Jarring Jack' Jackson (Eddie Mayehoff) was, twenty years earlier, Ridgeville University's greatest all-round athlete — a nine letter man and All-American on the football team. His wife (Ruth Hussey) was once Olympic swimming champion. At 17, their son, Junior (Jerry Lewis) is thin, anemic, a hypochondriac and can't see a thing without his glasses. Junior finds it very difficult to live up to the expectations of his strapping father. Jackson, however, still wants his son to enter Ridgeville and play for the football team. Although Junior is definitely not cut out to be an athlete, Jackson, as Ridgeville's richest alumnus, will fix it. Junior's roommate at Ridgeville is Bill Baker (Dean Martin) a terrific football player. The coach is thrilled to have Bill on the team, the only problem is he is also obliged to have Junior on the squad. Junior's parents come up to see him play in the first game of the season and are mortified to see Junior score a touchdown for the opposing team. (An understandable mistake to make without one's spectacles.) Before the next game, Bill coaches Junior in kicking a field goal and helps build up his morale. In the big game, Ridgeville is being badly beaten when Junior is sent into the game and amazes everyone by winning it for them. He proves to his father that he is 'a man'. (Inside every Jerry Lewis is a Dean Martin struggling to get out. In *The Nutty Professor* 1963 — Lewis does in fact turn into Martin.) Jerry Lewis is a talented comedian who can make one wriggle with delight

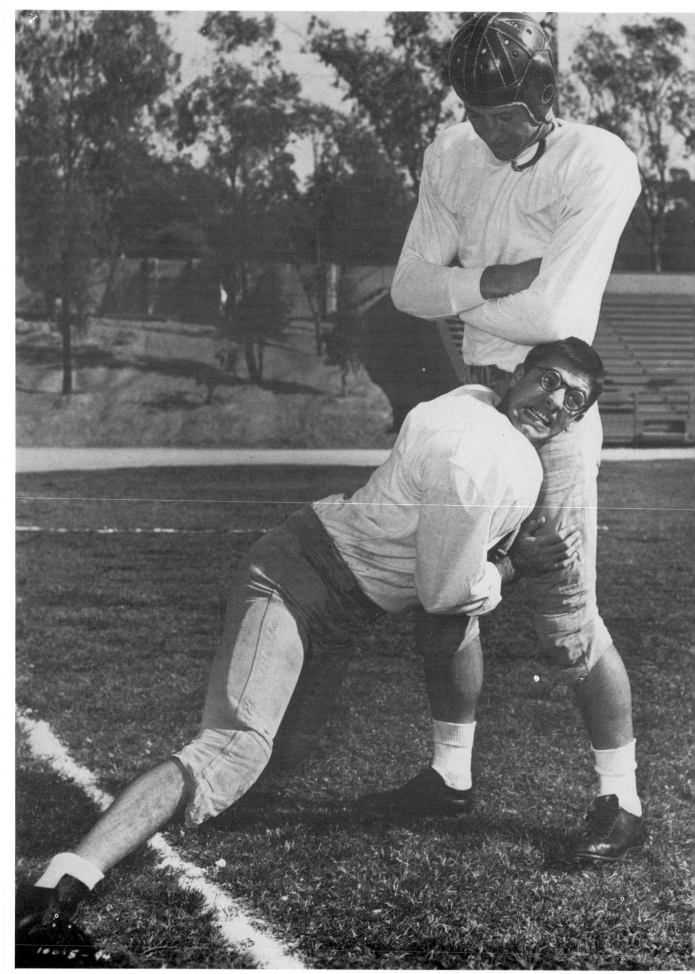

one moment and squirm with embarrassment the next. He is at his best when moving like a doll manipulated by a drunken puppeteer or when closest to his idol, Stan Laurel. Laurel, although he cried a lot, was never sentimental like Lewis. Eddie Mayehoff is very funny as the father who can finally speak the title of the movie with justification. For fact gatherers, the ref in the big game was played by Jane Russell's younger brother Jaime Russell and among the 29 USC and UCLA players featured were Al Carmichael, Howard Hansen and Frank Gifford.

It is refreshing for a college picture to put education before football, and *Saturday's Hero* (Col. 1951 — *Idols in the Dust* — GB) does just that. The only way that Steve Novak (John Derek) can get an education and hope to rise above his immigrant family's status is by playing football for tradition-bound Jackson College, where he is only valued for his sporting ability. In the inevitable Big Game, a tough opponent is paid to bring Steve down. His shoulder is badly injured but he continues to play with a kind of death-wish until he is permanently injured and out of football forever. He leaves for another college where he will be appreciated for his academic abilities. While being rather weighted in one direction, the film is a rather effective attack on the commercialism of college sport with its great demands on players. The games and training are covered at some length, but the injuries inflicted seem too melodramatically piled on and the local magnate (Sidney Blackmer) is too much the heavy to be convincing. Among the football players is Aldo Da Re (later Aldo Ray).

'You've heard about guys who can zig and zag, well Elroy Hirsch could zog with a couple of varieties of zugs,' so said a teammate of Elroy Hirsch known as *Crazylegs-All American* (Rep. 1953). Twice collegiate All-American, he was in 1950, as pass receiver for the LA Rams, the most valuable player in pro football. Hirsch plays himself skillfully in this straight story of his life. Also starring were members of the Rams and a few pro actors such as Lloyd Nolan as a coach. The picture begins with

Hirsch's high-school days, where the poor, shy and hard-working boy finds a parity with his fellows only on the football field. One of the very first films made in CinemaScope, it is filled with gridiron action with the wide screen giving plenty of room for the forward pass. Those who can't tell a pigskin from Miss Piggy, will not be too enthralled.

John Wayne was a football star at USC and appeared with his team (which included Ward Bond) in John Ford's *Salute* (1929). In *Trouble Along the Way* (WB 1953), Wayne plays an unemployed football coach, given the task of licking the team of a small Catholic college into shape. St Anthony's is in debt for 170,000 dollars and the rector (Charles Coburn) has the idea that the college can only be saved by means of a good football team. Coburn plays one of those oh-so-loveable clerics who shoots pool and is a football fan. (The title echoes *Going My Way*.) He finds a text in the Bible, 'the beloved grew fat and kicked', to justify his plans. Wayne, disillusioned by the game, decides to take on the job for the sake of his 11-year-old daughter (Sherry Jackson). Wayne and daughter go to St Anthony's, 'the bottom of the ivy-covered barrel' for one term. However, when the new coach meets the team, he realizes there is no way he can help them. 'How did you do last season?' he asks. 'We showed up at every game,' comes the reply from a scrawny youth. But because of Coburn's gentle faith in him, Wayne determines that the only method of helping the college would be to recruit pro players for the team. Coburn doesn't seem to notice the vast contrast between the giant crew-cut freshman and the other students. The team does amazingly well, beating Santa Clara 20—0. Unfortunately, the rector finds out that Wayne has transgressed the rules of college football. But all is forgiven when the school is saved by a church and state subsidy and it can revert back to its old ways of amateurism. The witty script by Melville Shavelson and Jack Rose, and the lively direction of Michael Curtiz, keeps the incipient sentimentality at bay. John Wayne is often the butt of the sophisticated, who see him as the embodiment of rightist ethics and the simplistic 'football mentality', but one cannot

forget, while watching *Trouble Along the Way*, what a fine screen actor he could be.

Injuries are an occupational hazard for football players, but injuries to spectators are unexpected. TV cameraman Jack Lemmon in Billy Wilder's *The Fortune Cookie* (UA 1966. *Meet Whiplash Willie* — GB) is bowled over on the sidelines by Cleveland Browns' Luther 'Boom-Boom' Jackson (Ron Rich). He is taken to hospital, but there's really nothing wrong with him that a hot bath won't cure. Enter shyster lawyer brother-in-law Walter Matthau who seizes the chance to make millions by suing the NFL and anyone else in sight.

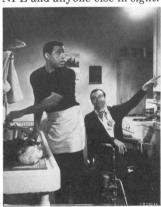
Ron Rich (left) looking after Jack Lemmon in *The Fortune Cookie*

'He's so full of twists. He starts to describe a doughnut and it comes out a pretzel.' He gets Lemmon to pretend he's been paralysed from the neck down. 'Boom-Boom' does everything possible to compensate for the accident he caused, by waiting on Lemmon hand and foot. His football playing begins to deteriorate, fumbling on the 12 yard line and losing a game for the Browns. 'Once a pro drops 3 punts in a row he's washed up.' Looking down at Lemmon in his wheelchair he sees the futility of everything. 'All for a lousy extra 5 yards.' Lemmon replies philosophically, 'Everybody tries for that extra 5 yards.' His conscience begins to prick vis-à-vis the contrite football player. Just when he has won his case, he decides to stand up (literally) for his principles and loses the compensation money, his wife and the respect of his brother-in-law. *The Fortune Cookie* is a wickedly funny moral tale in 15 chapters, with a highly-wrought script by Wilder and I.A.L. Diamond, helped by Walter Matthau's brilliantly caricatural Oscar-winning performance. Lemmon has the far more difficult 'Whose life is it

anyway' role. The film's problem lies in the fact that it has a steely surface and a soft center, the soft center (or rather wide-receiver) being 'Boom-Boom' Jackson. He is just too much the good-hearted, slightly simple black sportsman who wouldn't hurt a fly off the field, and his relationship with Lemmon, although essential to the plot, is unsubtle. Nevertheless, the ending with 'Boom-Boom' and Lemmon throwing a ball to each other in the empty Cleveland Stadium, has the right kind of sweetness to counteract the delicious acrimony of Walter Matthau's whiplash tongue.

How many Sunday afternoon arm-chair sportsmen have wanted to join in the game they are watching in order to change the sequence of events? George Plimpton, the journalist, did just that. Not content with merely being a spectator at the ringside or on the bleachers, he was willing to risk life and limb for a chance to realize his sporting fantasies, and also because it made good copy. *Paper Lion* (UA 1968) is the screen version of his bestseller which recounted his experiences in a pre-season tryout game with the Detroit Lions. The book was not only a personal document, but also an intricate study of professional football. The movie depends on a series of situations rather than an overall story-line, although it makes some concessions by adding female interest (Lauren Hutton) and some rather corny sight gags, but on the whole it is true to the spirit of the original. Alan Alda has the right combination of physical ineptitude and witty objectivity to make one change one's mind about ever contemplating doing the same thing, unless one's masochism was worth the price in doctor's fees. Great sportsmen make it look so easy, Alda makes it look difficult. Given the commercial considerations, it's still a pity that Plimpton himself could not have been filmed actually trying to do his own thing, instead of getting an actor to fake it. The documentary side is riveting and in one scene director Alex March lets the camera observe the Detroit Lions in the dressing room before a game. It is a study in tension and concentration until the game with the St Louis Cardinals explodes in color and energy. With the game sewn up, Joe Schmidt lets tyro quarterback Alda 'run out the clock'. In 3 plays he loses 42 yards, runs into his own goalpost and knocks himself out. It is rare to see a sports pic where sport is at the center of things and where the plot is on the sidelines. Vince Lombardi, Alex Karras, John Gordy and Mike Lucci and the Detroit Lions appear as themselves.

Number One (UA 1969) was a serious attempt to get inside the game of football. *Paper Lion* was a much more jokey affair. There's never very much to joke about when Charleton Heston's around. Perhaps it's that Roman profile and deep, solemn voice (the voice of God in *The Ten Commandments*) that keeps any kind of horseplay and backslapping in the locker-room down to a minimum. Heston plays veteran superstar quarterback Ron 'Cat' Catlan of the New Orleans Saints. His wife (Jessica Walter), who used to be out at his games, is now paying more attention to dress designing. (In the movies dress designing is the favorite occupation for wives who neglect their macho husbands.) Catlan injures his knee in a pre-season game and rumors begin to circulate that he is through as a football star. At 40, he is afraid to give it up and start a new life. (Heston was 45 years old.) At the NFL season opener he has a steel brace taped over his knee and is swallowing painkillers. When he is introduced into the stadium, he is booed loudly. After the opening kick-off, Catlan goes into a huddle determined to inspire his team. He completes two accurate passes that take the Saints to the 10-yard line. Catlan fades back to pass again but his receivers are covered and he runs for a touchdown as the crowd cheers him on. On the next exchange, the Saints regain the ball after a fumble. Taking over again, Catlan fades back but can't find an open receiver. Two huge defensive linemen and a linebacker drive him to the ground and he lies motionless. Catlan's career is over.

One of the problems of Tom Gries' direction is that it tries too hard to compete with TV and fails. TV techniques create the immediacy of the spectacle, moving rapidly from inside a huddle to the sidelines to instant replay. A movie which tries to use the same techniques will suffer by comparison,

lacking the spontaneity and excitement of the real thing. Film is a more analytical medium and should add a dimension to a sporting event that television cannot hope to do. It can penetrate the physical and psychological preparations necessary for a big game. It can take a closer look behind the scenes and behind the eyes that stare from a helmet. In *Number One*, the very real problem of the ageing sportsman is lost in soap operatics, neither does it reveal much more about the New Orleans Giants than the average Sunday afternoon viewer can get from CBS or NBC.

Fan *Noun* 1: an enthusiastic follower of a sport or entertainment; 2: an enthusiastic admirer (as of a celebrity). Fred Exley (Jerry Orbach) the anti-hero of *A Fan's Notes* (WB

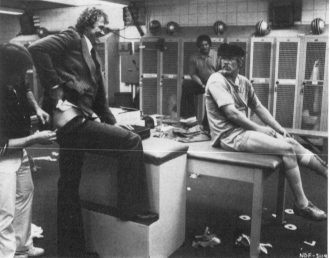

Bo Svenson (receiving an injection) and Nick Nolte (right) in *North Dallas 40*

1972) fits both definitions and some. He is more of a fanatic than a fan, dedicated to the point of mania to the game of football and especially his idol, Frank Gifford, star halfback of the New York Giants. One day on TV he sees, with one minute fifteen seconds to go, Gifford knocked into concussion by the Eagles' dreadnought, Chuck Bednarick, a shock that drives Exley from bar to bar that night. He comes to accept the fact that he is not a performer but one of life's fans. 'It's my fate, my destiny, my end, to be a fan.' This should strike a sympathetic chord with most of us who belong to that category and there is an interesting concept at the heart of this adaptation from Fred Exley's novel. Unfortunately, the self-pity, the flash flashback structure, the straining towards satire, make *A Fan's*

Notes merely an interesting failure. Eric Till directed.

North Dallas 40 (Par. 1974) seems a long way from the days when the likes of Dick Powell could touchdown in the last seconds or Pat O'Brien inspire his team with platitudes. *North Dallas 40* is not an imitation of football on television, but a complement to it. Directed by Ted Kotcheff, it has translated former Dallas Cowboy Peter Gent's whining novel into a witty and compassionate movie about the agony and ecstasy of the game, the accent being on the agony. Phil Elliott (Nick Nolte) is the veteran wide receiver on the North Dallas Bulls (based on the Dallas Cowboys). Midway through a gruelling season, Elliott, who starts each day with codeine tablets washed down with beer, realizes he has

reached a crisis in his life. His bones, muscles, ligaments and nerves have been fractured and dislocated after years of football, but he needs the excitement of the game as much as the drugs he takes. After meeting Charlotte (Dayle Haddon), he sees that there is another world outside the violent, masculine sport of football. He begins to question the brutality of the sport in which his body is battered and bruised each Sunday. Charlotte can't understand how Elliott can enjoy a sport that brings such physical pain. Football will remain his way of life as long as his body holds out. Controlling the game he loves, is an Orwellian organization dedicated through bureaucracy to keeping the players in line and in ignorance, treating them as not much more than data cards for the computer.

On his return to Chicago, Elliott learns that the organization has hired investigators to check out his rebellious life style. It is well-known that the Dallas Cowboys run the most sophisticated information-evaluation system in football. (In *Rollerball* 1975, an organization with a vastly dehumanizing effect is seen under the guise of science fiction, but mirrors the world of big business football gadgetry.) In the 1970s athletes began to query these monolithic structures and the time-honored values they represented. *North Dallas 40* suggests an alternative which extends towards a radical assessment of the state itself. Although it does not set out to be a political allegory, being more part of the Jock Liberation Front, it does, in the light of recent political developments in the USA, seem particularly relevant.

'I'd always wanted to do a football picture,' said Albert S. Ruddy, the producer of *The Longest Yard* (Par. 1974. *The Mean Machine* — GB) 'but with the game as the dramatic payoff to the story. You don't compete with the real thing on Sunday TV. In prison there's no question of who the winners and losers are. If you put prisoners in football uniforms against guards and order a game, you've got a whole new set of rules with built-in violence as the crux.' Virtually the whole picture takes place in Citrus State Prison, Georgia, so, for the price of one ticket, we are offered a football movie and a prison drama, the difference being that the cons instead of creating mutiny, bash the guards in a 'game', and instead of Yale we are expected to root for the team of prisoners. The movie aims to present the microcosmic Them vs Us situation, whereas, on reflection, we might well ask if We are They or They are Us. Almost everyone in the picture is violent and vicious and the anti-authoritarian stance only leads to the nihilistic view that the violence of authority is indistinguishable from the violence that opposes it. Robert Aldrich who made *The Dirty Dozen* (this is 'The Dirty Eleven') again collects an assortment of rogues and no-hopers and unites them into a team. The plot concerns one time pro football star quarter-

Right: Burt Reynolds (center) in *The Longest Yard*

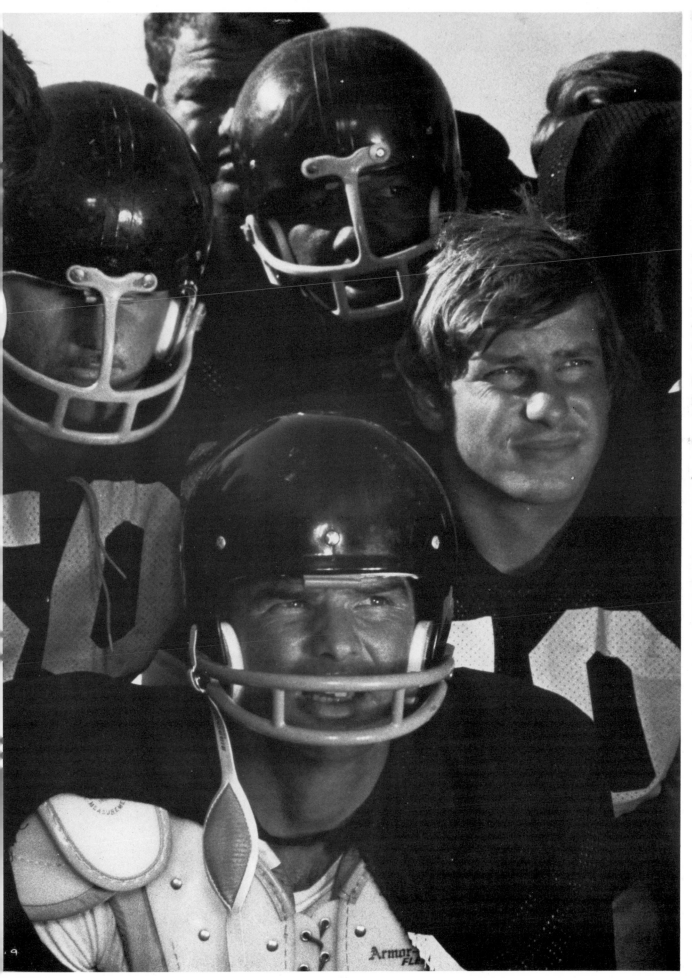

back, Paul Crewe (Burt Reynolds) convicted for auto theft. Warden Hazen (Eddie Albert) tries to persuade Crewe to coach the guards' semi-pro football team. The Warden wants the US championship. Crewe, under pressure, agrees to form a prisoners' team to play the guards for a practise match in 4 weeks, a seemingly impossible task. Crewe, with the help of an ex New York pro, starts getting a team into shape. Their training includes the study of stolen X-rays to determine which of their opponent's bones are most breakable. Each man not only wants to win but to maim. 'The way I figure it, we'll all be in the same place 1000 years from now, so what the hell!' says one profound individual. Crewe and his co-cons form The Mean Machine, but the guards boast the legendary Bogdanski (Ray Nitschke of the Green Bay Packers). Game day arrives. Civilians and guards' families crowd the stadium outside the walls. Inmates fill their own stands behind a wire screen. Soon after kickoff the Guards score. Bogdanski gets busy stomping on faces and gouging eyes. In the third quarter, as

the Guards score one touchdown after another, his teammates realize Crewe has sold out to the Warden in exchange for parole. But in the fourth quarter, Crewe suddenly knows that he has no guarantee of getting parole and he re-enters the game with renewed vigor. The guards try to stop him, but the Mean Machine, sensing the change, blocks for him. He executes incredible passes as casualties mount on both sides. There has not been such a crunching of bones on screen since Charles Laughton's *Henry VIII*. In the last few seconds of play, with the guards still leading, Crewe gets the ball, finds a hole and hits dirt for touchdown under a ton of bodies. The victory is with the cons today, whatever retribution tomorrow may bring. *The Longest Yard* was an enormous success in the USA. Burt Reynolds, who was a college football star headed for the Baltimore Colts when injury aborted his pro career, is pretty convincing in the role. His cool, devil-may-care brawn has established him as the Clark Gable of the 70s, although he has a much more knowing air that one wouldn't

be surprised to find him, like a cartoon character, making asides and winking at the audience.

Burt Reynolds reappears as a gridiron hero in *Semi-Tough* (UA 1977) another of director Michael Ritchie's semi-satires (*The Candidate* and *Smile* were others) on middle America. Walter Bernstein's script has a witty free-wheeling quality that counteracts Ritchie's way of taking one idea and hammering it into the ground. Burt Reynolds' persona is perfectly suited to the role of Billy Clyde of the Miami Bucks football team. He lives in a platonic threesome with teammate Skate (Kris Kristofferson) and Barbara Jane (Jill Clayburgh), until he catches Skate kissing Barbara Jane. Although Billy Clyde is told 'all you care about is fucking and football', as the title of the movie implies, underneath his hairy-chested macho exterior is a warm human being who would like to write a book and marry the girl he loves, Barbara Jane. Florida seems to be burgeoning with instant revelation cults such as Pyramid Power, Pelfing — a kind of massage administered by

Clara Pelf (Lotte Lenya at her butchest) where she sticks her fingers up his nose. ('The inside of the nose is a reflection of personality'), and a fad called Movagenics which obliges the follower to crawl around like a baby. (An amusing image of regression.) At the center of all this activity is the football team owned by Big Ed Brookman (Robert Preston). When he isn't crawling around the carpet of his office, on the walls of which hang pictures of Nixon, Vince Lombardi, J. Edgar Hoover and Joe McCarthy, he is listening to his favorite singer, Gene Autry, the red neck's Bob Dylan. Autry's cornball voice counterpoises the more flip side of Burt Reynolds. 'Back in the saddle again' and 'Silver-haired daddy of mine' accompanies the football games seen mostly in slow-motion. There is a lot of balletic blocking and tackling and not much scoring in order to demonstrate the unimportance of the result. The final game, almost a parody of the old college football picture, has Billy Clyde scoring a touchdown in the last second. One of the best scenes is a meeting with a classy publisher. ('Intel-

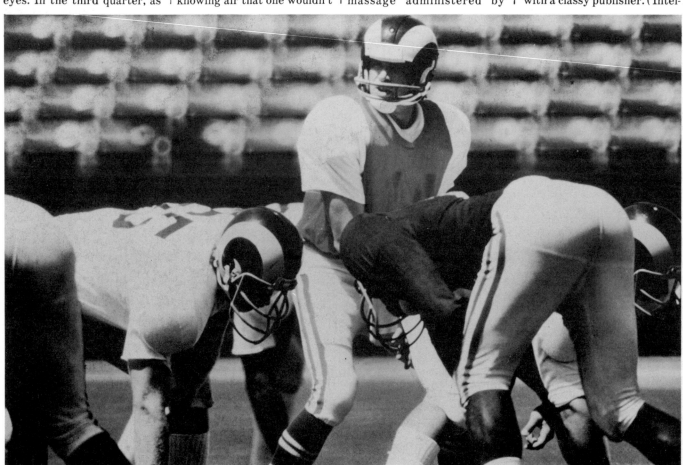

Warren Beatty at quarterback in *Heaven Can Wait*

52

lectuals are the jocks of the mind', he says trying to ingratiate himself with Reynolds.) He wants Billy Clyde to write a book on 'the football no one has ever seen. The real truth. What drugs the players take, how games are really fixed, the influence of the mafia, but no sensationalism.' 'Are gay footballers on the offence or defence?' he asks. 'Defence,' replies Reynolds. 'You can grope someone easier.'

California is really the breeding ground for such consciousness-movements as seen in *Semi-Tough* and with so many reborn Christians popping up all over that state, it was inevitable that there should be a movie about a reborn quarterback set in the capital of God's own country, Los Angeles. *Heaven Can Wait* (Par. 1978) is *Here Comes Mr Jordan* (Col. 1941) reborn. This time round Joe Pendleton is a football player and not a boxer. Joe (Warren Beatty) is just about to fulfil his ambition to play quarterback for the LA Rams, when he's taken to Heaven before his time in error. As his body has been cremated, he has to fill the body of a loathsome plutocrat. He returns to Earth and after several weeks of training feels he's ready, but the Rams refuse to give him a tryout. So using his fortune, he buys the Rams and announces his intention to play in the Super Bowl. There is no need to divulge the result. The story attempts to draw a comparison between the ethics of sport and those of big business; it also contains some romantic twaddle about love's destiny and some black comedy involving Dyan Cannon and Charles Grodin, but it's all really just a sunny Californian movie. Warren Beatty, producing, co-directing (with Buck Henry) and co-writing (with Elaine May), acts as if his mind or body is elsewhere. The 40-year-old Beatty still looks young enough to be playing ball at this level and he does his own quarterbacking in the film (he was All-Star Center at Washington Lee High School in Arlington Virginia) supported by the Rams team and former stars, Deacon Jones, Les Josephson, Jack Snow, Jim Boeke, Charlie Cowan, and Joe Corolla. The Super Bowl sequence was filmed during half-time in front of 60,000 fans at the LA Coliseum for an exhibition between the Rams and the Oakland Raiders.

OTHER FOOTBALL MOVIES

The College Widow WB 1927 played by Dolores Costello is a merry widow who makes goo-goo eyes at each member of a college football team, knowing that her interest will spur them on to great things on the day of the big game. A nicely turned silent comedy directed by Archie Mayo. (Remade as **Freshmen Love** — WB 1936 about rowing).

Forward Pass WB 1929 was thrown by Douglas Fairbanks Jr. at a crucial moment and helps win the big game and the girl (Loretta Young). As the blurb said about this all-talking college caper: 'The roar of the stands, the snap of signals, the thud of flying feet racing to the most dramatic touchdown ever filmed and every seat on the 50 yard line. It's a real man's picture that women will love.'

College Lovers WB 1930 was unconventional in that the hero does *Not* make a touchdown for the old Alma Mater in the last seconds. Otherwise it's a typical campus comedy about a flirt (Marion Nixon) who causes problems by winning the hearts of the two best players on the team. Like almost every movie of that period it included songs. Incidentally the big game ends in a tie, so does romance and football.

Maybe It's Love WB 1930 or maybe not. 'What is it that makes a football player battle fiercely on the field? Does he fight for honor? Or is it the hope of glory that spurs him on? **Maybe it's love** the billboards speculated. Upton College has not defeated their rival college Parsons for 12 years and if things don't improve the President will have to resign. His daughter (Joan Bennett), discards her horn-rimmed spectacles and prim clothes and begins to flirt with the eleven best footballers in America in order to lure them away from their various colleges to Upton. She seems to be able to wander into men's dorms and training quarters without questioning. The gridiron scenes are good as they feature the 1929 All-American team. Joe E. Brown is the football star at Upton who is replaced by one of the All-Americans. One of director William Wellman's minor efforts.

The Spirit of Notre Dame UI 1931, dedicated to the memory of Knute Rockne who died the same year, it starred Lew Ayres and Andy Devine. Devoted almost entirely to the game, it is patriotic, sentimental, romantic and not a dame in sight.

Hold 'em Jail 1932 was about as amusing as its title. Bert Wheeler and Robert Woolsey are prisoners at Bidemore prison who start a football team. **The Longest Yard** without the violence or laughs.

70,000 Witnesses Par. 1932 see a player (Johnny Mack Brown) get the ball, run for a touchdown, but as he reaches the 5 yard line he drops down dead. The detective (Charles Ruggles) asks that part of the game be re-enacted to see who dunnit.

College Coach WB 1933 (**Football Coach** — GB) was an aggressive Pat O'Brien who gets results but is not liked. William Wellman tried to get as much of the football milieu in as possible between the songs. Dick Powell's high tenor suggested that he had been tackled rather too low. John Wayne appears briefly (as he did in 14 other movies in 1933).

College Humor Par. 1933 is pretty puerile, if this is anything to go by. Bing Crosby is a crooning professor (not a professor of crooning) and Jack Oakie and Richard Arlen play football stars. Oakie cheerfully undergoes a brutal initiation ceremony before excelling on the football field.

Hold 'Em Yale Par. 1935, based on a Runyon story, showed a group of Broadway touts going to the Harvard-Yale game and not understanding how it could be amateur. Cesar Romero plays Gigolo Georgie.

Fighting Youth UI 1935 could have been a potentially dangerous movie if it had fallen into the hands of America's enemies. A college football star (Charles Farrell) falls for a girl (June Martell) and is put off his game. She is a spy for a political organization which believed that to break up college football would effec-

tively destroy the American constitution. But all is well in the end for the constitution and football, because the hero makes a sensational comeback and wins the game of the year for the college.

Pigskin Parade TCF 1936 (**Harmony Parade** — GB) had the distinction of being Judy Garland's first feature film. What story there was concerned two coaches (Jack Haley and Patsy Kelly) at a small college who discover a hillbilly (Stuart Erwin) whose football talents help them to win the Yale Bowl.

Life Begins in College TCF 1937 for lovers Joan Davis and Tony Martin. When a player is injured in the last few minutes of the game, the Ritz Brothers take to the field and save the game not the movie. The Ritz Brothers were the poverty-stricken man's Marx Brothers.

Hold That Co-Ed TCF 1938 was a pleasant satirical musical-comedy starring John Barrymore in one of the best of his late films. He plays a crooked politician who appears at a college during the football season to drum up votes. He seeks re-election as state governor which includes seeing that the college football teams wins. Barrymore traded on his debauched image and cured ham style of playing. He was supported by George Murphy, Joan Davis and Jack Haley.

The Cowboy Quarterback WB 1939 was a feeble remake of **Elmer the Great** 1933 with football replacing baseball and Bert Wheeler replacing Joe E. Brown as the hick who gets involved with gangsters. A long way from the original Ring Lardner story.

The Spirit of West Point Film Classics 1947 was embodied by two great football stars, Felix 'Doc' Blanchard and Glenn Davis. They play themselves in this story of their lives, which is full of gridiron action including a lengthy and well-photographed record of the 1946 Army-Navy game. The newsreel material is skillfully incorporated into the film.

Good News MGM 1947 was a breezy Technicolor musical which told the tale of a captain of football (Peter Lawford) at Tate College who doesn't realize until the end that June Allyson is much better for him than snob-by Patricia Marshall.

Yes Sir, That's My Baby UI 1949 sang Donald O'Connor while baby-sitting when his wife (Gloria de Haven) is at college. All the wives of the football team are studying, leaving their husbands little time for the game. Coach Charles Coburn gets them to show their wives who's boss. They do. They win the big game and the battle of the sexes.

Father was a Fullback TCF 1949, father being Fred MacMurray, coach of State U. football team. He not only has problems with a losing team but with his teenage daughter (Betty Lynn). The boy to win her favors is a garage hand called Hercules Smith, one of the finest quarterbacks in the country. He decides not to go to Notre Dame, but in order to be with his girl he enters State. A good vehicle for Fred MacMurray's homely character, this rather bland domestic comedy has a lively cast including Maureen O'Hara, Rudy Vallee, Thelma Ritter and 11-year-old Natalie Wood.

Peggy UI 1950 played by Diana Lynn can't tell her father (Charles Coburn) that she's married to a fullback from Ohio State (Rock Hudson) because he hates him so much. Undemanding.

The Guy Who Came Back TCF 1951 was Paul Douglas as a self-pitying ex-football star who, after being rejected by the navy, gets a job as a coach for their football team. Linda Darnell and Joan Bennett are the women in his life. Banal.

Bonzo goes to College UI 1952 after being brought up by Ronald Reagan in **Bedtime for Bonzo** 1951. Bonzo is a brainy chimp who passes the college entrance exams and whose immensely strong long arms make him the star of the football team. On the eve of the big game, he's kidnapped and substituted for by a less sportive chimp. Bonzo manages to escape in time to get into his uniform and save the team in the last minutes. He turns down an offer to become a pro, because he'd rather stay

with his 11-year-old friend (Gigi Perreau). A cross between Mickey Rooney and Spencer Tracy, Bonzo gives a performance equal to any of his co-stars.

The Rose Bowl Monogram 1952 was a sugar bowl story set in Pasadena of football player (Marshall Thompson) meets girl (Vera Miles), loses girl, gets girl (he wins the game by unselfishly blocking the way for his best friend to score.) The Rose Carnival backgrounds, filmed in color, helped the eye if not the mind.

I Love Melvin MGM 1953 contained a witty musical number entitled 'Saturday afternoon before the game' in which Debbie Reynolds dressed as a ball is tossed around by a dancing and singing football team.

The All-American UI 1953 (**The Winning Way** — GB) attempted little and achieved even less. Tony Curtis wins the title of All-American as a result of his spectacular performance in an important game. That day, however, his parents, en route to see their son play, are killed in an automobile accident. Tony gives up football but is finally persuaded by the Dean's secretary, Lori Nelson, to return to it. Most of the humor is limited to jokes about the length of Tony Curtis's hair.

Son of Flubber Disney 1963, or more precisely, a sequel to **The Absent-Minded Professor** 1961 which had Fred MacMurray inventing Flubber i.e. flying rubber. The Pentagon having clamped down on Flubber, the professor has invented Flubbergas. Trailing 37-35 Medfield College has the ball on its own 2 yard line, first down and 98 to go. The team comes out of a huddle and . . . They're trying a field goal! A 98 yard fieldgoal? The ball sails over the line of scrimmage, over the 50 yard line, over the goal posts, over the state line, over the Atlantic. It is seen orbiting the Earth. That's kicking for you!

John Goldfarb, please come home TCF 1965 was an extremely damp squib, full of heavy slapstick and awful acting. King Fawz (Peter Ustinov) is an aged, one-eyed despot with 80 sons who builds a football field in the middle of his oil-rich desert. John Goldfarb (Richard Crenna), flying a U.2. mission to Russia, crashlands on the football field. He becomes coach of Fawz's football team. The big game is between the home team and visiting Notre Dame. When Shirley Maclaine enters the line-up for the home team, the upright college boys are too much the gentlemen to tackle a lady and she scores the winning touchdown.

M*A*S*H TCF 1970 ends with an intraservice football game in which the corrupt way it is played reflects the values of the Korean war surrounding the camp. The ideals of sport are shattered in a comically well-choreographed game, where every foul practice is employed, while the reserve players sit on the sidelines passing 'joints'.

Gus Walt Disney 1976 is a mule from Yugoslavia who saves a sagging L.A. team by kicking 100 yard field goals. Gus is, of course, far more lovable and wise than the humans, and is able to elude the heavies Tom Bosley and Tim Conway throughout the film. The California Atoms are played by the Los Angeles Rams. A movie to please everyone from the age of 2 to 3.

Black Sunday Par. 1977 was the day on which the fanatic pilot (Bruce Dern) of a giant Goodyear airship used for TV coverage of football games, threatened the annihilation of 80,000 spectators including the President at the Miami Super Bowl. Despite previous warnings, the TV blimp had to be allowed to fly over the stadium, because that is what the network had promised the American people and to put off the Super Bowl would be like 'putting off Christmas'.

The One and Only Par. 1978 was a good description of extravert student Henry Winkler. He makes fun of the usual warm-up war cry before the game and then a little into the first quarter he's carried off on a stretcher. 'You faked a football injury', says a teammate. 'I wasn't faking. I was acting,' he replies.

The Great American Pastime

BASEBALL

In 1953, there was an extraordinary coming together of two myths when Marilyn Monroe married baseball hero, Joe Di Maggio. The marriage was not a happy one. The marriage between Hollywood and baseball, although it has lasted longer, has been only marginally more successful. In spite of baseball being the most loved sport in the USA and the favorite of America's literati, there have been fewer movies on baseball than on boxing, football or even horse-racing. Maybe it is more problematic to depict in dramatic and visual terms the duel between the pitcher and the batter than the head-on conflict in boxing and football. They also have more violence going for them, while most of the violence in baseball is the violent abuse hurled at the hated umpire.

Baseball movies have no equivalent to the puerile college football movie, nor any anti-Establishment stance as in *North Dallas 40*, nor any condemnation of the sport itself found in boxing pictures. The myth remains unsullied. The film-maker must, in Yeats' words, 'Tread softly or you walk on my dreams.' In common with religion; no blasphemy is tolerated, it has a tough side as well as a mawkish and sanctimonious side, and there is hardly an assertion on baseball that doesn't lead to argument. The Great American Pastime has been handled in a more sentimental and patriotic way than the more brutal and less democratic game of football. As part of the fabric of American life, people are more lyrical about it. From Walt Whitman's, 'I see great things in baseball. It's our game, the American game,' to Frank Sinatra, casting his blue eyes over a ball park in *Take Me Out To The Ball Game* (MGM 1949), saying 'Gee, what a sight! You gotta admit it's a great thrill. A kinda warm feeling comes over you, doesn't it? Happens to me every spring.' Browning got it wrong. In spr-

Take me out to the ball game
Take me out with the crowd,
Buy me some peanuts and crackerjack
I don't care if I never come back.
Let me root root for the home team
If they don't win it's a shame
'cos it's one, two, three strikes you're out
At the old ball game.

— ALBERT VON TILZER
and JACK NORWORTH.
(The national pastime's national anthem used in dozens of movies.)

ing, a young man's fancy turns to thoughts of baseball. Stars, stripes and diamonds set every patriotic heart aflutter. A baseball can produce tears in the eyes and a lump in the throat (and sometimes one on the head as in *The Winning Team* — WB 1952). It is all quite understandable because baseball is the most homegrown of American sports (at least according to the legend of General Doubleday). The sound of ash on horsehide has the same powerful effect on the American listener as the sound of willow on leather has on the Englishman. A baseball uniform is an essential element of Americana. The baseball bat was almost as important to a Norman Rockwell Saturday Evening Post cover as a guitar was to a cubist painting.

Nostalgia *is* what it used to be and the movies have tried to trade on it, although the vague memories of old men recalling the exploits of Christy Mathewson and Ty Cobb are far more accurate than, say, the disastrous *Babe Ruth Story* (AA 1948). For many American males, baseball is a link to their fathers and back to a distant past. (Philip Roth gives a poignant description of Portnoy's father playing baseball in *Portnoy's Complaint*.) In *Fear Strikes Out* (Par. 1957), this link between father and son through baseball is stretched to breaking point. Nostalgia is not baseball's only appeal. Baseball provides a structure of box-scores, strategy and planning. The probabilities, statistics and permutations are infinite. The game could last forever. In every game, a situation comes up that has never been seen before. Very little of the flavor of this has ever reached the screen, because most movies have to go against specialization in order to attract a wider audience. The domestic life of the ball players is important for box-office reasons which means enticing 'the little woman', who is fed-up with games on television, to go out and see a sports movie. The diamond is not a girl's best friend.

Often, so much time is taken up with the private lives of the ball players that the baseball fan wants to shout, 'Play ball!' or 'Kill the director!' Occasionally, however, the national pastime ceases to be a pastime and becomes the center of existence, the screenplay making a mountain out of a pitcher's mound. When the mountain was Paramount's, the hyperbole was justified because they produced, *Fear Strikes Out, Bang the Drum Slowly* (1973) and *The Bad News Bears* (1976), three of the best baseball pictures.

A cloud of morbidity hovers over quite a number of baseball movies. Lou Gehrig dying of multiple sclerosis in *The Pride of the Yankees* (RKO 1942), Babe Ruth entering hospital with throat cancer in *The Babe Ruth Story*, Monty Stratton having a leg amputated in *The Stratton Story* (MGM 1949), Grover Alexander suffering from double vision and fits in *The Winning Team*, Dizzy Dean finding solace in the bottle in *The Pride of St Louis* (TCF 1952), Jim Piersall finding himself in a straitjacket in *Fear Strikes Out*, and to top it all, the fictional catcher dying from Hodgkin's Disease in *Bang the Drum Slowly*.

Baseball, like death, comes to everyone in America. It is the most democratic of games. In *Talk of the Town* (1942), a cold, theoretical law professor (Ronald Coleman) is taken to a ball game to meet real people. 'A great thing this baseball. It gets the legal cobwebs out of the brain,' he comments. Whether played on the sandlots around the country, the little leagues, the minor leagues or the big leagues, it is close to the American people. The baseball movie is thus the sports equivalent of the small town movie, (e.g. the Andy Hardy perennials) featuring the average family of two adults, 2½ kids and a dog. Despite distortions, vulgarizations and over-sentimentality, Hollywood has managed to ex-

ract the mythology of baseball, keeping it intact.

In June 1888 in the 'San Francisco Examiner', there appeared a humorous ballad by
Ernest Thayer, called 'Casey
at the Bat'. The tragedy of the
mighty Casey who struck out
for the Mudville Nine when his
slugging was crucial, has been
set to music, made into an
opera, and filmed three times.
(Once as early as 1899.) In
Casey At The Bat (Par. 1927)
Wallace Beery played the most
famous sporting anti-hero of
them all. The adaptation of the
13 stanza comic-monologue into a full-length silent film was
done quite skilfully. Here
Casey is a junkman when he
isn't playing with Mudville.
'An idler 6 days a week, and an
idol on the seventh,' as a title
expresses it. Immodest about
his slugging ability, Casey brings to the plate a bottle of beer
and proceeds to knock the ball
into the grandstand or over the
fence using his one free hand.
But on the fatal day, the Pride
of Mudville comes before a fall.
After Casey has ignored the
first two offerings from the pitcher, on the third 'the air is
shattered by the force of
Casey's blow,' and 'the mighty
Casey has struck out.' In order
to provide the happy ending
deemed necessary by the
movie moguls ever since pictures moved, it is suggested
that drink and pride were his
downfall and that there will be
another game in which he will
triumph. The Nineties background is well caught and
Beery, a perfect Casey, is ably
supported by ZaSu Pitts, Ford
Sterling and Sterling Holloway.

Buster Keaton tries to get
on the baseball team in *College*
(UA 1927) although he doesn't
know one end of the bat from
the other. He does it to impress
Mary (Anne Cornwall) the
most popular girl at college
who is stuck on the athletic
hero, Jeff (Harold Goodwin).
Buster wears catcher's pads to
play 3rd and gets in everybody's way. Jeff sends him into
bat at the wrong time which
causes him to be ridiculed by
the other players. Buster's
stoical acceptance of what is
happening to him makes for
great comedy.

Joe E. Brown had a clause
written into his contract with
Warner Bros. which stated
that they were to supply him
with his own baseball team. It
was called the Joe E. Brown
All-Stars and included several

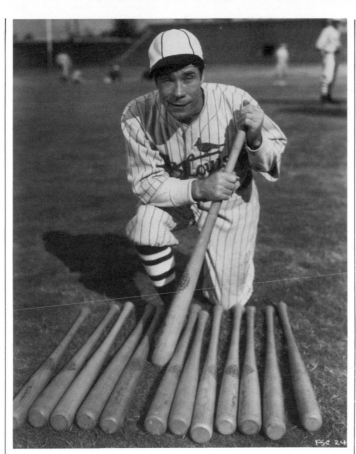

Joe E. Brown in *Fireman Save My Child*

pro ball players. Brown once
spent several weeks working
out with the New York Yankees. As someone remarked,
'Well, he's not the first comedian I've seen in a Yankee uniform.' But Joe E. Brown was
serious and divided his interests between show business and baseball. He was part
owner of the Kansas City Blues
and a friend of all time greats
such as Bill Dickey, Lou Gehrig
and Tris Speaker. Most of the
movies he made in the thirties
had a sporting subject: *Hold
Everything* and *When's your
Birthday?* (Boxing), *Sit Tight*
(Wrestling), *You Said a
Mouthful* (Swimming), *Maybe
It's Love* (Football), *Local Boy
Makes Good* (Athletics), *Six-
Day Bike Rider*, *Polo Joe*, and
three baseball pictures; *Fireman Save My Child*, *Elmer the
Great* and *Alibi Ike*.

Fireman Save My Child
(WB 1932) was the weakest of
the three, in which Brown
plays a dopey, peanut-
munching, hick fireman whose
hobby is playing baseball. He
manages to get to the big
league, pitching for the St
Louis Cardinals. Joe is torn
between two women and two
ways of life, the girl back home
(Evalyn Knapp) and the sophisticated city girl (Lillian Bond).
Simple values triumph in the

end of this serio-comic movie
directed by Lloyd Bacon. Joe
E. Brown was to the mouth,
what Jimmy Durante was to
the nose or Eddie Cantor to the
eyes, which meant that when
invention flagged, Brown's
mouth was always good for a
laugh. (In two senses.)

Both *Elmer the Great* and
Alibi Ike were adapted from
two classic Ring Lardner
baseball stories. *Elmer the
Great* (WB 1933 — adapted
from the play by Lardner and
George M. Cohan) was first
filmed as *Fast Company* (Par.
1929) and later, with a change
of sport, as *The Cowboy Quarterback* (WB 1939). Lardner, as
a baseball reporter, traveled
with the players and got to
know their off-the-diamond
characters. Elmer was based
on Big Ed Walsh, a pitcher with
the Chicago White Sox, who
was not renowned for his
modesty. The screenplay, for
some reason, changed Lardner's hero into a batter. Elmer
is a hayseed braggart who
knows how to handle a bat. He
first refuses to join the Chicago
Cubs because of his desire to be
near his girl-friend, Nellie
(Patricia Ellis). Elmer gets involved with a gang of crooks,
but after nearly missing the
big game, wins the day for the
Cubs against the Yankees. The

crucial match is both exciting
and funny and Mervyn Le-
Roy's capable direction kept
the film at a lively pace. Apart
from his mouth, Joe E. Brown
is less broad than usual.

Alibi Ike (WB 1935) was one
of Joe E. Brown's best, and
although the original Ring
Lardner story was coarsened
by the introduction of a gang of
gamblers, the dialogue was
sharp and witty. It tells the
story of a rookie who comes to
the Cubs with a fast ball, a good
batting eye and an excuse or
alibi for whatever happens to
him. When he's tired he doesn't
just say so; he'd say he had
gravel in his shoes and needs to
give his feet a rest. Journey-
man director Ray Enright
made a good job of it and Joe E.
Brown won new admirers.
Olivia de Havilland played her
first leading role as the romantic interest at the age of nine-
teen.

Those who have seen the
newsreel footage of Lou
Gehrig's farewell speech to the
62,000 fans gathered at Yankee Stadium, when he says,
'Most people think I've had a
tough break, but today, I feel
I'm the luckiest man on the face
of the earth', testify to it being
a most moving experience.
Here was one of America's
greatest sporting heroes, once
powerful and handsome, now
prematurely gray and painfully thin, stricken with multiple
sclerosis. It was quite a burden
on Gary Cooper's shoulders to
live up to that legend. In *The
Pride of the Yankees* (RKO
1942), within the context of a
Hollywood weepie, he created
his own kind of legend. Once
transmogrified into 'art', a
biography becomes a fiction.
Gary Cooper as Lou Gehrig is
as fictional as Cooper as Harry
Morgan in *For Whom the Bell
Tolls*, Mr Deeds, Beau Geste or
Peter Ibbotson. During Hollywood's heyday, nobody ex-
pected a movie star to sub-
merge himself in the personality, real or unreal, that he was
playing. *The Pride of the
Yankees* was a ball picture and
a box-office success, because
people didn't go to see Lou
Gehrig, they went to see Gary
Cooper. The speech that
Gehrig made on the newsreel
was moving to those fans of the
diamond who had followed
Gehrig's 2130 games for the
Yankees and knew the score,
but Cooper was able to move
those people who had never
heard of Gehrig and who
couldn't tell horsehide from

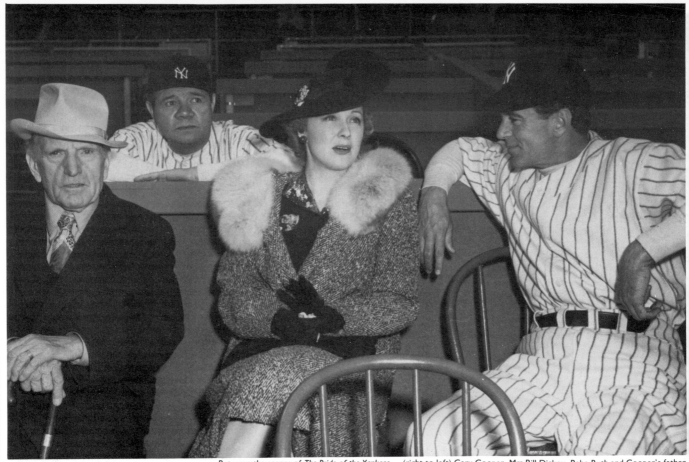

Between the scenes of *The Pride of the Yankees* — (right to left) Gary Cooper, Mrs Bill Dickey, Babe Ruth and Cooper's father

pigskin. Cooper's 'Aw shucks!' mannerisms might not have been Gehrig's but they suit the shy and earnest young fellow who loved his mother and worked hard to get ahead. According to reports after Gehrig's death, no-one knew that the disease was fatal. In the movie, Cooper and his brave wife (Teresa Wright) do know it, which makes more dramatic sense. In a tenement house in New York, eleven-year-old Lou Gehrig dreams of becoming a famous sportsman, while his parents want him to become an engineer. At Columbia University he works his way through school by waiting at table. Although a top athlete, Lou still plans to be an engineer but abandons his studies to become a professional ball player when his mother needs an operation. In his first important game, Lou trips up and a girl in the stand yells, 'Tanglefoot', a cry taken up by the crowd. That night Lou meets the girl, they fall in love and eventually marry. After a long and brilliant career, Lou collapses while training. His reflexes get worse and he decides to retire. He learns that he has a very serious illness (not spelled out)

that will soon kill him. It is the end of everything for him except for the girl who called him 'Tanglefoot' and after the farewell ceremony, he gropes through the gloom to where she is waiting for him in the sunshine at the end of the tunnel. Director Sam Wood pulls out all the stops at the end, and the public would have been very disappointed if he hadn't. Although Cooper was taught how to throw and bunt left-handed by Lefty O'Doul, who worked with him for many weeks, we are only given glimpses and montage sequences of Lou at bat and running bases. The film never catches the excitement of a real baseball game, nor gives any notion of how many are out, how many are on, or even the score. Babe Ruth, Billy Dickey and Mark Koenig play themselves, so does Gary Cooper.

The fact that Babe Ruth died in the same year as *The Babe Ruth Story* (AA 1948) was released is purely coincidental. 'The Sultan of Swat' died of throat cancer, a disillusioned man, shunned by the sport that he had made the most popular in America. If Gary Cooper was more famous than Lou Gehrig, then the opposite was

true of William Bendix playing the Babe. Babe Ruth was well-known even in countries around the world that didn't play baseball. In World War II, Japanese soldiers were said to have shouted, 'To Hell with Babe Ruth!' as the worst insult they could think up.

In the movie, many of the statistics are there and quite a few incidents on and off the diamond including his excesses and lack of discipline. Babe Ruth himself was said to have okayed the screenplay and coached Bendix but, on the whole, the movie was Ruthless. The Bambino deserved better than this. What little action there is on the playing field is perfunctory and studio-phony. It's too genteel and sentimental by half. Ruth was bigger than life. He drove faster, ate more, swore more and was a better ball player than any man living. The Yankees fined Ruth 52,000 dollars for flouting the club's regulations. In the movie, he is fined for missing a major game, because he was taking an injured dog to hospital. William Bendix plays him as a lumbering, good-hearted oaf, not unlike his *Life of Riley* persona, the very opposite of the Babe. The movie

begins in Baltimore's St Mary's Industrial School for Boys, where the baby Babe is under the special care of Brother Matthias (Charles Bickford). In his teens, Babe enters pro baseball as a pitcher with the Baltimore Orioles. Later, when with the Boston Red Sox, a girl in a restaurant tells him he has a habit of telegraphing a pitched curve. She disappears before Ruth can learn her name, but her advice starts him on his way to becoming baseball's greatest left-hand pitcher and home-run king. Finally Ruth meets the girl again. She is showgirl Claire Hodgson (Claire Trevor) and he proposes to her. They only marry after Ruth has achieved the hitherto unthinkable total of 60 home runs in the 1927 season. After 21 years a major league player, Ruth goes to the Boston Braves, but he is older and slower (so is Roy del Ruth's direction), and although he hits 3 home runs against Pittsburgh, he decides to quit. Ill and discouraged, he agrees to try a serum treatment, never before used, if it will help humanity and as he is rolled in-

William Bendix in *The Babe Ruth Story*

56

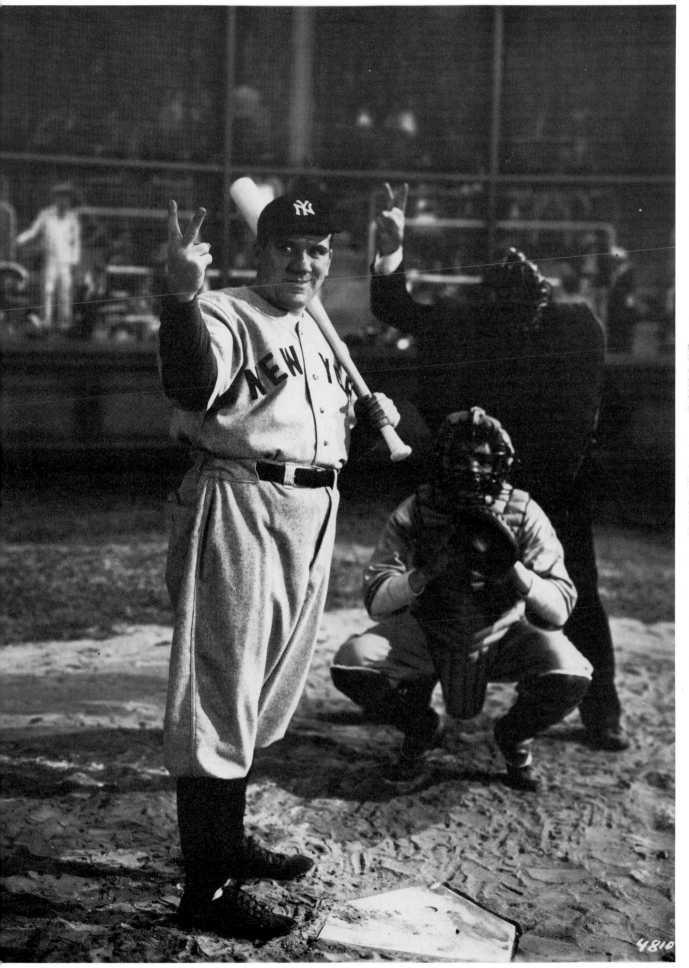

to the operating room, 'to make his greatest play far from baseball crowds,' there are sobs and angel voices on the soundtrack. It was characteristic of most Hollywood movies of the forties and fifties that attention to period detail was very superficial. Aside from newspaper headlines, it is difficult to believe that most of *The Babe Ruth Story* was set in the twenties and early thirties and not in the late forties.

Although some of the uniforms and costumes might have been turn-of-the-century, in *Take Me Out To The Ball Game* (MGM 1949 — *Everybody's Cheering* — GB), the language, attitudes and musical arrangement were pure late forties. Eddie O'Brien (Gene Kelly) and Dennis Ryan (Frank Sinatra) are a song 'n dance team by night and ball players by day. This is soon put an end to when the new owner-manager K.C. Higgins arrives. K.C. turns out to be Esther Williams whom Kelly immediately makes a play for. She shows little interest in him except in his ability to play ball. Inevitably, Esther soon thaws (after a swim) and falls for Kelly's rather blatant charms. Gene Kelly mugs like

mad in desperation with the material, and Betty Garrett chases shy Sinatra. It was Busby Berkeley's last film as director. (Gene Kelly and Stanley Donen, in fact, worked on most of the numbers which led producer Arthur Freed to allow them to direct the far superior *On The Town* — MGM 1949.) The best parts of *Take Me Out To The Ball Game* were the numbers such as 'O'Brien to Ryan to Goldberg'. This Technicolor musical is very much like the words of the flag-waving finale, 'Like a great big strawberry shortcake, or a turkey on Thanksgiving day, Like a 4th of July, or apple pie, It's strictly USA.'

Sam Wood, the guru of goo made *The Stratton Story* (MGM 1949) into rather a touching tale of the triumph over crushing odds, told in a sensitive manner. It is the 'true' story of Monty Stratton (Jimmy Stewart), an amateur baseball enthusiast who owns a small farm which he shares with his mother (Agnes Moorhead). After a particularly good display of his skill in a local game, he is spotted by a talent scout (Frank Morgan) who trains him to become a

first-rate pitcher. Eventually he leaves the farm and becomes a pro with the Chicago White Sox. At the beginning of his sporting career, he meets and marries Ethel (June Allyson) and they have a son. One day, Monty goes rabbit shooting on the farm, falls into a ditch and shoots himself through the leg. It has to be amputated and it's many months before he can walk again. He refuses to admit defeat and is able once more to take his place among the professional players. The movie is fortunate to have James Stewart in the lead (the role was meant for Van Johnson) who manages to suggest the growth from a gangling youth to an adult in mind and body. Agnes Moorhead gives a beautifully restrained performance and June Allyson exudes husky sweetness. There is not much footage of the national pastime, but what there is is quite effective especially when Stratton makes his dramatic comeback. Monty Stratton himself acted as technical advisor and Gene Bearden, Bill Dickey, Jimmy Dykes and Mervyn Shea play themselves.

It Happens Every Spring (TCF 1949) had the sort of idea

that the Disney studios later dreamt up for the kiddie market. This one contains the fantastical notion that chemistry professor, Ray Milland, discovers, by accident, a chemical compound which, when applied to a baseball, makes it repulsive to wood and therefore could baffle any batter who tried to make contact with it. The movie has one visually comic device, that being the sight of a batter swinging wildly at a ball that trickily dodges the bat. Milland smears the secret grease on before he pitches, thus making himself the ace of the big teams. Paul Douglas plays the dumb catcher who doesn't catch on. Naturally certain ethical considerations come into play, but they are resolved because the professor runs out of the compound, hurts his hand and goes back to teaching. Jean Peters is the spoil-sport girl who raises the ridiculous question of fair-play. The charm, like the compound, is spread rather thin and runs out before the end.

The cry to commit arbitercide is stronger than in any other sport. The umpire is not

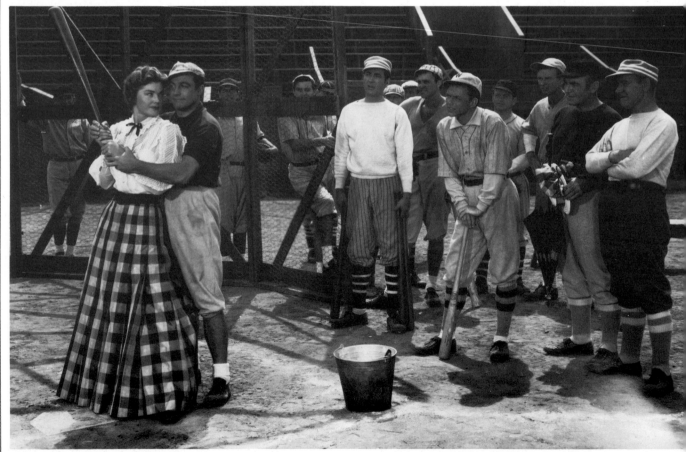

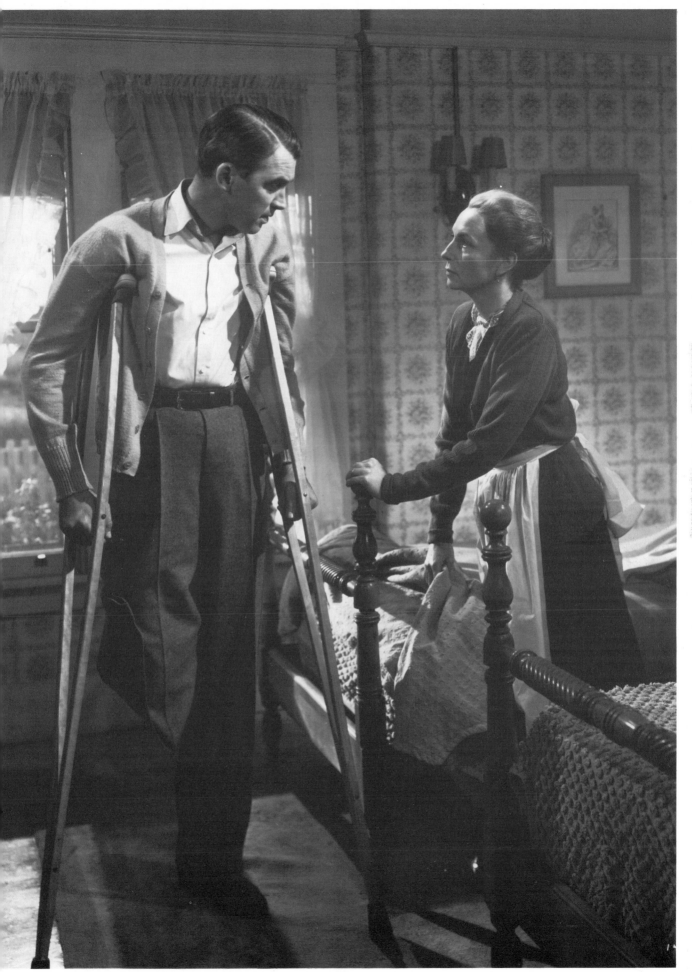

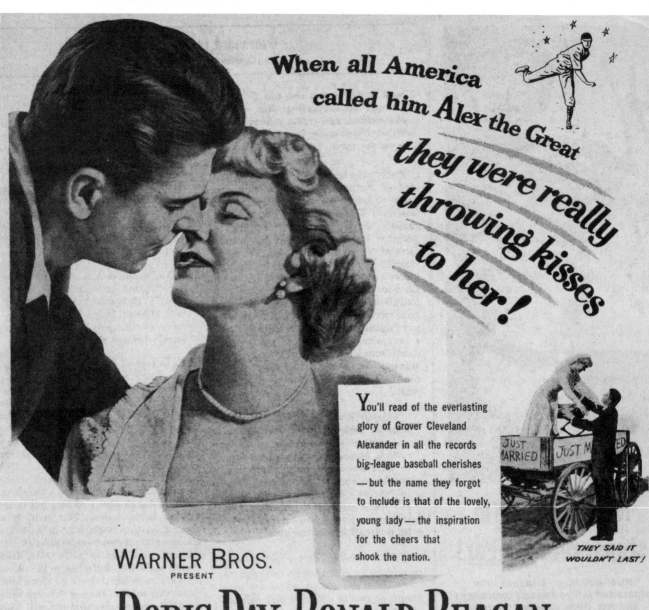

When all America called him Alex the Great they were really throwing kisses to her!

You'll read of the everlasting glory of Grover Cleveland Alexander in all the records big-league baseball cherishes —but the name they forgot to include is that of the lovely, young lady — the inspiration for the cheers that shook the nation.

THEY SAID IT WOULDN'T LAST!

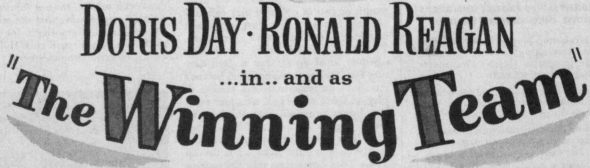

WARNER BROS.
PRESENT

DORIS DAY · RONALD REAGAN

...in.. and as

"The Winning Team"

ALSO STARRING

SCREEN PLAY BY
TED SHERDEMAN AND
SEELEG LESTER &
MERWIN GERARD

FRANK LOVEJOY

PRODUCED BY
BRYAN FOY
DIRECTED BY
LEWIS SEILER

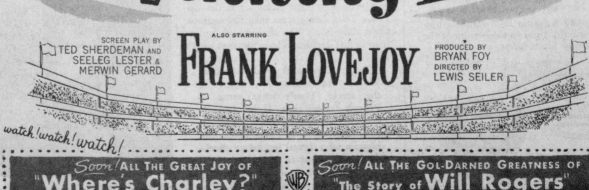

watch! watch! watch!

Soon! ALL THE GREAT JOY OF
"Where's Charley?"
COLOR BY TECHNICOLOR

Soon! ALL THE GOL-DARNED GREATNESS OF
"The Story of Will Rogers"
COLOR BY TECHNICOLOR

5

only the man in the iron mask, but a man in the stocks. Certain gentle souls who enjoy baseball and are passionately against violence, suddenly lose all control and would gladly see the umpire drawn and quartered for making a bad decision. Who in the world would want such a job? This is the initially amusing idea behind *Kill the Umpire* (Col. 1950). An ex-ballplayer who loves the game, becomes an umpire. William Bendix, more at home than as Babe Ruth, does as well as he can in a role which gets progressively less funny as the film deteriorates into farce. Of course when he becomes umpire in the Texas Interstate League, he's put upon by everyone including some shifty local gamblers. Frank Tashlin's frenetic screenplay works against director Lloyd Bacon's more solid virtues.

Black players were barred from the white professional leagues until 1947 when Jackie Robinson became the first black in the major leagues. *The Jackie Robinson Story* (Eagle Lion 1950) is a well-meaning movie which tells of Robinson's struggle against racism. Jackie Robinson himself gives a remarkably natural performance despite the inept script. The picture recounts the poverty of his California childhood, his all-round athletic record at UCLA, his service in the segregated army, and his difficulties in finding a job. He marries his college sweetheart (Ruby Dee) and travels with the all-black Kansas City Monarchs team, suffering prejudice as they travel through the south, before he is offered a contract with Branch Rickey, manager of the Brooklyn Dodgers. The best scenes are those between Robinson and Rickey (Minor Watson) in which Rickey warns him of what he will be up against in the white league. Everything will depend on his being able to take abuse from the other players and the hecklers in the stands without fighting back. 'Mister Rickey,' Robinson says, 'I got two cheeks, ain't I?' He knows that white pitchers will try to brain him and fielders will delight in treading on him with their spiked shoes. He takes on the job, because he doesn't want to be reduced like his brother to roadsweeping. Robinson is jeered when playing with Montreal (one of the

Dodger's farm clubs) and a black cat is thrown on the field. He finally silences the critics by his skills as a hitter, fielder and base runner. A non-smoker, non-drinker, Robinson was a man of extraordinary moral stamina who, by keeping his cool and playing the white man's game, opened up the sport for players like Willie Mays. The baseball scenes are not very convincing with sports announcers telling us things we should have been shown. Ploddingly directed by Alfred E. Green, the film never really gets near the heart of the problem, resolving itself with a tacked-on happy ending that can only seem superficial. A celestial voice inveighs against intolerance and informs us that 'America is a country where every boy has the opportunity to become President — or play for the Brooklyn Dodgers,' and you'd better believe it. Looking at it now from a distance of over 30 years, it does seem embarrassingly naive but it was a seed that finally grew 'Roots'.

How did the Pittsburgh Pirates win the National League pennant, when they were in 8th place in the early part of the season? It needed a miracle and according to *Angels in the Outfield* (MGM 1951), that is exactly what occurred. A combination of whimsy, sports, religion, and romance, it's not as icky as it sounds, only ickish. Helping to keep the gorge from rising is the direction of Clarence Brown (also the producer), and the performance of Paul Douglas as the Runyonesque

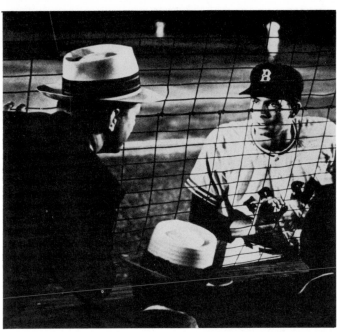

Anthony Perkins in *Fear Strikes Out*

Pirates manager, Guffy McGovern. He is a loud-mouthed, blaspheming, misanthropist. One evening, he is greeted by a celestial messenger who tells him that his team will start winning when he mends his ways. Douglas becomes kindness itself and miracles begin to happen on the diamond. The Pirates win 10 straight games, but the game is nearly up when an orphan girl (Donna Corcoran) sees an 'angel' behind each Pittsburgh player. This leads newspaper reporter, Janet Leigh, to investigate the possibility of heavenly intervention. In the end, of course, Douglas falls for Leigh and proves to be really on the side of the angels. There are brief appearances by Bing Crosby, Joe Di Maggio, Ty Cobb and Harry Ruby to enliven the proceedings.

Mrs Grover Cleveland Alexander is credited as Technical Advisor on *The Winning Team* (WB 1952), which leads one to suspect that it may not be the most objective view of the life of her husband or herself as played by Ronald Reagan and Doris Day. She is revealed as the real power behind 'Alex the Great's' pitching arm. Set in the first decades of the century, it recounts the tale of Grover Alexander's two loves, Aimee his wife, and baseball. A telephone linesman in a Nebraska farming town, he is spotted pitching for the local amateur team. He becomes a pro and tours the country sending his fiancee money to buy a farm. At the peak of his suc-

cess, Grover is hit on the head by a ball. He begins to suffer from double vision and his baseball career seems ended. Grover and Aimee settle down on the farm, but his mind is on baseball. One night, he wakes up to find that his sight has returned to normal. Grover joins the Philadelphia Phillies and is a sensation, winning 28 games in his first season. Home from World War I, Grover reports to his new owners, The Chicago Cubs. In the middle of a game, Grover collapses. The doctor advises him to quit baseball as there will be more seizures. Grover, not wanting Aimee to know the truth, pledges the doctor to secrecy. He takes to the bottle and Aimee, thinking him a lush, leaves him. (We are supposed to admire her resolve in leaving him, and his for not telling her.) When Aimee hears the truth, she pleads with a friend, Roger Hornby (Frank Lovejoy), manager of the St Louis Cardinals, to give her husband a chance. Mainly through Grover's pitching, the Cardinals go from success to success. (Cue for montage sequence.) Grover exhausted, manages to carry on until the final game is won. Aimee rushes into his arms for the final cliché clinch, proving that they are a winning team. Neither Day nor Reagan are terribly winning in this labored biopic, Day, because she spreads her charm too thickly and Reagan, because he hasn't very much to spread. Doris Day, after a race from downtown New York, arrives at Yankee stadium in the 9th inning, just in time to inspire Reagan to come through in the 1926 World Series. These are the important details that sports writers do not have the privilege of knowing when writing their articles. 'Due to the dramatic last minute arrival of Mrs Grover Alexander, her husband was able to pitch a no hitter for victory.' Of course, today it is impossible for any movie starring the President of the USA not to have marginal interest.

Another biopic of a Cardinals' player, but of a slightly less lugubrious nature than *The Winning Team*, was the life story of Dizzie Dean, *The Pride of St Louis* (TCF 1952). Dan Dailey plays the colorful character, famed as much for his unorthodox behavior and mangling of the English tongue, as for his pitching prowess.

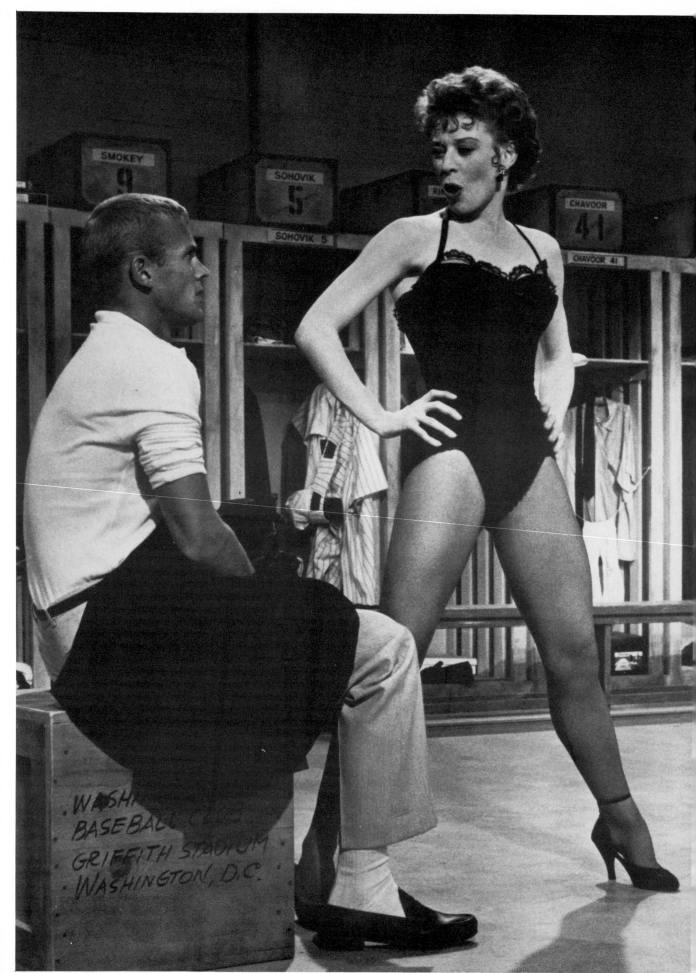

lthough there is quite a lot of ction on the diamond, the ovie concentrates more on izzy's antics away from the eld. Jerome Herman Dean oon to be dubbed 'Dizzy' by ns and sports writers) is scovered by a baseball scout tching in a small ground in rkansas. Soon Dean's pit-ing comes to the notice of the ardinals who offer him a con-act. He persuades them to gn up his brother Paul tichard Crenna), also a fine tcher. The Dean brothers ecome ace pitchers and bring eat success to the Cardinals. t the height of the brothers' iumphs, both Paul and Dizzy amage their pitching arms. Vhen he returns to the game ter recuperation, Dizzy is no nger the player he was. He arts gambling and drinking, his wife Pat (Joanne Dru) aves him. (Here we go again!) tunned by her departure, he ccepts a job as radio commen-ator of baseball games. His uthoritative but racy broad-asts are enjoyed by the fans ut not by the teaching frater-ity who complain that his nglish may have a detrimen-al effect on children. At the nd of his next broadcast, Diz-y bids a moving farewell to the steners. Pat, who had heard ne broadcast, returns to him nd the teachers' spokes-oman calls him to apologize.

A baseball movie that ends ith a great baseball star not inning a game but winning ac-eptance of colloquial English, an't be all bad. The sticky pat-nes come in the drinking, ambling, wife-leaving scenes hich screenwriter Herman J. lankiewicz *(Citizen Kane,* he Pride of the Yankees) uld not breathe any life into. lsewhere, the script and the awky appeal of Dan Dailey's erformance, make it reason-bly entertaining despite the edestrian direction by Har-on Jones. What was needed, s in the case of *The Babe Ruth tory,* was a little less everence and a lot more gusto. or the record, both Dailey and ean stood 6ft 4ins in bare feet nd weighed approximately 89 lbs. Dailey was trained by te Danning to give some idea f the famous jet-propelled pit-hing style of the dynamite ean of the 30s.

Dan Dailey, director Har-on Jones and baseball team-d up again for *The Kid from eft Field* (TCF 1953). It tells of

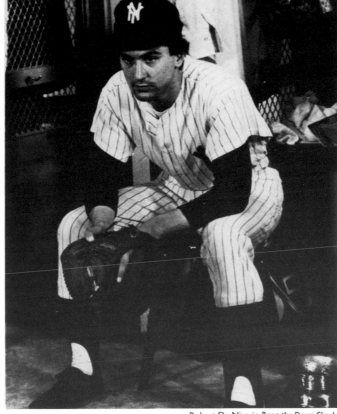

Robert De Niro in *Bang the Drum Slowly*

a has-been ball player (Dan Dailey) who works as a peanut vendor in a ball park. He passes on shrewd coaching tips to the team via his small son (Billy Chapin) who is batboy. Soon the team begins to win and the players demand that the boy be made their manager. The sight of a nine-year-old manag-ing a team of grown men has limited comic possibilities. The adults are so childish, the father so self-effacing, the boy so cute, that it proves once again that any attempt at satire on baseball is doomed to failure.

The interest of *The Big Leaguer* (MGM 1953) for cinephiles is the fact that this is the first feature directed by Robert Aldrich, and for base-ball fans there is a chance to see some of the training techni-ques of a New York Giants' farm club in Florida. Each year, hundreds of young hope-fuls from America's sandlots come to the training camp run by John Lobert (Edward G. Robinson in his worst period). He rates 3rd baseman Adam Polachuk (Jeff Richards) as the outstanding prospect of the year's crop. Aided by Lobert and his niece Christy (Vera-Ellen in her only non-musical), he becomes a home-run hero and signs for a future in the big leagues. Carl Hubbell, mem-

ber of the Baseball Hall of Fame, recreates his real life role as a Giant's scout. Most of the material is fairly routine, the father-son conflict, the romance, the gruff but good-hearted manager, and the hand on the heart respect for base-ball, but Aldrich has directed it with a competence that pro-mised better things. The best parts are the relationships bet-ween the baseball try-outs in the camp, the rivalry and fraternity and, believe it or not, the ball playing.

Fear Strikes Out (Par. 1957) was an auspicious film. It was Alan J. Paluka's first produc-tion, Robert Mulligan's first movie as director and it gave Anthony Perkins his first star-ring role. It also happens to be one of the more interesting of sporting biopics. In 1952, Jim Piersall, outfielder of the Boston Red Sox, suffered an emotional collapse. Piersall (with sportswriter Al Hirsh-berg) described the reasons for this crack-up in his auto-biography and Ted Berkman and Raphael Blair turned it in-to a taut screenplay. Holly-wood was always rather sim-ple about complexes, but the film avoids glib psychological theorizing while still making the reasons for Piersall's breakdown perfectly clear. In effect, Piersall suffered from

what has been called the Laius complex. Laius, the father of Oedipus, tried to kill his son at birth, but the boy grew up and killed his father instead. The Freudian expression 'Strike the father dead' (with its hint of baseball) is essential before the son can be a man in his own right. The father-son theme (the imitator of the father, the imaginary father etc) was popular in the mid-fifties. e.g. *Rebel without a Cause* (1955), *East of Eden* (1955) and *The Rack* (1956). The tie between nine-year-old Jim and his dad (Karl Malden) is strengthened by their shared love of base-ball. Dad Piersall, never hav-ing got beyond minor league status in his youth, is determin-ed to live out his own life through his son. Every day after school he coaches young Jim. 'We're going for the big leagues, boy,' he mutters. Jim is a highly-strung lad, always striving to please his father. At 17, his all-round talents help his high-school team to win the championship. 'How'd I do, dad?' he asks with the flush of victory on his face. 'Not bad, son. But you weren't on your toes all the time and you know it.' Jim is signed by the Red Sox and sent to the Scranton team for training. His father tells him that next year it has to be Boston. His batting wins Scranton the pennant, but the pressure on him is great. When he finally gets to play for the Red Sox, it is as shortstop, a position he has never filled. The fear of failure is so strong, that the strain of the past years takes its toll and he goes berserk attacking his team-mates and trying to climb the high wire fence. (A powerfully directed moment.) He wakes up in a straitjacket. The real irony of Piersall's dilemma is brought out when speaking of his father to the psychiatrist at the hospital he says, 'If it hadn't been for him standing behind me, pushing me and driving me, I wouldn't be where I am today.' When he realizes that it is his father's monomania that has driven him to the edge of madness, he begins on the road to recovery and success. Ob-viously there were con-tributory causes inherent in Piersall's nature, but for dramatic purposes the pater-nal cause eliminates the others. Perkins gives an edgy, angular performance, not without moments of tender-ness and wit. Karl Malden, his bulbous nose emoting, gives

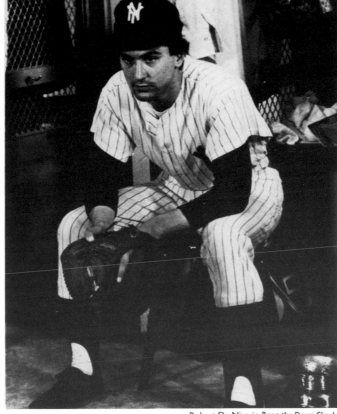

another of his intense performances. Although it is more about being bats than baseball bats, the scenes on the diamond are quite well done.

One advantage that the screen version of *Damn Yankees* (WB 1958. *What Lola Wants* — GB) had over the Broadway hit, was the genuine outdoor baseball sequences. Gwen Verdon repeats her stage role as the Devil's handmaiden given the job of vamping a rookie (Tab Hunter) on the Washington Senators, while Ray Walston as the Devil tries to fix it so that the Senators can beat the Yankees for the A.L. pennant so causing millions of people to go mad. Directed by Stanley Donen, it retains the vigor and tunefulness of the original. The Devil's side has the best tune with 'Whatever Lola wants, Lola gets,' but there is also singable advice to all ball players with 'You gotta have heart.' The only thing that dates the movie is Tab Hunter's crewcut. It is mercilessly free from the sentimental whimsy that other fantasies such as *Angels in the Outfield* and *Heaven Can Wait* (1978) engender.

In Ingmar Bergman's *The Seventh Seal* (1956), Death, one of the dramatis personae, plays chess with the hero until he can checkmate him. Death is no less a presence, albeit an invisible one, in *Bang the Drum Slowly* (Par. 1973). Here, instead of chess, he might have been seen pitching a hot one to the dying ball player, Bruce Pearson (Robert de Niro). Pearson is a dimwitted, tobacco-chewing hick who happens to be dying of Hodgkin's Disease. Unlike Lou Gehrig, this catcher is not a golden lad, but a born loser on the point of being sent down from the 'New York Mammoths' to the farm team. It is only the proximity of death that enables this gauche creature. Death also enables his roommate Henry Wiggen (Michael Moriarty), the antithesis of Bruce. He's got everything going for him. He's good-looking, well-dressed, self-assured, has a beautiful wife (Heather MacCrae) and is a 20 game winning ace pitcher. Suddenly, he is faced with the secret of Bruce's disease. 'You're driving along with a man who's been told he's dying. It was bad enough rooming

with him when he was well,' he narrates. Henry now feels an obligation towards Bruce. The rest of the team wonder at Henry's concern for the 'plumb dumb catcher' and insinuations abound. The manager claims that it has been a long time since he saw any 'fairies' in baseball. (There is nothing 'fairy' in their relationship, although the movie's implicit view seems to be that there is something unhealthy about close male friendships only justified in this case because Bruce is dying.) When the disease becomes common knowledge, the other players stop their ridicule and begin, for the first time, to include Bruce in their activities. Bruce even begins to play better. But the illness strikes. After visiting him in hospital, Henry goes to the airport to say goodbye to Bruce who is going home to Georgia. He promises to send him a series scorecard. The Mammoths win the playoffs and the series, but Bruce never receives the scorecard. At his funeral, Henry's voice over says, 'He wasn't a bad ballplayer when they gave him half a chance. From now on I rag

nobody.' Mark Harris' screen play, adapted from his 195? novel (from the series of Henry Wiggin novels), works on a number of levels. The superficial implication of the final lines is 'don't rag anyone in case he's dying of an incurable disease', but it also tries to teach us that we're all part of the same team and that the way to get on with other people is to understand them and look after them, rather than try to push them around. On the other hand, it is a superior weepie (a bit like a Bette Davis/Miriam Hopkins movie), and another buddy-buddy picture (*The Sting* and *Maurie* were made the same year), as well as brilliantly creating the almost Freemasonry of the locker room with its own language and signs, which naturally precludes women. The two main women, caught in the misogynistic web of the plot, are an ordinary wife and a gold digger. The male actors, who had to loosen up with an hour or two of baseball every day before shooting, are excellent especially Vincent Gardenia and Phil Foster as manager and coach, and Robert de Niro

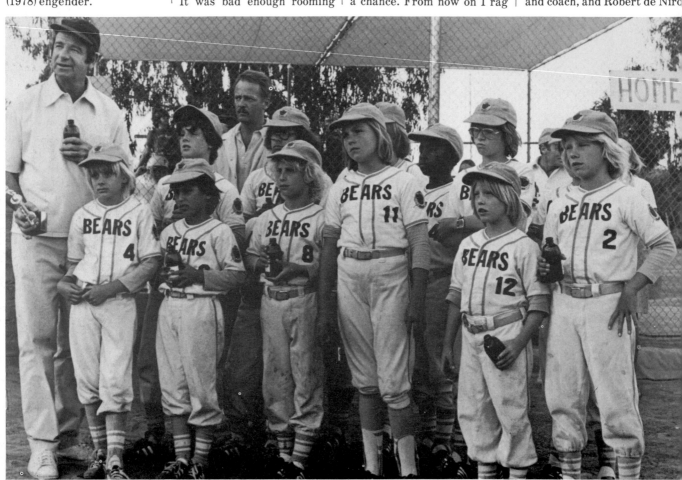

Walter Matthau with *The Bad News Bears*

his first important role. He ⟨w⟩ent several weeks with the ⟨C⟩incinnati Reds learning how a ⟨pi⟩tcher moves and taking pit⟨ch⟩es from a machine. He even ⟨tr⟩aveled in Georgia to study ⟨th⟩e speech patterns so that he ⟨so⟩unded as authentic as he ⟨lo⟩oked. John Hancock, the dir⟨e⟩ctor, was inclined to underline ⟨th⟩e pathos which was innate in ⟨th⟩e script and he also overdid ⟨th⟩e slow-motion so that we get ⟨m⟩ore instant replay than ac⟨tu⟩al play.

The main differences bet⟨w⟩een the Big Leagues and the ⟨Li⟩ttle Leagues seems to be the ⟨fa⟩ct that the Little Leaguers ⟨ar⟩e more competitive, swear ⟨m⟩ore, and the spectators get ⟨fa⟩r more involved, if we are to ⟨be⟩lieve The Bad News Bears ⟨Pa⟩r. 1976). The basic lesson of ⟨A⟩merican life is learnt early. ⟨W⟩in or die. The Bears are a ⟨te⟩am in the fictional Southern ⟨Ca⟩lifornia version of the Little ⟨Le⟩ague called the North Val⟨le⟩y League. It is made up of ⟨ne⟩ighborhood misfits, rejects ⟨fr⟩om other teams. The team in⟨cl⟩udes a huge fat boy, forever ⟨cr⟩unching chocolate bars, a ⟨co⟩uple of Mexicans who speak ⟨no⟩ English, a juvenile delin⟨qu⟩ent, a black kid who does ⟨H⟩ank Aaron impressions, a ⟨Je⟩wish boy, a near-sighted pit⟨ch⟩er and a 12-year-old retired ⟨pi⟩tcher named Amanda Whur⟨li⟩zer (Tatum O'Neal). This ⟨ra⟩gbag team is handed over to ⟨M⟩orris Buttermaker (Walter ⟨M⟩atthau) a beer-swilling, ⟨br⟩oken-down ex-minor league ⟨pr⟩o as coach. 'What do you ex⟨pe⟩ct — all we got is Jews, spics, ⟨ni⟩ggers and a boogie-eating ⟨m⟩oron,' says one of the little ⟨m⟩onsters when Buttermaker ⟨fi⟩rst confronts them. The open⟨in⟩g game against the perennial ⟨le⟩ague champs, the Yankees, ⟨pr⟩oves to be a disaster. Butter⟨m⟩aker calls the game off at the ⟨en⟩d of the first half innings. ⟨T⟩he score is Yankees 26 — ⟨B⟩ears 0. But he recognizes a ⟨ch⟩allenge when he sees one and ⟨is⟩ determined to turn them into ⟨th⟩e 'Bad News' Bears, teaching ⟨th⟩em to win at any price. Grad⟨u⟩ally, he sees that he is making ⟨th⟩em abide by society's cut⟨th⟩roat ethics instead of letting ⟨th⟩em lose blissfully in their ⟨o⟩wn way. They do not become ⟨la⟩st minute victors, only losing ⟨th⟩e championship by a hair. ⟨Y⟩ankees 7 — Bears 6. The club ⟨re⟩joices in the face of defeat, ⟨b⟩ut they give a warning to the ⟨w⟩inners, 'Wait till next year.' ⟨W⟩e. watch out for two sequels.) ⟨It⟩ is a delightfully wry comedy,

containing the un-American message that winning isn't everything and that one can play the game of life without dropping out or changing the rules, but without conforming either. The message is not rammed home, being an integral part of the story. The team is the most individualized bunch of kids since 'Our Gang', being cute only in the sense of smart. Walter Matthau, at the center, gives a superb comic performance, never noticeably playing for laughs nor trying to be loveable. The screenplay by Bill Lancaster (Burt's son) is shrewd and witty (even the many expletives) and director Michael Ritchie (whose first film was about the madness of competition in *Downhill Racer* 1969), manages to find a lighter touch than he did in his other satires on Middle-America.

The very nature of *The Bad News Bears* would seem to exclude any sequels, unless the whole philosophy behind it were eliminated. If they are seen to get better and better and become winners, the point is lost. That is basically the problem with the two sequels. *The Bad News Bears in Breaking Training* (Par. 1977) is without Matthau, Tatum O'Neal, Bill Lancaster and Michael Ritchie as director. (He is producer.) The screenplay is by Paul Brickman and the director is 26-year-old Michael Pressman. It tells of the Bears' efforts to get from California to Houston to play in the Astrodome, the winning team to play the Japanese champions in Japan. As the sequel is called *The Bad News Bears go to Japan* (Par. 1978), there is no need for the result to be given. William Devan is unamusing as the manager in the former film, while Tony Curtis in the latter provides some laughs as a conner conned by the Bears into going straight. Mush seems to have crept into both and the second looks as if it was produced by the Japanese Tourist Board. The good news is that the Bad News Bears have been disbanded or grown up and the bad news is that it spawned something called *Here Come the Tigers* (American International Pictures 1978) which is, believe it or not, about a Little League team of youngsters who cuss better than they play. The team contains a deaf pitcher and a karate-champ batter. The makers had the originality to call the team The Tigers and not The Bears.

The Bush Leaguer WB 1927 is Monte Blue who plays a gas-station owner who abandons his job for a career as a baseball player. He becomes a baseball ace, falls in love and sells a patent on a new-fangled gas pump he invented. Minor league stuff.

Fast Company Par. 1929 was the first of three versions of the Ring Lardner-George M. Cohan play, **Elmer the Great**. This one is a fairly fast-moving romp with Jack Oakie as the egocentric Elmer, who has been lifted from a bush league into a big one. He proves a natural home-run hitter but has to be kept, by unscrupulous means, from running home to his sweetheart.

Death on the Diamond MGM 1934 was not an earlier version of **Bang the Drum Slowly** but a murder mystery. First, the Cardinals' pitcher is shot through the heart after rounding 3rd base. Second, another pitcher is found strangled in the locker-room and third, the Cardinals' catcher dies of arsenic poisoning after eating a hot-dog. There are also two attempts on the life of star pitcher Kelly (Robert Young). One ingenious attempt was the placing of a small bomb in the pocket of his sweater. The suspects are the head of a gambling syndicate, a jealous ball player, and two members of the club expelled for taking bribes. It all goes to show what a dangerous sport baseball can be.

It Happened in Flatbush TCF 1942 was all about the Brooklyn Dodgers with Lloyd Nolan as their fictional coach. Dullsville.

Ladies Day RKO 1943 was the story of a love-smitten pitcher (Eddie Albert) who can't play ball when his wife's around and can't play any better when she isn't. As played by 'Mexican Spitfire' Lupe Velez at her loudest, who can blame him? Patsy Kelly and Max Baer also feature.

Make Mine Music RKO 1946 was Walt Disney's musical compendium, the hep-cat's answer to **Fantasia**. In one of the items, **A Musical Recitation**, the mighty Casey struck out again. Jerry Colonna's high-pitched banshee voice recited the immortal lines ending with:

And somewhere men are laughing, and somewhere children shout; But there is no joy in Mudville — mighty Casey has struck out.

The episode opens with the chorus singing the song, visualized by a series of old-fashioned lithographs reflecting the '90's. Then we see the ball park itself. Being a cartoon, there is even more hyperbole than in the poem, although it retains the spirit of the ballad. A bat gets caught in a batter's long waxed moustache and a ball slides up the first baseman's foot into his hand. When the fatal third strike occurs and 'the air is shattered by the force of Casey's blow,' a tremendous wind blows over the spectators. Finally, we see Casey alone in the ball park in the rain, going crazy chasing the ball around the field with his bat.

The Kid from Cleveland Rep. 1949 was 15-year-old Rusty Tamblyn (later Russ) making his film debut. He plays a baseball-loving delinquent child who is helped onto the straight and narrow by sports announcer, George Brent. In order to do this, Brent recruits the whole of the Cleveland Indian team plus Bill Veek, their owner. Veek, one of baseball's greatest showmen, should have been given the task of directing this harmless moral tale. A sort of movie equivalent of Bat day, it sets out to prove that there is nothing baseball won't cure. The Indians are seen warming up, in spring training, playing a bunch of wayward kids, and in a few disconnected newsreel shots. Bobby Feller and Tris Speaker turn up. George Brent is his usual uncharismatic self.

Rhubarb Par. 1951 was a cat that was left 30 million dollars and a ball team by an eccentric millionaire (Gene Lockhart). Sticking fairly closely to the story by H. Allen Smith, it tells of how the eponymous puss, helped by his guardians, (Ray Milland and Jan Sterling), triumphs over anti-feline fiends, bookies and gangsters,

to become a national mascot and the pride of Brooklyn. The ball team, the Brooklyn Loons, play better when their cat-owner is around. On the eve of the big game, Rhubarb is catnapped by gangsters but he manages to escape in time to bring luck to the team.

Strategic Air Command Par. 1955 calls up ex-World War II pilot, James Stewart while he's playing 3rd base for the St Louis Cardinals. Stewart, in blue-gray hair, looks the oldest ball player in the world. 'I'm no youngster any-more. I have a few more years of baseball left,' he says. Reluctant at first to rejoin the air-force, he's persuaded by General Frank Lovejoy of the necessity to keep America strong and that the qualities needed for a pilot are those of the baseball player. 'The B.47 is on third base, it'll be up to you to bring it home,' says Lovejoy. June Allyson is the waiting wife who was much happier watching her husband from the stands than looking up at the sky. 'So nice to see a young couple so gay,' someone says at an air-force party. There is nothing gay, in either sense, in the rest of the picture.

The Great American Pastime MGM 1956 was a waste of time. Tom Ewell is a lawyer who lets himself get talked into managing a Little League team. As the boys lose games, he loses friends. He finally pulls the club into shape and, never learning, embarks on a new career as a Scout leader. Anne Francis plays his wife and Ann Miller, an attractive widow. Nathaniel Benchley, son of Robert, wrote the contrived script.

The Bingo Long Traveling All-Stars and Motor Kings UI 1976 is an all-black baseball team barnstorming through Middle America in 1939. They have to deal with the prejudice of white spectators by clowning around on the field. 'You know how us niggers are,' says Billy Dee Williams as Bingo Long, founder of the troupe. Terrific performances also from James Earl Jones and Richard Pryor and cool direction by John Badham make this one of the most entertaining of social comedies.

65

Movies on HOOFS

The only thing missing from the cement outside Grauman's Chinese theater in Hollywood, among the handprints of the stars, is a hoof. Neither is there a tomb to the unknown horse at Forest Lawn Memorial Park. Horses have been in almost as many movies as bipeds. They appeared in *The Squaw Man* (1913), the first major film produced in Hollywood, and it was during the making of *Birth of a Nation* (1915), the first film masterpiece, that director D.W. Griffith gave the grandiose instruction, 'Move those 10,000 horses a little to the right.' Where would the cinema be without the horse? Nobody would have been headed off at the pass, the cavalry would not have arrived on time, knights in shining armor would have clanked around like out-of-order robots without their white chargers, and there would have been no horse-racing movies.

Like boxing, horse racing has attracted film makers, because of its crooked connections and the opportunity it gives for sudden success or ruin. Mainly, however, it has been an excuse to film that most photogenic of animals, the horse. Cameramen like to shoot horses, don't they? Horse racing being a most colorful spectacle, the studios were quick to lavish Technicolor on it. Today, one of the few delights to be derived from the horse pics of the thirties and forties, is the brilliant color photography (due principally to Natalie Kalmus, the color consultant), particularly in those from the Twentieth-Century-Fox studios, who made so many race-horse operas that they could easily have been renamed Twentieth-Century-Horse. These films made enough money to keep the studio in more than oats.

Most Hollywood race-track pictures suggest that it is not the honest sport most of us believed it to be. Jockeys seem to be under continual pressure from gangsters to ride a crook-

ed race. Poor jockeys, the Peter Pans of the sporting world, who have not only never grown up but have never grown! (Mickey Rooney's short stature cast him as a jockey in a number of movies.) To the horse player, the horse and rider are abstractions, as much alive as the kings, queens and jacks in a pack of cards. The gambler and the tipster often have a joker jockey up their sleeves. An aspiring jockey watching a race-track movie would learn that the best way to win is to allow the other horses to get a few furlongs ahead and then get the horse to make a superequine effort to pass them at the winning post. Alternatively, the rider or owner should make sure the horse is injured or even breaks a leg a few weeks before the big race. Apparently this gives the horse the extra incentive it needs to win.

It must be said at the outset that most horse-racing pictures are more pedestrian than equestrian which, with a fine disregard for the rules, would

shock the cognoscenti. One of the problems is that they have virtually one interchangeable plot. The prototype goes something like this:- In *Home in Indiana/Kentucky/Maryland/Wyoming* (TCF 1937-1947), the white mare, Zanuck, gives birth to a foal with only three legs. The wise, old horse-trainer (Walter Brennan), who delivered the foal, calls him Tripod. The trainer's grandson (Lon McAllister) falls in love with Tripod at first sight and, despite the colt's obvious disability, is determined to make him a champion racer. After a year's training, Tripod is ready to enter the Technicolor Grass Handicap. The owner of the rival stables is entering his own filly (Charlotte Greenwood). The week before the big race, Tripod has all 3 of his legs broken by racketeers. On the day, however, Lon carries Tripod across the winning line beating Charlotte by an acne pimple.

To pass the time, while watching these equine epics, one can always enjoy the switch

A four-legged friend
A four-legged friend
He'll never let you down
He's honest and faithful
Right up to the end
That one, two, three,
    four-legged friend

— JACK BROOKS, JACK HOPE,
LYLE MORRAIN.
Sung by BOB HOPE, ROY ROGERS in
Son of Paleface
(Par. 1952)

from back-projection to long shot of the stunt man on a real horse. The close-up generally shows an agonizing actor sitting on what could be the arm of a horse-hair sofa while the landscape rushes by behind him. If one is sharp enough, the stunt man's face can be seen to differ from that of the studio-bound rider.

The horse in a race-track movie is treated on a par with the humans, even being referred to by name. Horses in westerns are an anonymous, dispensable lot. Most cowboys treat their horses in a cavalier manner, except for a soppy singing cowboy like the Trigger-happy Roy Rogers. Basically, it is just something between a cowboy's legs, very useful for tossing corpses over or for jumping out of windows. Michael Curtiz was not far wrong when he shouted 'Bring on the empty horses.' But the western does not concern us here. The other category, besides the race-track movie, is the horse-worshiping film, where horses are ridden not for any functional purpose or for gain but solely for pleasure.

'There are people in this world to whom a horse is just a horse and not a thing of beauty and culture,' says Lilli Palmer in *The Miracle of the White Stallions* (Walt Disney 1963). The horse in art has a respectable lineage. Writers from Xenophon (365 B.C.) onwards have celebrated the horse. They have been painted by the greatest artists through the centuries. The horse is the tragic center of Picasso's Guernica representing, according to the artist, suffering humanity. A horse dies with Brunnhilde in the fire at the end of Wagner's Ring, Caligula made his horse a Consul and Richard III was prepared to give his kingdom for one. To D.H. Lawrence they were 'the kings of creation in the order below man,' and according to Swift's Gulliver they were far above man. The movies have inclined o worship the horse in the same manner. The horse has had to carry a burden of heavy symbols in such films as *The Misfits* (1961), where Arthur Miller's screenplay sees the wild horses being roped by cowboys as, among other things, the taming of the free spirit of America. Until the horse is set free in *The Electric Horseman* (1979), his rider will remain bound.

Another type in this category could be called the colt opera, which attempts to prove that a dog may be *man's* best friend but a horse is definitely a *boy's*. Little girls, too, are carried away by horses. There is something almost unhealthy in his catalogue of pre-pubescent lovers of horses. The boy's courtship of *The Black Stallion* (US 1979) is, if not homo-erotic, equusexual. Elizabeth Taylor's violet eyes have the glow of a love-sick girl's when they light on The Pi in *National Velvet* (MGM 1944). This near hysterical attraction of young girls for horses seems to suggest that they are only waiting until they are old enough before a stud comes along. It would be invidious to bring a Freudian interpretation to bear on these kiddie movies, but the signs are there to be read if one wished to do so. In adult horse fare, the film makers themselves provide the libidinal glossary. The horse and rider is a fairly obvious sexual image. 'There is no secret so close as that between a rider and his horse' asserted Surtees and D.H. Lawrence, who was no sloach in sexual matters, seemed to agree. The film adaptation of his 1934 short story *The Rocking-horse Winner* (Two Cities 1950) hardly disguises the masturbatory undertones of the young boy's furious riding of his wooden horse. The boy in *Equus* (US 1977) blinds six horses, because they witness his abortive sexual encounter with a young girl in the stables. In *Reflections in a Golden Eye* (WB 1967), Elizabeth Taylor, now very grown up but still horse-crazy, is contemptuous of the inability of her husband (Marlon Brando) to ride her stallion, Firebird. 'Firebird's a horse,' mumbles Brando. Miss Taylor glares at him. 'Firebird's a *stallion*,' she says in such a way as to cast aspersions on his own virility. As it happens, Brando's lack of horsemanship is linked to the character's homosexuality.

The horse, despite having been forced into allegories, anthropomorphized, asked to fulfil impossible tasks and slobbered over by generations of moppets, has managed to retain its dignity and beauty throughout the proceedings.

'Yankee Doodle came to London just to ride a pony,' went George M. Cohan's song from his 1904 hit musical, *Little Johnny Jones*, filmed by Warner Bros. in 1923 and again, with the advent of sound, in 1929. The plot of both versions told of an American horse's entry in the English Derby ridden by Johnny Jones. In the silent 'musical', Johnny Hines played the title role against absurd English backgrounds. The 1929 rendering, directed half-heartedly by Mervyn LeRoy, at least had the original songs to give it life. They included 'Yankee Doodle Dandy', 'Give my regards to Broadway', and one with the classic title of 'She was kicked on the head by a butterfly', which exactly describes the impression the film made. Eddie Buzzel played the Yankee jockey. Virtually the whole musical was telescoped into one production number in *Yankee Doodle Dandy* (WB 1942).

Although *Sporting Blood* (MGM 9131) was Clark Gable's first starring role, he was nuzzled out by a steed called

The Marx Brothers in *A Day at the Races*

Tommy Boy, who had the main part. The movie tells of the rise, fall and rise again of Tommy Boy, ending with a rousing Kentucky Derby race. Ernest Torrence plays a breeder who loves horses but hates to see them run in races and Madge Evans is the heroine who, on hearing that Tommy Boy's

jockey is going to throw the race, cuts the reins so that he can't pull the horse.

The race-track milieu really found its voice in Damon Runyon. The narrator of his stories is obsessed by horse race betting, an obsession shared by every other 'guy'. Even 'dolls' take second place. In fact Runyon's characters hardly ever think of anything else. Runyon was a great comic stylist, who scrupulously avoided using a past tense or contradictions, doing wonders with the historic present. The flavor of his particular lingo is difficult to capture on film, which provided merely ersatz Runyon. Nevertheless, the world of horse players, touts and bookies who hang around Mindy's on Broadway, has inspired many a screenplay including the expert musical *Guys and Dolls*. *Little Miss Marker* (TCF 1934 — *The Girl in Pawn* — GB) was the first screen version of Runyon's tragi-comic story. The others were *Sorrowful Jones* (Par: 1949), *40 Pounds of Trouble* (1963) and *Little Miss Marker* (UI 1980). Runyon describes the tightfisted bookie Sorrowful Jones thus: 'He is a tall, skinny guy with a long, sad, mean-looking kisser and a mournful voice. He is maybe sixty years old . . .' Of the four Sorrowfuls, Adolph Menjou, Bob Hope, Tony Curtis and Walter Matthau, only the latter comes close. In the 1934 version, Menjou had 6-year-old Shirley Temple to contend with. This was her first starring vehicle and made her into the world's biggest and smallest star from 1934-1938. Unlike Mae West, the other blonde star of the period, 'goodness' had every-

thing to do with Shirley's career, although they had much in common. Both had curly, blonde hair and dimples, both sang and both were teasers who had men falling over themselves to please them. In Runyon's story, the tiny tot dances whenever she can 'holding her little short skirt up in her hands and showing a pair of white panties underneath.' Shirley keeps her skirt decorously in place. Left in the hands of mean Menjou as a marker or IOU for her father's 20 dollar bet, she softens the hardest hearts in the racing world. Charles Bickford as the crook who causes her father's suicide, finds himself having to give his blood to Shirley after an accident, thus saving her life. (In the story she dies.) Although Runyon was able to strike the chord of pathos, he never became as sentimental as this reasonably charming picture becomes.

Another Runyon story, *The Lemon Drop Kid* (Par. 1934), was attempted with Lee Tracy as the young racing tipster who has to leave town pronto with the law at his heels. 3-year-old Baby Leroy, nearing the end of his acting career, was typecast as a brat and William Frawley had a shot at Runyonese. Like the remake (with Bob Hope in 1951), virtually the only thing it had in common with the original story was the title.

Broadway Bill (Col. 1934) was not a Runyon character but the name of a race horse. His owner (Warner Baxter) marries Myrna Loy of the upper crust and gives up racing. But the track is in his blood so he leaves his wife, taking with him the horse in which he has so much faith. After many complications, Bill is ready to be entered in a 25,000 dollar handicap but during a rain storm in a leaky shelter he runs a high fever and almost dies. Baxter lands in jail for not having paid the feed bills and the horse is claimed by the sheriff. By a series of implausible incidents, Broadway Bill passes the winning post first. Based on a Mark Hellinger story, it was directed by Frank Capra as well as could be expected. Capra liked the story so much that he filmed it again in 1950 under the title *Riding High* (Par.) with Bing Crosby.

Frank McHugh is a writer of

Overleaf: Shirley Temple and Adolph Menjou in *Little Miss Marker*

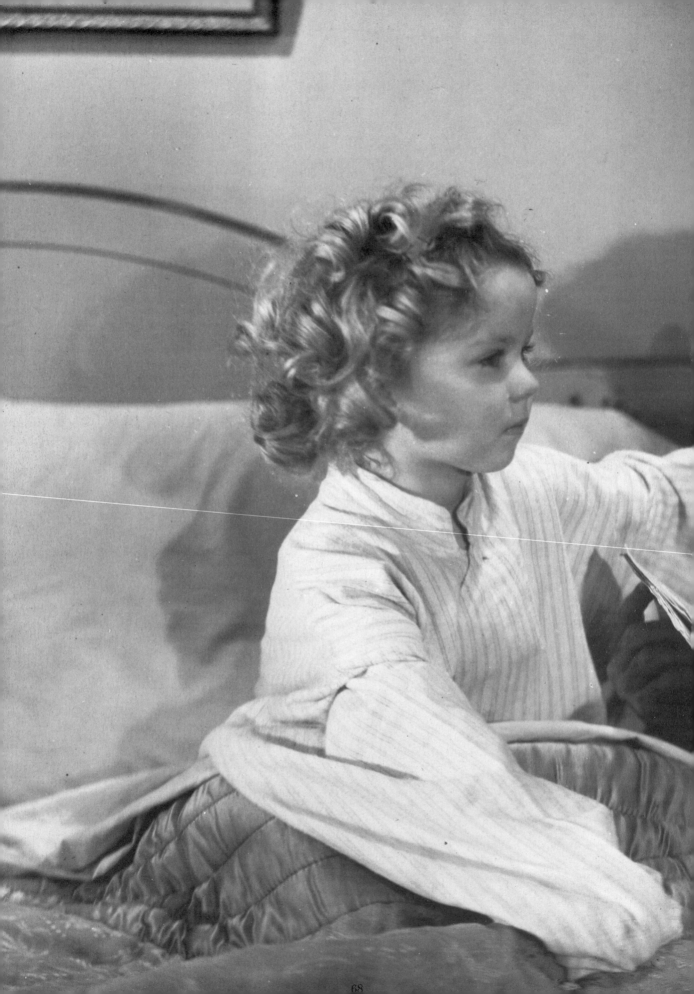

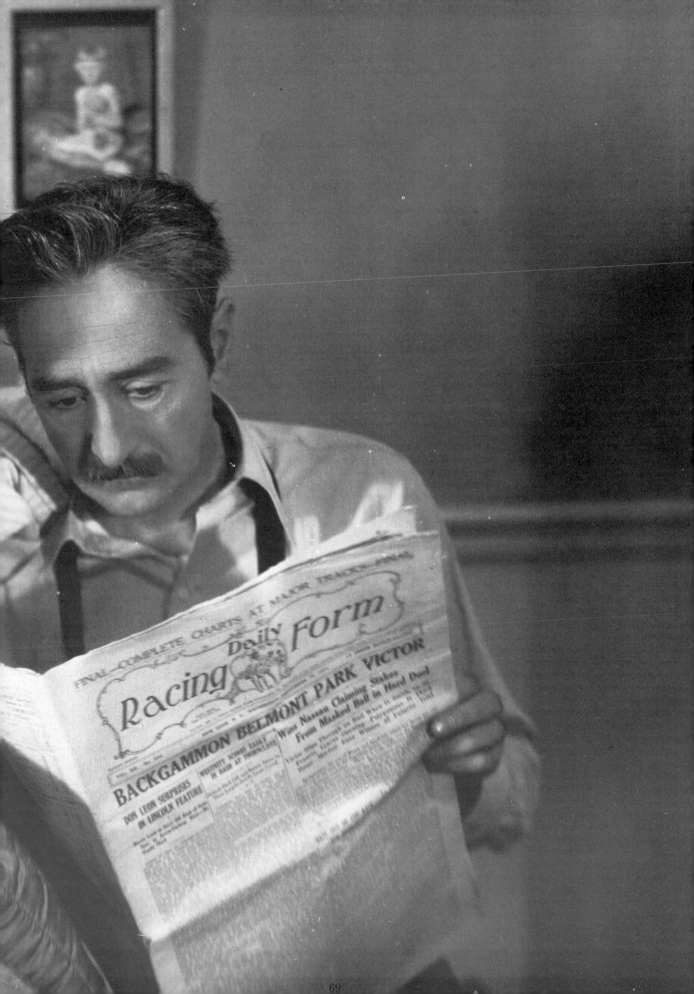

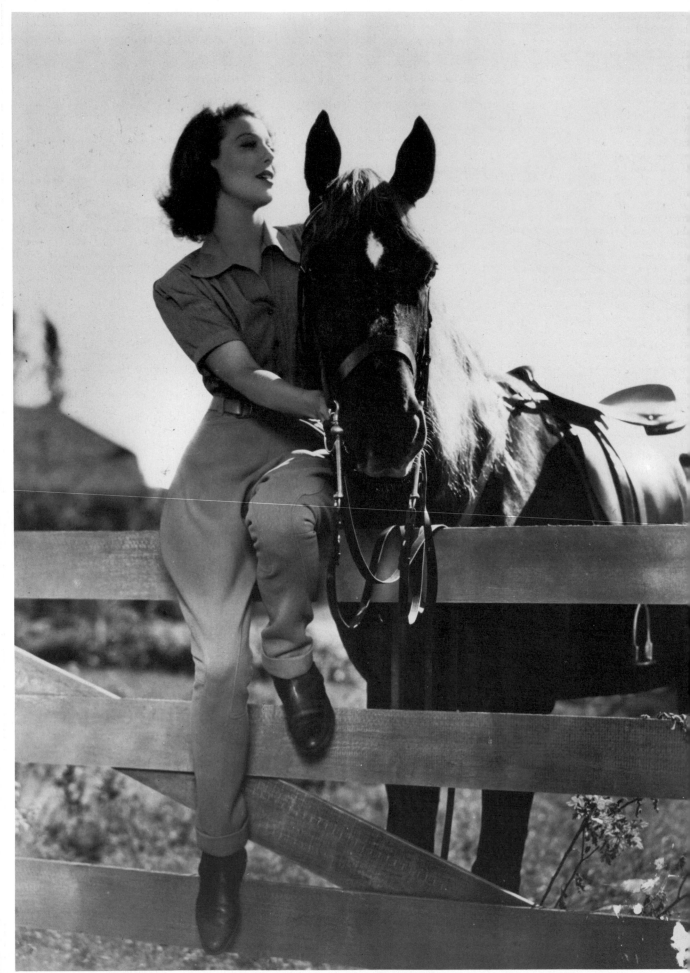

greeting-card verses who finds he can pick race-horse winners in *Three Men on a Horse* (WB 1936). Being a subconscious tipster, his oracular powers disappear when he bets on his own tips. Based on the George Abbott and John Cecil Holm farce, it is slickly directed by Mervyn LeRoy with a crack cast including Sam Levene (his screen debut), Joan Blondell, Guy Kibbee and Allen Jenkins.

Joe E. Brown's farewell movie for Warner Bros., *Polo Joe* (1936), fell as flat as he did from a polo pony. In order to impress a girl (Carol Hughes), Joe pretends to be an eleven-goal man although he's horse-shy. When one of the team breaks an arm before the big match, he is forced to take his place. The sight of Joe E. Brown practising on a bad-tempered donkey and then strapped to a polo pony by an elastic belt, would probably not even amuse Prince Charles. Joe E. Brown, to his credit, did most of his own stunt work although he had hardly been on a horse before.

From the ridiculous to the ridiculous, (albeit the sublimely ridiculous.) in *A Day at the Races* (MGM 1937). The story so far... Unless Judy Standish (Maureen O'Sullivan) can meet the mortgage payments on the Standish Santatorium, she'll have to sell it to the owner of a nearby racetrack (villainous Douglas Dumbrille) who wants to convert the home into a casino. Her only hope of making the money is for High Hat, a horse owned by her fiancé (Allan Jones), to win the steeplechase. Enter the Marx Brothers. Harpo is a jockey, Chico a tout ('Get your tutsi-frutsi ice-cream'), and Groucho is Dr Hugo Z. Hackenbush who, although a horse doctor, gets to run the clinic. One of his victims (i.e. patients) is Mrs Up-john (Margaret Dumont) to whom he gives horse pills. 'Isn't that awfully large for a pill?' asks a suspicious doctor. 'No. It was too small for a basketball and I didn't know what to do with it,' replies Groucho. 'Say, you're awfully large for a pill yourself.' When giving one of the pills to a horse he says, 'Take one of these every half mile and call me if there's any change.' After some popcorn-time songs from Allan Jones, a water-ballet, and a long 'darkie' number with Harpo, we finally reach

Left: Loretta Young in Kentucky

the race-track finale. To get High Hat to win, the brothers reroute the track into the country. To cut a long race short, Harpo seems to have ridden High Hat to defeat until it turns out that, after a fall, Harpo had switched horses with the winning jockey. At the happy ending Groucho proposes to Dumont. 'Marry me and I'll never look at another horse.'

Wings of the Morning (TCF 1937) was the first Technicolor film made in Britain and very pretty it was, if rather too fey. Annabella plays the dual role of a gypsy princess of 1889 and her granddaughter who falls for horse trainer, Henry Fonda. His preparations for a horse to win the Epsom Derby are interrupted by scenic views of the English and Irish countryside, gypsy lore, love scenes and songs sung by Irish tenor John McCormack.

Thoroughbreds Don't Cry (MGM 1937) was the first of ten films Mickey Rooney and Judy Garland were to appear in together. It was the start of a whole spate of wholesome kid-oriented movies. (Garland was a chubby 15, Rooney a small 17). The story tells of Sir Peter Calverton (C. Aubrey Smith) and his grandson Roger (Ronald Sinclair) who come to the USA with their horse The Pookah. Rooney rides the horse in a preliminary but throws the race. The old man dies of disappointment. (Exit C. Aubrey.) Roger is left with The Pookah on his boyish hands. Garland gets Rooney to repent his sins but the stewards bar him from the race-track. Roger (frightfully English) rides the mount himself and wins the big race. Rooney is fine as the cocky jockey, but Garland has to wait until *The Wizard of Oz* (1939) before her personality really came into focus.

Mickey Rooney turns up again in a racing story called *Stablemates* (MGM 1938) as a stable boy who unexpectedly becomes the owner of a race-horse called Lady Q. He attaches himself to old soak, Wallace Beery, who once knew everything there was to know about horses until he started seeing pink elephants. In a gooey scene, Rooney pleads tearfully with Beery to operate on Lady Q's injured hoofs. The movie ends happily with Beery, Rooney and Lady Q setting up a *menagerie à trois*. Sam Wood directed.

Bing Crosby was a racing en-

thusiast who owned some race horses in his time but he was better at backing vehicles for his talents in the movies. In *Sing You Sinners* (Par. 1938) he plays a country boy who comes to LA and makes a killing on his first day at the track. He picks up the 'Australian System' i.e. you put your money on the horse with the most i's and a's in its name. (Try it. It hardly ever fails.) Bing buys a horse and in order to save money on a jockey, he turns his 13-year-old kid brother Donald O'Connor into one. In spite of crooks, he wins a big race, making it possible for his other brother, Fred McMurray to marry Ellen Drew. Crosby is a little too urban to convince as a country boy, but the songs, races and performances are all lively even if it sags a bit in the middle.

Twentieth Century Fox's lushly photographed Technicolor racing story *Kentucky* (1938) created a mini genre. The white porticoed plantation house, the paddock, the track, horses streaming across wild fields, the faithful negro retainers, the black mammy, the young couple keen on horses, and the temperamental thoroughbred breaking his heart to win. The first 25 minutes of *Kentucky* deals with the American Civil War to show how it sowed the seeds of a family feud between two horse-breeding families. In this Montague-Capulet situation, the son of the Dillons (Richard Greene) falls in love with the daughter of the Goodwins (Loretta Young) only she doesn't know he's a Dillon. She's an expert rider and owns a champion trotter. Jack, disguising his origins, helps her train a two-year-old called Blue Grass. Blue Grass must be hand-ridden as he reacts violently to the whip. Just before the Kentucky Derby, Sally finds out that Jack is a Dillon. Boy loses girl. Boy wins race. Boy gets girl. Walter Brennan won the Oscar for best supporting actor as the crusty old head of the Goodwin family who does not live to see the reconciliation of the families. If Shakespeare had introduced a horse-race into 'Romeo and Juliet', all would have been well.

Some real horse non-sense was provided by *Going Places* (WB 1939). Dick Powell, masquerading as a famous Australian rider, arrives at the mansion of Colonel Withering

(Thurston Hall — the name of the actor not the mansion). The Colonel owns Jeepers Creepers, a man-devouring horse. The Colonel's niece (Anita Louise) asks Powell to ride Jeepers in the Maryland steeplechase. Powell finds out that music is the only thing that will soothe the savage beast, preferably the trumpet-playing of the horse's groom, Louis Armstrong. On the big day, Louis and his band follow the race in a car but when they get separated Powell has to sing to Jeepers until he becomes 'hoarse'. Jeepers goes haywire but when Louis and the musicians catch up again, Powell masters the horse, wins the race and the niece. 'Satchmo' is delightful in one of his rare featured roles. Allen Jenkins and Ronald Reagan were among the horse-lovers.

"Greater than *Kentucky*" proclaimed the posters for *Maryland* (TCF 1940), which might not have pleased the denizens of Blue Grass Country. Although a change of state didn't necessarily change the conditions, directed by Henry King it was a notch better. The blacks, as stereotyped as ever, are lazy and stupid with a passion for dice or religion. Hattie McDaniel, everybody's favorite black mammy, and Walter Brennan, everybody's favorite white pappy, provided the humor. When he is six, Lee Danfields's father (Sidney Blackmer) is thrown by Maryland Maid and killed. His mother Charlotte (Fay Bainter) decides to have Maryland Maid destroyed, sells all her horses and forbids her son ever to ride. Many years later, Lee (now John Payne) returns from England (the worst place to send anyone who has to keep away from horses), falls in love with Brennan's grand-daughter (now Brenda Joyce) and a horse called Cavalier. Despite his mother's opposition, he agrees to ride Cavalier in the Maryland Hunt Cup. Cavalier turns out to be the foal of Maryland Maid who wasn't shot at all. Charlotte is terrified for her son and she turns up at the track to see the race. They're off! At the beginning Payne is thrown. Quickly mounting his horse again, though twenty lengths behind, he makes up ground. In the stretch he is neck and neck with the leading horse. At the post Cavalier wins by a nose.

Overleaf: Mickey Rooney, Elizabeth Taylor and The Pi in National Velvet

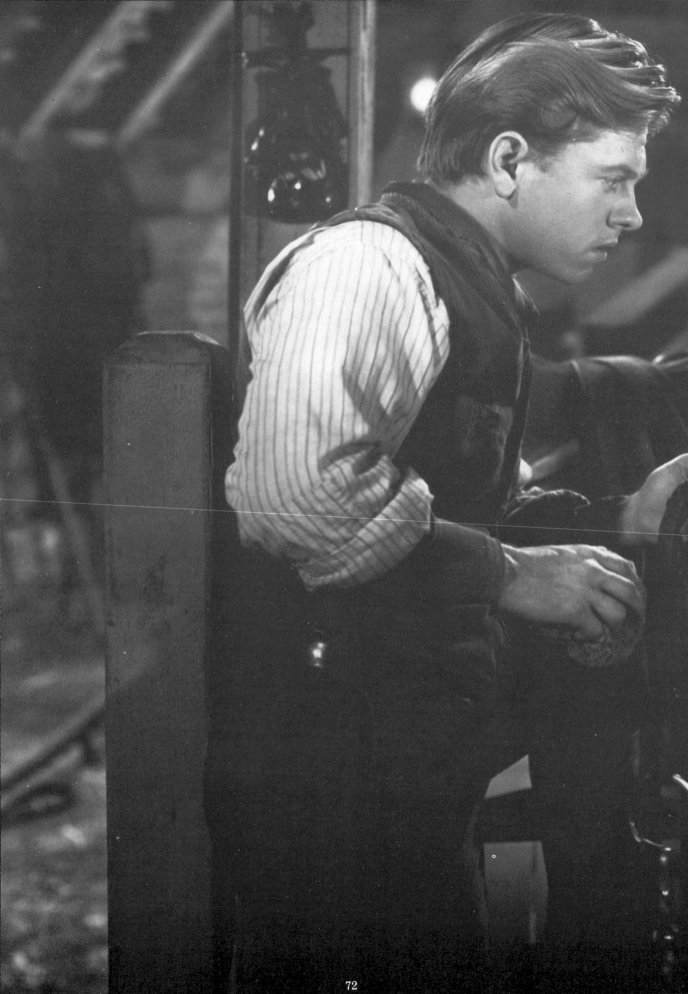

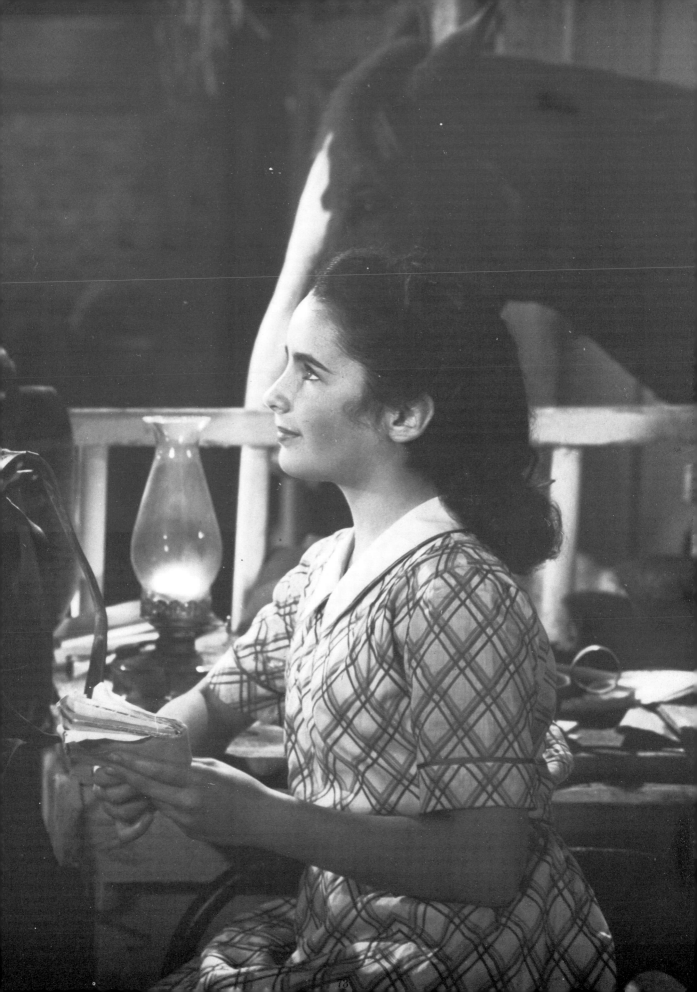

Unlike the western or race track story, the colt opera or kiddie weepie stresses the aesthetic qualities of the horse. *My Friend Flicka* (TCF 1943) is set against a ravishing Utah landscape. 15-year-old Roddy McDowell loves his colt Flicka. (Flicka is Swedish for little girl.) But Flicka proves to be a rebel and has to be trained to conform. Little Roddy proves himself a man by taming her (to an extent) with the approval of his stern father (Preston Foster) and soft-hearted mother (Rita Johnson). "It isn't just riding," explains Roddy, "I want a colt to be friends with me." Flicka nearly dies, Roddy sits up all night with her beside a river and then Roddy nearly dies. The film was a great success and adults in their forties remember it with affection. Today's children might not be so easily pleased.

Based extremely loosely on Damon Runyon's 'Princess O'Hara', *It Ain't Hay* (UI 1943. *Money for Jam* — GB) was one of Abbott and Costello's best outings. Lou gives candy to a horse in a horsedrawn cab and it falls sick and dies. Everyone in the neighborhood blames Lou. In order to replace the horse, he steals the famous winner Teabiscuit (Runyon would never have called it that) from the stables and gives it to the cab driver, Cecil Kellaway. He is overjoyed at getting such a fine specimen. But the hue and cry has been raised over the missing horse, and Bud and Lou hide him in the suite of a Saratoga hotel on the day before the famous races. Hounded by crooks and police, Lou puts Teabiscuit between the shafts of the cab, but the horse makes for the race-track at furious speed with Lou attached. The cab breaks away but Lou manages to mount the horse and enter the race. Among the dross, Abbott and Costello come up with some set-pieces of invention. One takes place in a betting shop where a commentary of a non-existent horse-race is relayed from the next room. The bookmaker guarantees Lou a win in a race with only one horse. It loses.

Perhaps the best known racing movie of all is *National Velvet* (MGM 1944). It is not difficult to see why. It has an exciting, fairy-tale story, children and animals, exotic settings (England, USA), bright child's picture-book color, the very popular Mickey Rooney, a new child star and all of it directed with know-how by the well-mannered but never mannered, Clarence Brown. It gave a fantasy vision of an England that Americans could believe was worth fighting for. When MGM decided to film Enid Bagnold's novel about a young English girl's fascination with horses, dozens of English refugee children then evacuated to North America were tested for the part of Velvet. (Shirley Williams, the British politician, was one of the unsuccessful candidates.) One of the reasons 12-year-old Elizabeth Taylor was chosen for the role was that she really could ride well, although Louis B. Mayer insisted she grow a further 3 inches before shooting. To the town of Sewels on the south coast of pre-war England comes former jockey Mi Taylor (Mickey Rooney). (Sewels is a mock-Tudor village set against a Technicolor backdrop of barns and fields.) He meets Velvet Brown, a girl whose dreams center on owning and riding horses one day. They admire a beautiful horse belonging to Farmer Ede. As they watch, the majestic animal easily jumps a high fence and is prevented from running away by Velvet. She has a way with horses. When Farmer Ede decides to raffle the horse, The Pi, Velvet wins by wishing very hard. She then confides her dream to her parents. She wants to enter The Pi in the Grand National. Velvet's mother (Ann Revere), who had swum the English Channel years before, gives her daughter the 100 sovereigns she had won as prize money for the entrance fee. She understands the 'importance of folly'. Velvet and Mi spend months training The Pi with Velvet always riding. Mi refuses to ride, because he had been blamed for the death of a fellow jockey after causing a spill in a race. He hires a jockey for The Pi, but the day before the National, the rider tells Velvet he doesn't think her horse has a chance. Furious, Velvet refuses to let him ride. Disguised as a boy, Velvet enters the race, rides brilliantly and wins. Immediately after she slips from the saddle in a faint. The doctor discovers that the 'unknown rider' is a girl. Although she is disqualified, Velvet and The Pi proved themselves champions and return home as heroes. We can even read a slight anti-sexist message behind the conventions of 1944. In the book, the race takes place in thick fog and Mi cannot see who wins. Thankfully, the race is excitingly filmed in bright sunshine (tropical plants are blooming at Aintree in March), but Mi still has difficulty in watching it, because he is so short, continually jostling Arthur Treacher. On the whole, Rooney's performance is closer to Thomas Hardy than Andy, although his visit to London is straight out of Dickens (London in the thirties?). Elizabeth Taylor radiates youth and a tooth brace.

Home in Indiana (TCF 1944) introduced 3 young stars to audiences for the first time; Jeanne Crain, June Haver and Lon McAllister, although Walter Brennan and Charlotte Greenwood got top billing. The only unconventional thing about the movie was that all the characters seemed to have the names of horses. Sparke, Thunder Bolt, Char, and Cri-Cri. Sparke (McAllister) arrives at the run-down farm of his great-uncle Thunder Bolt (Brennan) not intending to stay long until he catches sight of what is on the other side of a huge fence. There is Char (Crain), a girl who rides beautifully but looks like a boy in her overalls; Cri-Cri (Haver) who is older and more sophisticated; and magnificent stables. Sparke secretly breeds his uncle's mare with the great stallion next door. The filly is born blind but with the help of Sparke's 'whispering hands', the horse is soon ready to enter the big trotting race. The blind filly wins with Sparke driving. He also realises that under her overalls, Char is really a very pretty girl. The colorful backgrounds are splendid and the direction was in the capable hands of Henry Hathaway.

The son of... sequels are now a standing joke about Hollywood but in the thirties and forties sons of Dracula, Frankenstein, Kong, Monte Cristo and Lassie were produced with a straight face. *Thunderhead — Son of Flicka* (TCF 1945) contained most of the same ingredients as its dam. Beautiful Utah landscapes, a rebellious colt, a boy's love for a horse and his 'sentimental education'. Preston Foster and Rita Johnson are again the model parents and Roddy McDowell (now 17) played the boy. Thunderhead, the snow-white colt of Flicka, is even more bad-tempered than his mother and goes berserk probably from having to act with the insufferable Roddy McDowell. Instead of kicking son of Mrs McDowell where it hurts, son of Flicka attacks another stallion, presumably because the SPCA is easier to deal with than the SPCC. There are some spectacular riding scenes and Thunderhead is splendid in full flight.

Meanwhile from the ranch back at the race-track with a comedy-melo called *Salty O'Rourke* (Par. 1945) directed by Raoul Walsh in his usual extrovert manner. The title role sounds as if it should be played by someone like John Wayne or Victor McLaglen but it is played by dapper, unemotional Alan Ladd. The plot is an old boxing drama on horse-back. Ladd is a race-horse owner who is given 30 days by tough bookie Bruce Cabot to pay 20,000 dollars which he lost through the double-cross of a partner. Ladd knows of a world-beater horse, Whipper, that can be picked up cheap, because no one has ever been able to ride him. He finds a jockey, a tough youth played by Stanley Clements. They both fall for school-marm Gale Russell, whom no one has been able to ride either. The jockey, who is to ride Whipper in the 50,000 dollar Delington Handicap, agrees to lose the race. The race is on. Clements is pulling Whipper but half-way through he changes his mind and in a terrific burst of speed he wins by a neck thus risking his own neck. He is killed by Bruce Cabot's henchmen. Ladd exacts his revenge. Stanley Clements is said to have worked without a double.

Anna Sewell's novel *Black Beauty* had the distinction of being banned by the racist government of South Africa, who did not realize that the title referred to a horse. The screen version of *Black Beauty* (TCF 1946) was made in black and white. Mona Freeman is the young girl from Birtwick farm who is given the beautiful black colt. She breaks him in herself and enjoys riding him about the 'English' countryside. But one day she has to go off to finishing school and bids Black Beauty a tearful farewell. While she is being finished, the horse is sold as a carriage horse. On her return, after searching for him, she reaches a barn where he is kept only to find it in flames. She rushes in to save the horse, but it is the horse that rescues her. Black Beauty goes home to Birtwick and soon becomes a fine, glossy horse again. Black Beauty is played by Highland Dale.

Gallant Bess (MGM 1946) was not an historical romance about Queen Elizabeth I, but a ticky love story of a boy and a horse. Tex (Marshall Thompson) is a 17-year-old orphan who spends his time necking with his brown mare, Bess. But along comes the war and the navy recruits him. When he comes home on leave one stormy night, he finds Bess ill with pneumonia and dying. Back on the Jap-infested island in the Pacific, Tex moons over the dead animal while men die all around him. Tex thinks he's going crazy when he hears whinnying sounds way out in the jungle. But he isn't crazy.

There's an injured horse out there and she's the image of Bess. The C.O. decides to make the horse the unit mascot. 'I think she'll be good for us until we get back to what we are all thinking about,' he says. Bess II can count, roll over, and even carry her injured master out of the jungle. Directed by Andrew Marton, it was shot in the cheap two-color process called Cinecolor.

Back to glorious Technicolor with *The Homestretch* (TCF 1947), and a plot that moves from Maryland to London to Buenos Aires to Boston. As the poster said, 'Their eyes met in Boston. Their lips met in London.' The eyes and lips belonged to Cornel Wilde and Maureen O'Hara. Wilde owns a horse which he enters in 'The Ascot, England.' It happens to be Coronation Year which provides an excuse for scenes in London interspersed with

stock shots of the event. The horse goes lame in the Gold Cup after a magnificent start. Wilde decides to take his horse to Buenos Aires in the hope of her recovery for the Gran Premio Nacional. Maureen O'Hara leaves her Bostonian family to marry Wilde and then proceeds to reform him. She wants him to stop gambling and gallivanting and to settle down on his farm in Maryland to breed thoroughbreds and children. So they fight it out on and off the race-track until she finally shows him who wears the jodhpurs. There are plenty of good scenes of Wilde's horse in action.

Green Grass of Wyoming (TCF 1948) tells of the romance between a white stallion and a black mare. The stallion is none other than Thunderhead, son of Flicka, last seen three years earlier trying to get Roddy McDowell off his back. Thunder-

head has matured since and he's thinking of settling down with Crown Jewel. He keeps her mind off her work which is to train for an important trotting race. Crown Jewel fails to win, breaking down just as she approaches the winning line. This is because she and the stallion (who watches the race from the rails) will soon hear the patter of tiny hoofs. The humans involved are Peggy Cummins, Charles Coburn, Robert Arthur, Burl Ives and Lloyd Nolan. Entertaining in its way, it has some interesting scenes of the training of trotting horses.

Sorrowful Jones (Par. 1949) (the first remake of *Little Miss Marker*) was built around the personality of Bob Hope. He plays a penny-pinching Broadway bookie whose crusty surface hides a sentimental streak. This is revealed unashamedly when he is left

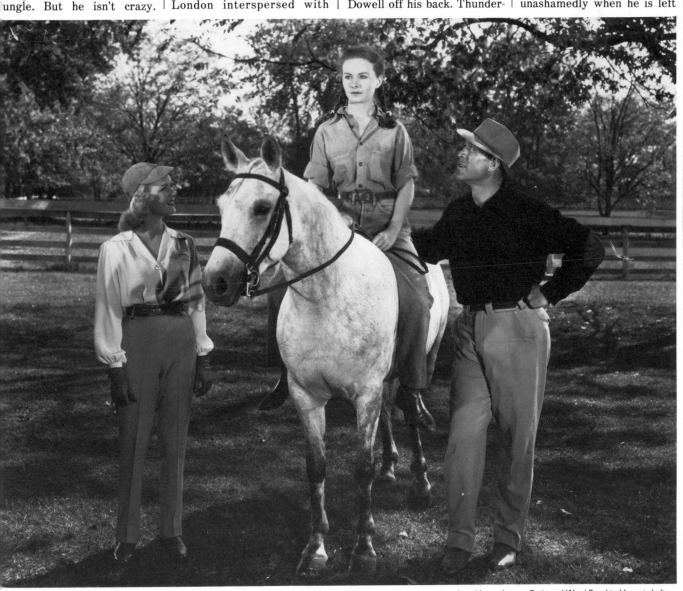

June Haver, Jeanne Crain and Ward Bond in *Home in Indiana*

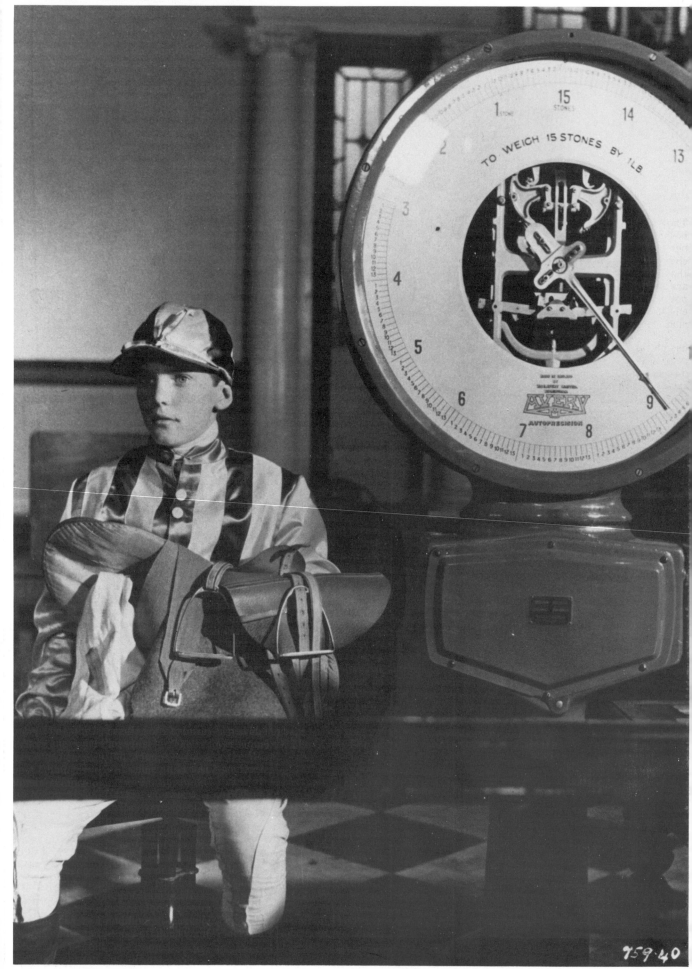

with a 4-year-old called Martha Jane (Mary Jane Saunders) whom he nicknames 'Shorts'. As gangster Big Steve (Bruce Cabot) has been barred from racing, he enters a horse called 'Dreamy Joe' under the little girl's name. She thinks the horse is hers. After an accident (she falls off a fire-escape), Martha Jane lies in hospital calling for her horse. Although only a few hours before the big race, Hope and side-kick Regret (William Demarest), go to the track and kidnap Dreamy Joe. They take the horse to the hospital and the child opens her eyes. Hope marries nightclub singer Lucille Ball and they adopt the moppet. There are amusing moments but it is not nearly as good as the earlier Shirley Temple version.

The twenty-one-year-old has-been Shirley Temple appeared in *The Story of Seabiscuit* (WB 1949. *Pride of Kentucky* — GB), one of her last films. In this biopic of one of America's most famous racehorses, Miss Temple battles with an Irish accent and the horse. Barry Fitzgerald is her uncle who trains Seabiscuit by taking advice from the leprechauns. Other little people appear called jockeys. Shirley falls for rider Lon McAllister who falls off a horse. She is the nurse at the LA hospital overlooking Santa Anita race-track and helps him to recover. Lon proposes to her but she says she will only marry him if he gives up racing. Fitzgerald with 'oirish' wisdom tells her that if she really loves Lon she won't try to change him. Lon rides Seabiscuit in the Santa Anita Handicap and wins by half a nose. The Technicolor is interrupted by actual newsreels of the horse himself, then back from monochrome to monotonous Irish whimsy. David Butler directed.

Another biopic of a racer was *The Great Dan Patch* (UA 1949). Dan Patch, as everyone knows, was the first horse in the world to run a mile in 2 mins 4 seconds in a trotting race. He keeps on breaking records until, with Dennis O'Keefe driving him, he ends his career by doing the mile in 1 min. 55 seconds. O'Keefe is a chemist who's mad about racing and horses but his socialite wife Ruth Warrick is against the expense of training horses on

their Indianapolis estate. He leaves her and marries Gail Russell, who shares his love for horses. Charlotte Greenwood supplied the human interest.

Hemingway's short story 'My Old Man', was a jaunty, colloquial and finally moving anecdote, in which a son's affectionate memories of his jockey father subtly reveals his old man as a crook. There was nothing subtle about *Under My Skin* (TCF 1950) based on the story. The only thing that John Garfield as the father has under his skin is fat. (It was one of his last roles.) To his 11-year-old motherless son, Joe (Orley Lindgren) he is a hero. After doublecrossing Italian gambler, Luther Adler, by winning a race he was supposed to throw, Garfield and his son flee to Paris. When Garfield is not at the Chantilly race-track, he is

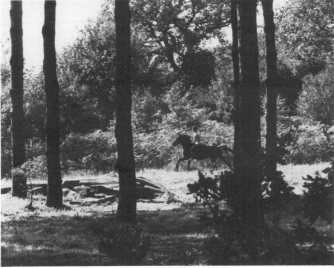

Bare-back riding in *Reflections in a Golden Eye*

at a 'leetle' bistro kept by Micheline Prelle. (Her name was simplified from Presle for American audiences.) She sings interminable French songs while everybody in the cabaret sways. Garfield looks like a cinch to win the big race until gambler Adler turns up again and asks him to lose or pay with his life. His hero-worshipping son is counting on him to win. In the same way as he won the fight he was supposed to lose in *Body and Soul*, Garfield wins the race, but as he streaks across the winning line he crashes into a riderless horse and is taken to hospital. In his dying breath he asks to be taken back to the old US of A. 'He meant eet about going 'ome, Joe,' says Micheline Prelle (or Prestle.) 'Don't you sink we owe it to eem to take eem zere.' Other delights in

this movie include the psychoanalysis of a 'mean' horse. It turns out to be untrainable, because it had an unhappy colthood. The back projection of the steeplechasing is better than that of the European locales. The film owes nothing to Hemingway except an apology. Jean Negulesco directed.

Bob Hope was back on form as a race-track tout in *The Lemon Drop Kid* (Par. 1951). At a Florida race meeting, he makes the mistake of persuading Moose Moran (Lloyd Nolan) to transfer a bet from the horse of his choice to the one tipped by Hope. When the horse loses, Moran threatens to kill Hope unless he can make good the 10,000 dollars he lost. Moran gives him until Christmas or else 'you'll find your own head in your stocking.' The rest of the picture strays from the race-track to follow Hope's attempts to get the money. One way is to disguise some typical Runyon characters, such as Harry the Horse and No Nose Cohen, as Santa Claus and to open a home for 'old dolls'.

The characters that hang around the race-track in William Dieterle's *Boots Malone* (Col. 1952) are not Runyonesque at all. Their hearts are as hard as their faces. The trainers, agents, touts and bookies have no sentimental affection for horses, grannies or cute kids. They're only after a fast buck. Even the hero (William Holden) as a busted jockey's agent thinks nothing of robbing a boy of a 100 dollar bill. He does reform, however, when he makes newsboy, Johnny Stewart and an unknown horse into a winning

combination. Dieterle effectively captures the flavor of the actual horse parks where a lot of the action was filmed.

This is the standard of some of the dialogue in *Money from Home* (Par. 1953). Dean Martin: 'Ain't he quaint?' Jerry Lewis (pretending to be English): 'You mean, isn't he quisn't?' Martin plays 'Honey Talk' Nelson who, in order to pay off his debts to a big-shot gangster, promises to see that My Sheba is withdrawn from the Gold Vase Steeplechase to be run at Tarryton, Maryland. He takes his cousin Virgil Yokum (Jerry Lewis) with him to Tarryton. On the way they meet Bertie Searles, My Sheba's English jockey. (A Bertie Wooster type with monocle. The kind of Englishman that went out of Hollywood movies in the thirties.) Fortunately, being overfond of the bottle, he spends most of the picture in a state of unconsciousness. (The best way to watch the movie.) Jerry pretends to be the jockey. Pat Crowley, the owner of the horse, sees through both his accent and his monocle. (Who wouldn't?) Virgil finds himself riding in the steeplechase and winning.

Authentic Englishmen were seen in a few British-made horse racing pictures in the early fifties. 'The Sport of Kings' not only brings out the best in man and horse but the worst of English snobbery. It gives the gentry, like the horses, the chance to dress up in their racing clothes and parade around. In the 1930 Derby, after suffragette Emily Davidson threw herself under George V's horse, the King's first question was to the condition of the horse and jockey. *The Galloping Major* (Romulus 1950) starred Basil Radford as Major Hill, an impoverished gentleman and lover of horse flesh, who runs a pet shop in the unlikely London suburb of Lamb's Green. He desperately wants to own a racer, so he forms a syndicate to buy one. The 300 syndicate owners (including choleric clubman A.E. Mathews) vote to enter the horse, 'The Galloping Major', in the Grand National. Major Hill himself ends up riding the horse, overweight as he is. The commentator describes it as 'the most incredible race I've seen'. Certainly there is nothing credible about it.

Based on a minor D.H. Lawrence short story, *The*

Rocking Horse Winner (Two Cities 1950) is an atmospheric little film about a young boy (John Howard Davis) and his mystical ability to pick winners by working himself up into a trance on his rocking horse. Valerie Hobson and John Mills play his worried parents. *Derby Day* (Br. Lion 1952) is one of those omnibus concoctions where one setting is used to tie up quite separate stories together on a string of coincidences. (e.g. *Grand Hotel*, *The V.I.P.'s* etc) It is a formula that seldom comes off, offering as it does an excuse for an all-star cast to do little work. To Epsom come recently-widowed Anna Neagle in a white lace gown, Michael Wilding as a newspaper cartoonist (his fiancée was killed in the same air crash as Miss Neagle's husband) and Googie Withers and John McCallum, who have just killed a man and

need to win enough money on the Derby to escape the country. *The Rainbow Jacket* (Ealing 1954) was in color and gave an almost documentary insight into the lives of jockeys. British comedy screenwriter T.E.B. Clarke *(Passport to Pimlico, The Lavender Hill Mob)* had wanted to write a racing picture for a long time and someone suggested it would make a good comedy. 'You don't joke about serious things,' he replied. Unfortunately, the melodramatic story of a warned-off jockey (Bill Owen) helping a cockney lad (Fella Edmonds) with 'the thing in his blood' to become a champion seems spurious against the realistic backgrounds of Newmarket and Sandown Park. Sir Gordon Richards (the first jockey to be knighted) appears on a few winners.

Pat Boone, the bland antidote to Elvis, was the goody-

goodys' idol. For his second movie, Twentieth Century Fox resuscitated the plot of *Home in Indiana* (1944), added songs, transferred it to Kentucky, and called it *April Love* (1957). While Elvis was doing things with his pelvis unseen outside a sex manual, Pat Boone was 23 and never been kissed. He plays a city boy who comes to his uncle's farm and falls for pretty Shirley Jones, the girl next door. He gets interested in trotting horses and wins a big race. It's all fairly easy on the eye and mind.

There were some exciting racing sequences in *Wall of Noise* (WB 1963) filmed at Hollywood Park and an attempt to understand the passion for the race-track, but it was more soap than race-horse opera. Ty Hardin is torn between married woman Suzanne Pleshette, model Dorothy Provine and a horse called

Escudero. His final choice depends on whether Escudero wins the Farewell Handicap or not. The horse falls badly, a gangster (Simon Oakland) dies of a heart attack, Pleshette goes back to her wealthy husband (Ralph Meeker), and Hardin ends up with Provine nursing the injured Escudero.

In the first episode of the trivial triptych, *The Yellow Rolls Royce* (MGM 1965), Rex Harrison plays a Lord who owns a French horse called June 10th, which he has entered for the Gold Cup at Ascot. He also has a French wife, Jeanne Moreau, who is having an affair with his secretary, Edmund Purdom. Not suspecting anything, he buys a yellow Rolls Royce (how vulgarly ostentatious!) for his wife's birthday. The Rolls is used for an assignation between Moreau and the caddish Purdom at Ascot while my Lord is

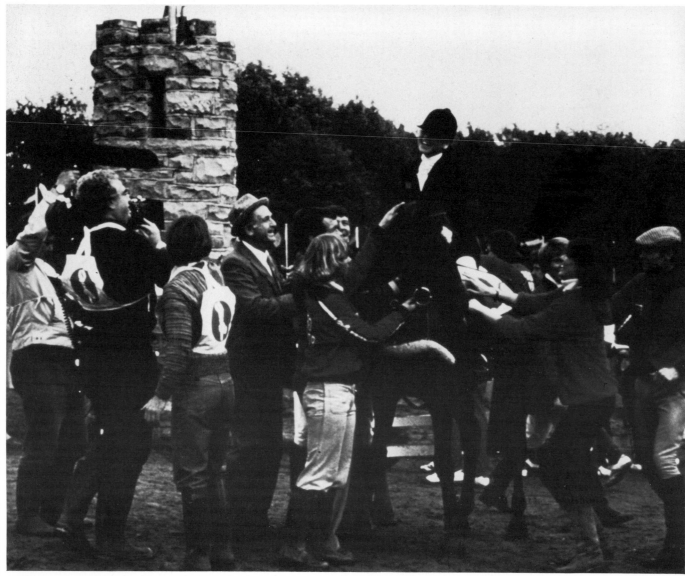

Tatum O'Neal at the Olympics in *International Velvet*

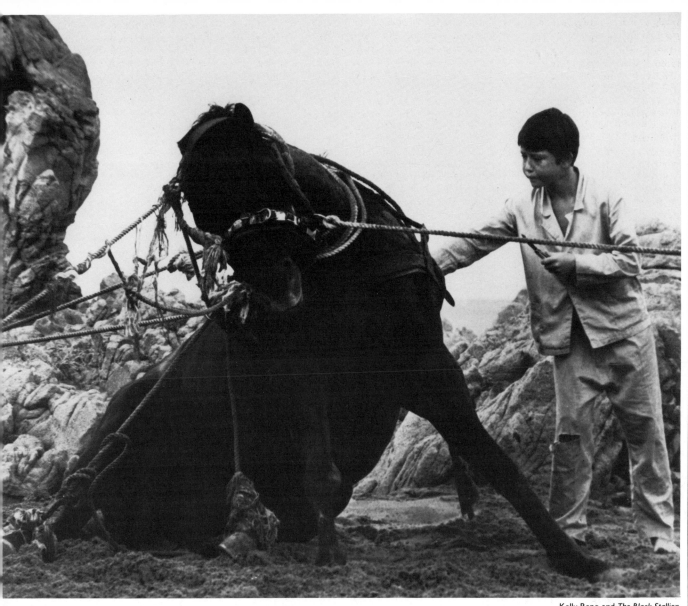

Kelly Reno and *The Black Stallion*

presumably watching the race. Tipped off by gossiping Lady, Moira Lister, he manages to tear himself away from the members' enclosure and discovers them together in the car. His horse wins but the cheers ring hollow in his ears and he asks his chauffeur to sell the Rolls the next morning. One of writer Terence Rattigan's snobbish confections, it is based on the tenet that the English love a Lord, especially when dressed up for Ascot. (See also the Ascot scene from *My Fair Lady* — WB 1964.)

Marlon Brando as the closet homosexual Major in *Reflections in a Golden Eye* (WB 1967) decides to prove himself by trying to ride his wife's stallion, Firebird. The fact that he is a poor rider diminishes him further in her eyes. She (Elizabeth Taylor) is having an affair with macho Lt Colonel Brian Keith and both of them

share a passion for riding, polo and good sex. Poor Brando cannot stay on Firebird so he beats the horse in frustration. To his horror, he sees he has been observed by Private Williams (Robert Forster) whom he secretly lusts after. When Brando returns home scratched and bruised, Miss Taylor lashes at him with her riding crop. The Private, who fancies Taylor, takes to riding Firebird in the forest around the camp barebacked and bareassed. In John Huston's absorbing movie, based closely on Carson McCullers' short novel, the horse comes into its own as a sex-object.

The young stable boy (Peter Firth) in *Equus* (UA 1977) is also given to riding in the nude at night when most 'normal' boys of his age go skinnydipping. He prays to a picture of a horse above his bed and this god, Equus, tells him that

'two shall be one' like a horse and rider. After blinding 6 horses, he consults psychiatrist Richard Burton. 'I'll erase the welts cut into his mind by flying manes . . . and one thing I promise you: he'll never touch hide again.' The eight monologues that Burton delivers are enough to bore a bronco to sleep. Playwright Peter Shaffer's woolly thinking is mercilessly exposed on the screen, whereas in the theater the imaginative use of actors in masks to represent horses, strengthened the ritualistic elements.

Who would have dreamt that sweet little Velvet Brown who won the Grand National in the 1944 film *National Velvet* could, according to *International Velvet* (MGM 1978), be 'living in sin' with cynical author, Christopher Plummer, who doesn't believe in marriage? She (Nanette Newman)

hasn't recovered from a miscarriage after falling from a horse, and he is suffering from writer's block. Velvet still lives in England's green and pleasant land, is around 40 and The Pi has just sired his last foal. Into her life comes orphaned niece, Sarah Brown (her middle name is Velvet to explain the title) from America. A difficult child, her heart is soon softened by the sight of a horse. As Francis Lai's syrupy music rises, Sarah Brown (Tatum O'Neil) and The Pi's heir, Arizona, embrace each other in slow motion. She soon becomes a top rider in the show-jumping world, and is even forgiven for being American. (At school when she first arrives, she is presented with what is supposed to be a Vietnamese's finger as a joke. Very socially conscious is director Bryan Forbes.) Defying a dislocated shoulder, Sarah Brown and

Arizona win a gold medal for Britain (she has a British passport) at the Montreal Olympics. The jumping is spectacular and exciting, but it's a long time coming and one has to endure almost two hours of slush before it. Other moments that should thrill children everywhere are the destruction of a horse that gets hysterical in the course of airfreighting and the burning to death of three young men in a car-crash after harrassing Sarah and her horse. Tatum O'Neil has to age eight years during the film (like the audience), but she's much more convincing as a 10-year-old brat than an 18-year-old bride.

On the face of it *Casey's Shadow* (Col. 1978) would seem just another horse-racing yarn, but because of Martin Ritt's astute direction, Carol Sobieski's screenwriting and the acting throughout, it manages to transcend the genre. The Louisiana and New Mexico settings also offer a change from the well-worn Kentucky or Hollywood milieus. Walter Matthau plays an impoverished Cajun, whose wife abandoned him years ago, living in a ramshackle farmhouse in the bayou country with his three refractory sons. He ekes out a meagre living by training and running quarter horses. His 7-year-old son Casey (Michael Hershewe) has developed a special kinship with a handsome and powerful quarter horse which is named Casey's Shadow. Matthau enters him in the forthcoming 1,000,000 dollar All-American Futurity race at Ruidoso, New Mex. on Labor Day. However, two months before the race, Shadow is injured and the vet tells Matthau that it will take nearly a year for him to recover. But Matthau is determined to get him fit for the race. 'They say that running quarter horses is only for the rich and fancy these days... This year *this* boy's going to do it!' he exclaims. The final race is in the best nail-biting tradition with a pointed use of the often misapplied slow-motion. The rituals of training and racing and the hangers-on are looked at in a humorous and sometimes caustic way. The relationship between the father and his sons never becomes sentimental thanks again to Matthau's marvellously expressive misanthropic mug. Alexis Smith is a raunchy horse-owner and Murray Hamilton and Robert Webber play the villains with relish.

The camera tracks around an exotic ship somewhere off the North African coast in 1946 at the beginning of *The Black Stallion* (UA 1979). Arabs in white djelabas guard the stallion. A boy is given a bronze model of Alexander's steed Bucephalus by his father, who tells him the story of how the young Alexander tamed the wild horse. The boy's name is Alex. Suddenly a great storm strikes and, in a brilliant sequence, the ship is wrecked, people burn to death or drown. Alex (Kelly Reno) and the black stallion, the sole survivors of the wreck, are washed up on an extremely picturesque island. There, as in most desert island movies, (e.g. *The Blue Lagoon* — 1949, 1980, where boy grows to love girl or *Heaven Knows Mr Allison* — 1957 and *Sea Wife* — 1957, where man grows to love nun,) the boy and the stallion develop an intimate relationship. They find food for each other, watch ex-

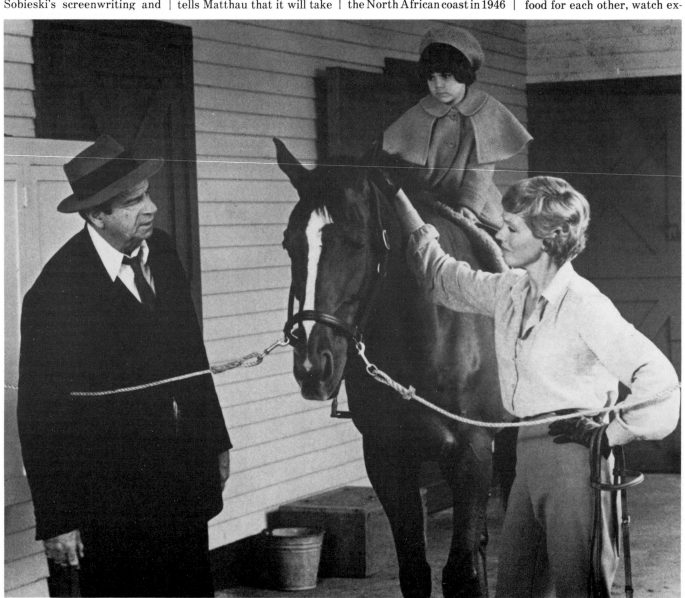

Walter Matthau, Sara Stimson and Julie Andrews in *Little Miss Marker* (1980)

quisite sunsets together and go for orgasmic rides along the beach. They could have made beautiful music together if the insistent musical score had let them. They certainly make a beautiful picture together and each romantic scene is wrung by director Carroll Ballard for every salty teardrop. Once they are rescued and return to small-town America, the film returns to more conventional territory. The young Crusoe and his black horse Friday find it difficult to adapt to the middle-class conventions imposed upon them and like Gulliver, Alex prefers to sleep out with his horse. (The film forces literary comparisons.) Then he meets old-time trainer Mickey Rooney who says he can make The Black into a champion racer. But Alex's old friend (a black) advises him to 'Let that horse stay wild, Alex,' and after the inevitable big race, the mysteriously bonded pair ride off like a centaur. Based on Walter Farley's slim novel of the fifties, the film embraces all the themes dear to horse pictures, forging them into a forceful Rousseauian myth. The arab steed was played by several powerful stallions. Alex was played by one freckle-faced boy.

Walter Bernstein (screenwriter of *The Front, Semi-Tough*) made his directorial debut with the fourth version of the Runyon story, *Little Miss Marker* (UI 1980). Although it still avoids the original ending (the girl dies of pneumonia and Sorrowful Jones reverts to his former parsimony) it is more astringent and wittier than the previous attempts plus having Walter Matthau as Sorrowful Jones. Not since W.C. Fields has such a lovable child-hater graced the screen. Faced with having to look after the little girl he cries, 'Buy her a soda, anything,' and then on contemplation, 'Forget the anything. Just a soda.' He is so stingy he gives the child cornflakes without milk and when told that his dog has been shot he mutters, 'See what you can get for the fur.' As a bedtime story, instead of reading from Black Beauty, Matthau reads to the girl from the Racing News. Sara Stimpson as the living IOU is just the right side of cute. What fouls up the movie is the 'adult' love interest between sweet racehorse owner, Julie Andrews and sour Matthau.

Sweepstakes (RKO 1931 contained the rather singular jockey (Eddie Quinlan) whose horse 6-shooter only wins when he shouts 'Whoop-te-do.' James Gleason plays a wise trainer. Hardly raised a 'Whoop-te-do.'

The Woman in Red WB 1935 was Barbara Stanwyck as a professional horsewoman who marries into the 'polo crowd' who find her vulgar. Stanwyck is worth watching even in this company.

Down The Stretch WB 1936 was the first time Mickey Rooney co-starred with a horse. (Unless one counts his meeting with the ass Bottom in **A Midsummer Night's Dream**.) Here, the 16-year-old Rooney has to live down his jockey father's bad reputation.

Checkers TCF 1937 was not about Nixon's dog but Jane Withers' horse. It breaks a leg so it naturally wins an important race. Una Merkel as a ranch owner helps keep boredom at bay.

Straight, Place and Show TCF 1938 with the Ritz Brothers seemed like a month at the races. When they hear that a trio of Russian jockeys plan to square a race, they imprison the Russians and take their places. Ethel Merman belted out a couple of songs.

Little Miss Thoroughbred WB 1938 was little Janet Chapman trying to step into Shirley Temple's buckled shoes in this doomed attempt to do a **Little Miss Marker**.

The Ladies from Kentucky Par. 1939 happily included Zasu Pitts as a Southern Belle. The other lady was the less interesting Ellen Drew trying to reform New York gambler George Raft. Of course, after being exposed to southern hospitality, he ends up a better and wiser man, thanks also to a horse called Roman Son.

Million Dollar Legs TCF 1939 were Betty Grable's and a winning horse's. This college caper also featured Donald O'Conner, Buster Crabbe, and Jackie Coogan.

Come on, George 1939 featured horse-faced ukulele-playing George Formby as a jokey jockey. Like his American equivalent, Joe E. Brown, Formby was cast in many sporting roles with mainly unfunny results.

Sporting Blood MGM 1940 had the same title as the 1931 Gable film but a different story. This predictable little picture starred Maureen O'Sullivan and Lewis Stone.

Down Argentine Way TCF 1940 went Betty Grable as a wealthy horse-owner who falls for Argentinian horse-breeder Don Ameche, although their families are opposed to each other. The Argentinians spend their time singing, dancing and watching colorful horse races. Carmen Miranda sings two night-club numbers in her first film and this Latin American confection made Grable into a star. Leonid Kinsky is funny as a comic gigolo and J. Carrol Naish is most unfunny as a horse trainer. Charlotte Greenwood kicks up her long legs once or twice.

Golden Hoofs TCF 1941 had Jane Withers' efforts to save a trotting horse farm from being sold off by Charles 'Buddy' Rogers. A soap opera that might have been better as a glue opera.

She Went to the Races MGM 1945 starred Frances Gifford who has a fool-proof betting system. A group of professors try to work out a scientific method of winning. Among the professors are Edmund Gwenn and Sig Rumann. Ava Gardner appeared in one of her pre 'love-goddess' roles.

The Bride Wore Boots Par. 1946 and the bride-groom wears a frown. She (Barbara Stanwyk) loves horses, he (Robert Cummings) hates them. In the end, (after a divorce), the husband rides to victory in a race, thus winning back his wife and his spurs. Irving Pichel directed this silly story.

The Fabulous Suzanne Rep. 1946 was a waitress at Bill's diner who could pick winners by closing her eyes and sticking a pin into a race card. But she can't afford to lose so she doesn't bet. Barbara Britton plays Suzanne and Rudy Vallee and Richard Denning are the men in her life.

My Brother Talks to Horses MGM 1946 and they tell him who's going to win. A reasonably amusing idea wears rather thin and gets sunk in sentimentality. Jackie 'Butch' Jenkins, making his third film for MGM in the same year (he retired not a moment too soon, at the age of ten), was the kid brother, and Peter Lawford the elder brother who exploited him. It was directed to his debit by Fred Zinnemann.

Neptune's Daughter MGM 1949 was, of course, Esther Williams. And her sister, Betty Garrett, both fall for polo stars. At least Garrett thinks Red Skelton is Jose O'Rourke, the S. American polo player. Red is only the polo club's masseur. As polo is not exactly the sport of the people, the only way such plebian types as Red Skelton or Joe E. Brown (see Polo Joe) can get near a pony is to pose as a player. Red helps the team win in the end despite never even having been near a clothes' horse. The high-light of the movie is 'Baby it's cold outside' sung by Ricardo Montalban, the real Jose, to Williams, and man-eating Betty Garrett to carrot-topped Skelton.

Riding High Par. 1950 cast Bing Crosby as an happy-go-lucky horse-player whose beloved horse dies after winning a race. An enjoyable remake of **Broadway Bill**, it featured many of the actors from the previous movie such as Charles Bickford, William Demarest, Raymond Walburn, directed again by Frank Capra. Oliver Hardy has a bit part. The racing milieu is lovingly captured.

Boy from Indiana 1950 was Lon McAllister, now 27 and still grooming a horse to win the big race. 66 minutes *long*.

Francis goes to the Races UI 1951 with Donald O'Connor and tips him off about the winner. Francis is, of course, the talking mule (the voice was Chill Wills') who made six movies with O'Connor.

Fast Company MGM 1953 was about a horse called Gay Fleet who minces to music and only wins when the jockey sings to it. He is owned by Polly Bergen, trained by Howard Keel and harried by Nina Foch.

Grand National Night Renown Pictures 1953 is a frightful frightfully British piece of horse manure. Babs (Moira Lister) is murdered on the night of the title after Star Mist, her husband's (Nigel Patrick) horse wins the National. Was it her jealous husband? Was it Pinkie, Joyce or Buns Darling?

Gypsy Colt MGM 1954, made in dreadful Anscocolor, was a virtual remake of **Lassie Come Home**. Donna Corcoran is the little girl to whom Gypsy keeps returning even though it's been sold to a racing stable hundreds of miles away. Ward Bond and Frances Dee are the dull parents (or maybe it's the color.)

Racing Blood TCF 1954 was the story of a stable boy (Jimmy Boyd) who helps a colt born with a split hoof to win a big race over the colt's more fortunate twin brother. Doubly awful.

Pride of Blue Grass 1954 starred Vera Miles and Lloyd Bridges. They breed race horses and familiarity breeds contempt.

The Fighting Chance 1955 had Rod Cameron as a horse trainer, Ben Cooper as a jockey and Julie London as the filly they both fall in love with.

Glory RKO 1956 heralded Margaret O'Brien's entry into adulthood with a tin horn. This was one of her last pictures and also one of the last productions of Howard Hughes' ailing RKO studios. This was the last straw that broke the horse's back. O'Brien plays Clarabel Tilbee and Charlotte Greenwood is Miz Tilbee her grandmother who nearly goes bankrupt because of her granddaughter's insistence that they enter Glory for the Kentucky Derby. Along comes old-time trainer, Walter Brennan, who discovers that the filly needs goggles to race properly. Glory wins the day. The horse not the film.

Just My Luck Rank 1957 was a painfully unfunny British comedy with Norman Wisdom as a jockey.

Who's Got the Action? Par. 1962 tells of Lana Turner's efforts to stop husband Dean Martin from playing the horses. 'You can't hate a man for liking animals', she says but when he loves them so much he spends 8000 dollars in a few months on horses, she decides to do something. She secretly takes her husband's bets by becoming a bookie. 'When he loses, I'll win.' Paul Ford is amusing as a horse-playing judge and Eddie Albert and Walter Matthau try hard to raise the material above average. Daniel Mann directed.

The Horse in the Gray Flannel Suit Buena Vista-Disney 1968 was so called, because ad agency exec. Dean Jones has the idea of finding a horse to serve the sales campaign for a new aspirin as a way of keeping his horse-mad daughter (Ellen Janov) and his boss (Fred Clark) happy at the same time. The last 26 minutes are given over to horse-jumping at a Washington D.C. show. The bottom of the oat bag.

The Reivers TCF 1969 was based on the minor William Faulkner novel of a Mississippi childhood in 1905. Directed by Mark Rydell, it is likable despite being too pretty and folksy. The 11-year-old hero (Mitch Vogel), after an adventurous sojourn in Memphis with his corrupting mentor Steve McQueen, rides a race while being cheered on by the local whores. He wins, because the horse just needs one whiff of a sardine to get him going. The race, black flanks in closeup and slow-motion, is described simultaneously by Burgess Meredith's narrative voice.

Run for the Roses 1978 had a boy, a horse, the Kentucky Derby zzzzzzzz. . . Panchito Gomez as the boy, Vera Miles and Stuart Whitman as step-parents. Henry Levin directed. Run for the exits.

Movies on WHEELS

Motor racing is about the same age as the cinema and they have evolved together. Both have undergone vast changes since the beginning of the century. Apart from the technical advances, no other sport has been transformed quite so visibly. Styles of dress may have altered slightly in tennis, baseball and soccer, but the general look of the game has remained essentially the same over the years. The difference between the baseball in, say, *Alibi Ike* (WB 1935) and *Bang the Drum Slowly* (Par. 1973) is minimal compared with the difference between the motor racing in *The Crowd Roars* (WB 1932) and *Winning* (UI 1969). 70 years ago, the fastest cars were 20-foot long leviathans with engines of up to 18 liters capacity. Now they are low, sleek machines, 12 feet long, weighing a mere 1,100 lbs, their 3-liter engines developing more than 375 hp. Then the drivers, wearing large goggles and cloth caps, bumped along rough and dusty roads. Now they lie almost prone, guiding their streamlined vehicles over macadam or concrete surfaces whose undulations are absorbed by independent four-wheel suspensions. In the old days, drivers and their mechanics frequently had to jump out of the car during a race to change a tire quickly or make repairs. Today, the driver sits alone concentrating on his highly skilled art, leaving the repairs and maintenance to his pit staff. Similarly, the cinema has evolved from the days of the crank camera (like cranking up a car engine), through the cumbersome and stationary cameras and poor sound recording of the late twenties to the world of wide-screen processes, color, Dolby sound, zooms, long-focus lenses and other space-age hardware, up to the point where movies such as *Star Wars* (1977) etc are ultimately high-technology show-offs.

Early cars were the equiva-

I used to go to pieces. I'd see an accident like that and feel so weak inside I'd want to quit, to stop the car and get out. I could hardly make myself go past it. But I'm older now. When I see something really horrible, I put my foot down — because I know everyone else is lifting his.

YVES MONTAND in **Grand Prix**
(MGM 1966)

We all have a secret prayer that the other fellow will crash so that we can get in on top.

KIRK DOUGLAS in **The Racers**
(TCF 1955)

lent of the Edison Kinetoscope and when the first cameras rolled, the first cars were there. Speeding automobiles immediately established themselves as primary elements in demonstrating the visual effectiveness of the medium. The car chase, comic or dramatic, has been camera fodder since the beginnings of the silent cinema. The shade of Mack Sennett has never strayed very far and in the 60's, car chases hit the screens with a bang in a string of films including *Bullitt* (1968), *The Italian Job* (1969) and the James Bond adventures. Unhappily, Henry Ford has had a greater influence on the cinema than John Ford. Just as gun-toting in America has become institutionalized, enshrined in law and even sanctified by the President, so too has the lethal potential of the automobile. This is positively encouraged by movies such as *Dirty Mary and Crazy Larry* (TCF 1975) and *The Cannonball Run* (TCF 1981). Cars have eaten up the landscape and in-

vaded the screens, edging out the humans. Some films are virtually vehicles for vehicles and a Volkswagen called Herbie has starred in four films to date, (*The Love Bug* — 1968, *Herbie Rides Again* — 1974, *Herbie goes to Monte-Carlo* — 1977, *Herbie goes Bananas* — 1981). Roger Corman realized in the 70's that 'sex was out — car crashes were in,' so he produced a series of crack-up movies culminating in *Death Race 2000* (1975), in which the winner is not only the fastest, but the one who has killed the most pedestrians *en route*. The car, of course, has always been used more spectacularly outside the confines of the race track, usually in the most inappropriate places, although movies such as *Le Mans* (Solar Cinema Center 1971) tried to see the car as more than just an instrument of escape and destruction.

Motor racing is merely a logical extension of everyday driving in a big city or on the highway. In a classic Disney cartoon, Goofy, a considerate

and gentle being, becomes a monstrous killer when he gets behind a steering wheel. Ordinary French drivers in Jean Luc Godard's apocalyptic *Weekend* (1967) resort to murder and cannibalism. W.C. Fields decides to use the money he inherits in *If I Had a Million* (Par. 1932) literally to drive road-hogs off the roads. This relationship of man to the mechanical power he has at his fingertips, is codified in motor racing. However, many top drivers have stated, not always in jest, that they feel safer on the track among their peers than among the amateur racers on the public highway. When the racing champion in *Stolen Hours* (UA 1963) is asked to hurry in his family car, he says, 'If I'm going to race, I'll do it on the track not here where every kid thinks he's Stirling Moss.'

Theoretically, motor racing should be the most cinematic of all sport. The camera can provide far more interesting perspectives on a race over a large distance or many laps, than a spectator can possibly get on the roadside or from the stands. It can take you inside the car, into the pits, give you a bird's eye view from a helicopter and a worm's eye view from the dirt. Film makers have made brave attempts to disguise the fact, to non-aficionados at least, that all races look the same, as do the cars and the drivers in their helmets. They are aware that many audiences agree with the sentiments expressed by Jessica Walter in *Grand Prix*. 'I suppose they're pretty to look at, the cars. Otherwise it's very boring, really. It's like some people one meets. They look very interesting and after ten minutes with them you're bored speechless.' A daring speech to put into the mouth of a character in a film where the racing sequences are far longer than ten minutes. Nevertheless, the director of *Grand Prix*, John Frankenheimer, stated, 'We can't afford only to interest car nuts. We're trying a mad idea in a way, mixing up real races, staged races, with a story...I hope that with our movie people who hate racing may understand it better. Those who like it may see some of the insanity of it.' A forlorn hope, Mr Frankenheimer. Those who hate racing would probably not go to see it in the first place, but if they do they will leave the theater still trying to figure out the point of the sport. Those who love it will get impatient with the story that interrupts it. (This applies to most car race movies.) Few people understand what racing means to the driver, and when the script-writer tries to explain it, it generally comes out in platitudes. 'The racing car is to me like some kind of great animal.' (*Red Line 7000* 1965), or 'Cheat death and you live higher.' (*Silver Dream Racer* 1980). Taciturn Steve McQueen struggles manfully in *Le Mans* to explain to a racing widow why he races, but it isn't worth the effort.

In the 30's and 40's, motor racing pictures used the race track as a convenient arena for melodrama in which the villain and the hero battled it out in the big race, the hero winning despite the villain's dirty tricks. In later films, motor racing itself provides the drama, although the Ben Hur chariot race syndrome is never totally absent. The number of deaths in racing has risen sharply since the 50's, so the spectre of Fear looms large, affecting the driver, his family and friends. As Death waits, so do the women. 'Every time you go out that door I never know whether I'll see you again,' they say. The moral point often made in car race pictures (and in boxing ones) is that all the risk and effort of the hero's profession is not worth the sacrifice of personal happiness (i.e. female, fraternal and family responsibilities). The hero must realize that his life is empty, that he has been exploited, and that the spectators are a bloodthirsty mob hoping to see him killed. Before this view is expressed, the director and the audience have revelled in the dangers, thrills and fatalities for 70 minutes.

Grand Prix racing is the most glamorous of all motorized sports. The money and the glory is well earned for what is a high risk job. It is also a rich man's sport. The Formula 1 is the king of racing cars, the

most sophisticated thing on wheels. They can cost about 100,000 dollars to build and as much to maintain for one season. No wonder motor racing has the image of a sport for playboys. It is significant that in *Notorious Gentleman* (UI 1946. *The Rake's Progress* — GB), the only achievement of insouciant playboy Rex Harrison in civilian life (he dies a war hero) is to win Le Mans. A playboy's life is in itself a risky affair — all those narrow escapes from husbands and marriage. But, as everyone knows, there are no more attractive men to women than racing drivers. The potent combina-

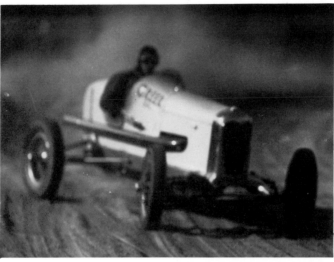

Auto-racing 1932 style in *The Crowd Roars*

tion of a man, the internal combustion engine, the smell of gasoline, and a silk scarf tied neatly round the neck, proves too much for any woman to resist. The winner kisses the Beauty Queen, shakes the phallic champagne bottle and ejaculates it over the crowd.

At the other end of the spectrum from Grand Prix racing are the demolition derbies and stock car races. The drivers operate at the lowest and least publicized levels of sport. Most exponents of the 'stox' circuit build their own cars, although they are, on the whole, men of modest means. The car has to be strong enough to hit a fence at 60 mph, turn two somersaults and keep going. The best cars can cost over 10,000 dollars to build and the drivers don't earn big money. The gritty independence of the participants, the risks involved for mean gains were presumably what attracted Howard Hawks to the sport in his *Red Line 7000* and supplied the perfect metaphor in *The Last American Hero* (TCF 1973).

The motor cycle is too anarchic a vehicle to have been much used as a sport in the movies. When it has, as in *Little Fauss and Big Halsy* (Par. 1970) or *C.C. and Company* (Avco 1970), the bikes start to dictate a road or gang movie. The motor cycle first emerged fully as a sexual symbol in *The Wild One* (Col. 1954) and has since become the icon of an erotic-narcotic esoteric religion. *Wild Angels* (American International 1966) deified the Hells Angels and in *Easy Rider* (Col. 1969) bikes and drugs combined to become the ultimate freedom machine. 'The Buddha, The Godhead, resides quite as comfortably in the circuits of a digital computor or the gears of a cycle transmission as he does at the top of a mountain or in the petals of a flower,' writes Robert Pirsig in 'Zen and the art of motor cycle maintenance.' This attitude to machines pervades most of the movies on wheels.

There are a few notable silent movies on motor racing (a silent motor race is rather like a silent musical) but Charlie Chaplin's first appearance in his tramp persona was in *Kid Auto Races* (1914) about a soapbox derby. The cars in *The Crowd Roars* (WB 1932) don't look much faster than the soapbox variety. Despite their long rectangular chassis and big wheels, the Greer Special and the Gilmore Lion were, of course, the last words in streamlining in 1932. The film, however, goes at a cracking pace even though the plot creaks a bit. James Cagney plays an obsessive racing driver, determined to keep his

younger brother (Eric Linden) out of motor racing. The brother is crazy about racing and resents Cagney. Frank McHugh, the pal who tried to bring the brothers together is killed on the track. The film ends with the brothers winning the Indianapolis 500 in the same car. Directed by Howard Hawks, it is an early example of his theme of the cameraderie of men who risk their lives for a living. The professional direction and Cagney's electric performance bring life to the trite story. Ann Dvorak and a wisecracking Joan Blondell are the siblings' dames. Linden: 'Did you see me drive?' Blondell (cooly): 'No. That's a thrill I'm saving up.'

Bicycles don't seem to have changed much since Joe E. Brown became a *6-Day Bike Rider* (WB 1934) in order to impress a girl (Maxine Doyle). The humor is rather dated, though. By means of a sponge full of chloroform, inadvertently thrown away by a race physician and caught behind the springs of his bike, Joe manages to win the race. He places his girl on the handlebars and they ride around the track in triumph. Directed by Lloyd Bacon, it was one of those rare films to deal with bicycle racing.

Only 7 years after *The Crowd Roars*, it was remade as *Indianapolis Speedway* (WB 1939), not that the cars had changed too noticeably. They seemed a little faster and lighter. The film, however, was slower and heavier than the Hawks version. Pat O'Brien, no substitute for Cagney, was the older brother in conflict with his younger brother, John Payne, until a fatal crash changes their lives. Ann Sheridan and Gale Page were the waiting women and it was directed by Warner Bros. stalwart, Lloyd Bacon.

The beautifully photographed Yorkshire countryside provided the background to a rather soggy British film, *A Boy, a Girl and a Bike* (Rank 1947). The boy was Patrick Holt, captain of a Yorkshire cycling club; the girl was Honor Blackman, a millgirl and enthusiastic member of the club, and the bike was a Raleigh. There was nothing special about any of the three, except that the boy wins the Moss Moor open race by half a length on the bike cheered on by the girl. Enter motorist John McCallum, a city slicker who forces cyclists off the road. He falls for the girl and even joins the club to be near her, but finally steps aside when he realizes that love between a cyclist and a motorist would never work. The screenplay was by that sentimentalizer of the working classes, Ted Willis (now Lord Willis) and the director was Ralph Smart.

From the calm of the English countryside to the roar of the dirt track and the brashness of Mickey Rooney in *The Big Wheel* (UA 1949). Mickey plays Billy Coy (coy he isn't!), son of Cannonball Coy, hottest car racer of his day, who was killed in the Indianapolis 500. Billy follows in his father's tracks much to the consternation of his mother (Spring Byington). She sits in the stands watching her son go round and round while being reminded by the announcer that her husband got killed doing the same thing. Mickey rises from garage mechanic to champion racing driver, losing some friends on the way, (some are killed, others avoid him). Naturally, in the end, he has to race at Indianapolis. He drives superbly, but as he reaches the last lap with victory in sight, his engine catches fire. The brave Mickey keeps driving. Despite the danger and the burns, he manages to finish the race in third place. However, the winner awards the trophy to little Mickey for the guts he displayed. Rooney was his usual energetic self, but the racing was distinctly under-powered. Jack Dempsey co-produced.

A similar nostalgia animates fans of old Hollywood movies and lovers of vintage cars. Both cry, 'they don't make 'em like they used to'. The London to Brighton vintage car race satisfies those for whom speed is not the prerequisite of an automobile. *Genevieve* (Rank 1954) tells of just such a race, following the adventures and misadventures of two couples who have a private race back to London for £100. The couples are John Gregson and his car-hating wife, Dinah Sheridan; Kenneth More and his trumpet-playing girl-friend, Kay Kendall. The film is really a number of variations on a single joke, the cars breaking down. The men are beastly to the women, getting them to push and blaming them for everything. 'All Ambrose thinks about are that silly old car and the other thing,' says Kay Kendall. 'My husband only thinks of the car,' replies the wife bleakly. The title role is taken by a capricious crimson 1904 Darracq and her opponent is a yellow 1904 Spyker.

Tony Curtis was placed by Universal International in a series of formula pictures in the early 50's until he managed to break away to do more varied work. After being a boxer in *The Flesh and The Fury* (1952), a football player in *All American* (1953), he became an auto-racing car designer in *Johnny Dark* (1954). The film investigates in a modest way, the problems of building a top class car. Johnny Dark (Curtis) designs a new type sports car for Fielding Motors, but Fielding (Sidney Blackmer) declines to approve it. With the help of Fielding's daughter (Piper Laurie), Johnny manages to sneak the car out of the factory. Johnny and his team enter it in the big three-day Border to Border race from Canada to Mexico. By excellent driving, Johnny brings his car home first. Fielding agrees to put the car into immediate production. The final race is reasonably well shot with subjective views and judiciously used back projection.

The first, big, expensive movie on motor racing was Henry Hathaway's *The Racers* (TCF 1955. *Such Men are Dangerous* — GB). In the early years of CinemaScope, the wide-screen process copyrighted by Fox, it was necessary for that studio to think of subjects in terms of filling the outsize screen. This gigantism led to top-heavy Biblical epics and empty Cook's tour romantic comedies. Alfa Romeos, Mercedes and Maseratis survived better in CinemaScope than people and *The Racers* was particularly successful when the yellow

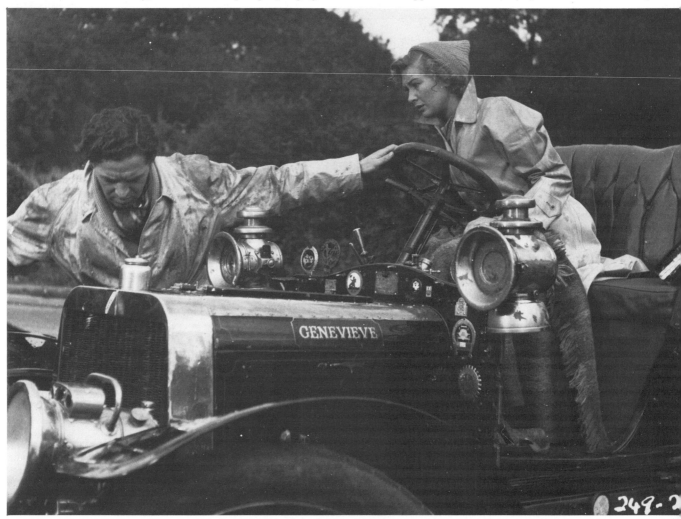

John Gregson, Dinah Sheridan and Genevieve

red and blue devils were screaming the curves and roaring towards the checkered flag. Cameras were fixed on the cars, even on the wheels of the autos in the actual Italian Mille Miglia. Stereophonic sound, the unsophisticated and rather gimmicky forerunner of Dolby, actually worked quite well in creating sound effects inseparable from the sport. The action takes place in Monaco, Rome, Berne and other European locations, but the director and actors never left Hollywood. These locales flash by like giant postcards. Kirk Douglas is seen in his car waiting for the start, while behind him is projected the crowd at the Grand Prix de Italia. Then cut to the race with closeups of Douglas in the studio. Nothing wrong with that, except that what takes place back in Hollywood between these expertly edited races, is a draggy love story, as banal as it's improbable. In his first race, Kirk Douglas (unconvincingly called Gino Borgesa) crashes when he swerves to avoid a dog belonging to ballet dancer, Bella Darvi. Later she seeks him out to apologize, but he tells her bitterly that all he wants is a new car. With the money she wins at roulette, Bella buys Kirk a racing car in which he wins a glorious victory in the Mille Miglia. On his way to becoming a ruthless champion, he gets out of his Ferrari and into Miss Darvi's bed and back into the car. When she leaves him to go back to ballet, he loses a string of races. In the end, however, during the Grand Prix de Italia, he looks up to see her standing there which gives him the inspiration to win again. Kirk Douglas, Gilbert Roland, Lee J. Cobb and Cesar Romeo all do their nuts, while Bella Darvi watches passively.

A feeble British attempt to make an auto-racing drama on similar lines was *Checkpoint* (Rank 1956), filmed in Italy in Eastman Color. Besides the views of Italy and the top races, there is an idiotic story of dastardly Stanley Baker stealing the blueprints of an Italian engine design for multimillionaire owner of racing cars, James Robertson Justice. Baker, wanted for murder, joins a racing team headed by ace driver, Anthony Steel. Steel is an upright, gentleman driver who spends his free time wooing Odile Versois and righting wrongs.

Finally, Steel has Baker as his co-driver, not knowing that Baker wants to use the car to escape the police. On a high cliff, Steel and Baker struggle for the steering wheel. The car is precariously balanced on the edge. It slips. Steel flings himself clear, but Baker is carried over the edge with it. The car kills James Robertson Justice who is at the bottom of the cliff and thus two baddies are killed for the price of one car.

Cornel Wilde was producer, director, part author and star of *The Devil's Hairpin* (Par. 1957) with his wife, Jean Wallace as co-star, so it is easy to know where to apportion any blame. Cornel Wilde constructed for himself one of those unsympathetic, self-centered roles that Kirk Douglas enjoyed playing. Wilde, however, is an expressionless stick of an actor who doesn't have to try too hard to alienate an audience. Of course, the difficulty arises when he has to gain their sympathy at the end. He portrays a former world racing champion who retired 2 years before after forcing his brother over the dreaded Devil's Hairpin bend during a race. His brother is now a mental and physical wreck and his mother (Mary Astor, equipped with granny-glasses and knitting) won't speak to him. He is goaded by the new world champion into making a comeback. The big race is about to start. Many of the world's best racers arrive out of hatred for him. Everyone wants to see him get beaten. Mary Astor listens to the race on the radio. Towards the end of an exciting, if not entirely realistic race, Wilde is on the Devil's Hairpin and could eliminate his closest rival, but he decides to give way rather than cause an accident. In the last lap, however, he goes on to win. A cheering crowd surges around him.

MGM's ventures into producing British films were mostly pretty dismal. The films, generally shot in Europe with English stars and perhaps one American, had a distinctly vapid air about them. *The Green Helmet* (MGM 1961) was no exception. Adapted by Jon Cleary from his own best seller, it starred stodgy Bill Travers as a racing champion compelled to race despite the fact that his nerves are beginning to show. His girl-friend, Nancy Walters, is terrified for him, and his mother, Ursula

Jeans, has to live with the fact that she has another son who wants to be a racing driver. Sidney James provides 'comic relief' as a cockney mechanic and the American 'name' Ed Begley, plays a business magnate unconcerned for the lives of the men who test his tires. Despite the predictability of the plot, there is some interest for lovers of horsepower in the shots of the Mille Miglia, Le Mans and the Florida 12 hour race and the presence of former world champion Jack Brabham in a speaking role.

Roger Corman, director of *The Viking Women and the Sea Serpent* (1957), *Teenage Caveman* (1958), *She-Gods of Shark Reef* (1958), the inventor of the Z-movie and schlock, went more up-market with his Poe adaptations in the 60's, but still had time to direct and produce youth orientated movies such as *The Young Racers* (American International 1963). The Monte Carlo Grand Prix is won by Joe Machin (William Campbell) in his Lotus, the victory being accomplished by reckless driving which endangers his own life and those of his fellow drivers. A one-time driver turned writer called Steve Children (Mark Damon) is doing an exposé on Machin. In order to get the lowdown, Steve joins the Lotus team. During a race at Aintree, Steve and Joe participate in a grudge match. Joe is out to knock Steve's car off the track, but when Steve's car swerves wildly, Joe has a change of heart and spins his own car off the track in order to avoid hitting him. You see, Joe, under his bravado, is an extremely sensitive and confused personality (unlike the film). There is some good location shooting around the Grand Prix circuit. The girls appear under the heading of The International Playgirls.

In 1939, Bette Davis in *Dark Victory* (WB) went blind just before dying radiantly. In the remake, *Stolen Hours* (UA 1963), Susan Hayward does the same in an even more cloying manner than her predecessor. However, an attempt is made to draw an analogy between the possible death of a racing driver and Miss Hayward's certain one. Her racing-driver friend (Edward Judd) knows that he could be killed at any time, but he says, 'I don't want to be told "you're going to get yours in the 10th lap".' Susan

marries kind doctor, Michael Craig and there are more comparisons made. 'A doctor like a driver needs good hands, strong nerves and death is never very far away.' 'There's a difference,' replies the doctor. 'A doctor never perishes in the operating room.' Poor Susan wants to grasp at life, so she goes to Italy to see her friend race. Drivers dice with death all around her, while she wanders carelessly almost onto the track. There is a crash. A spectator is killed. 'Don't cover his face,' she yells tearfully. 'Let him see as long as he can.' Luckily, she is rich enough to make her last days comfortable and death is seen as an enobling agent.

The Lively Set (UI 1964) had rather attractive young players, pleasant color and a reasonably exciting treatment of racing and speed trials, although the college scenes are a trifle fatuous and dated. Get those haircuts! James Darren is a builder and driver of racing cars who returns home after 2 years in the army and is persuaded to attend college by his mother (Marilyn Maxwell, in reality 15 years older than Darren). He has converted a J-47 jet engine into a trophy-winning 'dragster'. He meets student auto-engineer, Doug McClure who also has a 'dragster' and they challenge each other in their respective 'hot-rods'. Darren wins when McClure's car blows up. He soon quits college and in his jet car becomes a national celebrity. After failing to break the land-speed record on the Bonneville Salt Flats, he wins the Tri-Star race in a new gas turbine car. Pamela Tiffin agrees to marry him after he convinces her that she means as much to him as engines. Darren and McClure are last seen, having given up cars, experimenting on space travel. Perhaps they hoped for a sequel — 'The Lively Set on the Moon'.

Dedicated rather pompously to 'Mr Laurel and Mr Hardy', Blake Edwards' *The Great Race* (WB 1965) only rarely touches the genius of its dedicatees. It tells of an improbable race from New York to Paris via Siberia and Ruritania in 1918 in wildly improbable cars. The first part is an affectionate spoof of silent film comedy, and the second degenerates into an unfunny take off of 'The Prisoner of Zenda' and Victorian

Overleaf: Charles Goldner (left) and Kirk Douglas in *The Racers*

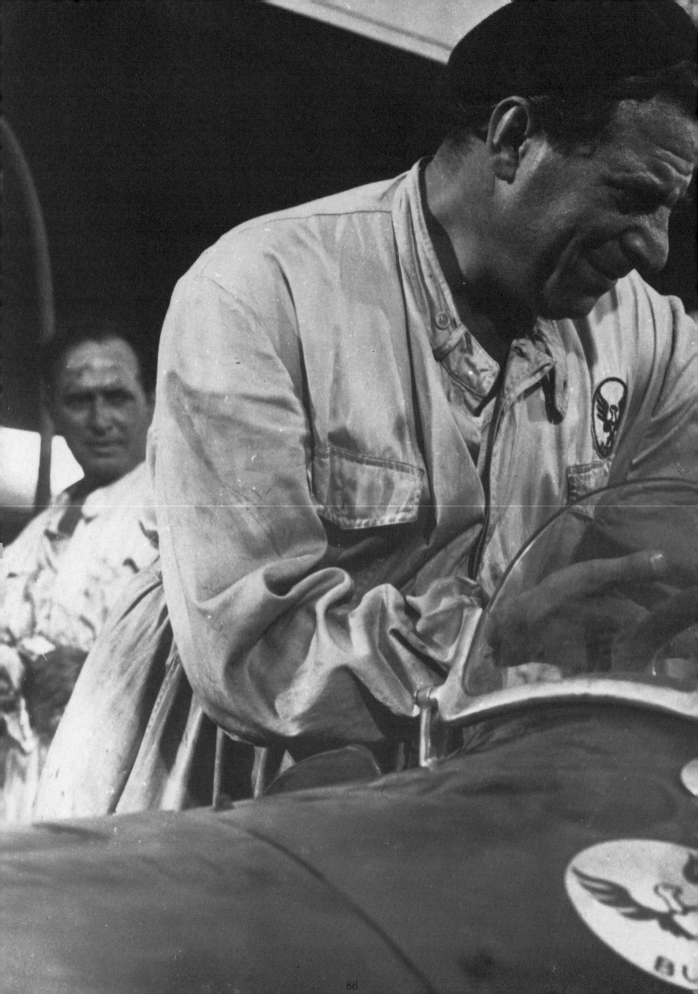

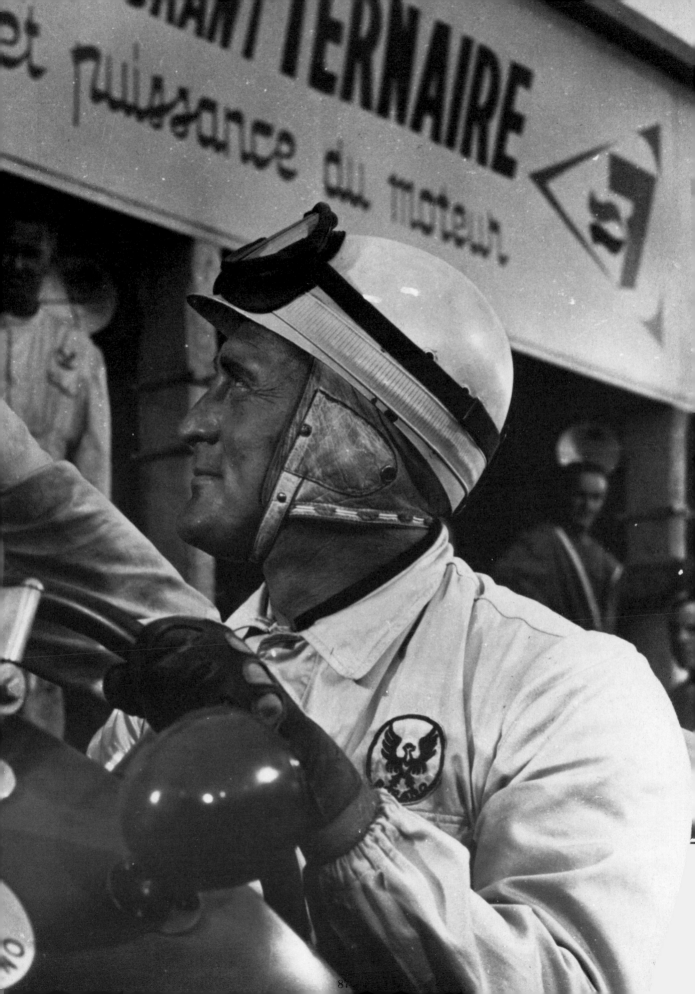

melodrama. Tony Curtis is The Hero, immaculate in white with glinting teeth, and Jack Lemmon is the Villain, evil in black with drooping moustache. Curtis drives a sleek, white car while Lemmon's car has a small canon in the front and can emit a smoke-screen. Natalie Wood is The Heroine who, although she has only a small traveling bag, changes her wardrobe virtually from shot to shot.

Admirers of director Howard Hawks might be hard put to it to find much to like about *Red Line 7000* (Par. 1965). Admirers of stock car racing might have more to cheer. The sport provides Hawks with his favorite theme — men who live dangerously, the fraternity that develops between them and the waiting women. The almost plotless and witless screenplay concentrates on the love affairs of three drivers 'each one seeking happiness.' (Like a melodramatic *Three Coins in the Fountain*.) 'Love, like a tachometer, has its red line

7000.' One girl (Gail Hire) believes she's a jinx to race-car drivers who fall for her and blames herself for any accident that occurs. A driver (John Robert Crawford) loses an arm, but believes he can drive just as well with a hook. Another driver (James Caan in his first leading role) after an accident, apologizes to the driver he had tried to kill, asking him to hit him. The man punches him. 'That's all I came for,' says Caan satisfied. All three couples have a problem which is conveniently resolved by the end when the three girls happily watch their men on the track. The racing scenes are quite exciting (there are some spectacular crashes), but the continuity is confusing. Ford cars seem to win all the races and there are billboards advertising Fords everywhere.

Visually, John Frankenheimer's *Grand Prix* (MGM 1966) must be the most successful race-car movie ever made. The Super Panavision screen is sometimes divided into halfs, thirds, fourths,

eighths, sixteenths etc. Zooms, filters, prismatic reflections and slow motion are all used to make auto racing into a vivid cinematic experience. A camera attached to a car was lowered to within an inch of the track to give the spectator a bumper's eye-view of the race at 150 mph. Saul Bass, the noted credit-title designer, was the visual consultant and his contribution to the look of the film is inestimable. The opening 25 minutes is of the Monte Carlo 'Round the Houses' run with its treacherous curves and hills. There are helicopter shots, subjective views and a crash of a car tumbling into the sea. The film begins with Monte Carlo in May, taking in Spa (Belgium), Brand's Hatch (England), Clermont-Ferrand (France) and ends with Monza (Italy) in September where it is virtually impossible to tell the difference between the simulated races and the real thing. If only that were all! Because of commercial considerations there had to be a plot to go with it. It

tells 'the story of four drivers, the women behind them, the cars beneath them.' (Not vice versa?) They are The American (James Garner), The Corsican (Yves Montand), The Englishman (Brian Bedford) and The Sicilian (Antonio Sabato). Garner is the ruthless driver who risks his personal happiness for driving. At the end, in the empty race-track after winning at Monza, he realizes, predictably, that his life is a sham without the woman he loves. Garner wins because he lost the girl, Bedford loses because he got the girl, Montand is killed because he can't decide between his wife and mistress. The women are Fashion Editor, Eve Marie-Saint; ex-model Jessica Walter and a race track groupie Francoise Hardy. Toshiro Mifune (dubbed) is a Japanese car manufacturer who sponsors Garner in his Yamura (the only invented car in the film.) Maurice Jarre wrote the repetitious music.

On the subject of repetitious music, Francis Lai wrote the

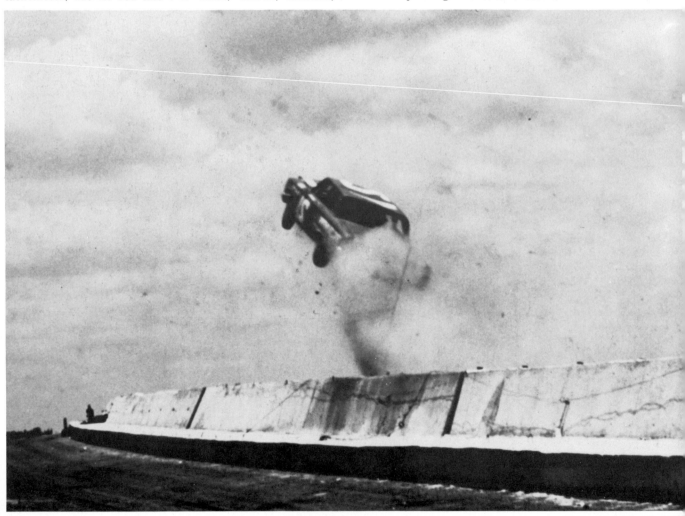

'Lift-off' *Red Line 2000*

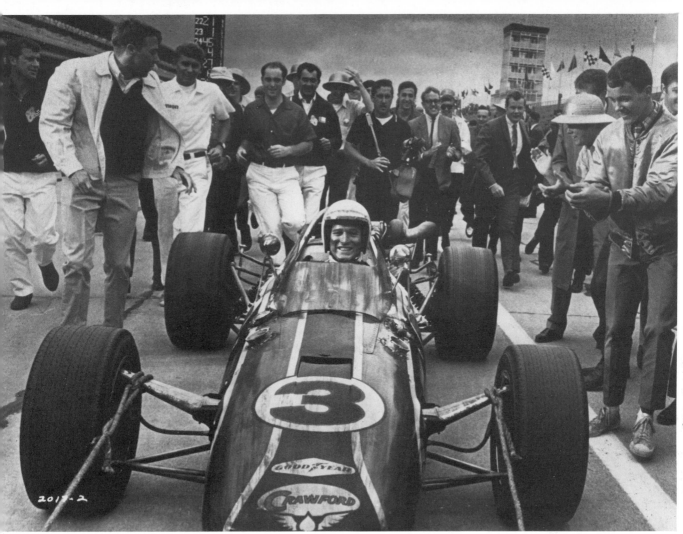

vell known doo-bee-doo theme or *A Man and a Woman* (UA 1966 — *Un Homme et une Femme*). It is an ultra-chic women's magazine love story between a racing driver widower (Jean-Louis Trinting-nant) and a film continuity-girl widow (Anouk Aimée). His wife committed suicide prema-urely when she thought he had been killed during the 1963 Le Mans Grand Prix; and her stunt-man husband was blown up during the making of a war film. Both these marriages are cold with extensive use of flash-back. Thus Trintignant fears for the wife of a racing driver, and Anouk, having been married to a man in a dangerous profession, finds herself in love with another. These problems keep creeping in while they carry out a court-ship in the *très snob* seaside resort of Deauville. Will they or won't they make it together? Doo-bee-doo. He enters the Monte Carlo Rally and manages to win despite all the flashbacks he has. She waits anxiously for him. Some-

times they appear in Eastman color and at others in sepia. Very artistic, except that the director Claude Lelouch later admitted that he had run out of funds and couldn't afford any more color stock. Doo-bee-doo-bee-doo.

'Go, go, go, on the speedway. Go for the money and lead the pack. Curve and swerve like you do at a dance,' sings Elvis Presley over the titles of *Speedway* (MGM 1968). Stock car racing merely provides Elvis with another stock vehi-cle. Elvis is a racer with a heart of gold and a silver crash hel-met. He supports 5 revoltingly cute little girls, buys their father a station wagon, and rescues 'chicks' from the arms of his Casanova manager, Bill Bixby. Elvis is 'a real hot dog' and wins almost every race, so the tax man sends an inves-tigator in the shape of Nancy Sinatra. They go go go for each other and Elvis decides to play Uncle Sam. 'He's your uncle not your dad. He's the best friend you ever had,' he sings. A more sanitized entertain-

ment would be hard to find and when Elvis is ahead in a race it's a case of the bland leading the bland. The movie ends with the tamest race ever filmed. When the commentator says, 'there's something wrong with the weight distribution,' he's not referring to Elvis' midriff. The differences between the studio sets and the shots of the track (featuring champions Buddy Baker, Richard Petty, Tiny Lund and Roy Mayne) is marked. Others featured are Miss Beverley Hills (playing Miss Charlotte Speedway) and someone called Poncie Ponce.

Producer Roger Corman continued to angle for the youth market with *The Wild Racers* (American Interna-tional 1968) directed by Daniel Haller, who was art-director on Corman's Poe films. Fabian plays an unpopular racing driver, banned from the American circuit, who spends his time in Europe racing and skirt-chasing. Mimsy Farmer is the only girl who gets to see him a second night. While driv-ing, the hero has short

flashbacks or flash-ins about how to ditch his girl-friend. The footage of the Grand Prix rac-ing is grainy and over-exposed which is either to give the im-pression of a newsreel or it's just badly filmed. The Spanish Grand Prix, the climax of the film, is shot entirely in red filter. This might create the feeling of the heat during the race or what it would look like through cheap sunglasses. Another fraudulent sports movie that uses the subject and then proceeds to criticize it as an empty and negative pur-suit. However, a Canadian critic called it 'the best auto-racing picture ever,' and 'Variety' called it 'an inane car meller'. One of them could be right.

After *The Great Race* (1965), *Those Daring Young Men in their Flying Machines* (1965) and *Chitty, Chitty, Bang, Bang* (1968), which looked into a fan-tastical past of the pioneering days of automobiles and planes, came *Those Daring*

Overleaf: A fatal accident in *Grand Prix*

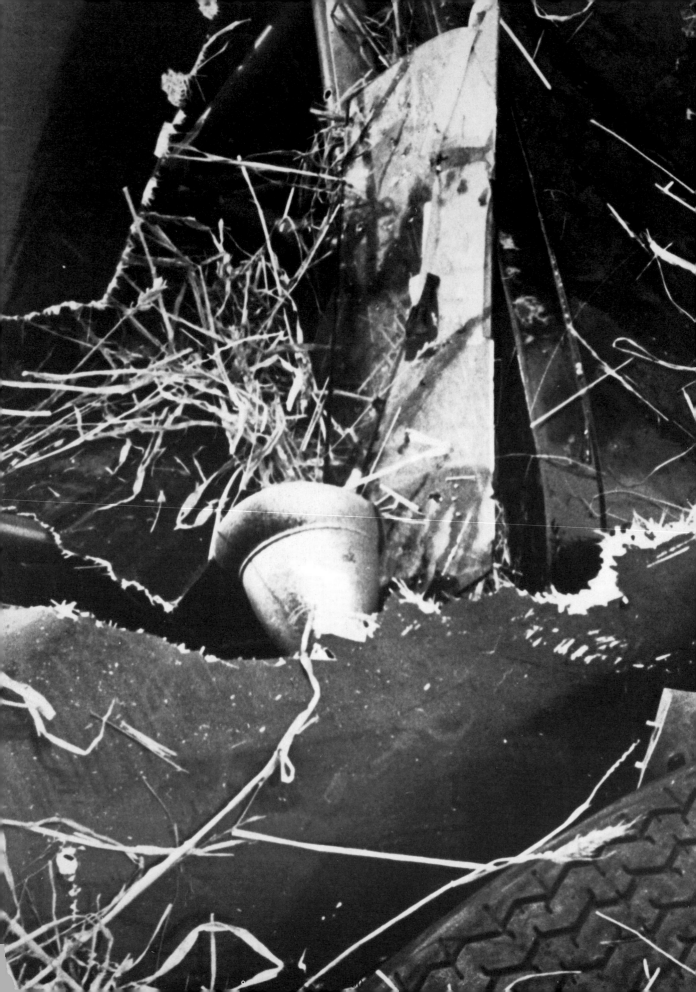

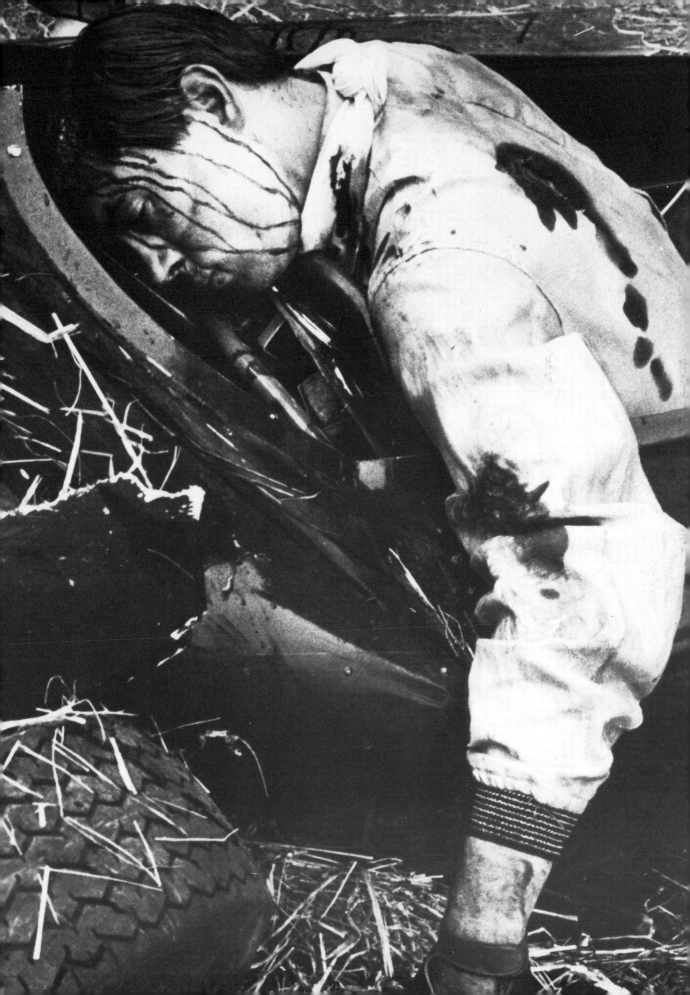

Young Men in their Jaunty Jalopies (Par. 1969 *Monte Carlo or Bust* — GB), another nostalgic, slapstick, inflated all-star co-production. 20 autos from the golden period of 1926-1929 were specially designed by David Watson (all with modern Fiat 2,300 engines) for this Monte Carlo Rally of the twenties. With its routes covering 1500 miles of the most terrible roads in Europe, it was a great test of skill and ingenuity on the part of the drivers. The race in the film is far too broad to have much authenticity. Participating are villainous Terry-Thomas in his 'Nifty Nine', Tony Curtis in his Triple S, an American type speedster, a German (Gert Frobe) in his Mercedes with stolen jewels in the spare tire, and two pukka British officers (Peter Cook and Dudley Moore). Tony Curtis wins after being pushed over the line by aristocratic Susan Hampshire. If only the film had as much wit as Ronald Searle's credit titles.

'I'm driving good, but my life is crap,' says Paul Newman in *Winning* (UI 1969), which just about sums up the movie. Newman's knowledge and practical experience of top class racing must have helped him to identify with the Formula One racing driver he plays, and a genuine passion for the sport shines through those blue eyes. What little plot there is doesn't slow up too much of the action, and unlike *Red Line 7000* and *Grand Prix*, the dialogue is fairly lively and adult even though the situations are trite. Joanne Woodward, Newman's estranged wife (in reality his unestranged wife), doesn't want their 17-year-old son (Richard Thomas Jr.) to get interested in racing, and tries to steer him away from his father. She has a point. He takes the boy drinking, encourages him to drive, and gives him the very useful advice, 'always trust the seat of your pants'. While Newman is busy knocking seconds off his speed record, Robert Wagner, rival driver, is knocking up his wife. The final showdown has

Newman and Wagner pitted against one another in the big race. Set in and around the Indianapolis 500, there are many documentary aspects to the film. Newman drives around the empty Indy Oval in his Ford on what is almost a sight-seeing tour. There is all the showmanship that surrounds the race. Parades, balloons, and a Goodyear airship. (Motor-racing pictures are full of free plugs.) We see the work in the pits and the real race itself including crashes with tires bouncing into the crowd.

Football Superstar Joe Namath, after failing in the restaurant business where he peddled things like Quarter-back Burgers and Football Hero Sandwiches, signed a film contract. (Paul Newman eat your heart out.) Instead of appearing in a football picture, he opted for a bike movie, *C.C. and Company* (Avco Embassy 1970). Namath plays C.C. Ryder (get it?), a motorcyclist wandering the country in search of his identity (and perhaps Dennis Hopper and

Peter Fonda). He joins a marauding gang of bikers, led by the giant Moon (William Smith), who call themselves The Heads. But Joe is really a goodie and saves fashion-magazine writer Ann-Margret from being raped by his leather-clad buddies. They meet again at a motorcross event which she is using as a background for a fashion layout. C.C. does a trial run around the course and is immediately offered a sponsorship on the motocross circuit by the Kawasaki team. He wins his first race in spectacular style, but when he refuses to hand over his winnings to Moon, he is viciously beaten up. The climax comes with a challenge race between Moon and himself in an empty football stadium. As they go into the final turn, Moon loses control of his bike, crashes into a fence and is killed. C.C. escapes with his girl. The gang is portrayed as Neanderthals on wheels who 'give motorcycling a bad name', in contrast to Namath's newly-found legit

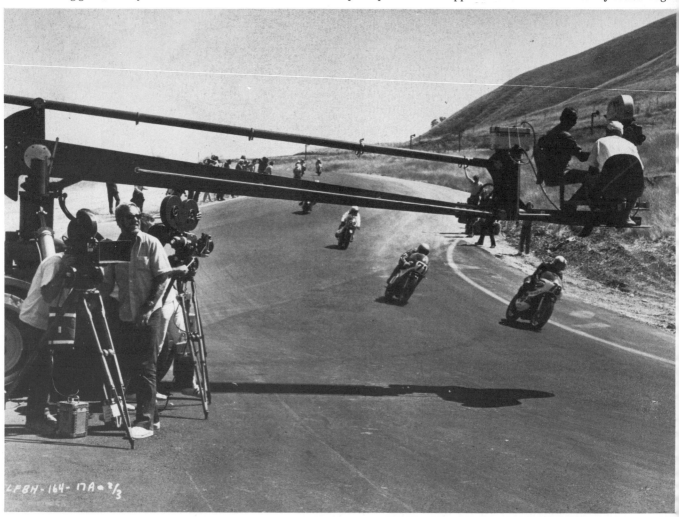

The filming of *Little Fauss and Big Halsy*

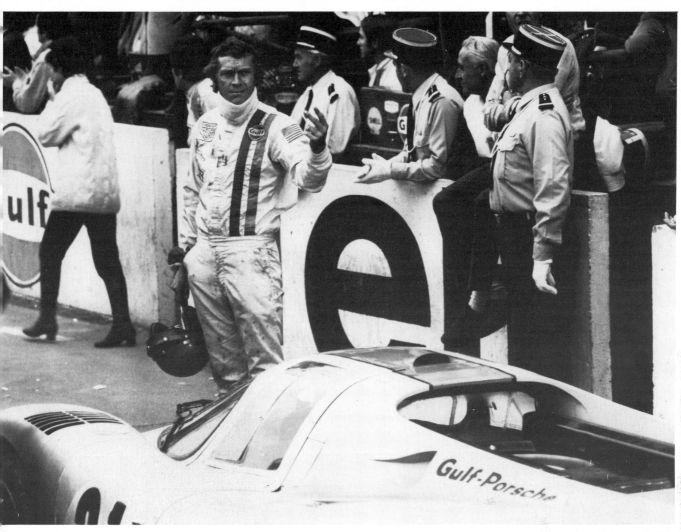

Steve McQueen in *Le Mans*

way of life. There is plenty of bike action, but the sex and violence is half-cocked. Although Namath is likable and looks at home on a high-powered machine, his acting is of the tricycle variety. There is one good joke, though. One of the girls of the gang, trying to stall a security officer at the stadium, tells him they are filming a 'youth-oriented raunchy motor-cycle movie'.

A far superior motor-cycle movie is *Little Fauss and Big Halsy* (Par. 1970) played by Michael J. Pollard and Robert Redford respectively. Little, as he is called, is a gauche, bespectacled, amateur motor-cycle racer ('I was goin' as fast as I've ever been in my life, but I fell off') and mechanical wizard who lives with his Maw and Paw (Lucille Benson and Noah Beery Jnr.). Halsy is a pro-racer scraping a living by traveling across America from one small-time dirt-track to the next. He's an unscrupulous bum, who swaggers around boozing and screwing track groupies'. Naturally, the naive

Little is attracted to his lifestyle and leaves home to follow him as his tuner. Halsy exploits Little as they travel around. Rita Nevraska (Lauren Hutton), first seen running towards the track in the nude, attaches herself to them and Little falls for her. When Halsy beds her, Little begins to see through him and leaves. The climax takes place at Sears Point race track in San Francisco where Little, who has become as callous as his one-time hero, beats Halsy in the race. Sidney J. Furie's direction and Charles Eastman's script contain echoes of past successes, *Bonnie and Clyde* (1967), *Butch Cassidy and the Sundance Kid* (1969). Robert Redford's ego-tripper has similarities with his role in *Downhill Racer* (1969), although his performance does capture the pathetic grandeur of the character. His relationship with Pollard is not very far from that in a Dean Martin-Jerry Lewis comedy, which rather undercuts the seriousness of the film's intentions.

The Johnny Cash songs counterpoint the action ironically. The pessimistic but moral ending stresses what Redford says. 'Cycles is a mean toy, lady'.

About 8 million dollars was spent on *Le Mans* (Cinema Center Films 1971) and it certainly makes for an expensive looking package. Without going in for all the visual pyrotechnics of *Grand Prix*, director Lee H. Katzin captures on the wide screen, with zooms and vivid closeups, the excitement and tensions of Formula One racing. The plot is minimal. The drama comes from the struggle between Porsche and Ferrari, engine failure, time lost in the pits and the crashes. Slow motion is used to show in minute detail what happens to a car crashing at speed. The metal disintegrates, the car bursts into flames and the driver tries desperately to get away from the vehicle. Steve McQueen, no mean driver himself, plays a member of the Porsche team. He is drawn to the widow (Elga

Anderson) of a driver killed in the race the year before. They exchange long, lingering looks, speaking in monosyllables after significant pauses. This was undoubtedly an attempt to give audiences a break from the amount of decibels in the rest of the movie. Unfortunately, McQueen's attempts to explain to her what makes racers tick, is unconvincing. The action on the track speaks louder than words. The camera work is so good that even autophobes might get an inkling of what attracts those who are driven to drive. In a direct crib from *Tokyo Olympiad* (1966), at the countdown to the start of the race, the noise of the crowd is faded out and only the amplified sound of the driver's heartbeat is heard. So that's what makes them tick!

In the Road movies of the late sixties and seventies (unlike those with Crosby, Hope and Lamour) no one stays anywhere for very long. It's 'keep on trucking' or as a character says in *Two-Lane Blacktop* (UI 1971), 'The thing

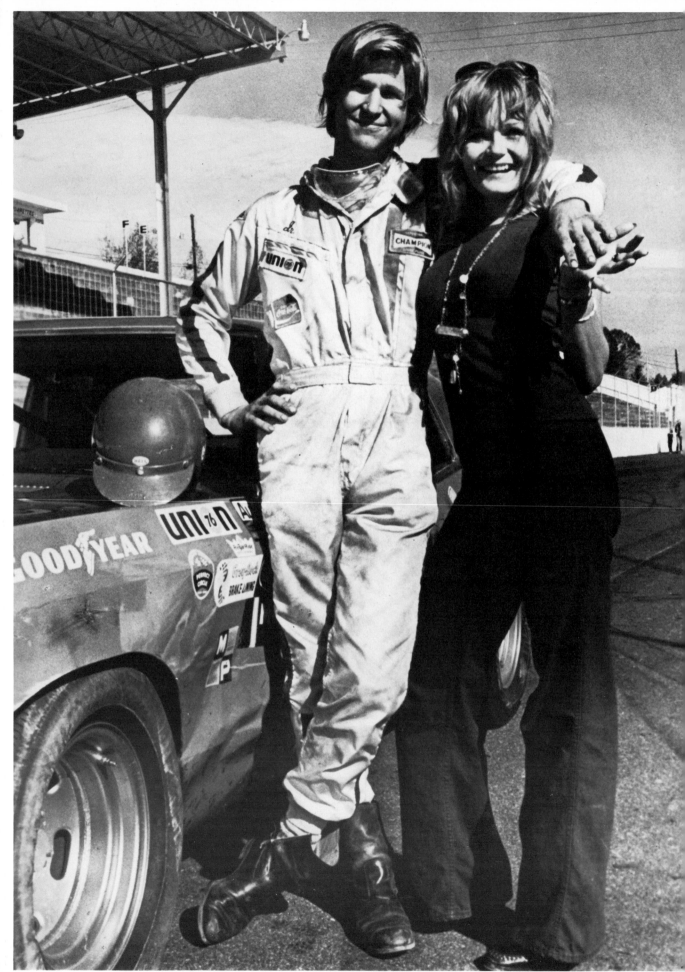

s you've got to keep moving.' The road movies are really about the vastness of American space, its variety and monotony. In other words, a vroom with a view. The nomads in their shining souped-up autos try to break away from the restrictions of time and space. Two long-haired car freaks (James Taylor and Dennis Wilson) head east from California in their 1955 Chev. They are street racers who race for small bets between midnight and dawn. On the way to Sante Fe, they challenge and beat other roadsters. Finally, there is a confrontation with an ageing playboy (Warren Oates) in a bright orange Pontiac GTO. The director, Monte Hellman, captures beautifully the empty car-lots, late-night diners, the open country and the two-lane backdrop to this American sub-culture. The film's structure is as linear as the road it follows, although its allegorical pretensions are inclined to side-track it. The fact that the cast consists of nameless characters is always a danger sign for pseud spotters. They are merely called The Driver, The Mechanic, The Girl and GTO. What is effective is Hellman's detachment from his subject and although the characters are given representative labels they remain individuals. Laurie Bird is The Girl who gradually replaces the 300 dollar prize-money to the winner.

Stock car racing has its superstars and its fanatics, but it is a sport that holds very little attraction for the liberal-minded middle-classes. It has an immutable red-neck image. *Corky* (MGM 1972) was filmed on location in Dallas where stock car racing was said to have begun. Corky (Robert Blake) is an auto mechanic and small time dirt-track racer who aspires to the life of a Grand National driver. Corky's hero is the famous champion, Richard Petty. Although he loves his wife (Charlotte Rampling with a Texas drawl) and two kids, he loves his 1967 Plymouth Barracuda street racer much more. Painted in pink with black racing stripes, it takes most of his time and money. The atmosphere of southern white middle-class life and of the minor league races is well caught by director

Leonard Horn, but the film descends into crude melodrama. Fuelled by jealousy over his wife, Corky goes berserk with a gun. While being chased by the cops, what should he see ahead of him but a sign which reads 'Demolition Derby Tonite'. He heads for the track and enters the raceway at the beginning of the Derby. The police surround the track. Other cars crash into him, and as he has no seat belt he winces in pain. Finally, he crashes trying to make a getaway. Robert Blake, following his other 'loser' role in *In Cold Blood* (1967), gives a riveting performance.

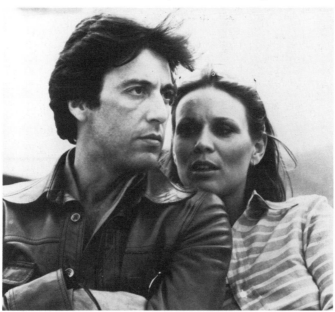

Al Pacino and Marthe Keller in *Bobby Deerfield*

Stock car racing also features in a big way in *The Last American Hero* (TCF 1973). However, the portentous title promises much more than it delivers. Presumably, Junior Jackson (Jeff Bridges) is the last American hero, because he is an individualist who holds out to the very last before giving in to the exigencies of the Establishment. He is a North Carolina mountain boy who makes his way from petty crime to fame and fortune as a stock car racer. He builds his own engines and runs them against factory-built cars, and has nothing but contempt for the drivers with Coca Cola and Goodyear all over their automobiles. For how long can Junior remain outside the system? The film starts to move inexorably towards its cynical ending. Rebuilding, replenishing racing machines costs money. A man can be his own man for just so long.

Junior signs with the big firm, Colt Automative. 'Where are you going from here, Junior?' asks a reporter. The question remains unanswered. The movie was adapted from a Tom Wolfe Esquire article on the life of racing star Junior Johnson, who is credited as technical advisor. Lamont Johnson directs it in a cool but flat manner. Although good-looking, Jeff Bridges is never film-starry and suggests the seediness of the character's rural background. Valerie Perrine plays a 'groupie' who has the hots for any driver who wins.

After churning out dozens of pictures for American International, producer/director Roger Corman set up his own company, New World, and continued to make cheap formula pictures for the youth market i.e. 'exploitation' movies in film jargon. Less solemn that the same year's *Rollerball*, *Death Race 2000* (New World 1975) is a campy, sci-fi comedy which, like the best comic books, caricatures the horrors of contemporary society. In the year 2000, the population of the United Provinces of America has been emotionally dulled by the horrendous war and the effects of the Great Depression of 1979. Only the annual transcontinental Death Race, in which every pedestrian is fair game, creates some excitement. The winner is determined by the quickest time and the highest body count. For example, women — 10 points, teenagers — 40, toddlers — 70, oldies — 100. (Logically in

sporting terms, the most agile should be worth the most points.) It's a way of keeping the population down, like in our own society. (There are over 25,000 deaths in the USA p.a.) The 5 drivers in the race are Calamity Jane Kelly in her Stud Bull car, Mathilda 'The Hun' Morris in her Buzz Bomb, Nero 'The Hero' Lonigan in The Lion, 'Machine Gun' Joe Viterbo (Sylvester Stallone) in his Peacemaker and Frankenstein (David Carradine) in his Monster. The race is complicated by a band of revolutionaries led by 90-year-old Thomasina Paine. Paul Bartel directed.

The illegal rallies that take place across the States was looked at with a certain amount of artistry in *Two-Lane Blacktop*. There is very little to be said for the mindless extended car chases that are *Gumball Rally* (WB 1976) and *Cannonball* (New World 1976. *Carquake* — GB). The former is a race from New York to Long Beach Cal. run by bored business executive Michael Sarrazin. Among the rest of the cast are a Porsche Targa, a Rolls Royce, a Mercedes 300SL roadster, a Kawasaki motorcycle and a van loaded with 50 gallon drums of gasoline. *Cannonball* has a few more amusing moments although the comedy is even broader. Entering for this no-holds-barred cross country race are a mad German who hums 'The Blue Danube' while dodging the police, comic feminists, crooked country-and-western singers. For those 'in' on the joke, Martin Scorsese, Roger Corman, Sylvester Stallone (a few months prior to *Rocky*) and the director Paul Bartel all play minor roles. David Carradine is again behind the wheel.

Another Roger Corman production to appeal to the juvenile drive-in market where youngsters can watch a movie from their cars about cars, *Eat My Dust* (New World 1976) takes place in the small mid-Western town of Puckerbush, where the stock car race has attracted most of the populace. Among them is Hoover Niebold (Ron Howard) a recent high school grad whose passion for racing is almost as strong as his passion for the town's teenage vamp. Legendary racer Big Bubba Jones (Dave Madden) tells Hoover that 'race driving is for outlaws, inlaws and ass-holes.' But

Left: Jeff Bridges and Valerie Perrine in *The Last American Hero*

Hoover steals Bubba's car and a Keystone Kops chase ensues. After destroying half of Puckerbush, he is arrested. Bubba agrees to drop the charges and takes Hoover on as his assistant.

To paraphrase Oscar Wilde, one would have to have a heart of stone if, on watching Marthe Keller dying in *Bobby Deerfield* (WB 1977) one doesn't burst into laughter. The title role is taken uncomfortably by Al Pacino as a Formula One racing champion who meets and falls for the above-mentioned Miss Keller in a clinic in the Swiss Alps. She's dying of leukemia, although he doesn't know it. As he is a racing driver, she hopes to find out from him what he knows about death. But he is cold and unemotional and thinks about death as little as he thinks about life. After winning races throughout Europe because 'he has an almost feminine touch at the wheel of a car' (*and* he does bad Mae West imitations), he returns to Keller from whom he has learnt love.

Throughout this unactable and ludicrous melodrama directed by Sidney Pollock and written by Alvin Sargeant, Pacino looks far less healthy that the strapping Marthe Keller. In a scene worthy of Buster Keaton, Pacino, in bed with Keller, reaches over her sleeping body to stroke her hair, but when he pulls his hand away it is holding a large tuft of hair. Shocked, he tries to replace it on her head.

Imagine being black in the Deep South in 1947 and wanting to enter the stock car races. You meet abuse, and prejudice from all sides, but you get your chance on the small, rural dirt-tracks, only because promoters think crowds might want to see a Negro crash and burn. You would expect no mercy from the white drivers who would be out to kill you. *Greased Lightning* (WB 1977) is the true story of Wendell Scott, the man who went from taxi driver and moonshine runner to winner of the 1963 NASCAR Grand National Championship. Scott, like

Jackie Robinson, was the first man to cross the color line in sport at the risk of his life. Stock car racing is dangerous at the best of times. Michael Schultz, who made the bouncy *Car Wash* (1967), makes the most of the action sequences and the talented cast, but falls into the conventional traps of the biopic. Early hopes, struggles, heartbreaks and final triumph. Richard Pryor, one of the most anarchic and original comedians around, does wonders within the worthy limitations of the role. Beau Bridges is fine as the redneck driver who befriends him and Pam Grier suffers as his wife.

Prejudice also exists in *Breaking Away* (TCF 1979), although not to the cruel extent of *Greased Lightning*. The prejudice here is prevalent among the WASPish college kids at Indiana U. against the children of the stone cutters of the town of Bloomington. Four of the 'Cutters' are Cyril (Daniel Stern), Mooch (James Earl Haley), Mike (Dennis Quaid), and Dave (Dennis

Christopher), all 19 years old and in limbo between high school and work. 'At 16 they call it sweet 16. At 18 you get to drink, to vote, to see dirty movies. What the hell do you get when you're 19?' asks one of the boys. Mike is bitter when he watches the college kids playing football, because he was a great quarterback at high school and now he's a nobody whom his cop brother calls a bum. But the film centers around Dave. Dave is a cycling fanatic who shaves his legs and pretends to be Italian all of which drives his used-car salesman father (Paul Dooley) nuts. One of the most original and amusing elements in Steve Tesich's screenplay is the contrast between the Italian persona that Dave has created for himself, out of the necessity to identify with a predominantly European sport and as escapism, and the typical American small town that surrounds him. Peter Yates' direction, with the help of Mendelssohn and Rossini, creates the feeling of the exhilaration of riding a

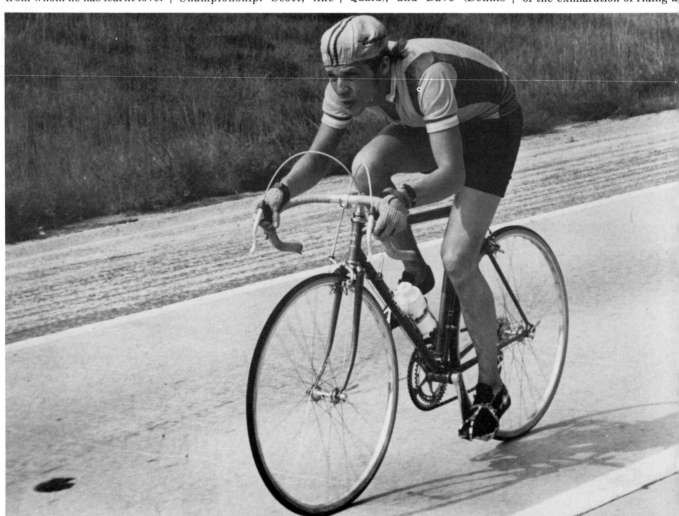

Dennis Christopher, *Breaking Away*

cycle at top speed. One day an Italian team comes to town to take part in the Cinzano 100 and Dave enters. To the strains of The Barber of Seville overture, he chases the Italians. They are contemptuous of his peasant greeting of 'Bon Giorno' and give him the sign that means 'get lost'. One of them puts his pump between the spokes of Dave's bike and he takes a spill. From then on the film goes down hill. Dave is disillusioned. 'Everybody cheats. I just didn't know,' he says weeping in his father's arms. He drops his Italian mannerisms and becomes what he is — a 'Cutter' and proud of it. He and his 3 buddies decide to enter for the little 500 Bicycle race against sponsored college teams. On the big day, as everybody sings 'America, America' with their hands on their hearts, Sport, that other great democratic institution, unites both 'Cutters' and college kids. What follows is as improbable as one finds in many a corny, old racing movie. After 200 laps (25 miles), while the other teams have changed riders, Dave is out in front and yet to come in for an exchange. However, a bad fall forces him to give up the bike to his extremely inexperienced teammates. Naturally they fall behind, but Dave, almost single-handedly (or single-leggedly) has beaten a fit, crack college team. Families embrace their sons and even the stereotyped college kids manage a smile. Dave is soon to join them, having passed his college entrance exam. The subject of class consciousness, not a common theme of American movies, is raised and then ironed away by the ending which confuses democracy with necromancy. The moral climate of the film is Cartesian. i.e. Jimmy Carter not Descartes.

'Anything you can do, I can do the same,' seems to be the motto of certain British film makers as regards America. Silver Dream Racer (Rank 1980) has the American market stamped all over it as well as Dunlop, Marlboro and Goodyear. The announcer at the big motor-cycle race at Silverstone, UK is American, the hero's rival 'the bad boy of International racing' is American Beau Bridges, the hero's girl-friend with whom he romps romantically is American actress Christina Raines and his black mechanic

(Clarke Peters) has an American accent. Boys play basketball around a gas station as police sirens scream. Mention of London or Brand's Hatch hardly dispels the feeling of displacement. But the producers want to have their apple-pie and eat it. The hero is British 'rock superstar' David Essex and, as in Chariots of Fire (1981), he triumphs over the American thus boosting flagging British morale. After his brother is killed in a pre-credit sequence, Essex inherits the bike of the title. When his mechanic sees it, he exclaims, 'Wow, man! That's not a bike, it's a work of art.' Our working-class hero David tries to get a sponsor, because he is determined to ride at Silverstone, 'the greatest race in the world.' Beau Bridges, in his stars and stripes helmet, is on his 500cc Suzuki and David is on his Silver Dream. Too many closeups make the race difficult to follow, but David must win. He does, but the makers, thinking perhaps that it was all too conventional up to then and not willing to offend the Americans or Suzuki, decide that the hero should crash after he passes the finishing line and be killed. But 'even if he had known he was going to die, he would've gone anyway.' David Essex, a motor-cycle freak since the age of 14, did some of the less dangerous riding and did all his own acting. The movie was made at Pinewood, England, and cost 5,000,000 dollars.

Following the facetious Gumball Rally and Cannonball, comes the asinine The Cannonball Run (TCF 1981). The race this time is the 3000 miles from Chicago to California. It's the kind of movie where frightening pedestrians, crashing into buildings and riding motor-cycles in hotel lobbies is considered hilarious. All the cops are cretins, all the girls luscious. They have only to bare their breasts to have the cops eating out of their . . . hands. The anti-car brigade or Friends of Nature are held up to ridicule. Dean Martin (64 years old), dressed as a priest, is busy chasing chicks; Roger Moore, who thinks he's Roger Moore, has a different girl of a different nationality every few miles; Burt Reynolds (half-asleep), Sammy Davis Jr., and Farrah Fawcett are also involved. Peter Fonda 'guests' as a Hell's Angel.

OTHER MOVIES ON WHEELS

Red Hot Tires WB 1935 (**Racing Luck** — GB) was a luke warm racing drama with Lyle Talbot as a racing star trying to prove that he was innocent of murder. Others who got away with murder were Mary Astor and Roscoe Karns.

No Limit GB 1935 was what British comedies, featuring Lancashire comedian George Formby, would go in order to provide a laugh. It takes place on the Isle of Man during the famous TT races in which George proves his prowess as a motor cycle rider. He is as funny as a serious accident.

Daredevil Drivers WB 1938 ran out of gas half-way through. It starred Dick Purcell in love with dirt-track racing and Beverley Roberts, in that order — it also featured Joan Blondell's sister, Gloria.

Road Demon TCF 1938 was about dirty tricks on the dirt track. Henry Arthur plays a young driver who wins against all odds. The one bright spot was Bill 'Bo Jangles' Robinson doing a tap dance.

Danger on Wheels UI 1940 was hot-headed daredevil driver, Richard Arlen who wins the Indy 500 with the help of faithful side-kick mechanic Andy Devine.

Excuse My Dust MGM 1951 was a mildly amusing Technicolor comedy about the inventor of a horseless carriage in 1895. Red Skelton, whose comedy consists mostly of twitching, wins a cross-country auto race to prove to his girl-friend's father (William Demarest) that the car was not just a passing fad.

Roar of the Crowd AA 1953 and the smell of grease had, according to the publicity, 'All the drama of the biggest race thrills on earth.' This tale of a racing driver (Howard Duff) who after an injury becomes a spark-plug salesman and then finishes ninth at Indianapolis, was somewhat less than earth-shattering. Famous drivers of the day, Johnny Parsons, Henry Banks, Duke Nalon and Manuel Ayalo, appear as themselves.

Drive a Crooked Road Col. 1954 had a screenplay by Blake Edwards, was directed by Richard Quine and starred Mickey Rooney. Rooney uses his skills as a racing driver to drive a getaway car in a robbery master-minded by Kevin McCarthy. Pedestrian.

Hot Rod Girl AA 1956 was Lori Nelson trying to persuade youngsters to do their racing on the drag-strips and not in the streets. Pretty tame stuff after reading the come-ons the posters provided. 'See: Teenage terrorists tearing up the streets. See: Raw violence in America's thrill-packed snake-pit for women. See: Speed crazy Rock 'n Roll Rampage.'

Hot Rod Rumble AA 1957 had Richard Hartunian proving that he was innocent of killing a member of his hot-rod gang during a race. The publicity boys could only come up with, "you'll need shock absorbers for this one." Shocking.

Hot Rod Gang AA 1958 (**Fury Unleashed** — GB) entices model teenager John Ashley to join them. With the help of Gene Vincent (as himself), he starts a Rock 'n Roll band, wins a drag race with the super de-luxe hot rod he designed himself.

Speed Crazy AA 1959 told the edifying story of two racing drivers in love with the same girl. It ends happily with one of them stepping aside by plunging himself and his car over a cliff. Brett Halsey, Charles Willcox and Yvonne Lime were the protagonists.

Thunder in Carolina Darlington Films 1960 dealt with the 'Southern 500', a stock car event that attracts 100,000 people every Labor Day to Darlington. S.C. Rory Calhoun deliberately crashes his car to save the life of a former protege. Plenty of footage of the actual race.

Fireball 500 AI 1966 mixed stock-car racing with pop music. Frankie Avalon competes on the track and off with Fabian for the affections of Annette Funicello. Some documentary footage of the various speedways.

Spinout MGM 1966 (**California Holiday** — GB) starred Elvis Presley as a singer and racing driver caught between three girls and his Dusenberg. 'I'll really travel and hit the gravel,' he sings, 'But I'll be back.' He was back for nine more movies of the same type.

Hot Rods to Hell MGM 1967 could have been retitled To Hell with Hot Rods. 74-year-old John Brahm directed ageing stars Dana Andrews and Jeanne Crain as parents terrified by young people with hot rods.

Thunder Alley American International 1967 featured Fabian as a stock car racer who blacks out at the most inconvenient moments, like in the middle of a race. In a Spellbinding moment near the end, he realizes in his sub-conscious mind that as a child he had been boxed in and injured during a go-cart race. Schlock car racing.

Track of Thunder UA 1968 had former Disney kid Tommy Kirk (now Tom) opposing Ray Stricklyn in small-town stock car racing.

The Love Bug Walt Disney 1968 was not about an aphrodisiac, but a cute Volkswagon called Herbie, who is the fastest car in the world if he approves of his driver. He unaccountably approves of dreary Dean Jones as a wreckless racing driver.

The Gang Who Couldn't Shoot Straight MGM 1971 was a hit and miss satire on the Mafia. Hapless gangster, Jerry Orbach, organizes a gala bicycle race using cyclists especially imported from Italy in order to impress the underworld bigwigs. A half-finished track thwarts his plan, but one of the cyclists, gifted con man Robert de Niro, manages to stay in America.

Steelyard Blues WB 1973 starred Donald Sutherland as a Demolition Derby fanatic who dreams of a derby in which he can smash school buses, campers and mobile homes. Peter Boyle takes off Brando in **The Wild One**.

Dirty Mary and Crazy Larry TCF 1975 were Susan George and Peter Fonda. Fonda is a young stock car driver who needs money to advance his racing ambitions. Instead of asking his bank manager for a loan, he robs a bank and, using his skills as a racer, evades the cops in a long chase. A crash course in destructive driving.

Sidecar Racers UI 1975 gave a rare glimpse into the sport of sidecar racing. Not much plot, but plenty of bike action and it all takes place Down Under.

Crash WB 1977 was set in the Phillipines and had good location photography, plus an interminable 1,000 mile race across 'the most difficult terrain ever.' Larry Hagman plays the race promoter who dreams it up. Joe Don Baker and Susan Sarandon win, despite crashes and torrential rain.

SideWinder I. Avco-Embassy 1977 contained a lot of motocross action unimaginatively filmed. Rich bitch Susan Howard takes over undisciplined motocross troupe including Michael Parks and Alex Cord.

Deathsport New World 1978 was a 1000-years-after sequel to **Death Race 2000**. Powerful combat motorcycles called 'Death Machines' are used in a 'sport' that is a substitute for capital punishment. David Carradine and Claudia Jennings battle it out. The reductio ad absurdum of all bike movies.

OLYMPIA!

It was Lenin who realized early in the Russian Revolution that 'of all the arts film is for us the most important,' and Hitler and Goebbels perceived the immense propaganda potential of the 1936 Olympic Games in Berlin and its propagation through the medium of film. Both film and sport have become part of *every* nation's propaganda machine. When Baron de Courbertin first had the idea of a Modern Olympics in 1894, 1500 years after the original Games, he conceived it as a coming together of the youth of the world in friendly competition where differences of class, religion, politics and race would be forgotten. Much high-flown language has since been used about 'the family of man' while at the same time exalting nationalism. *Chariots of Fire* (TCF 1981) manages to have it both ways, and even the Nazi *Olympia* (Olympia Film 1938) pays lip-service to internationalism. Pieties continue to be mouthed about sport bringing people together, while ignoring the passionate chauvinism involved. The Games have not been a substitution for war but a preparation for it.

TV and radio commentators in each country concentrate on and get excited by a competitor from their own nation, making no pretence of wanting the best man to win. It's as futile as the bride wanting the best man to win at a wedding. There are national interests at stake. It is no longer possible, however, to report on a sporting extravaganza such as the Olympic Games as merely a festival of sport or as the living proof of the brotherhood of nations without considering the political environment in which it takes place. It may not be integral to sport but it is a part of the event and its significance must be acknowledged. Politics, commercialism, professionalism, drug abuse, sex abuse and foul play have existed in The Games since its in-

> The most important thing in the Olympic Games is not to win but to take part. Just as the most important thing in life is not the triumph but the struggle.
>
> — BARON PIERRE DE COURBERTIN (1863-1937). Founder of The Modern Olympics.

> Once every 4 years the world goes to war and they call it The Games.
>
> — Blurb on poster for **The Games** (TCF 1970)

ception in 1896. One of America's greatest athletes, the American-Indian, Jim Thorpe, was stripped of the two titles he won at Stockholm in 1912 because he had taken part in some professional baseball matches (vide *Jim Thorpe — All American* WB 1951). In Antwerp 1920, a Czech soccer team walked off the field in protest against the referee's evident bias towards the home team. The British athletes Harold Abrahams and Eric Liddell both had to fight for their beliefs against various forms of prejudice before the Paris Olympics of 1924 (vide *Chariots of Fire*). In 1928 at the Amsterdam Olympics, a protest was launched against the presence of professional soccer players among the teams. The Berlin Olympics of 1936, with the help of Leni Riefenstahl's film *Olympia*, was a shop-window for the Hitler regime. Japan, Germany and Russia were excluded from the London Olympics of 1948. In 1956 at Melbourne, the Hungarian rebellion made itself felt in the water-polo final between Hun-

gary and the Soviet Union and police had to be brought in to stem the bloody battle. (This is not shown in the film of the *Melbourne Olympiad* — 1956.) A Danish cyclist collapsed and died, possibly from the effects of drugs, during the 1960 Rome Olympics. The story of how triple Olympic swimming champion Dawn Fraser was suspended for 10 years for stealing a flag in 1964 in Tokyo is told in detail in *Dawn!* (SAFCOR 1979). In the same Olympics a boxer was suspended for life for assaulting a referee. Sex tests for women were first used at the 1968 Mexican Olympics (not seen in the official film of those Games) and the Palestinian raid at Munich in 1972 is barely touched upon in *Visions of Eight* (1973), while the black power protest is completely ignored in the same film. Perhaps one day an honest, all-embracing documentary or fictional film will be made of this heady and stimulating quadrennial occasion, accepting the fact that, although there is mutual respect among athletes, there is also fear and

hatred of their rivals, natural components of all competition where, contrary to the old Baron's theme song, the important thing is to win and not only to take part.

It may be that the two most memorable Olympics of the twentieth-century (there are only four more) will be the Berlin and Tokyo Games because of the films that were made of them. A great artist can confer immortality on an event. (e.g. Napoleon's invasion of Russia in *War and Peace*, Picasso's *Guernica*, Eisenstein's *Battleship Potemkin* etc.) As literature endures over newspaper articles, so newsreels die the next morning while *Olympia* and the *Tokyo Olympiad* (1965) will keep those Games alive. The official film of the London Olympics of 1948, *The Glory of Sport* (Rank 1948) was straightforward newsreel reporting, an extended Gaumont British News. But, as television became more expert at bringing sport live into people's homes, the scope and purpose of the documentary film, and of sports movies in general had to change. They had to be more structured, contemplative and technically superior to the telecast. Kon Ichikawa, the director of *Tokyo Olympiad*, had color, a fantastic range of lenses and stereophonic sound. Nevertheless, technique was merely a means to an end and the hundred or so cameras looked at the Games with only one eye. But, with all the technical means at the director's command these days, a future Olympic film might come out as *Star Games*.

The documentary or biopic (i.e. *The Bob Mathias Story*, *Chariots of Fire*) dominate this chapter, although athletics has provided social parables in *The Loneliness of the Long Distance Runner* (Br. Lion 1962) and *The Jericho Mile* (ABC Pictures I. 1979), as well as comedy for Buster Keaton and W.C. Fields.

Summer Games

Buster Keaton was such an athletic performer that it was inevitable that he should make comedy in which track and field events play a large part. *College* (UA 1927) was given over almost exclusively to Buster's athletic achievements and misachievements. However, Keaton could never do anything without grace, and when he's being supposedly inept at sports, he performs with as much skill, beauty and timing as the best of sportsmen and he gets laughs. When the plot demands his sudden metamorphosis from bungler to remarkable athlete, this usually implausible act becomes believable. Buster plays Ronald, a book-worm whose speech at his high-school graduation is on the 'Curse of Athletics'. 'The student who wastes his time on athletics rather than study shows his ignorance,' he says in the inter-titles). 'Future generations depend upon brains and not upon jumping the discus or hurling the javelin. What have Ty Ruth or Babe Dempsey done for science?' Naturally, the speech is met with scorn by the students and, presumably, by the movie-theater audience. As his girl-friend Mary (Anne Cornwall) says after the speech, 'Anyone prefers an athlete to a weak-kneed teacher's pet. When you change your mind about athletics then I'll change my mind about you.' The rest of the film consists of Buster's attempts to make her change her mind about him. He neglects his studies in order to take part in sporting activities. His tryout for the track team is a disaster. The comedy comes not from his inadequacies, but from the difference between the serious intensity with which he performs his actions and the minimal results of his efforts. Buster tries to time himself in a sprint. At the same time, two small boys begin to fight beside the track and one chases the other. As Buster runs his fastest, the boys easily overtake him. His attempts at the shot put begin and end with his falling over backwards from the weight of the put. His discus throw knocks the dean's top-hat off and the javelin he hurls lands about 15 feet in front of him. His efforts at the high jump, long jump, pole-vault, hammer and hurdles are all inversely effective. But

later, when Mary cries to him for help on the telephone for she has been locked in her room by Jeff (Harold Goodwin) star-athlete and rival for her affections, Buster is able to perform extraordinary athletic feats in order to rescue her. He springs out of the locker-room window (high jump), sprints along the sidewalk, leaps a tall hedge, jumps a pond (long jump), grabs a pole supporting a clothes line and pole-vaults up to Mary's second-story window. Jeff is up to no good with Mary so Buster hurls a plate at him like a discus, and as Jeff

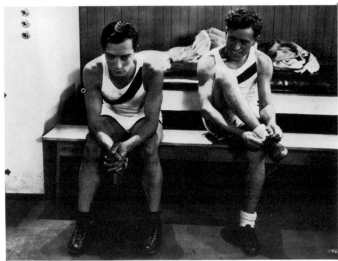

Buster Keaton (left) in *College*

escapes through the window, Buster throws a lamp as a javelin at him. Again as in *Battling Butler* (UA 1924), Buster is able to transcend himself physically when roused but, unlike the earlier movie, this wish-fulfilment fantasy makes a comic point elegantly.

Elegance is not a word that comes to mind when describing the slapdash slapstick sporting antics of Joe E. Brown. In *Local Boy Makes Good* (WB 1931) he is a bookish botanist who is mistaken for the best athlete on the campus. It trod the already well-worn path of the weakling winning a sporting contest he reluctantly finds himself in, because of the passive heroine. Dorothy Lee was the inspiration behind the perspiration.

One of Joseph L. Mankiewicz's first scripts, almost 14 years before he became a director, was a crazy comedy called *Million Dollar Legs* (Par. 1932) starring W.C. Fields as the President of the small country of Klopstokia. 'What this country needs,' pronounces President Fields, 'is money.' Everyone in Klopstokia is a sports ad-

dict. Babies can jump 6 feet and most adults can run the mile in a few seconds. But the country is broke and the cabinet is ready to overthrow the president by feats of strength, when an American brush salesman (Jack Oakie) suggests they enter a team for the forthcoming Olympic Games in Los Angeles. (The Olympics were held in LA in 1932 with 40 countries represented. Klopstokia is not in the record books.) Despite the presence of the spy, Mata Machree (played by Lyda Roberti, cruelly taking off Garbo's Mata Hari of the

same year), Klopstokia brings home gold medals, Fields winning one of them by throwing a 1000 lb weight. Andy Clyde, Ben Turpin and Billy Gilbert add to the madness.

The 1936 Olympic Games in Berlin took place a few months after Hitler's armies reoccupied the Rhineland. Hitler spared no expense in making it the best organized and most efficiently equipped in the history of the Olympics. After *Triumph of the Will* (1935), a documentary of the 1934 Nuremberg Rally, the director Leni Riefenstahl became established as Germany's foremost 'ideological film propagandist'. In 1936 she was commissioned to film the Games 'as a song of praise to the ideals of National Socialism.' The result was a 4-hour documentary *Olympia* (Olympia Film 1938) shown in 2 parts. I. The Festival of Nations, concentrating on the track events in the Olympic Stadium. II. The Festival of Beauty, filmed in the Olympic Village and taking in the other events around the stadium. As there would be no retakes for the great moments,

the filming was meticulously organized before hand. Riefenstahl had over 30 cameramen, planes and airships at her disposal and spent 2 years in the cutting room. She proclaimed 'I wished to undertake a synthesis between the cinema and sport ... I realized that I had to approach the Games from a perspective other than topicality in order to capture not only the events themselves, but also their spirit and form ... I started to observe each sport with the eye of the camera.' A grandiloquent prologue links the ideals of beauty in Greek antiquity with those of the Third Reich. In a 'Summertime for Hitler' parade, the nations file past the Führer. Despite the insistence on Aryan splendor, Riefenstahl could not avoid showing the victories of Jesse Owens, the 'Tan Streak' from Ohio State, who won the 100 and 200 meters and the Long Jump. The German champion Luz Long watches as Owens breaks the Olympic Long Jump record by a foot. Legend has it that Hitler snubbed Owens for having shown up the Nazi philosophy of Aryan supremacy. When Owens returned home to the America of the 30's he said, 'I wasn't invited to shake hands with Hitler. But I wasn't invited to the White House to shake hands with the President either.' A German girl drops a baton in the last lap of the relay and Hitler turning to Goebbels says something. Is he perhaps suggesting that her lack of concentration could be rectified in a concentration camp? The pole vault duel between the Americans and the Japanese continues as day changes to night. The sun setting behind the flame and the flags waving in the glow of light ends Part I. Part II opens in the pastoral setting of the Olympic village away from the clamor of the stadium. There is a lyrical sequence of blond young men swimming and taking a sauna together. They rejoice in their health and strength as future heroes of the coming war. The French title of the film was *Les Dieux du Stade* (The gods of the stadium). 'I teach you superman. Man is something that shall be surpassed', thus spoke Nietzche and 50 years later his prophecy is fulfilled on film. The ideals of the Olympic movement were transferred and corrupted into the ideals of the Nazi movement. It is easy

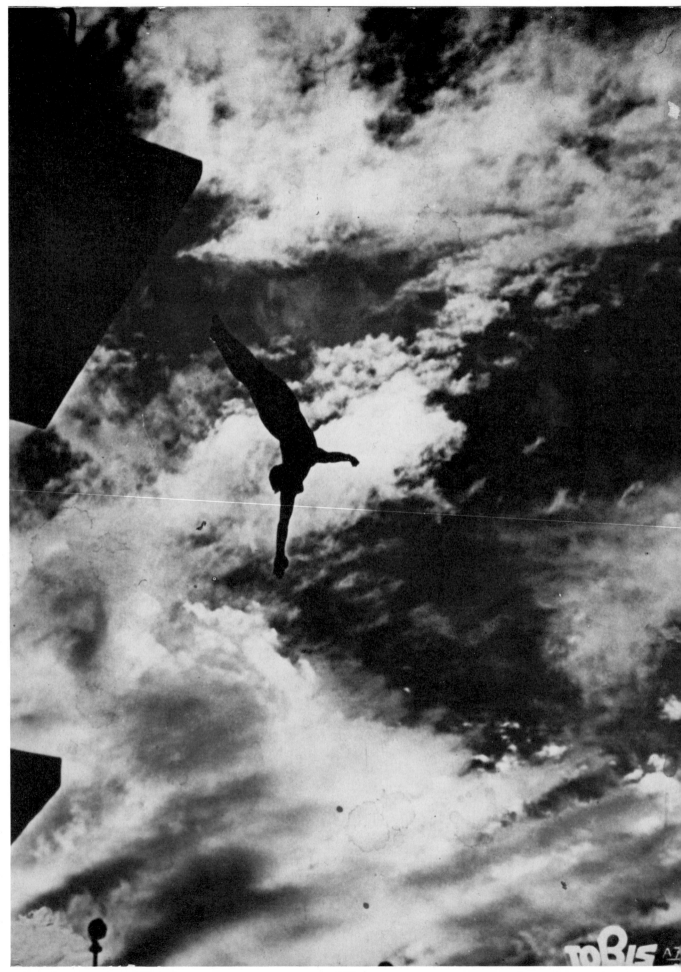

be seduced by the beauty of many of the images of the film into ignoring the sinister significance of the swastikas on the arms of the officials or to forget the persecution of the Jews that was taking place outside the walls of the stadium. The bad taste it leaves in the mouth derives also from much of the grandiose 'bad taste' of Nazi art. However, one cannot be blind to the exceptional technique of the film. Slow and reverse motion make the diving section a 'tour de force', the Marathon 'an epic hymn to endurance and the will to win', the comedy of horses and riders plunging into deep water, the yacht racing at Kiel under a darkened sky, the screen filling with thousands of girls swinging clubs all blend in what many consider to be one of the greatest documentary films ever made.

The winner of both the pentathlon and the decathlon at the 1912 Olympics in Stockholm, an unheard of feat before or since, was Jim Thorpe, although his name was not to be found in the record books. It was revealed that he had played one or two semi-professional baseball games before going to the Olympics and was ordered to return his medals. The story of one of America's greatest all-round athletes is told in *Jim Thorpe - All American* (WB 1951. *Man of Bronze* — GB). Burt Lancaster impersonates the famous American Indian with vigor and a certain pathos. The movie ends with Thorpe, after having turned to drink and unable to hold down a job, watching the 1932 Olympics in LA (See Chapter II.)

One of the biggest surprises of the 1948 London Olympics was the brilliant win in the decathlon of the 17-year-old American Bob Mathias. Both Mathias and his wife Melba play themselves in *The Bob Mathias Story* (AA 1954. *The Flaming Torch* — GB). Young Bob is determined to enter for the Olympic tryouts. Guided by his local high-school coach (Ward Bond) and supported by his parents and girl-friend Melba, he goes into vigorous training and succeeds in qualifying. At the Olympics (newsreel clips alternate with studio shots) he wins the decathlon with 7,139 points beating his nearest rival by 165 points and

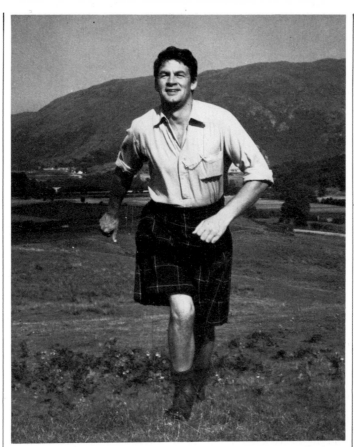

Bill Travers in *Wee Geordie*

returns home a hero. To make up for lost time in his studies, he enters Stanford U. where football seems to be his main preoccupation. After marrying Melba, he's asked to defend his title at the 1952 Games in Helsinki but he declines because he wishes to devote more time to his family. However, his old Bible-quoting coach explains to Bob that he has greater responsibilities to his country. The eloquence of the coach and the music on the sound track convince him and he goes to Finland where he wins the decathlon for the second time, the only athlete ever to accomplish this. Being 1954, in the midst of the First Cold War, the Helsinki Games are conceived in terms of American-Russian rivalry. The film is a simple dramatization of events we know to be true, such as the victories at the two Olympics, and others which we must take on trust. As the real-life protagonist is also the star, one must presume that his parents, coach and wife all behaved as if they were in a minor Hollywood movie. Bob Mathias looks as though he'd rather be doing something more virile than acting.

The Melbourne Olympics provided the climax of *Wee Geordie* (Br. Lion 1956. *Geor-*

die — GB). 'Wee' Geordie is a giant of a man who wins the gold medal in the hammer for Britain, more especially for Scotland. But he wasn't always so herculean. At 12, Geordie, way up in the picturesque and Technicolor Highlands, is small for his age until he sends for a correspondence course in Physical Culture run by a Mr Samson (Francis de Wolff) and they make beautiful muscles together. At Mr Samson's suggestion, Geordie takes up the hammer. After winning the event by a huge margin at the Highland Games, he is visited by the Olympic selectors and asked to represent Britain at the Games in Australia. Geordie, who has never been further than the next parish, doesn't want to leave his bonny Scotland or his braw Jean (Norah Gorson). He is finally persuaded to leave by the local Laird (Alastair Sim). But on board ship to Australia, poor Geordie falls into the clutches of buxom Danish shot putter, Helga (Doris Goddard). After Geordie wins the hammer throw in his Dad's kilt, inspired by Jean shouting into the radio at home, Helga embraces him, an act which is described by the radio commentator. When he returns to his village, he is shunned by the locals despite

the glory he had brought to them, until he explains himself. It's a typically cosy and whimsical product of the British film industry, which doesn't lack charm. Bill Travers as Geordie confuses dullness with naivity. (In the actual Melbourne Olympics, the hammer was won by the American Harold Connolly who fell for the charms of Olga Fikotova, the Czech discus gold medalist and they were married the following year.)

In the late 50's and early 60's, there emerged in England a movement of playwrights, novelists and film makers who were labelled 'angry young men'. Many of their works dealt honestly and vigorously with working-class life, containing an overt criticism of the 'never had it so good' philosophy of the Conservative government of the day. Alan Sillitoe's short story on which the film *The Loneliness of the Long Distance Runner* (Br. Lion 1962) was based, was a tough, concise study of the mind of a rebel, using the metaphor of sports. Colin Smith (Tom Courtney) is sent to reform school (Borstal) for stealing. His factory-worker dad dies of cancer, and his mum blows the insurance money on a telly and a fancy-man. Colin is a good runner and catches the eye of the governor of Borstal (Michael Redgrave). 'My family has been running ever since I can remember and what we have usually been running from is the police,' Smith explains. The governor hopes to enter Smith for the Borstal all-England Prize Cup for Long Distance Cross Country Running. Smith is good enough to win, but as he reaches the winning line, far ahead of his nearest rival, he deliberately and openly throws the race in order to show the governor just what he thinks of him and the system he represents. Unfortunately, Sillitoe's screenplay and Tony Richardson's busy direction try to hit too many targets at once which dissipates the offensive. There is an attack on the consumer society by filming the mother's spending spree in the style of TV commercials. Borstal is likened to a Public School (when they meet in a match, the two sets of boys from different social classes find their schools have much in common) and there is a heavy irony in the constant singing of 'Jerusalem', implying that dirty things are going on despite

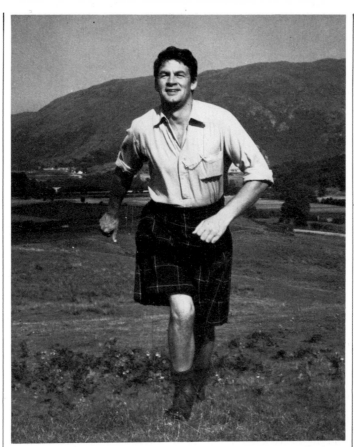

Left: Diving from Leni Riefenstahl's *Olympia*

101

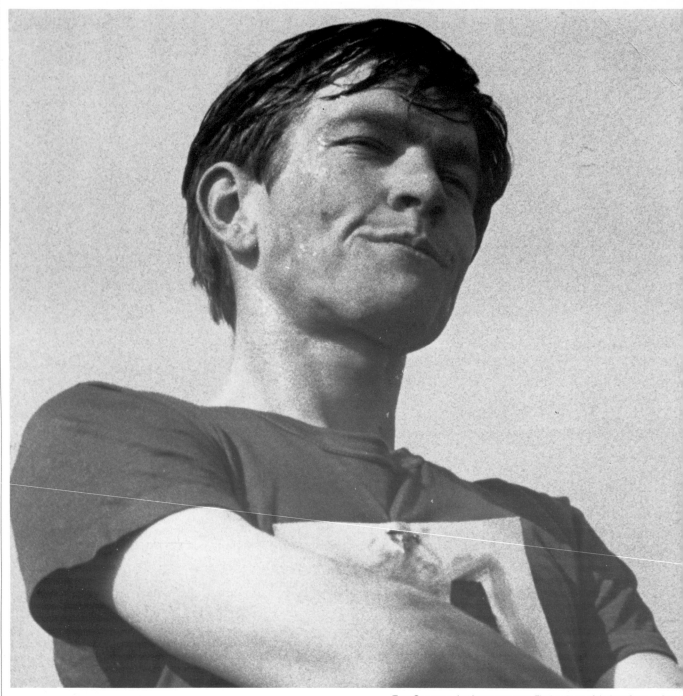

Tom Courtenay decides not to win in *The Loneliness of the Long Distance Runner*

the noble sentiments expressed in the song. (It is used in the same way in *If* (1969) and *Chariots of Fire*.) The big race, the final anti-authoritarian act, is broken up by flash-backs, not so much of Smith's thoughts, but as short reminders to the audience for the motivation behind what he is about to do. Tom Courtney, in his film debut, makes this symbol, this boy named Smith, into a rounded character. Michael Redgrave as the main target of his rebellion, is much too sympathetic in the role of the 'pot-bellied pop-eyed bastard' of the story. Richardson's style is obviously influenced by the

French 'nouvelle vague' directors, particularly Truffaut, but it is much less true than *faux*.

'I have attempted to capture the solemnity of the moment when man defies his limits. And to express the solitude of the man who, to succeed, fights against himself. I have tried to penetrate human nature not through fiction but in the truth of the Games.' This statement of intention made by Kon Ichikawa is justified in his *Tokyo Olympiad* (1965). Not since the Berlin Games had a great film been made of the great event. Most of the other Olympics were made competently by experienced newsreel

teams, but the Japanese producers had the vision to give the 1964 Olympics to one of Japan's leading feature directors. To achieve his aims, Ichikawa employed 164 cameramen who used 232 different lenses. Special viewfinders and exposure meters had to be developed to bring competitors into close close-ups under all conditions and to shoot at night. Above all, the 15 day event involving 6,000 competitors had to be compressed into a 2 hour 10 minute film. The result was a crystalization of Japanese technical wizardry and creative genius. Not much factual information is given,

such as Dawn Frazer winning her third successive gold medal in the 100 metres freestyle or Joe Frazier winning the heavyweight boxing — television and the press were for that, but it does get nearer to the body and soul of the athlete than any previous attempt. Unlike Riefenstahl Ichikawa presents the human rather than the god-like qualities of the participants although they are no less heroic. 'The camera must capture, in all its living reality, the reflection of the skins of colored athletes... the blond child-like hair of a white athlete in the sun... the sharp piercing look from oriental eyes... We must rediscover, almost with surprise, this marvel which is a human being.' He observes the absurd as well as the sublime. There is the Soviet shot putter pulling at his pants, the comical weight-lifters, the different ways in which the marathon runners take their drinks and sponges on the way. The lyrical gymnasts, the intense breathing of a black runner, the look of joy on Ann Packer's features when she realizes she has won the 800 metres, the German-American duel in the pole-vault (won by Fred Hanson), the entry into the stadium of Abebe Bikila, the marathon winner breaking his own record, and the progression of the torch across the Middle East to the Far East, with its arrival in Hiroshima.

Among the people at the Tokyo Olympics according to *Walk, Don't Run* (Col. 1966) were Cary Grant, Samantha Eggar and Jim Hutton. Grant in his last film before retirement) plays an English industrialist in Tokyo on business unable to obtain hotel accommodation and Samantha Eggar is the girl who has an apartment to let. Grant ends up on the divan, but this still enrages Samantha's stuffy English fiancé, John Standing. Also sharing the appartment is gangling Jim Hutton, US entry for the 30 mile walk. Grant plays Cupid between Samantha and Hutton, even to the extent of walking beside Jim during the race to persuade him of her charms. Charles Walters' direction of this light-weight comedy goes at a walking pace. Grant is considered too old at 62 to get the girl, but he's still capable of creating sexual jealousy.

The commercial and political exploitation of athletes is dealt with in a superficial and hammy manner in *The Games* (TCF 1970). Directed by the misnamed Michael Winner and written by Erich Segal (presumably chosen for his jogging rather than literary achievements), it concentrates on 4 men in 4 different parts of the world each preparing for the Olympic Marathon to be held in Rome. Until the final race, the 4 characters never come together so the movie spends most of its 97 minutes jumping from one to another in order to sketch in their backgrounds. First to a small British town where a young milkman (Michael Crawford) is spotted by a fanatical trainer (Stanley Baker). It is implied that the trainer is homosexual, because he glares at any woman that approaches his protegé and seems to get more than job satisfaction from the massage sessions. The milkman becomes the cream of British long distance runners. Will he win the marathon? In New Haven, Connecticut, a Yale undergraduate (Ryan O'Neal) proves to be the top US athlete on the track and in bed. He seems to be one of nature's winners, but will he be one of Winner's winners? In the desert of Australia, two kangaroo hunters see their aborigine mechanic (Athol Compton) running as fast as their truck. They give up looking for kangaroos and decide to enter him for the Olympics for their own profit. Will the noble savage triumph? In Prague, an ageing Czech runner (Charles Aznavour) is pressed by the State to train once again to reach the physical condition that made him the world champion long distance runner. Will the Czech cross the line first? Does it depend on which country you see the movie in? No. In intense heat, the All-American boy, stuffed with drugs and having trained on beer and women, has a heart attack. The brave Briton collapses in the last lap, the dogged Czech comes in second. But, despite being shunned by his white team-mates and feeling homesick down under, the aborigine finishes first thus establishing the film's liberal credentials. In the long run, it's too busy puffing and panting to be able to say very much.

In case anyone wonders why the official film of the 1972 Olympics was called *Visions of Eight* (EMI 1973), it is prefaced by the following: 'Sunflowers are familiar to millions, yet no-one ever saw them the way Van Gogh did. So with the Olympics — a recurring spectacle familiar to people around the world. There is no chronological record, no summary of winners and losers. Rather, it is the seperate visions of 8 singular film artists.' The 8 'singular' film artists were in alphabetical order: Milos Foreman (Czechoslovakia), Kon Ichikawa (Japan), Claude Lelouch (France), Yuri Ozerov

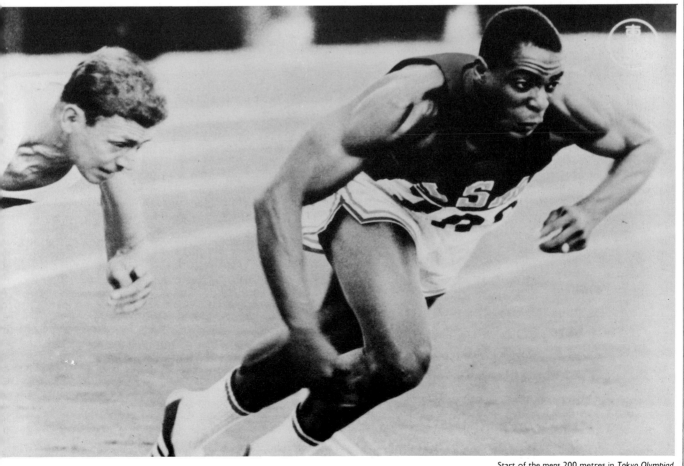

Start of the mens 200 metres in *Tokyo Olympiad*

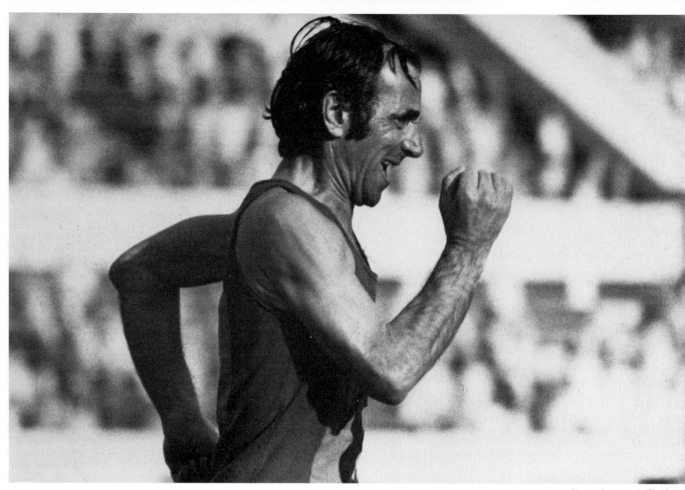

(USSR), Arthur Penn (USA), Michael Pfleghar (W. Germany), John Schlesinger (UK) and Mai Zetterling (Sweden), spoiling the broth. Part of the thinking behind this project was that 8 directors of different nationalities working on one film was somehow symbolic of the internationalism of the sportsmen and women themselves. The result was a mishmash which neither gave statistics nor expressed any of the excitement of the events. Instead we were given a series of arty, tricksy and often spectacular moments created in a vacuum, subtracting the aims from the Games. Franco Zefferelli was to have shot the opening ceremony but dropped out because he thought the Games had become a 'platform for political protest'. Little did he know how much. A squad of Palestinian guerillas invaded the Israeli team headquarters and claimed hostages. The outcome of the whole affair was the killing of eleven members of the Israeli team, five Arabs and a policeman. This is touched upon with a short glimpse of the memorial service for the Israelis and marathon runner Ron Hill's comment that the

tragedy meant 'putting my race a day later'. Ozerov filmed the athletes at the starting line, waiting for Go. 'All are bound by a common fraternity. They carry the flags of hope,' says the commentary. Foreman took on the high jump and the decathlon going in for jokey cross-cutting. Ichikawa concentrated on the 10.14 seconds of the 100 meters final with a very slow-motion repeat that took a minute of the film's time. Lelouch turned his camera on the losers with few psychological revelations. Arthur Penn watched the poetry in slow motion of the pole-vaulters. Pflegar paid homage to the women athletes and spectators. John Schlesinger got some mileage out of the marathon mainly following British marathon man Ron Hill; and Mai Zetterling, claiming not to be interested in sport but obsessions, had the easy and large targets of the weight-lifters to aim her camera at. The film was produced by Stan Margulies and David L. Wolper with the best intentions.

While Merrivale College athletics coach John Amos and his oafish assistant Tim Con-

way are on safari somewhere in Zambia, they come across *The World's Greatest Athlete* (Disney 1973). He is a long-haired blond youth in a loincloth racing a cheetah and passing it. They realize what a shot in the arm Nanu (Jan-Michael Vincent) would be for Merrivale's ailing sports teams. They persuade him to leave his jungle gym and come to America. He arrives at the college with his pet tiger Harry, and promptly wins the 100 yard dash in 8 seconds flat. He inevitably meets a girl called Jane in order to get in the line, 'Me Nanu, you Jane,' and there are a lot of double-takes with Tiger Harry dressed as a student. At the NCAA Track and Field Competition, Nanu is Merrivale's only athlete for all events. But his witch-doctor god-father (Roscoe Lee Brown) arrives from Africa and, with the help of the Disney studios special effects department, makes him fly backwards and reverses a javelin in flight. However, Nanu manages to win through in the end, but he goes back to Africa a sadder and wiser jungle boy. Lion County Safari Park south of Disneyland doubled for Zam-

bia. Of Jan-Michael Vincent's performance, Variety said it was 'beefcake and little else' but a teenage girl correspondent taking a newspaper critic to task for his slighting comments on Vincent's performance deserves the last word 'It was not only his dreamy person that turned me on, but his mysterious, great acting.'

The gold medalist of the women's 100 meter freestyle at Melbourne in 1956, Rome in 1960 and Tokyo in 1964 was the remarkable Australian swimmer Dawn Fraser, 'the human fish'. Her story up to the age of 42 is told in a movie simply entitled *Dawn!* (SAFCOR 1979, and she certainly merits that exclamation mark. Although it was made with the assistance of Dawn herself, it is no hackneyed eulogy, but an extremely honest and often moving look at a high-spirited non-conformist girl who was one of the world's greatest women swimmers. It was high-spirits and rebelliousness that lead to her downfall in the extremely conservative world of international sport. She was a girl who made waves. Dawn is played brilliantly by an extraordinary giant of a girl called Bronwyn

Mackay-Payne. Brought up in a working-class suburb of Sydney without much schooling, Dawn is discovered at the age of 15 by a swimming coach when he sees her beat a group of boys he was training and he asks her to join the squad. A little boy tells her, 'My mum says you're a boy, but I told her you were a girl 'cos I've seen your tits.' She wins her first gold medal at the age of 19. Her father dies and she's arrested for speeding and swearing. Her mother is killed in an accident in a car Dawn was driving. At the Tokyo Olympics, she 'souvenired' a flag from the Emperor's palace for a lark, but the Australian Swimming Association didn't see the joke and banned her for 10 years from competitive swimming. Her marriage breaks up and she enters a relationship with a woman. None of this is told mawkishly or coyly, and there is a great deal of humor in the film directed by Ken Hannan. Even such cliches as 'getting there's easy, it's staying there that's tough,' have meaning in this context and are counterbalanced by Dawn Fraser's frank admission that 'sex just before the race gave me the edge on the other girls.'

'Running feels good, like a love affair. It is like a relationship — you get out of it, what you put into it,' says Michael Douglas in *Running* (Buena Vista 1979). Douglas plays a 32-year-old marathon runner who has lost his job, his wife (Susan Anspach) and his credibility. 10 years earlier he failed to turn up for a big race at the Pan-American Games and now it is his last chance to prove something to himself in the Olympic Marathon. In the risible ending, he staggers home despite frightful injuries in an effort to show he still has guts. It ends on a freeze-frame of Douglas with his wife within shot. There was always an element of pretentiousness in Kirk Douglas' performances, but it was tempered with a dynamic personality. His son, Michael, has inherited one side of his father's personality without the other. Directed by Steven Hilliard Stern, the characters would be at home in a Doonesbury strip.

The title of the made-for-TV movie *The Jericho Mile* (distributed in theaters by ABC Pictures International 1979) symbolizes the use a prisoner makes of his track ability to break down the walls of the prison. Rain Murphy (Peter Strauss), a lifer, runs the mile on a self-made track in slightly over four minutes. He is trained by a coach from the local university and soon turns in a sub four-minute mile. A loner of a long-distance runner, his only friend is a black named O.C. Stiles (Richard Lawson). This creates racial tension in the prison and only the blacks and chicanos help build a track for him to train on. He goes outside to compete in a race that could qualify him for the Olympics. He beats the 3 minute 50.6 mile, but refuses to go to the Olympics, because he will leave prison only to return to it. Directed forcefully by Michael Mann and shot in Folsom Penitentiary with real inmates playing roles, it manages to side-step many of the cliches of prison drama even though certain issues are resolved a little easily.

The revolutionary sentiments expressed in the poem by William Blake from which *Chariots of Fire* (TCF 1981) takes its title (Bring me my Spear: O clouds unfold! Bring me my Chariot of fire' — Preface to Milton) are reduced to a mild jibe at the English Establishment. Shown at the Royal Command Performance of 1981, it became an immediate box-office smash in Britain. It is a classic English tale told in classic English terms, containing a nostalgia for Empire and ending with a whopping great dose of good old-fashioned patriotism. A romantic glow, familiar from BBC television's Edwardian sagas, surrounds the film. A young aristocrat jumps hurdles while picking up a glass of champagne from each hurdle without spilling it. The story tells of how Harold Abrahams and Eric Liddell managed to overcome a series of figurative hurdles to win the 100 and 400 meters respectively for Britain at the 1924 Paris Olympics. Abrahams had to fight against anti-semitism and snobbery at Oxford, and Liddell had to persuade the powers that be (including a smoothie Prince of Wales) that his strict Scottish Presbyterianism would not allow him to run on a Sunday as God comes before King and country. 'I believe God made me for a purpose,' he explains. 'He

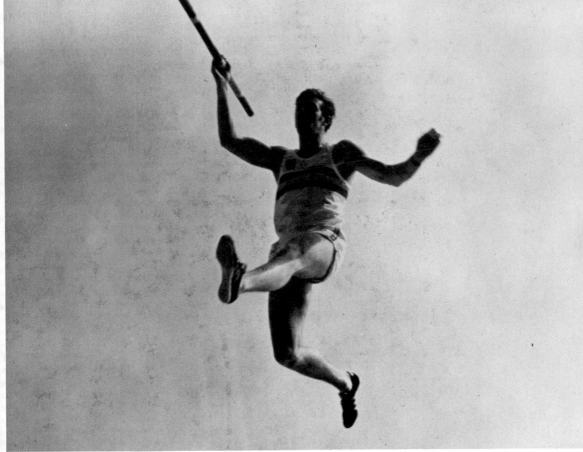

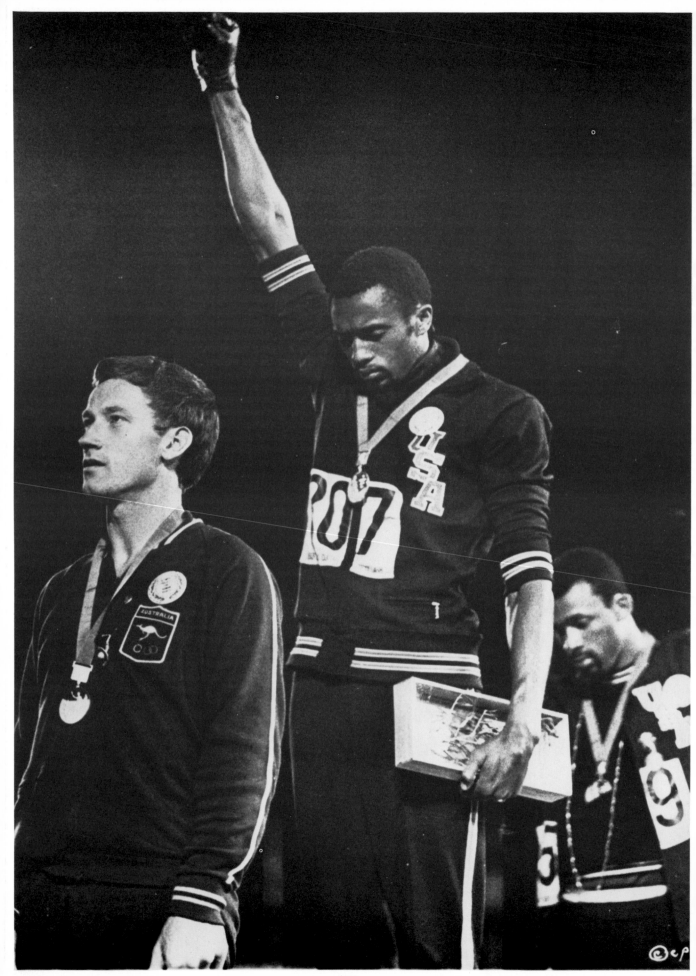

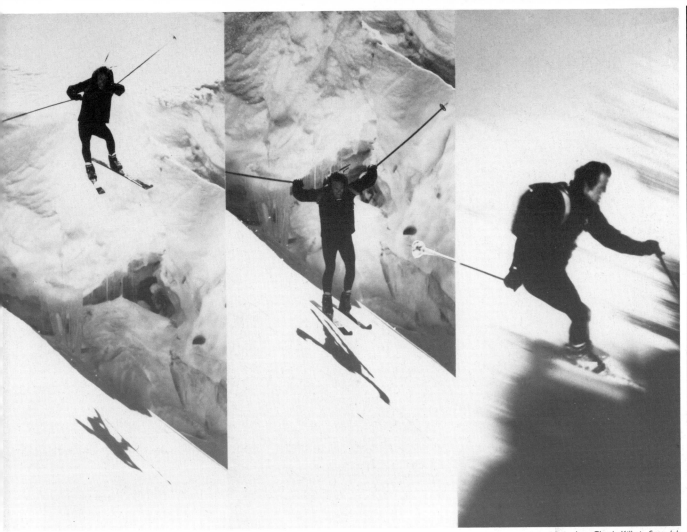

Jean-Claude Killy in *Snow Job*

made me fast. To win is to honor God' but never on a Sunday. The contrast and similarities between the Jew and the Scot are well delineated by the acting and by Colin Welland's terse script. John Gielgud and Lindsay Anderson play the reactionary Oxford Masters as if they had a stench under their noses. The film opens with runners in white vests and long white shorts cantering along a beach like white horses and ends with the Olympic victories. The structural problem of the film, having to build to a climax of two races instead of one, is solved cannily by editing them in different ways, in different time sequences using slow-motion juxtaposed with normal speed. The director, Hugh Hudson, pulls out all the devices of manipulative cinema for the final sporting triumph so that even American audiences would find it difficult not to be conditioned into wanting the British

Left: Black Power salutes on the winners rostrum in *The Olympics in Mexico*

to beat their American adversaries, Jackson Schultz and Charles H. Paddock. Nonetheless, running has seldom looked so exhilarating on film and the slogan could have been, 'You'll believe a man can fly.' A pre-condition of getting the parts in the film was actually to be able to run fast so that there would be no cutting from a face to someone else's body. Both Ben Cross (Abrahams) and Ian Charleton (Liddell) are totally convincing in their roles. So convincing was Cross that Liddell's widow came up to the actor after the preview and told him how much her husband used to talk about him.

Winter Games

The Winter Olympics, established in 1924, is more circumscribed in global terms than the Summer Olympics, mainly because of geographical considerations. There have been two technically brilliant documentaries on the Games, *13 Days in France* on Grenoble 1968 and *White Rock*

on Innsbruck 1976, one major feature on skiing, *Downhill Racer* (1969) and one on ice-hockey, *Slap-Shot* (1977). Ice skating increased in popularity in the thirties because of the three-times Olympic figure skating champion Sonja Henie's ice musicals. The image of skiing and skiing resorts in the movies has given the expression 'high life' a new meaning. The 'beautiful' people are as necessary to a ski resort as snow. International thieves and their pursuers all handle themselves well on the slopes. Gentleman jewel thief, David Niven, is first seen on skis in *The Pink Panther* (UA 1963) and James Bond is as fast down a slope as he is with women. The great moment in Hitchcock's *Spellbound* (UA 1945) is Gregory Peck's realization while skiing, as to why he goes crazy every time he sees black lines on a white surface.

Ice-hockey, although an extremely popular spectator sport in North America, has seldom been the subject of a feature film. Ryan O'Neal

played it in *Love Story* (1970), and *Slap-Shot* (1977) did nothing to damage its reputation for being a virile, if not dirty, contact sport, but before then a puck had rarely been struck on screen. No wonder if *King of Hockey* (WB 1936 *King of the Ice Rink* — GB) is anything to go by. A bit of hockey hokum about how an unpopular player (Dick Purcell) is punched in the eye by a team-mate (Wayne Morris) which damages an optic nerve, thus keeping him out of the team. He is saved from degradation by his girl-friend (Anne Nagel) and sister (Ann Gilles) who scrape up enough money for an eye operation. He comes back onto the ice a nicer man.

Idol of the Crowds (UI 1937) was marginally better, mainly because of star-in-embryo, John Wayne. Interrupting his appearances in a string of cheap westerns, Wayne plays a hick hockey player who agrees to join the New York Panthers for 100 dollars a week in order to help his chicken farm. He soon proves himself their star

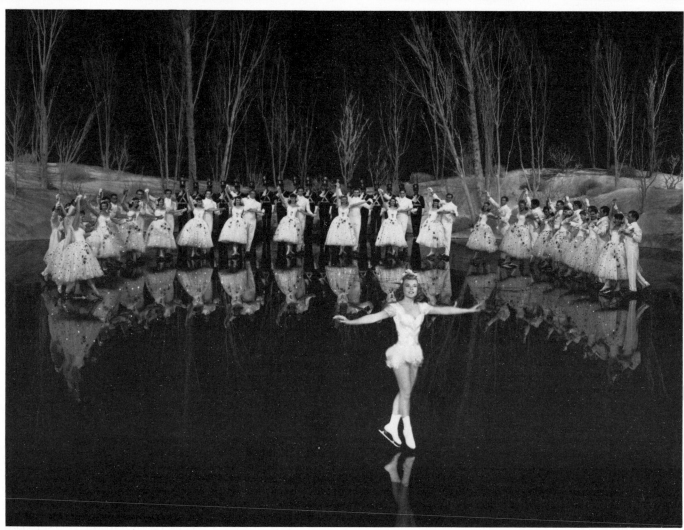

Sonja Henie in *Sun Valley Serenade*

player and meets a pretty roller-skater (Sheila Brady), who has been paid by a gangster to put him off his game. He's also offered a considerable sum to throw a match. Wayne refuses, of course, and saves the game in the last period. He goes back to his chicken farm in the end, exchanging pucks for clucks.

Norway's Sonja Henie began skating at 8, she was her country's champion at 14 and won her first gold medal at the age of 16 at the Olympics at St Moritz in 1928. She also won gold medals at the 1932 Games at Lake Placid and at Garmisch in 1936. Darryl F. Zanuck, head of Twentieth Century Fox, offered her 75,000 dollars to make her screen debut in *One in a Million* (1937). She went on to skate through another 7 pictures for the studio and became one of their top moneymakers. Most of them were sugar-coated thin ice-musicals which suited her uncomplex and wholesome personality. In her first movie, she plays a skater being trained for the

Olympics by her Swiss innkeeper father (Jean Hersholt). Don Ameche wins her heart. Roy del Ruth directed. In *Thin Ice* (1937) she's a skating instructress at a large Swiss hotel. Tyrone Power, as a Prince disguised as a newspaperman, wins her heart. Sidney Lanfield directed. Sonja Henie shifts from heel bandleader Cesar Romero to pilot Don Ameche in *Happy Landing* (1938) in which there are several ballet-on-ice sequences. Roy del Ruth directed this and also *My Lucky Star* (1938) which finds Sonja working in a department store, but when the boss's son (Cesar Romero) discovers what an incredible skater she is, he sends her to a sports-minded college. The finale, 'Alice in Wonderland Ice Ballet', takes place in the store. *Second Fiddle* (1939) started as an amusing satire on Hollywood and ended as something to satirize. Tyrone Power is her beau and Sidney Lanfield directed. *Sun Valley Serenade* (1941) had a slightly different formula. It featured

Glenn Miller and his orchestra playing some of his greatest hits. The climax was a ballet on black ice performed by Henie and company. On the last day of shooting, Henie fell and got covered in black dye. Instead of reshooting, the film cuts away just before the fall to her and boy-friend, John Payne, skiing down a Sun Valley slope. It was directed by H. Bruce Humberstone. *Iceland* (1942 — *Katina* — GB) had her falling for John Payne again. This time there was a little icing but no cake and the sequence of 8 movies in 7 years ended with *Wintertime* (1943) in which Sonja plays a Norwegian skating star who saves a winter resort from ruin. Nothing could save the film, however, and Henie hung up her skates for 5 years before appearing in her last American movie, *The Countess of Monte Cristo* (UI 1948). Although there were 6 skating numbers, it was a puerile period piece and her least successful picture. Sonja Henie, perhaps the most famous figure skater ever, died in 1969 of leukemia.

The Winter Olympics in Grenoble was filmed as *Thirteen Days in France* (1968 *Treize Jours en France*) by directors Claude LeLouch and Francois Reichenbach. Although much of it has the look of a Martini or toothpaste ad, there is a lot of virtuoso camerawork in this mostly impressionistic view of the Games. Both the film and the Games were dominated by Jean-Claude Killy, who won three gold medals — the downhill, the slalom and the giant slalom. General de Gaulle makes a haughty cameo appearance.

An American has never won a gold medal in the downhill event at the Winter Olympics, at least, not until Robert Redford in *Downhill Racer* (Par. 1969). Redford, just breaking into super-stardom, gives one of his cool, self-centered, cynical performances that made him seem perfect casting for *The Great Gatsby* (1974). Michael Ritchie, whose first

Right: Robert Redford in *Downhill Racer*

108

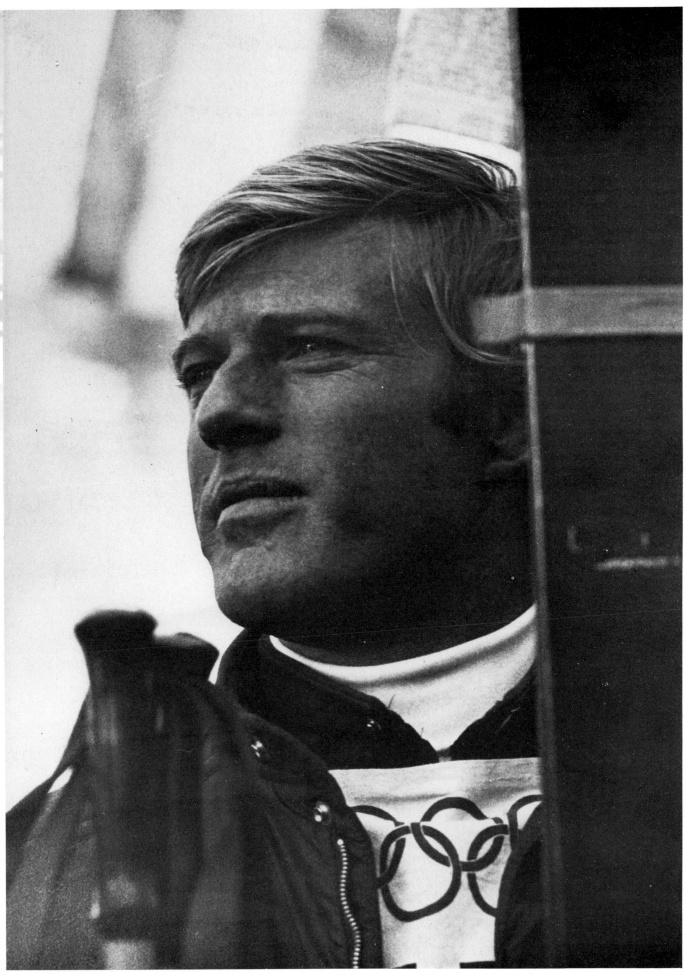

film as director this is, has some of the same characteristics in his direction as his star. The movie claims to be 'the first American feature to tackle the subject of ski-racing,' and by using a semi-documentary style, mixing 16 mm with 35 mm, it gives a rare insight into the sport. Redford plays a tough, undisciplined skier from Colorado who is called to Europe as a replacement on the American team when one of their members is injured. He's very soon at odds with the team's coach (Gene Hackman) and other members of the team. Given 88th starting position for his first race, he refuses to go, protesting that it would be impossible to win because the slopes will be rutted by runs made by the preceding skiers. But the next time he is started at 79, he finishes 4th and is hailed as one of America's hopes. In Kitzbuhel he fails and the coach tells him, 'It takes more than a sudden urge to beat the Europeans. It's their whole life we're trying to beat them out of.' Season follows season on

the ski circuit and finally it's the Olympics. To win is everything, to come second is nothing. Redford wins and he savors his moment of glory. The scenarist, James Salter, has written a laconic script sometimes bordering on the sententious. There are too many obvious pointers to Redford's character. In a bleak scene, he tries to explain to his father his obsession with skiing. The father hardly looks at him. Unlike his team-mates, Redford hasn't a university background which the coach throws in his face. 'You never had any education, did you? All you ever had were your skis — and that's not enough.' Underneath his cock-sureness, he has a heart of gold not only a gold-medal heart. However, it is during the downhill races that interest mounts. There was no studio filming, no back-projection. Joe Jay Jalbert, a racer from Seattle, filmed most of the shots of flying skis at speeds of 60-80 mph while holding a 151 lb camera.

There is also some terrific photography of a skier in flight

in *Snow Job* (WB 1972), the skier being the incomparable Jean-Claude Killy. The sexual pun of the title refers, in fact, to a heist carried out on skis and a snowmobile. 'You need the brains of a Yak to go hunting for robbers in this weather,' says detective Vittorio de Sica. The script might have been written by a Yak, and if Killy skied as well as he acted, he'd be dead by now. The rest of the cast consists of beautiful rich women and handsome ski-instructors. But there is plenty of footage showing off Killy's skiing skills. After the heist, he does an invigorating dance of joy on skies seen from a helicopter. The opening aerial shot of snow, sky and a lone skier, a miniscule figure, skiing nearer and nearer the camera is almost worth the price of a seat. The end titles state that 'All of Jean-Claude Killy's skiing was done by himself.' So was his acting, alas.

'This is a true story' begins *The Other Side of the Mountain* Part I. (UI 1975. *A Window to the Sky* — GB) which only goes to prove the saying that

'Life is a bad movie.' Yet, though it is directed with self-conscious sentimentality by Larry Peerce like an emcee holding up a sign to an audience 'Cry!', the facts of the story and the acting are moving enough to please Kleenex and Co. Jill Kinmont (Marilyn Hassett) of Bishop, California was an up-and-coming woman skier in the early 50's. In 1954, she won both the national junior and women's slalom and was tipped to go to the 1956 Olympics at Cortina. But, at the age of 18, she had a tragic accident during the Snow Cup race in January 1955. Her neck was broken, her spinal chord damaged, leaving her totally paralyzed from the neck down. The rest of the movie is taken up with the morally uplifting process of rehabilitation. Jill meets another skier, 'Mad Dog' Buek (Beau Bridges) who helps her and asks her to marry him. His proposal is greeted with the obligatory speech about pity, but she finally agrees. Hurrying to be by her side, he's killed in an aircrash. This disaster movie ends on the kind of hope

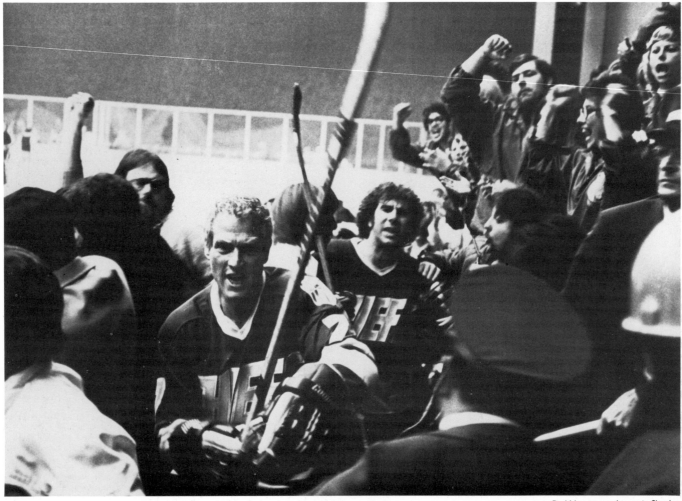

Paul Newman and team in *Slapshot*

hat can only come from a cock-eyed optimist.

The official film of the 12th Winter Olympics at Innsbruck, *White Rock* (Worldmok-Samuelson 1976), was so dominated by the musical score of Rick Wakeman, featuring the drummer Tony Fernandez and the Choir of St Paul's Cathedral, that it is surprising there was no avalanche. When the music stops momentarily, James Coburn intones on the sound-track things like 'Yours is not a jump for glory. It's a jump for joy,' or he's popping up on screen all over the place acting as mine host. He has enough skill in winter sports to try out a few events such as the two-man bob or an ice-hockey match, although he leaves the downhill to Klammer. Coburn is the representative of the ordinary man on the slope and one is tempted to toss a snow-ball at him in order to let the champions get on with it. Only 6 events are covered by some breathtaking photography. Cameras were nailed to skis or held by skiers as they hurtled down the slopes or down the ski jump.

Slap-Shot (UI 1977) expounds the principle of 'Speak dirty and carry a big stick.' The stick is a hockey stick or, more appropriately in this context, a slap-stick. Paul Newman is the coach of a demoralized minor-league hockey team called the Charleston Chiefs about to be sold off. The macho men booze, gamble and philander, while their wives do the same out of boredom. Newman decides that the only way they can get back a following is to play dirty. All their pent-up frustration explodes on the ice as they slam into their opponents. Three bespectacled brothers enjoy breaking rules and bones with the most relish. Only the one college-educated member (Michael Ontkean) of the team resists. Naturally the Chiefs become league champions. The sardonic message of the movie is clear. The public doesn't want to see skill in sport but violence presented with showmanship which is exactly what the movie does, and a very enjoyable hymn to vulgarity, brutality and obscenity it is. Unfortunately, there is always a little angel that sits on one shoulder of a Hollywood director, making sure the little devil on his other shoulder doesn't have it all his own way. The little angel tells George Roy Hill to make sure the audience

understands that, although it seemed as if the director admired these sporting oafs by making us laugh with them, for instance when they stick their asses out of the bus windows at hecklers or when they maim their opponents, their behavior is not condoned in the end. Newman must tell his team to go out and play 'old-time hockey' and the one good guy must show that he has been corrupted by their values by doing a strip-tease on the ice during a farcical game. Like the film, however, he retains his jock-strap. It bares almost all until it gets cold feet. Nancy Dowd, who wrote the earthy script, seems to have spent some time in men's locker-rooms, although her brother, Ned Dowd, a Johnstown Jet, served as technical advisor on the picture. Paul Newman is too intelligent an actor not to be able to act dumb, but this character of an ageing infantile jock eludes him.

The Other Side of the Mountain Part 2 (UI 1978) shows the same side as the other *Other Side*. Jill Kinmont (still played by Marilyn Hassett in a wheelchair) strives to be accepted as a person and relives Part 1. i.e. her skiing triumphs, her accident, her recovery. She is named 'Woman of the Year' and takes a vacation. She meets and falls in love with a long-haul trucker, played by a miscast Timothy Bottoms. Jill Kinmont now teaches remedial reading at a school in Beverly Hills which is very convenient in case Universal studios need her as technical advisor for a third dose.

Another box-office winner in the disability stakes was *Ice Castles* (Col. 1979). This is the story of a young girl from a small mid-western town who, just as she is about to realize her ambition of representing the USA in the figure skating at the Olympics, goes almost totally blind in an accident. The inspiration to triumph over this obstacle comes from the love of a young hockey player. She regains her sight and skills. It's not as maudlin as it sounds, mainly because Donald Wrye's direction keeps it cool and Lynn-Holly Johnson and Robby Benson are likeable in the leads. 19-year-old Lynn-Holly was the 1974 Novice Free Style Champion of the USA and later appeared as an ice-skater in the James Bond movie, *For Your Eyes Only* (1981).

OTHER FUN AND GAMES MOVIES

Charlie Chan at the Olympics TCF 1937, the Berlin Olympics that is, where his number one son, Sam Lee, is on the US swimming team and wins the 100 meters. Warner Oland as Chan also has time to solve a crime.

Feudin', Fussin' and A-Fightin' U 1948 was not, despite its title, about the International Olympic Committee, but a minor musi-comedy starring Donald O'Connor. Donald plays a fleet-footed traveling hair-tonic salesman who is coerced into running for the village of Rimrock in the annual cross-country race against the rival town of Big Bend. As the mayor of Rimrock is crow-voiced Marjorie Main, he can hardly refuse. As well as winning the race, Donald dances through two tap numbers.

High Time TCF 1960 has 57-year-old millionaire Bing Crosby, realizing that his education had been sadly neglected through the pursuit of riches, deciding to enrol at college. (See **Mr Belvedere Goes to College** — TCF 1949 — for the same weak joke.) The curriculum includes gymnastics, but Bing breaks the school record on the parallel bars. Other embarrassing things for Bing and the audience are his efforts on the track and his appearance as a Southern Belle at a local ball. It ends with the homily, 'Age is not a matter of years.' Fabian, Richard Beymer and Tuesday Weld are other students. Blake Edwards directed.

Billie UA 1965 is a tomboyish teenager who can run faster, jump higher, and throw further than any of the boys on the Harding High School athletic team. This embarrasses her father (Jim Backus) who is running for mayor on a 'male supremacy' platform. Billie's success on the athletic field is a result of a subconscious 'beat' in her brain. She teaches the 'beat' to her boy-friend (Warren Berlinger) with the result that he outshines all the other boys but still takes second place to Billie in all the events she enters. He is a male chauvinist prig and asks her to leave the team. Billie (Patty Duke) and the movie resist for a while, but finally give in to male brow-beating. The director was Don Weis.

Animalympics Lisberger 1980 was a feeble cartoon feature written and directed by Steve Lisberger in the year of the Moscow Olympics. The coverage of the Games by Channel ZOO includes pole-vaulting alligators and bob-sleighing squids.

Other Winter Sports Movies

Ice-Follies of 1939 MGM consisted of a series of lavish skating sequences (in Technicolor) performed by the International Ice Follies. The tiresome plot told of small-time skater, James Stewart, becoming a Hollywood producer, and marrying actress Joan Crawford.

Ski-Patrol UI 1940 starts with the Olympic Games ski marathon at Garmisch in 1936. Philip Dorn is the champion who later becomes a war hero in the ski-patrol facing his former skiing rival on the opposite side. War (and the picture) is Hell.

Ice Capades Republic 1941 featured skating stars Belita and Vera Hruba Ralston in a story of a newsreel cameraman (James Ellison) who, after ruining his film at Lake Placid, fakes another at Central Park pond.

Two-faced Woman MGM 1941 was Greta Garbo in her very last film. She retired after this flop at the age of 36 never to show either of her faces again. While on holiday at a winter sports resort, Melvyn Douglas, a New York publisher, falls in love and marries wholesome, idealistic Garbo, his ski instructress. Their honeymoon is short-lived, however, as he has to return to New York and his old flame, Constance Bennett. Garbo follows him to New York, pretending to be her own twin sister. Douglas falls for her, decides to divorce his wife and marry 'her sister.' Garbo is miscast in both roles but GARBO SKIES!

Ice-Capades Revue Republic 1942 (**Rhythm Hits the Ice** — GB) contained several dazzling skating sequences, performed by top class show skaters including Vera Hruba Ralston, the former Czech skating champion who was married to Herbert Yates, head of Republic studios.

Hit the Ice UI 1943 was exactly what the public expected from Abbott and Costello. They play press photographers mistaken for gangsters and ending up at a winter resort. There is a lot of falling about on ice and in the snow.

Silver Skates Monogram 1943 belonged to Belita, ice star of a routine ice revue.

Lake Placid Serenade Republic 1944 allowed Vera Hruba Ralston to do her bit on the ice, thankfully interrupting the boring boy-meets-girl screenplay.

Lady Let's Dance Monogram 1944 was a showcase for the skating talents of Belita in five full-scale production numbers staged by Dave Gould.

Ski-Party American International 1965 had college students Frankie Avalon and Dwayne Hickman joining a ski party although they've never skied before. They masquerade as girls and join the ladies ski lessons. Set in Sun Valley, it's the pits.

Winter-A-Go-Go Col. 1965 has a ski-lodge full of young people with snowman's brains trying to save the lodge from being closed down. Unhappily, they succeed.

The Double Man WB 1967 is set in the picturesque Voralberg in the Austrian Tyrol with its cable-cars and ski-lifts. Yul Brynner plays a CIA man and his double in this ski-run-of-the-mill espionage story. Britt Ekland was the girl in the case.

Ski-Fever 1969 stars Dean Martin's daughter Claudia Martin at a ski resort in Austria with Martin Milner as a ski instructor.

Last of the Ski-Bums UI 1969 is only for ski freaks. The movie follows three members of the ski-bum fraternity around the Alps. They relive past adventures in the US and New Zealand and learn new techniques. There's a lot of footage of fine skiing and bad acting. The three bums are Ron Funk, Mike Zuettel and Ed Ricks.

Ski Bum 1971, unfortunately, does not take the title of the previous picture seriously. Based on a Romain Gary novel, it tells of a young skier's non-commitment to life and finds he has nowhere to go but down. Zalman King and Charlotte Rampling ski through this drek.

Snowball Express Disney 1972 takes place in the Rockies where Dean Jones tries to convert a hotel into a ski-lodge. There's a lot of knockabout on skis, a snowmobile race and a St Bernard called Stoutheart. Adults in the audience will need rescuing with brandy.

Paperback Hero Agincourt Prod. 1973 takes us from a soft-corn movie (above) to a hard-corn movie. Keir Dullea plays a hockey hero in Delisle, Saskatuan. (pop. 700). He plays a fierce but mediocre game and he's the key man of the team. Dubbed 'the marshall', he likes to dress up in cowboy gear in his spare time and shoot at targets. He wants to prove that a man with a gun still stands for something in the West. It's a movie that's not only about a Walter Mitty, it seems to have been made by one.

The Man Who Skied Down Everest Ishihara 1976 was Japanese skier, Yuichiro Miura. This is the documentary record of the 1970 expedition to Mt. Everest which culminated in Miura's bid to ski down part of the mountain's upper slopes. He covered 6,600 feet, but his attempt was considered partly as a fall. During the expedition 6 Sherpa porters died in an ice fall. The first 80 minutes of the film is a travelogue, whereas the *raison d'être* of the whole enterprise takes only 2 minutes 20 seconds. It was filmed in a single take and is projected twice. First in silence and then with the man describing what it felt like. It won the Oscar for the Best Documentary of 1976, which tells you something about the film or the Oscars.

Anyone for...
TENNIS? GOLF? SOCCER? RUGBY? CRICKET?

British sports, such as cricket and rugby, hardly figure in the film lists, because of the predominance of American movies. Tennis and golf are as international as any sport, but their origins are very British, as in the cry, 'Anyone for Tennis?' or 'Tennis, anyone?' (the latter phrase is actually attributed to Humphrey Bogart.) Film makers have barely bothered to answer that question. Few countries play the American sports of baseball and football, whereas soccer is the dominant sport in almost every country in the world except the USA. Interest in soccer picked up a little in 1975 when Brazilian ace Pele joined the New York Cosmos. Pele visited Nixon in the White House and was even on the Johnny Carson Show. There must be something besides balls in the air, when an American film company is prepared to put money into a big production such as *Escape to Victory* (Lorimar 1981), in which Pele is co-starred with Sylvester Stallone and Michael Caine. Cricket's only tentative appearance in the USA was the team set up in Hollywood in the thirties by such English exiles as Sir C. Aubrey Smith, Ronald Coleman and David Niven, but it's too slow a sport for Americans. Soccer and rugby too are slower than football or basketball. In football one is allowed only 4 plays in which to advance the ball 10 yards. In basketball a team has to attempt a shot within 24 seconds of getting the ball. In baseball the pitcher is allowed only 3 inaccurate pitches and the batter faces a maximum of 5 balls before he's out or moves. Compare that to cricket where no runs need be scored from any number of balls. As Eartha Kitt used to sing, 'An Englishman needs time'. Cricket, like chess, is a game for the contemplative, something not easily transferable to the screen. It appears more often as a necessary adjunct to

the creation of an English atmosphere, (e.g. *Accident*).

Although the US championship and the Wimbledon fortnight attract vast TV audiences, tennis does not immediately spring to mind as a sport particularly suited to the big screen. There's not much a director can do with all that toing and froing, like a domestic argument in a cheap movie with the camera merely panning from one character to the other. Hitchcock used this very problem to his advantage in *Strangers on a Train* (WB 1951). Ida Lupino's *Hard, Fast and Beautiful* (RKO 1951) purports to be an exposé of the corruption behind amateur tennis (it was made in the days before the big open championships), but could easily have been a back-stage musical with a stage mother instead of a tennis one and production

numbers in place of the tennis matches. *Players* (Par. 1979) makes good use of Pancho Gonzales as a trainer, but, inevitably, a five-setter has to be reduced to about 10 minutes, intercut with frequent shots of the spectators (among them some well-known faces to make it more interesting). Neither does tennis lend itself to comedy, (witness the witless game in *California Suite* — Col. 1978), although Jacques Tati's M. Hulot could make a game of checkers seem hilarious.

Golf, however, in intrinsically much funnier than tennis, just as certain place names are more amusing than others. P.G. Wodehouse's golf stories fill a couple of volumes, while W.C. Fields' golf act turned up in at least three movies. John McEnroe might smash a racket in a temper on the tennis court, but such exhibitions are not

the done thing. Golfers, however, are expected to lose their tempers on the golf course. Perhaps it is because the anger is directed against themselves and not against an umpire or referee. The character of the golfer is perfectly embodied by Donald Duck in *Donald's Golf Game*, a Disney cartoon of the forties. Irascible Donald, in a golf cap and his habitual sailor suit, is made even more irascible on the golf course. His triplet nephews add to his frustration by substituting goofy golf clubs that turn into fish nets or umbrellas, which is exactly how a club feels in a golfer's hands after a fluffed shot. The nephews put a grasshopper in a ball, making it more difficult to hit than usual. Donald Duck reflects us all on a golf course on an off day. Not many laughs in *Follow the Sun* (TCF 1951), an uplift movie on the return to golf of Ben Hogan after a serious accident. World War II flying ace, Douglas Bader, had been an excellent cricketer and rugby player before the plane crash in which he lost both his legs. Golf is the only game he can play on his newly fitted artificial legs. In *Reach for the Sky* (1956), Bader (Kenneth More) is seen falling down every time he drives off the tee. 'Now let's have another whack at that golf ball,' he says, getting up until he finally manages to move the ball around the course.

In the nineteenth century, athletic excellence and noble qualities of character were equated. Boy's books like *Tom Brown's Schooldays* (filmed in 1940 and 1951) and others with titles such as *From Fag to Monitor* or *Through Thick and Thin for the Sake of a Chum*, taught that games developed manliness, patriotism and virtue. Today, TV cameras have now exposed this fallacy, even in games like rugby and cricket that were the models, thus leaving the movies to perpetuate the idea that sport develops character.

There was a breathless hush in the Close tonight —
Ten to make and the match to win,
A bumping pitch and a blinding light,
An hour to play and the last man in.
And it's not for the sake of a ribboned coat,
Or the selfish hope of a season's fame,
But his captain's hand on his shoulder smote —
'Play up! Play up! and play the game!'

from **Vitaï Lampada**
by SIR HENRY NEWBOLT

Tennis

Patsy Ruth Miller, now forgotten star of the silent screen, played tennis as well as she acted. That is to say she never got to Wimbledon, but was okay in the Hollywood tournaments. In *What Every Girl Should Know* (WB 1927), she is seen playing against Hollywood tennis champion Carmelita Geraghty in a tournament. This had nothing whatsoever to do with the plot about a brother and sister being put into two separate child institutions nor was any answer given to the question implicit in the title.

Jacques Tati used to do a number of mimes on the music-hall stage in France. One was a goal-keeper and the other was *Oscar — Champion de Tennis* (1931), his earliest experiment on film. It remained uncompleted, but it served as the basis for Tati's tennis match in *M. Hulot's Holiday* (1954).

Nuns in Hollywood movies are nicer, braver, wittier, tougher and sometimes sexier than other women, with the implication that nuns are fun. Ingrid Bergman could handle a baseball bat in *The Bells of St Mary's* (Par. 1945) and in *Come to the Stable* (TCF 1949). Sister Celeste Holm used to be a seeded tennis player before she took her vows. For a bet of 500 dollars in order to help build a children's dispensary, she enters a mixed doubles match. Despite the handicap of her habit, she lobs, volleys and smashes her way to near victory. (Love games are taboo.) Based on a story by Clare Booth Luce and directed by Henry Koster, it also has Loretta Young as a nun who drives like the devil. Actresses playing nuns are probably only marginally better than the other way round.

It says something about Alfred Hitchcock's attitude to tennis players in that in both *Dial M for Murder* (WB 1954) and *Strangers on a Train* (WB 1951), tennis pros, who have married well, try to get someone to murder their wives. Ray Milland, in the former, fails to get Grace Kelly killed and, in the latter, things go wrong for Farley Granger. In one of Hitchcock's most memorable set-pieces, Granger has to win his match as quickly as possible in order to get away to stop Robert Walker from incriminating him. As he plays his match, the spectators' heads move from side to side following the ball, except for one solitary head, that of Robert Walker's, who is staring straight ahead at Granger. It is not only a visual joke of the first order, but also a sinister image that makes sense in terms of the plot. Hitchcock would have preferred William Holden in the role of the tennis pro rather than the effete Farley Granger.

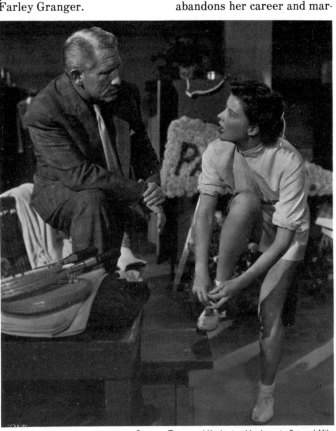

Spencer Tracy and Katharine Hepburn in *Pat and Mike*

The first (and virtually the last) picture about tennis was Ida Lupino's *Hard, Fast and Beautiful* (RKO 1951). Lupino, whose highly emotional performances made her reputation in low-key low-budget movies, directed about half a dozen movies of the same type. One of the very few women directors in Hollywood, her films are decidedly anti-feminist in nature. Sally Forrest as a tennis champion in *Hard, Fast and Beautiful* gives up her career, because she realizes that a home and husband is all she really wants. A tennis champion in high-school and devoted to the game, Sally is selected by her club to go to Philadelphia for the Girl's Junior Title tournament. Her mother (Claire Trevor) goes along too at the club's expense. In Philadelphia, the mother meets a promoter (Carleton G. Young) who sees in Sally a future champion. Sally wins the tournament and goes on to win the National Title after a hard-fought match. The promoter, the mother and Sally go off to Europe, but it's the mother who gets all the money earned by promotions. She is living off her daughter in the manner to which she is not accustomed. When Sally realizes she has been exploited, she abandons her career and marries her prim boyfriend (Robert Clarke). The shoe-string budget of the film sometimes shows through in the European scenes, but it's reasonably brisk, and the tennis sequences are well handled (filmed at Forest Hills) even if Miss Forrest might not convince tennis fans of her abilities. The social message exposing the corruption in amateur tennis is less effective. The neglected father and the boy-friend are there to make sure that Sally doesn't end up like her mother i.e. neglecting the home. Claire Trevor (splendid) is left all alone with the US Championship Cup on an empty court, forsaken by her daughter like the stage mother at the end of *Gypsy* (WB 1962).

Katharine Hepburn wears trousers in *Pat and Mike* (MGM 1952), but she doesn't wear *the* trousers. She's a professional golfer and tennis player, but whenever her sexist fiancé (William Ching) is around she feels inferior and her game deteriorates. Her guilt manifests itself in a tennis match against 'Gorgeous' Gussie Moran. She is playing well until her fiancé arrives. Suddenly the net appears to be way above her head, Moran has a gigantic racket, while hers is reduced to the size of a ping-pong bat. When she returns a ball, the other side of the court seems miles away. Many balls come at her at once, and to complete the nightmare, she imagines her fiancé in the umpire's chair. By the end of the picture, she has dumped him and married sports promoter Spencer Tracy, although she has to prove she's weaker than him in order to protect his male ego. Another example in a Hollywood movie of struggling feminism, manacled in the end by a patriarchal ideology. Tennis champs, Donald Budge, Pancho Gonzales, Frankie Parker and Alice Marble appear as themselves. It was directed by George Cukor from a script by Ruth Gordon and Garson Kanin.

M. Hulot, alias Jacques Tati, wearing a hat made of newspaper, a jacket and long trousers, serves unreturnable balls in an eccentric manner, driving everyone off the court in *M. Hulot's Holiday* (Cady Films 1954). Equally amusing, but unintentionally so, is the tennis match 'sensitive' John Kerr plays in *Tea and Sympathy* (MGM 1956). He embarasses his father (Edward Andrews), who is worried about his son's virility (i.e. he thinks he's a 'faggot'), by putting a spin on the ball and playing from the back-line instead of the more masculine type of game. Deborah Kerr makes a man of him in the end, while there is definitely something not quite right with the sexuality of her butch football-coach husband (Lief Erikson).

Stephen Potter, the English humorist and inventor of Lifemanship and Oneupmanship, was the inspiration behind *School for Scoundrels* (Associated British 1960) or How to win without actually cheating. Ian Carmichael plays the classic dupe, the used-car salesman's dream. When he introduces his girl-friend

Overleaf: Farley Granger and Ruth Roman in *Strangers on a Train*

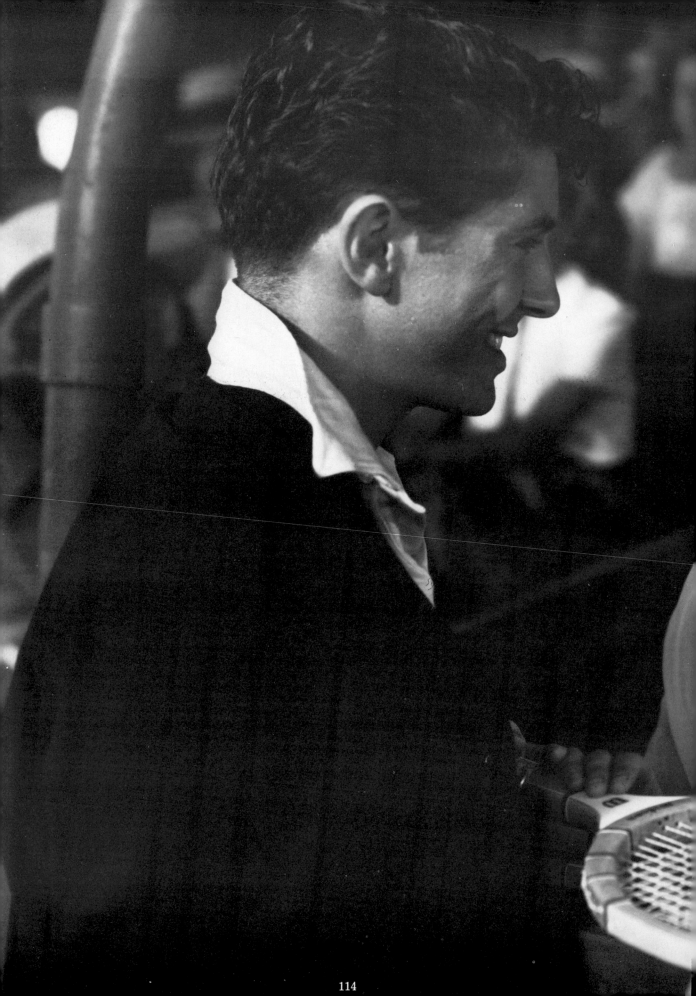

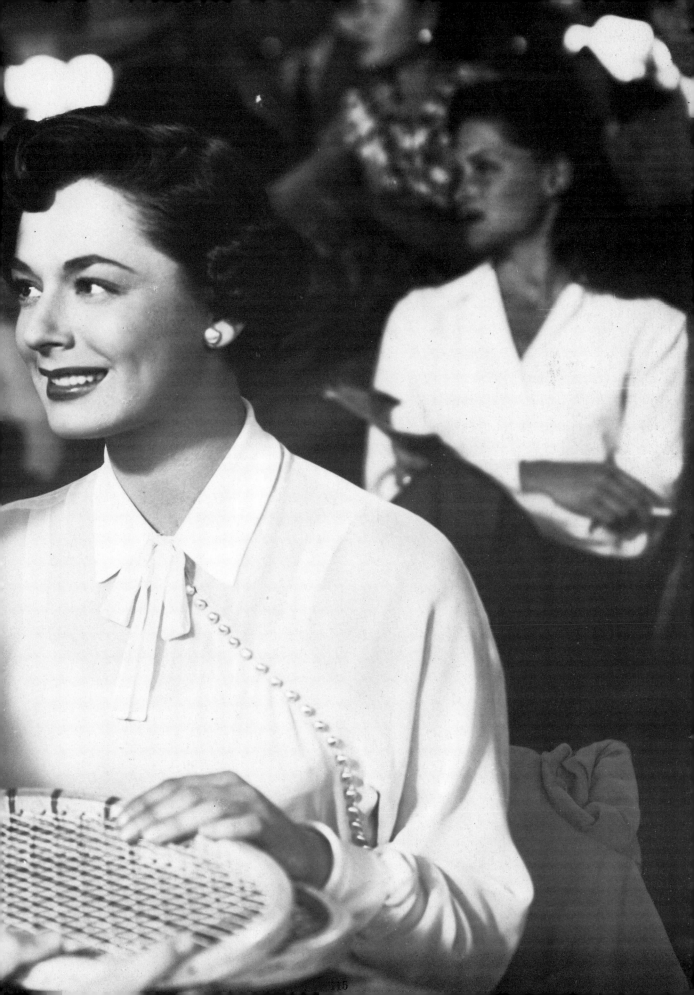

(Janette Scott) to caddish Terry-Thomas, he hasn't a chance. A tennis match is arranged between them with Janette watching. Immediately, Terry-Thomas makes Carmichael feel small by offering him 15 points start, and arranges it so that the sun is in his opponent's eyes. Every time he wins a point he shouts, 'Hard cheese!' and stands nonchalantly at the net to receive a service. Terry-Thomas hardly moves as Carmichael runs around the court, finally collapsing over the net in defeat. Desperate, he enrolls at Stephen Potter's college of Lifemanship where he is taught by Potter (Alastair Sim) such things as 'If you're outclassed, you must try to take your opponent's eye off the ball.' After graduating, Carmichael challenges Terry-Thomas to a return match. Using every trick of oneupmanship, he sends Terry-Thomas scurrying all over the court. The result is a 6-0 victory for Ian Carmichael and the school. (Are Nastase and McEnroe alumni of the same college?) The kind of modest comedy the British did best, it was wittily directed by Robert Hamer.

Michelangelo Antonioni's negative exposure of 'swinging London', *Blow Up* (MGM 1966), contains less than meets the eye. A fashionable photographer (David Hemmings) returns to the park where he first photographed what he believed to be a dead body. The body is gone. Was it ever there? Did he imagine it? Where does reality end and fantasy begin? He watches a student group in clown's make-up, miming a tennis match on a court. He begins to hear the sound of the ball on the non-existent rackets. He runs to retrieve an imaginary ball, near the place where he first photographed the 'body'.

In *The Sweet Ride* (TCF 1968), Tony Franciosa is a youngish forty-year-old who earns his 'bread' by taking on suckers at the tennis courts at Malibu. He shares a beach hut with a surfer (Michael Sarrazin who makes the 'sweet ride' of the title on his surf board) and a bandleader (Bob Denver). He ends up lonely when the other two cut out after realizing they're not kids anymore. Most of the audience over voting age might do the same before the end.

Wimbledon is used as a setting for a dramatic scene in *The High Commissioner* (Rank 1968, *Nobody Runs Forever* — GB). Christopher Plummer, in the title role, is sitting in the Royal Box at the Center Court, when Australian detective Rod Taylor spots a man among the TV cameramen whom he believes to be a terrorist. As the would-be assassin raises his gun, Taylor shouts for Plummer to get down. The criminal doesn't even have the courtesy to use a silencer on the gun during a match. Sub sub-Hitchcock.

When Woody Allen first meets Diane Keaton in *Annie Hall* (UA 1977) on an indoor tennis court, it's the beginning of a beautiful friendship. When doctors Bill Cosby and Richard Pryor and their wives (Gloria Gifford and Sheila Frazier) meet in a mixed doubles match in *California Suite* (Col. 1978), it is the end of a beautiful friendship. Written by Neil Simon, it is one of 4 sketches set at the Beverly Hills Hotel and stands out dimly in a bright movie. The slapstick 'black' comedy tennis match is very Simple Simon.

An old joke has two cats wat-

ching a tennis match and one saying to the other, 'My father's in that racket.' An offspring of Bjorn Borg will not be so quick to boast that their father was in *Racket* (Cal. Am. Prod. 1979). Not that the five-times Wimbledon champion has very much to do in this silly tale of a former Wimbledon champion (Bert Convy) turned instructor who is searching for a woman with enough money to buy him his own tennis court. Others involved are Edie Adams, Lynda Day George, Susan Tyrrell and Phil Silvers. Bobby Riggs, another tennis great, puts in a welcome appearance.

Most of the pleasure in *Players* (Par. 1979) comes from trying to identify the big tennis names who appear as themselves, rather like in those wartime all-star musicals such as *Hollywood Canteen* (WB 1944). In this *Wimbledon Canteen*, one can spot Ion Tiriac, Tom Gullikson, Dennis Ralston, Vijay Amitraj, Jimmy Connors and Jim McManus. Britain's John Lloyd is among the last sixteen and John McEnroe hardly speaks. (It is fiction after all). The most authentic moment in the movie is the

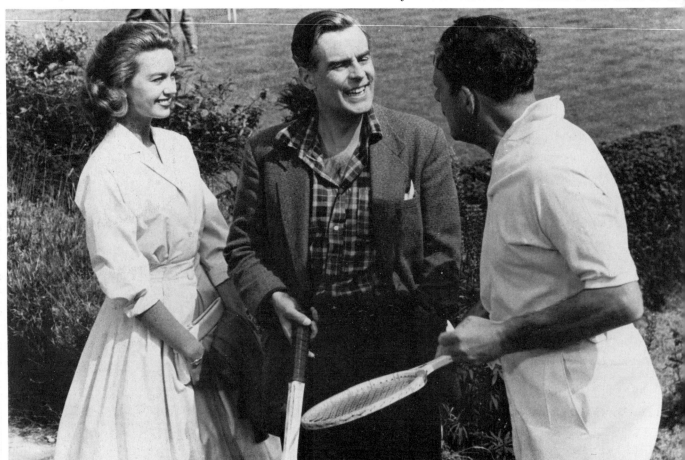

Janette Scott, Ian Carmichael and Terry-Thomas in *School for Scoundrels*

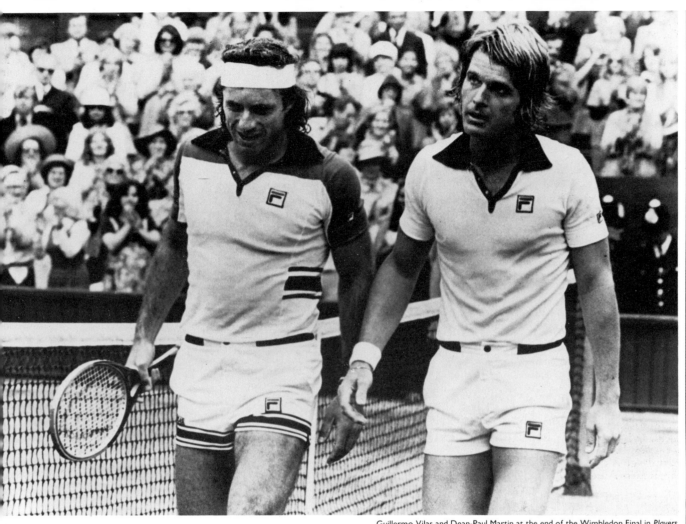

Guillermo Vilas and Dean-Paul Martin at the end of the Wimbledon Final in *Players*

sight of Ilie Nastase throwing a tantrum. Borg is absent, (presumably because he was appearing in *Racket* at the time). The Wimbledon final is between the favorite Guillermo Vilas and Dean-Paul Martin (son of Dean), an unseeded newcomer ranked 250th in world tennis. Martin is two sets down and he looks gloomily at an empty seat in the stands. As the movie starts with the Wimbledon final, we know we're in for a long flashback. We soon learn that the empty seat belonged to Ali MacGraw whom Martin met in Mexico where she has a lovely house full of her own soft-sculptures. He's a bit of a hustler who uses tennis as a con game to grab what he wants and to whom love means only zero points. Until he meets Miss MacGraw, that is. They're soon under the blankets together where presumably he's not unseeded. But, after romping around to Jerry Goldsmith's mushy music, she goes off to the yacht of her tycoon protector, Maxmillian Schell in Monte Carlo.

She really loves Martin, but she's pushing 40 and he's 26. Back to Wimbledon, where Dean-Paul is out to prove that he's not just a tennis-playboy, but a boy who can play tennis. As the music rises, so does he towards the final. BBC's Dan Maskell commentates as Vilas and Martin battle it out. Although he loses after 5 sets, (quite gripping), True Love had inspired him and he decides to give up hustling for serious tennis. Producer Robert Evans (Ali MacGraw's spouse) said, 'It is a unique love story with tennis as a strong foreground.' There is nothing unique about the love story with a strong forehand and foreplay. Dean-Paul Martin acts playing better than he play acts. Arnold Schulman's script has the bounce of an old, wet, tennis ball. Anthony Harvey's direction won't please anyone for tennis or against. Ali MacGraw acts as well as one of her stuffed-cloth sculptures. Only Pancho Gonzales, US champ of the 40's as Martin's coach, brings some life into the movie.

Golf

Golf provided P.G. Wodehouse with the subject for some of his funniest stories. Transferring the Wodehouse prose to the screen, has never really succeeded. A little of its flavor is retained in four silent short films (about 22 minutes each) made in 1924, based on his golfing stories. They are *The Clicking of Cuthbert*, *Chester Forgets Himself*, *Ordeal by Golf*, and *Rodney Fails to Qualify*.

When Laurel and Hardy ventured onto the golf course, the result was a foregone conclusion. Mayhem. In the reasonably posed question of the title, *Should Married Men Go Home?* (1928), the answer is an undoubted No, given the wives that Mr.L and H are generally saddled with. In this two-reeler, they both get into another fine mess. On the links, they insist that the apoplectic Edgar Kennedy play his ball where it lies. In the four feet of mud. Of course, it ends up with more mud slinging than a political campaign.

W.C. Fields' first sound picture was a two-reeler called *The Golf Specialist* (RKO 1930) in which he juggled with a recalcitrant golf club. In *You're Telling Me* (Par. 1934), Fields introduced a totally irrelevant golfing sequence into a plot about a European princess coming to Fields' small town. Nobody complained as it was the funniest thing in the movie. This time Fields has trouble with a piece of paper when trying to tee off. As almost everything was unrelated to the plot of *The Big Broadcast of 1938* (Par. 1938), Fields is first seen trying to set a world speed record on the golf course. He goes around on a motor-scooter to save time between shots. On finishing the game, he presses a button, the scooter turns into a miniature airplane and he takes off, landing on the deck of an ocean liner.

Most people would be quite happy to hit a ball straight down the fairway as Fred Astaire does in *Carefree* (RKO 1938), although he manages to hit about eight in a row, danc-

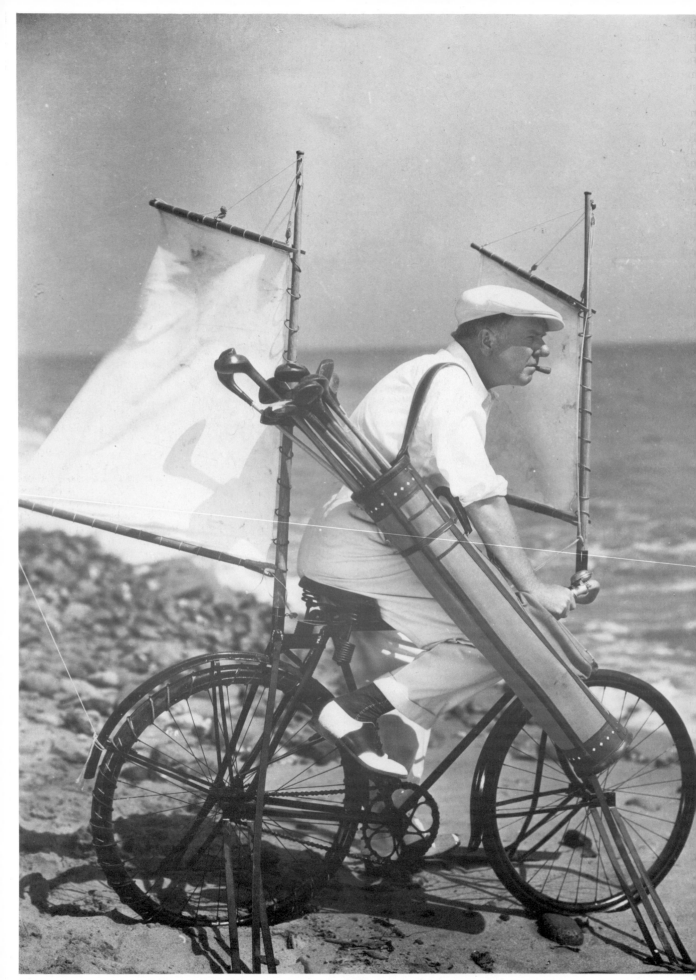

ng and singing at the same time. 'Since they turned Loch Lomond into swing' (by Irving Berlin) is an extraordinary number even by Astaire's standards.

Five tales of the supernatural are told in *Dead of Night* (Ealing 1945) by four top British directors. The one directed by Charles Crichton provides light relief. Based on a story by H.G. Wells, it is about two golfing buddies, Parratt and Potter (the irreplaceable duo, Basil Radford and Naunton Wayne) who fall in love with the same girl. They play a round of golf to decide which will marry her. (The winner, that is.) Potter loses and drowns himself. In the other world he learns that Parratt had cheated and returns to haunt him. The reappearance of Potter ruins Parratt's game no end. This is not the kind of bogie he wants on the golf course. Being an inexperienced ghost, Potter forgets the pass to make himself invisible again. Parratt, trying to help, makes the right pass and vanishes leaving Potter with the girl.

Years ago, Sammy Davis Jr. was asked on the golf course what his handicap was. He replied, 'I'm a one-eyed negro Jew.' Ben Hogan's handicap in *Follow the Sun* (TCF 1951) were the legs he had injured in a car accident. Another of those unctuously ingratiating biopics about a man's moral courage in overcoming difficulties with the help of a loyal wife who stands by him, it has the distinction of being the only movie to date to be devoted to the life of a golfer. Golf is a rich vein for comedy, but it is difficult, when watching these cool characters in their loud clothes on the green, to believe there are dramatic tales to be unfolded about them. *Follow the Sun* reveals all. Golfers want to be loved by the gallery and if they believe they're unpopular they sulk a lot. They sometimes let their best friends win so as not to cause hurt. As you watch a guy in checked pants and two-tone shoes miss a putt, remember that his wife is sitting alone in the club house waiting to see if he will win enough for the housekeeping money. Glenn Ford plays Ben Hogan soberly and Anne Baxter, as his wife Valerie, proves she can simper with the best of them. Hogan,

Left: W.C. Fields on his own version of a golf cart

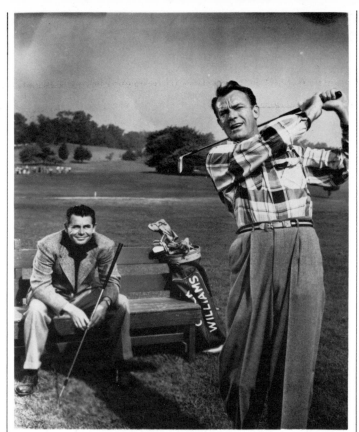

Glenn Ford (as Ben Hogan) watches Dennis O'Keefe in *Follow the Sun*

the young son of poor parents, has one ambition since he took up caddying — to become a golf pro. His dream comes true after winning a caddy's championship. He marries his childhood sweetheart and they do the golf circuits, starting in Canada and working their way down to California, which explains, in part, the film's title. All his spare time is spent practicing. He even perfects his putting in the bedroom, which goes to show how understanding his wife is. Hogan is dubbed 'The Texas Iceberg', because of his calculating approach to golf and his seeming aloofness from the press and the crowds. One day, driving home to Texas with Valerie in a fog, their car crashes into a bus. Valerie escapes with minor injuries, but Ben is seriously hurt. There are doubts about whether he will ever walk again. After many long and painful months, Ben is able to play golf again. Amazingly he manages to tie with Sam Snead in the LA Open. There is a playoff, but his legs cannot stand the strain and he loses. At the dinner afterwards, the chairman says, 'Ben didn't lose today. His legs weren't strong enough to carry his heart around.' Sidney Lanfield directed it and Sam Snead, Jimmy Demaret and Gary Mid-

dlecoff appeared as themselves. Pity the greens were black and white.

'Lady wrestlers that's something that shouldn't be allowed. Women golfers are alright,' says a shifty promoter in *Pat and Mike* (MGM 1952). Katharine Hepburn as the golf pro is asked what her handicap is. 'A fellow', she replies. (See Tennis section). Hepburn looks as though she can really hit a golf ball. Almost ten minutes of the picture is spent on the US Women's Match Play Championship in which top women golfers, Betty Hicks, Helen Dertweiler and Babe Didrikson are seen taking part.

At the beginning of *The Caddy* (Par. 1953), crowds mob the Paramount theater where comedians Joe Anthony (Dean Martin) and Harvey Miller (Jerry Lewis) are performing. A magazine writer asks them how they met and became a 'riot in show biz.' Flashback. Harvey could have been one of the world's greatest golfers, if it were not for the fact that he is too nervous to play before a crowd. He shares his room with Joe, who has the makings of a champion. Harvey persuades Joe to enter a Santa Barbara tournament with himself as coach and caddy. Joe wins despite Harvey's blunders. Joe then enters for the 10,000

dollars tournament at Montery Beach, but he is beginning to be embarrassed by Harvey's clumsiness. (So is the audience.) During the match, they begin to fight over which golf clubs to use. Unwittingly they start a riot which is so 'funny' they decide to give up golf and become a comedy team. Some of Jerry Lewis' mugging is amusing and Dean Martin sings the big hit of the year, 'That's Amore' (or was it 'that's a Moron'?). Donna Reed and Barbara Bates were the girls and Norman Taurog directed.

Jerry Lewis has troubles again with a golf ball in the inventive Frank Tashlin comedy, *Who's Minding the Store?* (Par. 1963). Jerry works in a department store and is demonstrating the Futurascope Fairway, a machine that registers the length of one's drive by the force of the club hitting a stationary ball. Jerry naturally hits the ball off its stand, into the street where it strikes a policeman and ricochets off buildings, knocking out people. When the machine registers 1300 yards, it blows up. The golf ball returns to its original position and explodes.

Banning (UI 1967) is not about the American New Right's confrontation with libraries, but about the Old Right and an ex-pro golfer called Mike Banning (Robert Wagner). He hasn't played in a competition for 5 years and is employed at the exclusive El President Country Club, teaching golf to bored and sexually frustrated wives of prominent members. They're interested in Banning's prominent members. In order to help a friend pay off his IOU's to a gangster, Banning accepts a challenge on the golf course against the powerful millionaire who controls the El President (Howard Duff) and a jealous husband (Guy Stockwell). There is plenty of personal animosity on both sides. The tense event ends in a tie and a sudden death playoff. Banning and his partner win, he pays off his friends debts and drives off (in his car) like the Lone Golfer. Anjanette Comer, Jill St John and Susan Clark are the women who try to bed our hero. Somewhere under its TV soap opera surface is an indictment of the LA upper crust whispering to get out.

The El President Country Club in *Banning* has a lot in common with the Bushwood Country Club in *Caddyshack*.

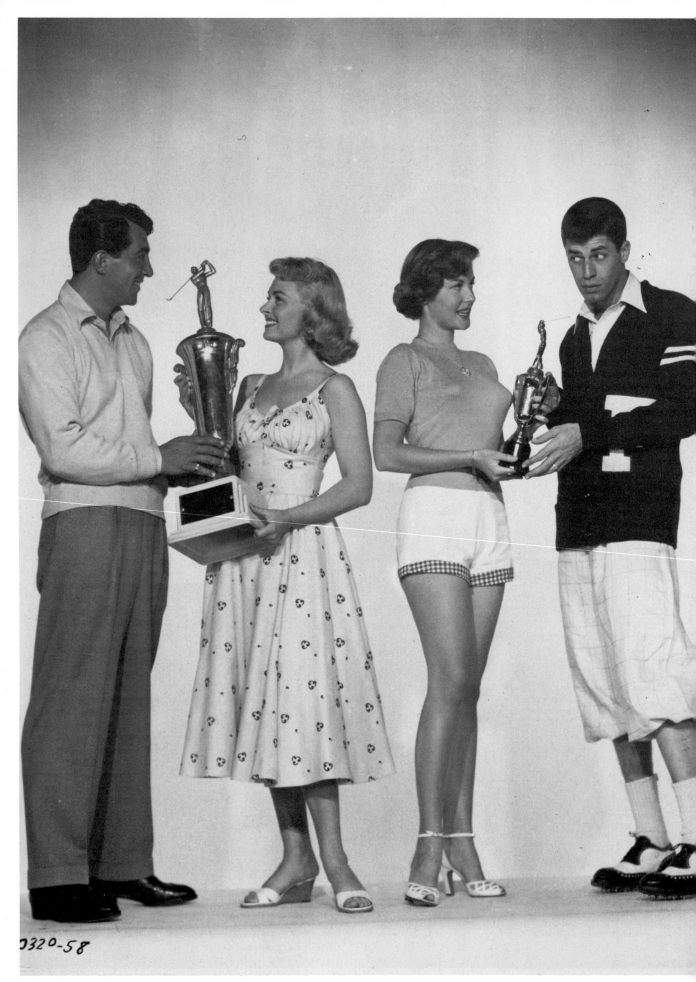

0320-58

120

WB 1980). Bushwood is run with an iron rod by Judge Smails (Ted Knight), a bigoted and arrogant stuffed shirt who pronounces 'golf' — 'gof'. Rodney Dangerfield, in a sportsjacket that's gaudy even to golfers, is a loud-mouthed millionaire who is as insulting as he is rich, and Chevvy Chase is a playboy who can play blindfolded, backwards and between his legs, but never completes a hole. The assistant greenkeeper is a loony who spends his time trying to rid the course of gophers with a variety of weapons including dynamite. (Mr Gopher is played cheekily by Chuck Rodent.) There is an aged golfer who, in attempting to break the course record, dies in a convulsion as he misses his vital putt on the last green. Directed by Harold Ramis, it's all good, dirty fun, more coarse golf than golf course. In the tradition of Mad Magazine, *Animal House*, and *Meatballs*, its sophomore humor is fairly miss and hit. Unfunny — a college boy throwing up in a convertible, so that someone who sits down on it slides off the seat. Funny — a parody of *Jaws*, when a bather drops a chocolate bar into the swanky pool and panic ensues as the swimmers think it's a turd.

Soccer

If England hadn't won the 1966 World Cup at Wembley Stadium, London, then *Goal! World Cup 1966* (Col. 1966) would have have been a completely different movie. British produced, with a commentary written by English sportswriter and novelist Brian Glanville and narrated by Nigel Patrick, it is not exactly an unpartisan view of the event. But England's victory worked to the film's advantage, giving it a structure that a victory for, say, Russia or Brazil would not have done. We see the host team, before their own crowd, eliminate Argentina and Portugal on their way to the final against West Germany. The final is filmed impressively by directors Abidine Dino and Ross Devenish like a rerun of World War II. Using 117 cameras, color and wide screen, England's 4-2 win is seen more vividly (close-ups of facial expressions, physical effort and pain) than was appreciated on the black and white television of the time.

The Russians produced three goals in the title of an interesting soccer film, *Goal! Goal! Another Goal!* (Lenfilm 1968). Starting during the siege of Leningrad in 1942, it tells the story of the origins of a team in the city, of its progress and tribulations — until final triumph in the European championships. The film reveals Soviet attitudes to sport and there are some good soccer sequences.

The Goalkeeper's Fear of the Penalty (*Die Angst des Tormans beim elf meter* — 1971), is not about soccer, but uses the sporting metaphor as a starting point to express the *angst* of everyday life in a border town in Germany. Joseph Bloch (Arthur Brauss) is a veteran goalkeeper who lets in a penalty without moving a muscle and then walks distraughtly off the field. He meets up with a cinema cashier, goes to bed with her, and in the morning calmly strangles her. In the end he explains why he didn't save that penalty at the beginning of the film. He had become immobile by the pressures of modern life. Like the goalkeeper, the camera of director Wim Wenders hardly moves. Every scene is separated by slow fades so that everything has the air of suspended animation. Based on the first novel of Peter Handke, it creates an atmosphere that is mid-way between hypnotic and soporific.

Most young boys imagine themselves playing for their national team as they kick a ball around a park. Bo Widerberg has realized this fantasy in the Swedish film, *Stubby* (*Fimpen* 1974). On his way past a children's playground, the winger of the Hammerby soccer team stops to sign autograph books for the boys and joins in their game for a few moments, until his famous 'two-step' is thwarted by a tiny 6-year-old boy nicknamed Stubby. Stubby soon earns a place in the senior team and scores the winning goal in an important match. One day, playing with his toys at home, he receives a call from the manager of the Swedish National Team. He is to play for Sweden in the World Cup qualification matches. Thanks to Stubby, the team beats Hungary, Austria, France and Russia, and he becomes a national hero with his name on billboards everywhere, but . . .

when he's asked for his autograph, he cannot sign his own name. Soccer has taken him away from his school work. The film, which is reasonable family entertainment, has basically one visual joke. The same sort of joke that has Mohammed Ali knocked out by a tiny tot. Johan Bergman plays this Tom Foot, and his own mother and father, the Hammerby Football Club, the Swedish National Team and the Moscow Dynamos participate good-humoredly in the enterprise. The action in which the boy takes part was developed from actual movements initiated during the real cup matches and filmed straight after the match.

The Boys in Company C (EMI/Raymond Chow 1977), the first of a number of movies set in Vietnam since the jingoistic *Green Berets* (WB 1968), was a mish-M*A*S*H* of the archetypal World War II movie and the more cynical attitudes of the seventies. It involves a bunch of raw recruits to the U.S. Marine Corps in 1967, who are knocked into shape by rigorous basic training and pitched into Vietnam. Among the recruits is a pro-footballer (Andrew Stevens), who agrees to captain a soccer XI against the local S. Vietnamese team. Washington informs them that if they win, they will be removed from active duty and sent on a prestige tour of Japan and other neutral countries of S.E. Asia. The Americans, far superior to the Vietnamese, are ahead by half-time. (Both teams are unbelievably bad. How the Americans who have never played soccer seriously can be better than the Vietnamese who have been playing soccer for years, is not explained. That would spoil the parable.) But the conditions of the bargain have been changed and, as a means of boosting Vietnamese morale, the team is now expected to lose the match. In almost a replica of the situation in *The Longest Yard* (Par. 1974), they allow the Vietnamese to take the lead by such obvious means as scoring own goals, tying their shoelaces at crucial moments and flagrantly not trying. Suddenly, amidst the jeers of the crowd, they decide to play for real and win, although it means returning to the combat zone. They have now become a real team who unite to fight the Viet Cong. Opting out, after all,

was only for long-haired students and leftist draft dodgers.

From bad soccer in a so-so movie, to good soccer in a bad movie with *Yesterday's Hero* (Col-EMI-Warner 1979.) The title refers to Rod Turner (Ian McShane), one-time soccer star, turned 35, now consoling himself with whiskey and fading press-clippings. When The Saint's leading striker is injured, their owner, rock-idol Clint Simon (Paul Nicholas), remembers his boyhood hero, Rod Turner. Rod has a chance of making it back into the big time, but The Saints' tough manager Jake (Adam Faith) thinks he's too 'old, slow and drunk.' During the F.A. Cup semi-final, Rod scores a goal but, at half-time, he's caught swigging whiskey and suspended. However, he makes it back into the team after training hard and giving up drink. For the Cup Final, he's on the reserve bench. Ten minutes from the final whistle with the teams drawn, a Saints' player is injured. You've guessed it. Rod runs onto the field to a tremendous roar from the crowd and plays as well as he did ten years ago. The tawdry script is by Jackie Collins whose scorn for her audience is apparent in this mixture of sex, sport, the jet-set and pop music which also includes a little black orphan child with a clubfoot who worships our yesterday's hero. The soccer sequences are well staged, but it would be far better to be standing in the icy rain on a Saturday afternoon at a third division match in the north of England.

British films like *Yesterday's Hero* help to put another nail into the coffin of the British film industry, whereas films like *Gregory's Girl* (ITC 1980) rise to prove that it was a premature burial. Gregory (Gordon John Sinclair) is a lanky 16-year-old school-boy, living in Cumbernauld-New Town outside Glasgow, Scotland. He has two overriding interests — girls and soccer. The school team is doing so badly that 'when they were awarded a corner, they took a lap of honor'. Gregory is told that he must lose his place as striker . . . to a girl. She is Dorothy (Dee Hepburn), an extremely attractive blonde with a very female figure and a tremendous boot. There is slight resistance at first to having a girl on the team. 'It's not right,

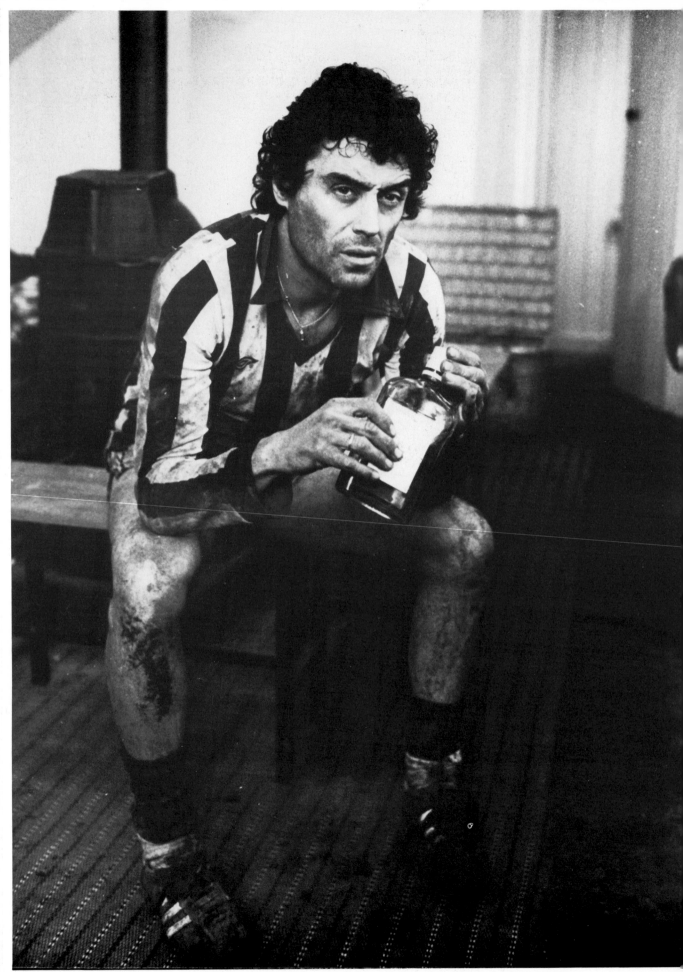

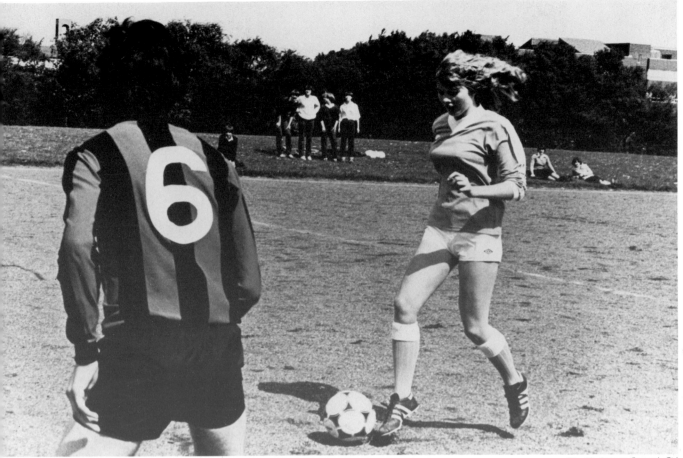

Dee Hepburn in *Gregory's Girl*

it's not natural,' comments one of the boys. 'It doesn't look nice. If women were meant to play football they'd have had their tits somewhere else.' But she soon convinces them that she's as good, if not better, than any boy, although when she scores a goal even the opposition rush up to kiss her. Gregory is infatuated with her and can hardly keep his eye on the ball as she fires shots at him in goal from all angles during practice. He finally gets a date with her and, dressed up in his friend's smart white sports jacket, he waits for her under a huge clock which resounds with each minute he is kept waiting. After being stood up, he ends up happily with another girl. The slight tale is packed full of witty details by writer/director Bill Forsyth. Even the rather consistent gender role-reversal (girl as soccer star, boys in cookery class, girl gets boy etc) is done without a hint of rhetoric. It is, however, a little too goody-goody to be true. There are no punks, no delinquents. Everyone, even the mostly absent adults, is so nice. Forsyth is looking back on an idealized

Left: Ian McShane in *Yesterday's Hero*

adolescence consisting of long, warm, summer days and nights (Despite the fact that soccer is played in winter.) Gregory tells a tiny boy who is calling on his little sister, 'Act your age. Go and demolish some phone-boxes. Break some windows.' No-one in this film would ever dream of doing such a thing which, in a way, is part of its charm.

'If nations could settle their differences on the football pitch, wouldn't that be a challenge?' says 'good' Nazi commandant Max von Sydow to P.O.W. Michael Caine in *Escape to Victory* (Lorimar 1981). As an ex-German soccer international, he has the idea for a challenge match between a German team and one picked from the P.O.W's, to be held at Colombes Stadium in Paris as a vast propaganda excercise for the Nazis. Caine, previously of West Ham United, agrees, if they get proper training facilities, better gear and plenty to eat and that certain East European players be allowed to join the team. The camp is rather like a summer resort in the Catskills, only less regimented. Only once does the real war intrude upon the film. The East Europeans ar-

rive at the camp as living skeletons. Meanwhile, an American (Sylvester Stallone) escapes (rather too easily) and contacts the French Resistance in Paris. They will dig a tunnel to come up inside the bath in the changing room so that the team can escape at half-time. In one of the more preposterous elements in an already implausible plot, Stallone is purposely recaptured in order to give the team the message about the escape plans. On the day of the match, the stadium (actually filmed in Budapest) is hung with Nazi flags. The Germans can't afford to lose, so they've bought the referee. The Allies include Pele, Argentinian Ardiles, former England captain Bobby Moore and Stallone as goalkeeper, although he's never played soccer before. He soon learns that it's not 'a game for fairies', when he gets kicked in the head. The referee turns a blind eye to the numerous German fouls and score at half-time is Germany 2 — Allies 0. In the changing room they get ready to escape. The Resistance have spent all night digging a tunnel. But the team decide they don't want to escape as they feel they have a

good chance of winning. 'The game means a lot to us,' says Pele. (It's not just a soccer match, you see, but a microcosm of the war.) So, with injuries and the ref against them, they take to the field for the second half. Ardiles shows his stuff and the Allies score. Pele, with a broken arm, scores the equalizer with a spectacular back flip. The French crowd begin to chant, 'Victoire! Victoire!' and sing the Marseillaise. There's not a collaborator among them. The Germans are given a penalty in the last moment. Stallone has to save the goal to save the match. The German stares at him with hatred as he gets ready to take the kick. Stallone stops it, the crowd invades the field and the team escapes with them.

The film, combining the cliches of the P.O.W. escape movie with those of a sports movie, is a commercial package made for a family audience. No swearing ('This frigging game,' says Stallone), no nudity (the men take showers virtually in the dark with their backs to the cameras), and no sex. Pele, who gets third billing, doesn't have much to say, but is credited with designing

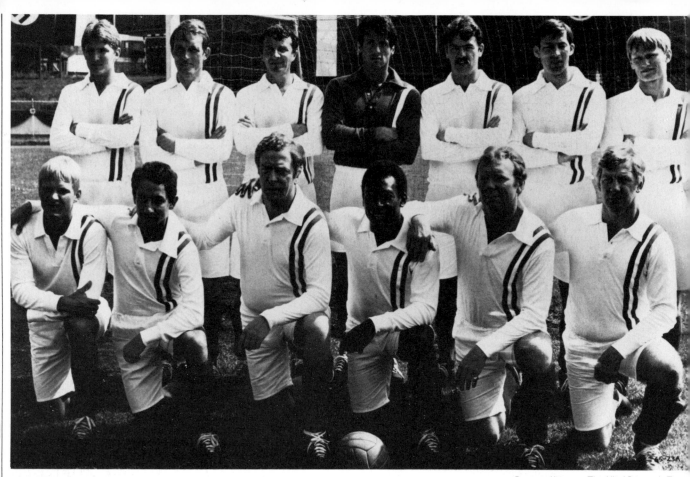

Escape to Victory — The Allied Prisoner's Team

the soccer plays. The soccer plays are, in fact, the most effective part of the film, with the real players being given a chance to show their skills. Unbelievably, it was directed by the once-distinguished John Huston. At least there won't be any bad movies about World War III.

Rugby

Pain pervades *This Sporting Life* (Rank 1963). On the rugby field where men are hurled to the ground, stamped upon, crushed and kicked. In the dentist's chair where a player is having his broken teeth ruggedly extracted. In the bleak northern industrial English town where the only light and warmth comes from the pubs. The widow, racked with a sense of failure and guilt, unwilling to alleviate the pain of the man who loves her and who inflicts pain on her. Lindsay Anderson, in his first feature, has attempted to make a modern tragedy with a working class hero. He succeeds to a certain degree. The grimy northern background had already become a cliché in British films of the late fifties and early sixties. The means by which

Anderson presents this lugubrious tale, tend to underline the already highly-charged material. Flashy flashbacks, characters shot in such a way as immediately to establish them as corrupt, weak, heroic, unhappy etc., and a continual clash between a bigger-than-life style and a realistic one. Nevertheless, it carries an emotional power rarely attained in British films and gives a picture, if a rather selective one, of the fierce matches, the shower-room fraternity, the hangers-on and the unscrupulous tycoons who run the Rugby League clubs. (Rugby League, as distinct from Rugby Union, is professional and the teams consists of 13 players instead of 15. The rules also vary.) David Storey, from whose novel the film was based, wrote the screenplay. Storey was a professional Rugby League player at Leeds in 1952 so he wrote from inside-the-scrum experience. The movie begins with Frank Machin (Richard Harris) lying on the ground of a rugby field, his mouth bleeding and semi-conscious. In the dentist's chair, under gas, Machin recalls his past. The conventions of the cinema allow the

memories to be reasonably lucid and chronological. Frank was a miner, lodging with Mrs Hammond (Rachel Roberts), a widow with two children, until he joins the City Rugby team and begins to earn money. Sport gives him a status he could never have achieved in any other field. He is a big, strong, aggressive and inarticulate man who develops an *amour fou* for his dour, bitter and dowdy landlady, a relationship as violent (and often as inexplicable) as the game he plays. When she dies (a trickle of blood from her mouth), he realizes the emptiness of success and, in the end, he sinks to his knees, this time in mental pain. Richard Harris' animalism is given free rein in one of his best performances and Rachel Roberts bravely copes with an almost impossible role.

Rugby Union is the background of a French comedy set in London called *Allez France!* (Films Borderie 1964). Produced, directed and written by Robert Dhery (of *La Plume de ma Tante* fame) with his wife Colette Brosset, Diana Dors and a collection of English and French character actors, it follows the inane adventures of

a French rugby supporter (Dhery) who crosses the Channel for the England-France match, gets lost, finds himself in a bobby's uniform and at the dentist's.

Cricket

The imcomparable Basil Radford and Naunton Wayne were teamed up for the first time in Alfred Hitchcock's *The Lady Vanishes* (1938) as the Punch-cartoon like Englishmen abroad, Caldicott and Charters, more worried about England's chances against Australia in the Test Match than in the murder, espionage and intrigue going on around them in a small European country. When they finally get back to England, hoping to catch some play, they are greeted with the headline 'Test Match Abandoned. Floods.' Arthur Lowe and Ian Carmichael had the unenviable task of topping Radford and Wayne in the 1979 remake, but, although they're good, they're much further down the batting order than their predecessors.

Radford and Wayne appear again as Major Bright and Cap-

Right: Rugby League in *This Sporting Life*

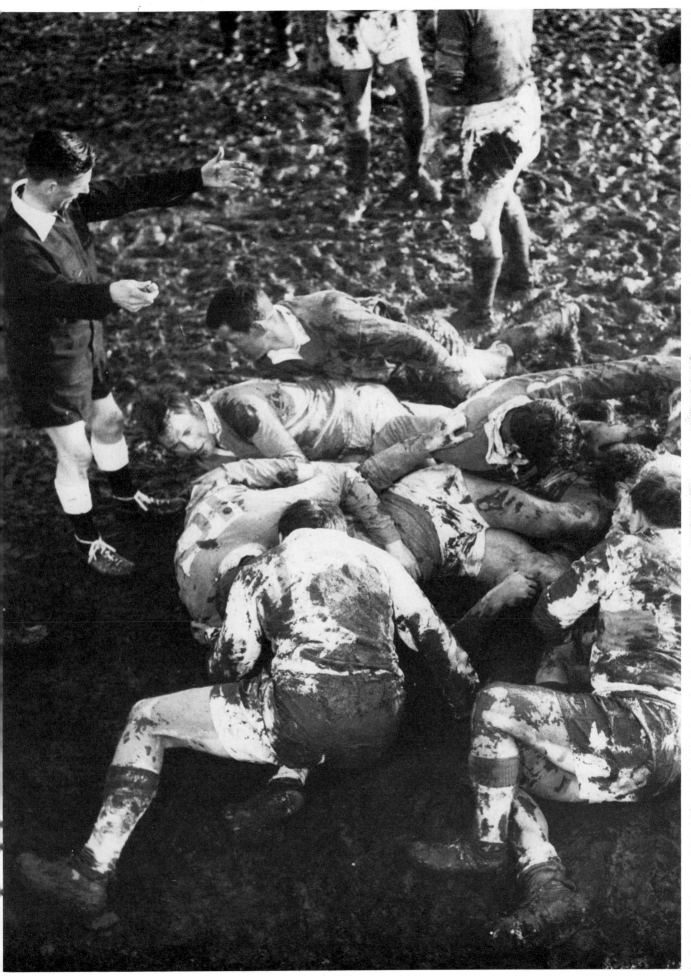

tain Early in *It's Not Cricket* (Gainsborough 1948). They play two British Intelligence men in occupied Germany on the track of one, Otto Fisch (Maurice Denham), a fugitive Nazi. Fisch gets to England, steals the famous Rothstein diamond and conceals it in a hollow cricket ball. By accident the ball is taken to be used for a match to be played at a country house where the guests happen to be Bright and Early. Among the men on the field is Otto Fisch determined to recover the diamond at all costs. (A German playing cricket is not only comic but downright blasphemous.) When the ball is hit in his direction, he makes off with it while the dumbfounded team give chase, ruining the wicket in the process. Bright and Early retrieve the ball, discover the diamond and unmask the villain. The pleasure to be derived from the throwaway delivery of Radford and Wayne, makes up for the idiocies of the plot.

Director Anthony Asquith and writer Terence Rattigan collaborated on over half-a-dozen films, all as English as county cricket and told with a slightly quivering stiff upper-lip. Rattigan was an above-average cricketer himself and his screenplay for *The Final Test* (Rank 1953) is shot through with his love for the game which fails, however, to disguise the smugness of much of the writing and the plot. Veteran England cricketer Sam Palmer (a 59-year-old Jack Warner!) is making his last appearance for his country against Australia in the Fifth Test at the Oval. He knows he's past his best, but hopes to give a good account of himself. A widower for many years, he has an only son Reggie (Ray Jackson) who, much to Sam's disappointment, is more interested in poetry than cricket. Instead of going to see his father play, Reggie is at home waiting to receive the eminent poet, Alexander Whitehead (Robert Morley) to whom he wishes to sell a poem. When Whitehead arrives and discovers that Reggie's father is Sam Palmer, he insists they go to the match. (Whitehead swings both ways. He likes art as well as sport.) They arrive at the Oval just in time to see Sam out third ball. The silence is oppressive as Sam makes his way back to the pavillion, but as he reaches the gate, the huge crowd rises to him. He is reconciled with his son and meets and likes the poet. Sam's career ends happily. 'It's a funny thing, you know, Reg, when Syd Thompson (the umpire) lifted his finger this morning, I thought to myself this is it, Sam Palmer, this is the finish. Well, you know, I'm wondering now whether it wasn't really the beginning.' What about the second innings? It's best not to ask, the film's long enough. Famous English cricketers Len Hutton, Denis Compton, Alec Bedser, Godfrey Evans and Jim Laker all make appearances.

A cricket match was introduced into *Three Men in a Boat* (Romulus 1956) based on Jerome K. Jerome's classic comic novel in which no such scene exists. The Three Men (Laurence Harvey, Jimmy Edwards and David Tomlinson) while trying to win the hearts of Three Girls (Jill Ireland, Shirley Eaton and Adrienne Corri) come face to face in the match with Three Old Boys (A.E. Matthews, Ernest Thesiger, and Miles Malleson). 'To say nothing of the dog' (the book's subtitle), Montmorency who chases the ball causing havoc. Directed by Ken An-

nakin, it deserves Two Cheers.

A summer's day in England. The sound of a leather ball on a bat. Sporadic clapping and cries of 'Good shot!' and 'Howzat!'. White flannels, green grass, cucumber sandwiches for tea. What could be more reassuring? This is how *The Shout* (Rank 1979) opens. Gradually, however one begins to notice that all is not what it seems. Some of the spectators and players seem a bit odd. It is, in fact, the annual match between the villagers of Lampton and the local lunatic asylum. In the scoring hut sit Charles Crossley (Alan Bates) and Robert Graves (Tim Curry) recording the runs. Crossley, introduced as 'the most intelligent inmate', begins to tell Graves a strange story about a man who could kill with the power of his shout. It is directed by Jerzy Skolimowski with the help of Dolby sound (take earplugs), and good actors (Bates, John Hurt, Susanna York, Robert Stephens). Based on a short-story by Robert Graves, it exploits the underlying menace of the seeming innocence of the English countryside.

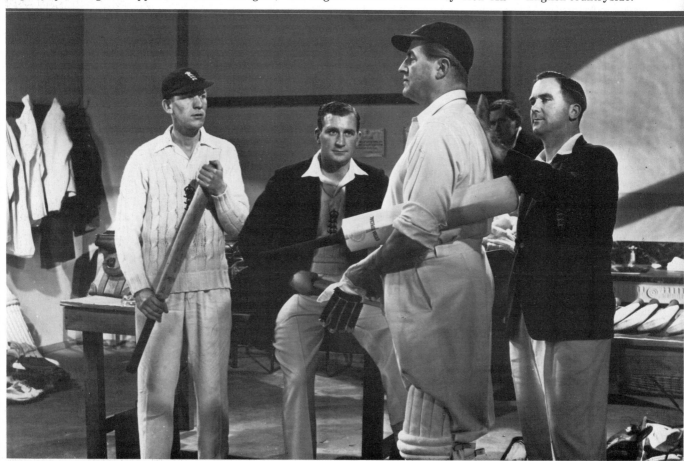

Jack Warner (bat under arm) ready for *The Final Test*. Jim Laker is seated and Godfrey Evans pats the ingoing batsman on the back

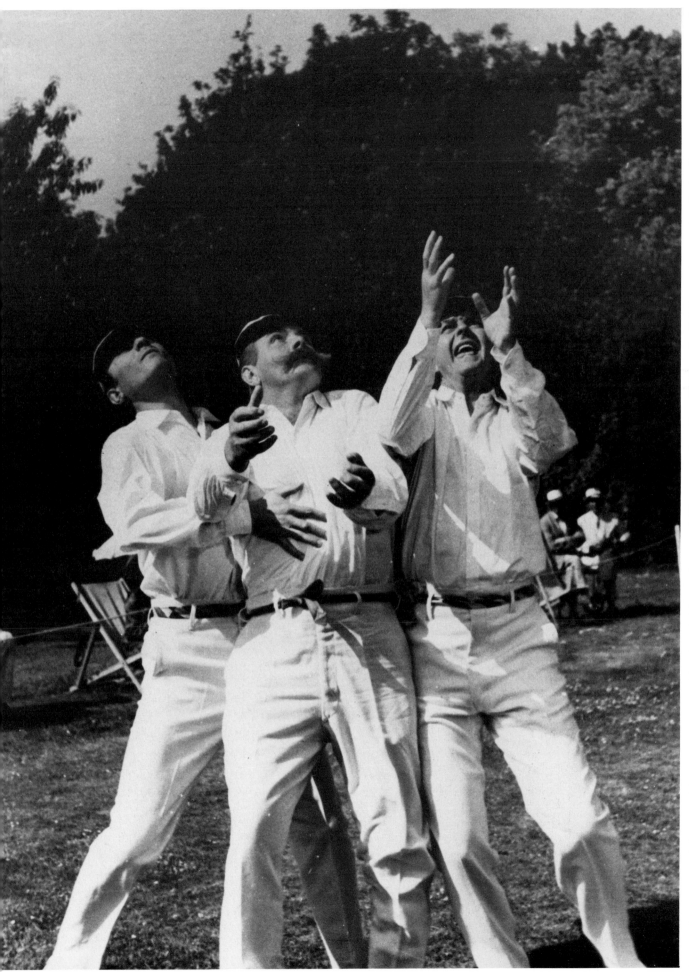

HUNTIN', SHOOTIN' & FICTION

From its beginnings American Literature was essentially a frontier literature, with protagonists testing their valor against the rigors of frontier life, of solitary heroes pitting themselves against nature. Hollywood has imitated, paralleled, continued, vulgarized and even transcended this literary tradition. The popular cowboy figure of the literature of the West, found in the novels of Zane Gray, reached its apotheosis in the Hollywood Western. The frontier experience is of great importance in the American psyche. To Howard Hawks it was America's most exciting time 'when people were forced to take law into their own hands, kill or be killed.' Shooting Indians, outlaws or mountain lions kept a man on his toes and allowed little time for intellectual activities. By 1870, however, the frontier was fast disappearing and America changed from being an agrarian society to an industrial one centered in the large cities. 'America is the country that still believed in heroes — Washington, Billy the Kid, Lincoln, Jefferson, Twain, Jack London, Hemingway, Joe Louis — athletes, aviators, even lovers... And when the West was filled, the expression turned inward, became part of an agitated, over-excited, super-heated dream life,' wrote Norman Mailer in *The White Negro* (1955). Where today in 'the home of the brave' can a man test his courage? Sport is the last frontier, the refuge for the he-man. But can a modern Daniel Boone satisfy his lust for adventure inside the institutionalized sports? For Hemingway the only way a man could prove himself was through hunting, deep-sea fishing and bull-fighting. Survival and dignity depend on this virile code. A man is nothing if not a man of action. The shadow of Hemingway looms large over movies with a blood-sports theme, and extends beyond. Even a Califor-

'Keep my head clear. I am a tired old man. But I have killed the fish which is my brother and now I must do the slave work.'

— SPENCER TRACY in
The Old Man and the Sea
(WB 1958)

Tens of thousands of elephants are killed in Africa every year. Soon we'll be alone on this earth with nothing else to destroy but ourselves.

— TREVOR HOWARD in
The Roots of Heaven
(TCF 1958)

nian surf movie such as *Big Wednesday* (WB 1978) treats the surfers going towards the rollers with the mystique that Hemingway reserved for bull-fighters in *Death in the Afternoon* (1932). Hemingway, like most major writers, has not been well served by the movies. His novels and stories have been put through the Hollywood machine, softened, stretched and flattened by it. However, one of his weakest novels provided the material for two fine films. *To Have and Have Not* (WB 1944) could hardly fail with Howard Hawks directing, William Faulkner and Jules Furthman writing the script and Humphrey Bogart and Lauren Bacall starring. Much was changed from the novel, but the spirit remained. The opening boat trip still depicts Harry Morgan's (Bogart) contempt for the rich tourists who hire his boat to go deep-sea fishing. It was remade excellently as *Breaking Point* (WB 1950) directed by Michael Curtiz with John Garfield as Morgan.

Man the Hunter is often confronted with the ineffective city dweller who decides to go on safari to prove his virility to the girl he brings along, presumably because he hasn't been able to prove it in bed. She soon discovers an authentic man. The white hunter Gregory Peck makes Robert Preston pathetic in his wife's (Joan Bennett) eyes in *The Macomber Affair* (UA 1947). Roland Culver in *Safari* (Col. 1956) hasn't a chance with Janet Leigh once hunter Victor Mature arrives on the scene with his gun erect. Cowardice = Impotence, Courage = Virility is a constant proposition. Urban man has been away from the frontier for too long and has become softened. Man's desire to escape the jungle of the cities for a purer, simpler condition is explored in *Deliverance* (WN 1972) in which four Atlanta businessmen spend a weekend canoeing in the Appalachians on 'the last, untamed, unpolluted, unfucked river in the South.' But their sporting trip turns very

nasty when they are shot at, terrorized and sodomized by mountain men.

'What more manly exercise than hunting the Wild Boar, the Stag, the Buck, the Fox, or the Hare? How doth it preserve health, and increase strength and activity!' said Izaac Walton's Venator in the 17th century. The 20th century fox need also be wary of the hunter. The English see hunting and fishing, less as an expression of masculinity than as an example of breeding. A gentleman is one who shoots grouse and rides to hounds. In Fritz Lang's *Man Hunt* (TCF 1941), a British game hunter (Walter Pidgeon) is parachuted into Gemany to kill the largest quarry of his life — Hitler. The gentleman, using the techniques that served him well in Africa, stalks evil with his rifle. History tells us that he failed in his mission, although Hitler did die in a foxhole some years later. Except for *The Wild Heart* (Selznick 1951. *Gone to Earth* — GB), fox-hunting is seldom considered from the point of view of Oscar Wilde's definition as 'the unspeakable in pursuit of the uneatable.' The hunts in 'rollicking' films like *Tom Jones* (1963) and *Sinful Davy* (1969) are all tally-ho and picturesqueness. Both Bob Hope in *Fancy Pants* (Par. 1950), masquerading as an English nobleman, and Lucille Ball in *Mame* (WB 1974) manage to nab the fox because of their incompetence, not in spite of it. In John Huston's *The List of Adrian Messenger* (1971), the villain of the piece (Kirk Douglas) is quite rightly killed gruesomely while fox-hunting. Jean Renoir used the rabbit hunt in *The Rules of the Game* (1938 *La Regle de Jeu*) to demonstrate the unthinking cruelty of his aristocratic characters, whereas the message of *Roots of Heaven* (TCF 1958) links the hunting of elephants with nuclear annihilation.

Mountains have always pro-

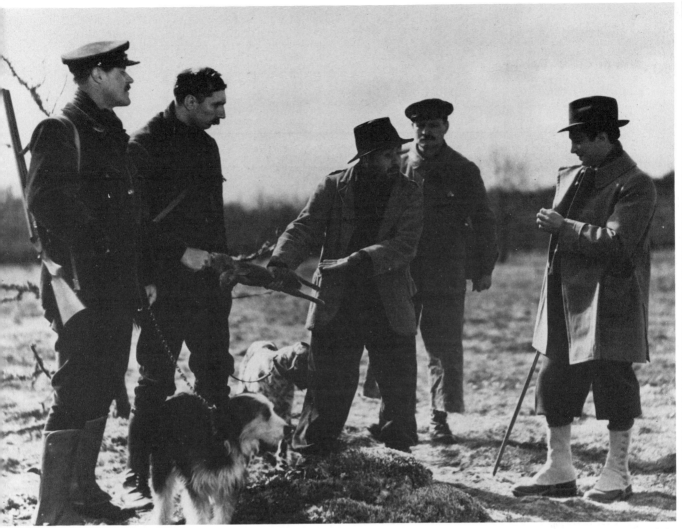

vided a symbol for man's striving for greater things. A nun exhorted others to 'Climb every mountain' in *The Sound of Music* (TCF 1965) and Julie Andrews seemed to take her literally. Nobody in movies climbs a mountain, in Mallory's phrase, 'because it's there,' but for philosophical and psychological reasons. The same mythology seems to inform surfers as alpinists. They compete to become 'king of the mountain' and refer to waves as Everests. The waves are moving mountains and if the surfers don't go to them then they will come to the surfers. In documentaries such as *Endless Summer* (Bruce Brown Films 1966), the act of filming is part of the challenge and experience of surfing. 'A whole new youth movement and transport system rolled into one,' Michael Blackmore calls it in his *Personal History of the Australian Surf* (Adams Packer Films 1981).

Swimming on screens has been dominated by the very free style of the ever-smiling Esther Williams. Synchronized swimming, influenced by the aquatic ballets in her films, has now become accepted as a bona fide sport in the 1984 Olympics. In the 1924 Paris Olympics, the gold medal winner of the 100 and 400 meters freestyle was the future Tarzan, Johnny Weissmuller. Four years later he retained his 100 meters title in Amsterdam, all of which stood him in good stead to outswim crocodiles.

Hunting

The title of Ernest B. Schoedsack and Irving Pichel's chiller *The Most Dangerous Game* (RKO 1932. *The Hounds of Zaroff* — GB), has a double meaning. Count Zaroff (Leslie Banks), a crazy sportsman living on a tropical island, lures people there so he can hunt them like animals and then display their heads as trophies. Man being the most dangerous animal would therefore be the most dangerous game to hunt, and the literal man-hunt also merits that appellation. Joel McCrae and Fay Wray are the prey. Richard Connell's short story, with all its possible interpretations of meaning, has provided at least four pictures with a scenario. Robert Wise directed a cheap remake called *Game of Death* (1946) with John Loder and Audrey Long on the run, and in *Run for the Sun* (1956), Trevor Howard, as an exiled Nazi, gets his kicks from hunting down Richard Widmark and Jane Greer. The same theme was employed in *The Naked Prey* (1966), directed by Cornel Wilde, with Wilde in the wild experiencing what it's like to be a hunted animal. African headhunters allow him a head-start before going after him.

Love Me Tonight (Par. 1932), one of the greatest of all Hollywood musicals, was visualized by the director Rouben Mamoulian in musical terms. In a hunt scene, horses and stags seem to be dancing. The huntsmen and their mounts come to a cottage where Maurice Chevalier and Jean-ette MacDonald are in each other's arms. They retreat in slow motion so as not to disturb the lovers. The scene ends with a view of the fox having taken refuge in a bed.

A munitions magnate, (Wilfred Lawson) flies to the heart of Africa for a month's shooting, taking along his new wife (Gail Patrick). The Safari captain (Warner Baxter) turns out to be none other than his wife's former suitor whom he had hounded out of England. This served as the basis for the plot of *White Hunter* (TCF 1936), directed by Irving Cummings. The plot of *King Soloman's Mines* (1937) kept being interupted by the singing of Paul Robeson. Although it was always a pleasure to hear his voice, the songs were ludicrously out of place even in front of the painted backdrops of darkest Africa. Cedric Hardwicke played the hunter Alan Quartermaine.

In what many consider to be Jean Renoir's finest film, *Rules of The Game* (Nouvelle Edition Francais 1939 *La Regle de*

Jeu), the country house comedy begins to take on a more serious tone during the shooting-party sequence as the aristocrats shoot rabbits with great relish and the pairs of lovers begin to tear into each other. The imagery of the hunt is more emotive than the rest of the film. This is, in part, explained by the director. 'The Sologne is a region of marshes entirely devoted to hunting, a sport which I detest. I consider it an abominable exercise in cruelty. By situating my story amid these vapours I gave myself a chance to depict a shooting-party.'

'An enthralling story of hunters and hunted and primitive love and passion in the heart of the Dark Continent' was how the posters described *Safari* (Par. 1940). Douglas Fairbanks Jr., 'the best hunter in West Africa', accompanies rich tourist Madeleine Carroll and her aristocratic boy-friend Tullio Carminati, on a safari. During a lion hunt, the Count has an easy shot at a lion and only wounds it. Fairbanks goes in to make the kill and is badly mauled. He recovers and decides to give up animal hunting and go Hun-hunting in Europe instead. Miss Carroll goes with him.

When Hemingway returned from a hunting trip to Africa, he attempted 'to write an absolutely true book to see whether the shape of a country and the pattern of a month's action can, if truly presented compete with a work of the imagination.' But *Green Hills of Africa* (1935) is far less interesting than the two short stories that were inspired by the trip. They got 'the shape and pattern' that was missing from his travel book. The stories were 'The Short Happy Life of Francis Macomber' (1936) and 'The Snows of Kilamanjaro' (1936). The former came out on celluloid as *The Macomber Affair* (UA 1947). Directed by Zoltan Korda, it's best when it sticks to Papa and not so good when it strays. By casting Gregory Peck as the white hunter, the contrast between the red-faced English hunter of the story and the American tourist couple is lost. In the story, Mrs Macomber is a floozie to the last whom the hunter rejects. In the movie, as played by Joan Bennett, she changes into a remorseful woman whom Peck falls in love with. (It doesn't make the film any the less

misogynistic.) The Macombers arrive in Nairobi on a hunting expedition as a last attempt at reconciliation. She suspects that her husband Francis (Robert Preston) is cowardly and unmanly beneath his bravado. She compares the assured manner of the hunter Robert Wilson (Peck) with her husband's nervous attitude. Macomber shows his cowardice on a lion hunt. She is disgusted by the spectacle and becomes even more attracted to Wilson. Francis is determined to prove his manhood in the coming dangerous wild buffalo hunt. His fear vanishes and he shoots three buffalos, but is informed that one of them is still alive in the bush. He follows bravely, standing his ground as the animal stampedes. Just as he shoots the buffalo, he himself is shot dead. His wife, thinking to save him, missed the buffalo and hit her husband instead. Was she a good shot or a bad one? In the story it seems like murder, but the film suggests it was an accident. The movie ends with her standing trial. Does she go to prison? Is she aquitted? We are not told, but a critic of the time came up with an answer. He pointed out that the last thing on the screen was 'Released by United Artists'.

Lou Costello plays a book salesman called Stanley Livingstone in *Africa Screams* (UA 1949) who is passed off by fellow clerk Bud Abbott as a big game hunter. They are forced to join a safari to Africa for the purpose of capturing an immense orang-outang. Lou has never been outside New York City and is terrified of mice. Inevitably, Lou and Bud are beset by lions, chimps, alligators, cannibals — and eventually the gigantic orang-outang. The boys and the ape end up back in New York. (From cardboard jungle to asphalt jungle.) Whenever Lou is scared (which is often) he gasps for air like a drowning man and then screams like a castrated hyena. Animal trainer Clyde Beatty, famous explorer Frank Buck and ex-boxers Max and Buddy Baer went along too.

King Solomon's Mines (MGM 1950) was just as remotely connected with the H. Rider Haggard novel as the 1937 version. Stewart Granger as Alan Quartermaine sets out on 'the most dangerous safari of my career' to look for Deborah Kerr's husband who

disappeared during his search for the legendary mines. He is a hunter who does not kill unnecessarily. However, he keeps shooting at animals and creepy-crawlies that make Miss Kerr scream. 'There are times when I prefer animals to humans,' says Granger bitterly. There is a spectacular animal stampede that is not unlike a sale at a big store.

The Wild Heart (Selznick 1952. *Gone to Earth* — GB 1951) ran into a lot of trouble during and after shooting. The British Field Sports Society tried to make it impossible for the film to be made and sent a message to every Master of Foxhounds. 'The film has an anti foxhunting theme. Do not lend the company your pack of hounds.' The horsy set of Much Wenlock (pop. 2,087) in Shropshire where much of the film was made, were uncooperative because of the message contained in Mary Webb's 1917 novel, 'Gone to Earth' on which it was based. In 1950, David O. Selznick (who obtained the western hemisphere rights for allowing his wife Jennifer Jones to appear in it), sued the film's producer Alexander Korda to stop release of the film overseas. Selznick lost the case, but hired Rouben Mamoulian to reshoot almost a third of the picture in Hollywood for US release. The original was an extremely handsome object, gloriously photographed in Technicolor by Christopher Challis often evoking the best of English landscape painters. Like most of the films directed by Michael Powell and Emeric Pressburger (*The Red Shoes*, *The Tales of Hoffman*), it is flamboyant and literate. The story, however, is the type of bucolic melodrama satirized by Stella Gibbons in *Cold Comfort Farm*. Jennifer Jones lives in the Shropshire hills with her widowed father (Esmond Knight). All her love is centered on her pet fox cub which she rescued and reared. Like the fox, she is wild and innocent. She marries a Baptist minister (Cyril Cusack), but is seduced by the wicked squire (David Farrar. Hiss! Hiss!) She goes back to her pale husband when she realizes that the unspeakable squire likes foxhunting. 'I'll hunt you down wherever you'll be,' he smirks. He inadvertantly hunts her to death while she's trying to rescue her fox from the hounds. Jennifer Jones gives one of her most alluring gypsy

performances. The rest of th[e] cast do what they can with th[e] stereotypes of Victoria[n] melodrama.

The best thing about *Wher[e] No Vultures Fly* (Ealing 1951) was its title. It also has an ant[i] hunting message, but this tim[e] the film's guns are trained o[n] big game hunters and ivor[y] poachers. Anthony Steel, lik[e] an English public-school pre[-]fect keeping order in th[e] playground, plays a forme[r] game warden who, sickened b[y] constantly having to ki[ll] animals, sets up a game re[-]serve. The script, the actin[g] and the color are uneven. Th[e] sequel, *West of Zanzibar* (Eal[-]ing 1954) provides the sam[e] formula as before with ele[-]phants as the name of th[e] game. Harry Wyatt, outdoors[y] British director, made the[m] both.

Big white hunter Victo[r] Mature, with glamorous Jane[t] Leigh and crazed Englishma[n] Roland Culver in tow, hacks hi[s] way through a cliché-ridde[n] jungle in *Safari* (Col. 1956). Culver is obsessed with th[e] desire to kill the famous lio[n] Hatari and is seriously maule[d] in the attempt. Mature is mor[e] interested in hunting down th[e] Mau-Mau general (Earl Cam[-]eron) who murdered his family[.] Janet Leigh paddles nude i[n] jungle pools as crocodiles mov[e] towards her like randy life[-]guards. Mature kills a[n] elephant, a rhino and a Mau[-]Mau. A Mau-Mau kills Culver[,] leaving Mature free to engul[f] Janet Leigh in his arms[.] Terence Young directed this rather offensive hokum in CinemaScope and color.

Steward Granger reappears as a hunter in India in *Harry Black and the Tiger* (TCF 1958). The tiger descends on a[n] Indian village, stalking the empty streets like a gun[-]fighter. He grabs a woman i[n] his mouth and runs off with her. Enter Harry Black (Granger) and his whisky-loving Indian servant Bapu (I.S. Johar). Granger tries to kill the woman-eating tiger[,] but is jumped on as he shoots[.] Both Harry Black and the tiger are wounded. Black is nursed back to health by Barbara Rush who is married to coward[ly] Anthony Steel. He finally kills the tiger, leaves Barbara, and lives happily ever after with his Indian servant. Hugo Fregonese misdirected.

In Sheridan's *The Rivals*, Mrs Malaprop spoke of 'allegories on the banks of the

Nile.' Roots of Heaven (TCF 1958) is an allegory in the jungle. Idealist Trevor Howard goes round the small town of Fort Lamy in French Equatorial Africa searching for people to sign his petition to stop the slaughter of elephants. 'I live with them. I like them. I like looking at them and listening to them. As a matter of fact, I'd give anything to become an elephant myself,' he tells sympathetic bargirl Juliette Greco. He soon realizes he won't get people on his side by peaceful means so he decides on stronger measures. He sets fire to the local ivory dealer's store and shoots US commentator-hunter Orson Welles with buckshot in his ample backside. He forms a motley band including Greco, drunken Englishman Errol Flynn (his penultimate role), a Baron Olivier Hussenot) who refuses to speak because of his disgust for mankind and a Black Na-

tionalist Edric Connor using the group for his own political ends. Later they are joined by American photographer Eddie Albert who, after seeing elephants shot, discards his camera and follows Trevor Howard into the bush. Although each character has symbolic value and the story, based on Romain Gary's novel, is a bit overblown, John Huston and his cast have made an entertaining spectacle. Leaving aside the dubious attitude to anti-colonialists, the image of the doomed elephant in a real African landscape comes over strongly. It was filmed in the Lake Chad area in 10 weeks of shooting with temperatures of 140 degrees F in the shade. Special icing machines were used to keep the color film from melting. Some members of the crew caught malaria and beri-beri, proving once again that film-making is a dangerous sport in itself.

Robert Mitchum is Captain Wade Hunnicutt in *Home from the Hill* (MGM 1960), a big man, big landowner, womanizer and the best hunter in the county. During a hunting trip outside the small Southern town where he has his estate, he is shot at by a jealous husband. It's all part of being a Man. Hunnicott's teenage son, Theron (George Hamilton) is too influenced by his mother (Eleanor Parker) and the Captain is determined to make a man of him. Under the tutelage of his father and backwoods boy Rafe (George Peppard), he learns to hunt, proving his manhood by slaughtering a huge, black boar. The killing of the boar is the significant event that enables him to shun the world of his mother and enter the macho world of his father. The great thing, he is told, is 'to be known in these parts as a man.' Later when Theron rebels against his father's masculine code, he also

abandons hunting. Pretty steamy stuff, directed steamily by Vincente Minnelli from the novel by William Humphrey.

The Last Safari (Par. 1967) is a title that may create joy or regret depending on one's attitude to the 'sport' of big game hunting. Suntanned, gray-haired Stewart Granger is wheeled out again to play a hunter. Is it his prominent jaw, English accent, and ruddy features that cast him so often as a hunter? Here he is disillusioned by the sweeping changes that have overtaken Kenya. He feels he is nothing more than a paid escort for trigger-happy tourists. He decides to go off on his last safari to destroy Big Red, an elephant that killed his closest friend. Tagging along with him are a rich American (Kaz Garas) and his half-caste companion (Gabriella Licudi), creating the familar triangular tension. When Granger finally has Big Red within his sights, he

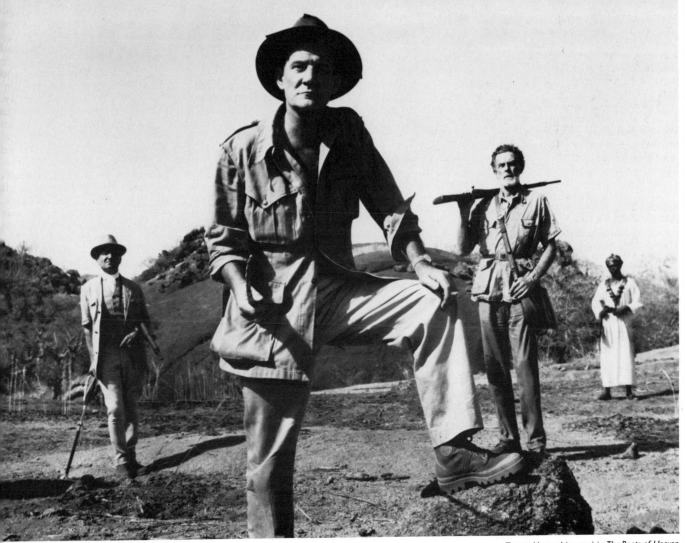

Trevor Howard (center) in *The Roots of Heaven*

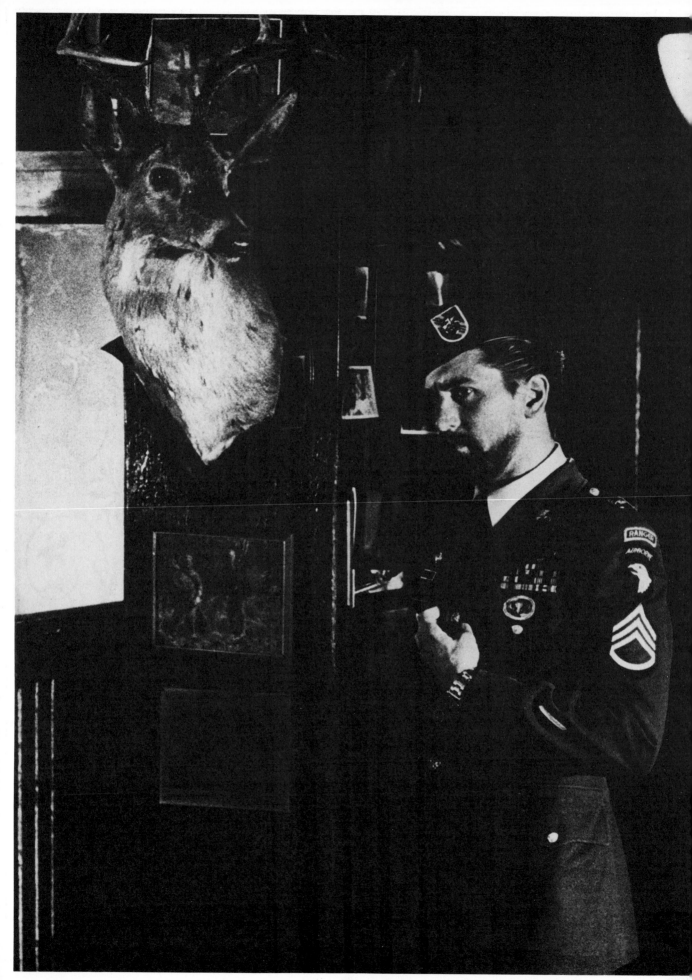

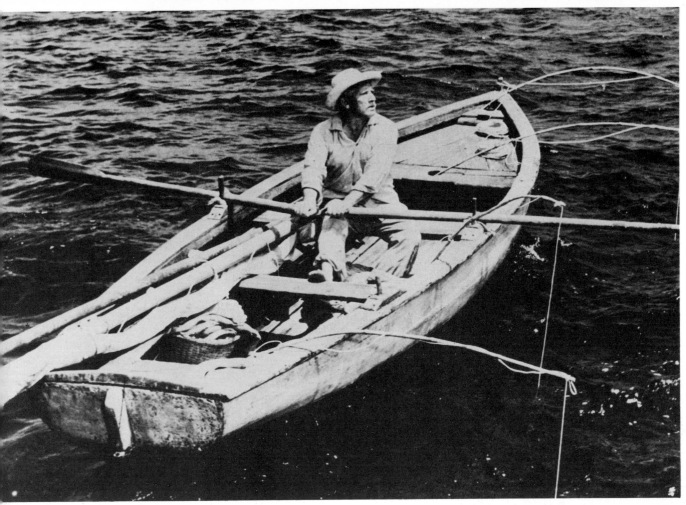

Spencer Tracy in *The Old Man and the Sea*

esitates, refusing to press the trigger. Big Red goes free. The safari party is over. Somehow by not shooting he has regained his status as a hunter. Produced and directed by Henry Hathaway from Gerald Haney's novel, *Gilligan's Last Elephant*, filmed on location in Kenya, the script is lumbering, the direction elephantine.

'There is perhaps no other literature quite so patriotic (as American literature) because none is so damning of the failure of a country to live up to its dreams and expectations', wrote Norman Mailer, author of *The Naked and the Dead*, arguably the best American novel of World War II. Mailer's novel *Why are we in Vietnam?* takes place during a hunting trip. The hunt in *The Deer Hunter* (MGM 1978) is the last possibility for the young men to practice the traditional masculine rites of the frontiersman before being cast into a bloody war that has no part in that tradition. The men fool around before the hunt until Robert de Niro, already show-

ing signs of leadership, begins to stalk the deer. The joking among friends is over. The fir trees, lakes, mists and rocks seem much further away from their small industrial town than they really are. The hunt takes on an epic quality as a Russian hymn rises on the soundtrack. De Niro shoots the deer with one bullet. 'One shot is what hunting's all about,' he says and it is a motif that runs through the movie with its games of Russian Roulette. When de Niro returns home from the Vietnam war, he goes up to the same spot as before. This time he is alone. (One of his friends is dead, the other crippled.) It is winter. There is snow on the ground. The Russian hymn rises again, but the scene has a different perspective. He stalks the deer and when he sees the beautiful creature, he fires into the air. The killing has to stop. He throws the gun away. Michael Cimino's film ends with the singing of 'God Bless America.' Dr Johnson said that 'Patriotism is the last refuge of the scoundrel' — for the people in *The Deer Hunter* who have

been hurt by the war, it is merely a last refuge.

In the past (up to about 1960), adults would accompany their children to the latest Walt Disney cartoon feature with enthusiasm. Nowadays, neither generation could get much excitement from the conventional animation, the coy songs, the cuteness and cuddliness of it all. Trying for some kind of moral fable, *The Fox and the Hound* (Disney 1981) tells of how a fox cub and a hound pup spend a happy childhood together, but because of the laws of nature (man?), they have to become sworn enemies, the hunted and the hunter. Among those who give voice to the drawings are Mickey Rooney, Pearl Bailey and Jack Albertson.

Fishing

Raymie (Allied Artists 1950) is an 8-year-old boy (David Ladd, Alan's lad) who lives with his widowed mother (Julie Adams) in a small fishing village on the Pacific coast. He is an avid fisherman and never tires of the legend concerning Old

Moe, a giant barracuda. He dreams of catching Old Moe one day. Because his friend (Charles Winninger) suffers a heart attack and has to give up fishing, he gives his expensive fishing gear to Raymie. It's not long before Raymie lands Old Moe. They struggle, but suddenly a change comes over the boy. He no longer wants the fish destroyed and as Old Moe is hauled in, he cuts the line. The other fishermen are furious, but his mother's boyfriend (John Agar) understands. 'The kid taught us all a great lesson. Like making your mind up and having the courage to sacrifice for it,' he moralizes. (He's fishing for compliments as he wants to marry Raymie's mother.) Charles Winninger and Raymie smile cheesily as Julie Adams and John Agar walk away from the pier hand in hand. Jerry Lewis singing the title song is enough to scare the fish away.

The message of *The Old Man and the Sea* (WB 1958) is 'Man can be destroyed but not defeated.' Unfortunately, Leland Hayward's production,

Left: Robert De Niro and the deer he shot before going to Vietnam in *The Deer Hunter*

133

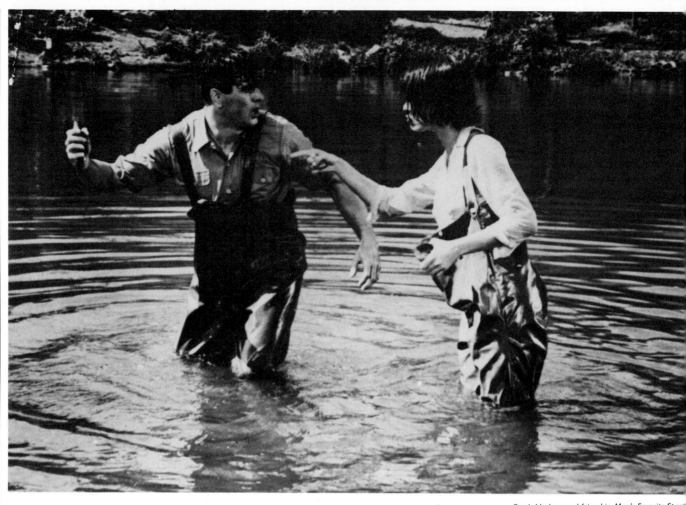

Rock Hudson and friend in *Man's Favorite Sport*

John Sturges' direction and Peter Viertel's adaptation belie that message. They were not destroyed but defeated by the task of transferring Hemingway's short parable-novel to the screen. Like the old man's efforts to land the giant marlin, John Sturges and his team (excepting James Wong Howe's splendid camerawork) grappled with the material and ended up with only a large skeleton. Also like the old man's struggle with the fish, it was a noble failure. The producers avoided the temptation to add feminine interest, a villain, a happy ending and to open it out more. But over-fidelity, in any sphere, can cloy and there are other ways of transmuting prose into film than this picturalization. The novel, although written in the third person, is almost an interior monologue and the filmmakers have resorted to the narrational device in order to use as much of Hemingway's language as possible. Spencer Tracy narrates well, but most of the time either the narration or the images are redundant. A humble Cuban fisherman has gone 84 days without catching

a fish. He goes out once more in his skiff alone and hooks a marlin. His line is unbelievably heavy as he tries to pull the fish in. It pulls the skiff out to sea, with the old man holding on. Four hours later, the man is still holding it, his right hand bleeding. On the third day, the old man harpoons it. It is the biggest fish he has ever seen, weighing over 1,500 lbs. It is bigger than the boat. He lashes the fish to the stern and starts for home. Sharks begin to attack and eat away the marlin. During his battle with the sharks, he is stripped of everything — his harpoon, his knife, his oar, and finally he is left with nothing but a skeleton. Tracy is as convincing as any film star could be in the rôle. His leathery, lined face is virtually the only face one sees for three-quarters of the film. It was filmed with Hemingway's guidance in the actual locations of the novel.

There is a slight snigger in the question mark in the title of Howard Hawks' *Man's Favorite Sport?* (UI 1964). The implication being that Man isn't mankind, nor the sport a sport in the strictest sense. Osten-

sibly the movie is about fishing. Rock Hudson plays the author of a best-selling book on fishing and is also top fishing-equipment salesman for Abercrombie and Fitch. A retired army officer (Roscoe Karns), a fishing fanatic, wants Hudson's advice on how to win the big tournament at Lake Wakapoogee. Paula Prentiss, a P.R. for the tournament, suggests that Hudson should enter as publicity for the store. He confesses to her that he has never fished in his life and that all his knowledge of fishing was obtained through research and conversations with fishing stars. Prentiss promises that in three days he will have enough practical training to make a good show in the tournament. Overloaded with the latest style of fishing and camping gear, he camps out near Lake Wakapoogee so that he can practice fishing in secret. He has trouble putting up a tent, he falls in the water but can't swim and has to contend with a jealous fiancée. During the tournament he manages to catch a trout by snagging his line on a tree branch and the hungry fish

jumps out at the bait. On the third day, with the help of a bear, he lands the biggest fish and wins the tournament. Other even less funny gags in this two-hour long comedy are Hudson catching his tie in a girl's dress zipper, being unable to unzip a sleeping bag he is in and having to hop around in it, and trying to fake a broken arm (to get out of the tournament) but the plaster cast freezes his arm into a salute position. The movie satisfies the film critics' favorite sport of 'hunt the symbol'. Substitute fishing for sex and we have a perfect thesis. Hudson has never fished (he's a virgin) but has written a book about it. He has all the equipment but he doesn't know how to use it until he is taught technique by nature-girl Paula Prentiss. A fish (phallic symbol) gets inside his pants and he jerks around trying to get rid of it. His tent is pink(!). These interpretations don't make the movie any better or funnier, but they make for a good parlor game.

Islands in the Stream (Par. 1977) was another attempt to adapt Ernest Hemingway to he screen. The novel, left unfinished, was published nine years after Hemingway killed himself in 1961. It contains some of his worst writing, thin psychology, and virile posturings. The best parts are his descriptions of deep sea fishing and the hero's relationship with his sons. The same applies to Franklin Schaffner's direction and Denne Bart Peticlerc's screenplay, but where the book is bad, the film is worse. At least the novel had Hemingway's authentic faux-naif style. The islands of the title are the Bahamas (in the Gulf Stream) and also, as in *For Whom the Bell Tolls*, that which no man is. Living there is the semi-autobiographical figure of Thomas Hudson (George C. Scott), painter and sculptor, who spends most of his time boozing, hunting and fishing. In 1940 he is visited by his three young sons (Hart Buckner, Michael-James Wixted, Brad Savage) and sets out to put them through a course of manliness. When they go spear fishing, the eldest boy is confronted with a hammerhead shark. He is able to take the fish off his spear gun and throw it in the path of the shark before it is shot from the shore. On a deep-sea fishing trip, the second son hooks a marlin and the enormous fish gives him a tremendous fight. His father stands behind him encouraging the young man as the hours pass. Seeing his son's bleeding hands and feet, he offers to take the line, but the boy will not quit. Just as the fish is pulled up, it escapes to the depths of the sea. The boy is not defeated by the experience, but realizes that the way he performed was more important than the result. Sententious maybe, but it is nothing to the sentimental tosh and false heroics that follow. The oldest son proves himself by being killed while serving as a fighter pilot and there is an embarrassing episode between Hudson and his ex-wife (Claire Bloom). It ends with Hudson fighting Nazis off the Cuba coast while carrying Jewish refugees by boat to safety. George C. Scott, with his gruff voice and exterior hiding a heart beneath the figurative chest-wig, comes as near to the Hemingway persona as one could wish.

Mountaineering

In the Germany of the 20's, a group of film makers led by Dr Arnold Fanck produced a sequence of mountain films. They were both vivid documentaries as well as symbolic and didactic melodramas. (Fanck was later prominent in Nazi films.) Leni Riefenstahl, the director of *Olympia 1936*, appeared in four of Fanck's mountain films. The best was *The White Hell of Pitz Palu* (released by Universal 1929) directed by Fanck and G.W. Pabst. Most of the film was shot in conditions of extreme cold during a 5-month location trip to the 12,000 ft high Pitz Palu in the Alps. It tells of a honeymoon couple (Riefenstahl, Gustav Diessel) who attempt the ascent of Pitz Palu. The wife is lost in a crevasse and every year after the husband returns to the spot. Many years later he is caught in a storm and finds himself reunited with his young bride. Universal used much of the footage in many B movies and serials, and later mountain films copied certain scenes. It was remade in 1953 with Hans Albers and Liselotte Pulver also using footage from the old silent version. Leni Riefenstahl's first film as director was *The Blue Light* (Sokal-Riefenstahl 1932) in which a strange young woman (Riefenstahl) sleepwalks in the mountains, finally killing herself. The films emphasized a heroic idealism that conquers nature's powers and achieves a mystical union with it.

The Challenge (London Films 1938) purports to tell the story of the original conquest of Matterhorn on the 14th July 1865 by a British team led by Edward Whymper. Three members of the team and a guide perished during the descent. (Bodies are seen bouncing from rock to rock.) The film, directed by Milton Rosmer with Robert Douglas as Whymper, tells of the exciting race between the British attacking the ascent from the Swiss side and an Italian team from the Italian side. (The Matterhorn, south-west of the town of Zermatt, is on the frontier between Switzerland and Italy.) Unfortunately, the film is saddled with an anticlimactic and somewhat

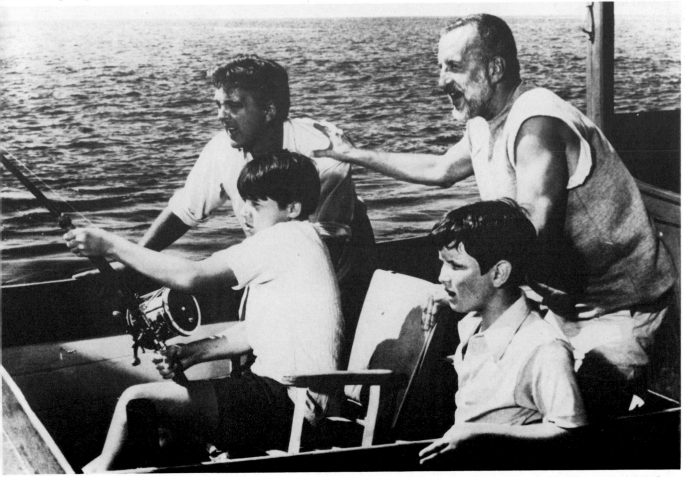

Michael-James Wixted (with rod), David Hemmings, George C. Scott and Brad Savage in *Islands in the Stream*

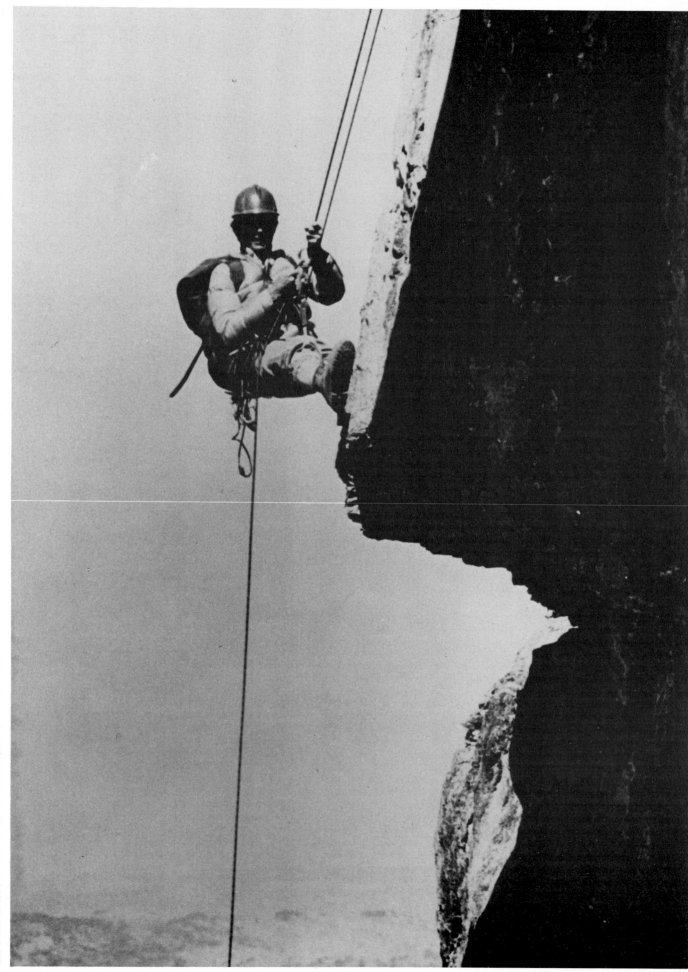

ridiculous court case in which Whymper is accused by an Italian of cutting the rope of his team-mates. His friend, an Italian guide (Luis Trenker), climbs the mountain himself to retrieve the broken strands of the rope arriving in the nick of time to prove Whymper's innocence. It ends not with a bang but a . . . .

The Matterhorn again provides the white background to *High Conquest* (Monogram 1947) and the bête noir of American mountaineer Warren Douglas. Since his father was killed on the mountain, he has refused to climb it. He is helped to overcome his fear by C. Aubrey Smith of the Alpine Club in London and by the love of Anna Lee. He returns to Switzerland and climbs the mountain with jealous guide Gilbert Roland. Roland tries to kill him, but he himself topples off the mountain. Irving Allen produced and directed this minor actioner.

High in the Swiss Alps, in the village of Kandermatt, at the base of the mountain known as *The White Tower* (RKO 1950), six people prepare for the climb. In the valley is Valli, daughter of a world-famous climber who saw her father die on the mountain a few hundred yards from the summit and so wants to carry on his dream; Claude Rains a drink-sodden writer who hopes the climb will provide him with the inspiration to finish a novel and also prove to his wife his is not a coward; Sir Cedric Hardwicke wants to climb to compensate for a life of failure and Lloyd Bridges is a German with Nazi sympathies who wishes to be the first to reach the summit for personal pride and national glory. Glenn Ford, an American, tags along because he is in love with Valli. Oscar Holmolka is the guide who has seen better days. They set off with not only their backpacks but with the burden of a heavy philosophical message. What a group to climb an unconquered mountain! The guide is fat and short of breath, Rains is a drunk, Hardwicke is ancient, the German doesn't believe in teamwork, and the American has never even done any social climbing. None of them look as though they could scale a fish. Half-way up the mountain, Glenn Ford proposes to Valli and Claude Rains finishes his novel and then

Left: Clint Eastwood in The Eiger Sanction

throws it and himself off a precipice. Towards the summit there is a race between the German and the American. The German is too proud to take help from the American and falls to his death. Directed by Ted Tetziaff, some of the Swiss mountain photography in Technicolor is pleasant and there are some wonderfully unlifelike papier maché rocks for the intimate scenes. However, fingers straining to hold onto the side of a mountain never fails to create high anxiety.

A few days before Queen Elizabeth II was crowned on June 2nd 1953, news came that the highest peak in the world had been climbed by a British team led by Colonel John Hunt. With them went a young photographer called Thomas Stobart who, with the aid of director Leon Clore, assembled the material to make *The Conquest of Everest* (Rank 1953), a splendid documentary of the event. The distinguished Irish poet Louis MacNiece wrote the commentary (spoken by Welsh actor Meredith Edwards) and Australian composer Arthur Benjamin wrote the inspirational music. Unfortunately, the one thing we don't see is the conquest of Everest. The commentary and the music try to make up for not being able to film the final assault. Who was the first man on the top? Was it the New Zealander Edward Hillary or the Sherpa Tensing. Did they both step on it in unison? 'Look Ma, top of the world!'

While the British climbed real mountains, the Americans continued to conquer fictional ones. Strictly speaking, Spencer Tracy in *The Mountain* (Par. 1956) is supposed to be Swiss. He wears a beret, wide corduroys tucked into mountain boots and guards a flock of sheep at the foot of Mont Bald which looks like the Paramount logo but is, in fact, Mont Blanc. Claire Trevor, his girlfriend of many years, is about as Swiss as a Hershy bar. He has a dissolute younger brother played by Robert Wagner. When a plane carrying gold from Calcutta to Paris crashes on top of the mountain young Wagner decides to climb the mountain to get his greedy hands on it. Tracy goes to keep an eye on his kid brother. The climb is a hazardous one. Extremely gripping are fingers and feet exploring an ice-packed rock for a hold.

They find a young Indian girl (Anna Kashfi), badly hurt but still alive. While the bad brother rummages among the dead bodies for money, the good one tends to the girl and improvises a sled. Wagner leaves alone and is killed in an avalanche. Tracy returns to the village with the girl and tells the villagers that his brother was a hero. Although they don't tell the noble Tracy, they don't believe a word of it. The rest is pretty hard to swallow too. Edward Dmytryk produced and directed.

Another American movie with a Swiss accent was *Third Man on the Mountain* (Walt Disney 1959) about a Swiss boy with an American accent. He is James McArthur who lives with his mamma and uncle in the village of Kurtal in 1865. He is determined to become as famous a guide as his father who was killed in an attempt to conquer The Citadel. Despite opposition from his family, he manages to get up the mountain, save a man's life and prove himself. Actually filmed in the Alps, the climbing sequences are of a high standard. The actors, including Michael Rennie, James Donald and Herbert Lom, do what they can with the stilted dialogue. Ken Annakin directed competently.

'He could climb all over me any time,' writes one of Clint Eastwood's female students in *The Eiger Sanction* (UI 1975). He is a professor of art at an American university. The mild-mannered Eastwood (called Dr Jonathan Hemlock) has a terrific collection of Impressionists obtained with money he has earned from murder. Tempted by the offer of a Pissarro, he agrees to perform one more sanction (a euphemism for assassination). He has to kill a member of an international alpine expedition which is to climb the north face of the Eiger. He is to join the party, discover the identity of his victim and find a propitious moment, while on the mountain, to do the deed. Eastwood goes into training in Arizona with his old pal George Kennedy who happens to be managing the expedition. One would have thought that practicing on hot sandstone in the desert wouldn't be particularly good training for the icy slopes of the Eiger, but it makes for some excellent desert scenery to contrast with the later alpine variety. On the way to the nail-biting climax,

Mr Eastwood beds a bevy of beauties, disposes of a wicked homosexual and his dog Faggot, escapes a hyperdermic needle and throws someone out of a window. All the while the director of the picture looks at the star with increasing admiration. As they are one and the same person it is not surprising. On the Eiger there is plenty going on but most of it is over the top. Falling rocks, loose ropes, the dreadful Fohn wind and people trying to kill each other. Good scenery behind the bad James Bondage.

Water Sports

Competitive rowing appears only fleetingly in Hollywood movies. More frequently, rowing is of the *On Moonlight Bay* (WB 1951) variety. Boy romancing girl while pulling on the oars. The roles are reversed in *Horse Feathers* (Par. 1932) when Groucho lies languidly in the boat, his hand trailing in the water, as Thelma Todd does the rowing. The most famous rowing trip is the one on which Monty Clift drowned his unwanted girlfriend Shelley Winters in *A Place in the Sun* (1951). (Phillips Holms did the same to Silvia Sydney in *An American Tragedy* — 1931.) Valentino was more often to be seen stroking women than a boat, but in *The Young Rajah* (Par. 1922) he plays an Indian Prince at Harvard who helps stroke the college team to victory. In *Freshman Love* (WB 1936, *Rhythm on the River* — GB), Frank McHugh is a college coach whose attempts to turn his rowing team into winners is beyond him until he gets Patricia Ellis to vamp two of the best oarsmen in the country in order to make them join the team. Jealousy between them causes problems, but all is smoothed out in time to save the day for the college team. It was a remake of the football comedy *The College Widow* (WB 1927). Robert Taylor is the Yank from Nebraska in *A Yank at Oxford* (MGM 1938) who shines in the Oxford-Cambridge Boat Race. The *Three Men in a Boat* (Romulus 1956) foul up the Henley Regatta during their trip up the English waterways, one of the many amusing incidents on the way.

Mistaken identity was an essential ingredient in a Joe E. Brown scenario, and in *Top*

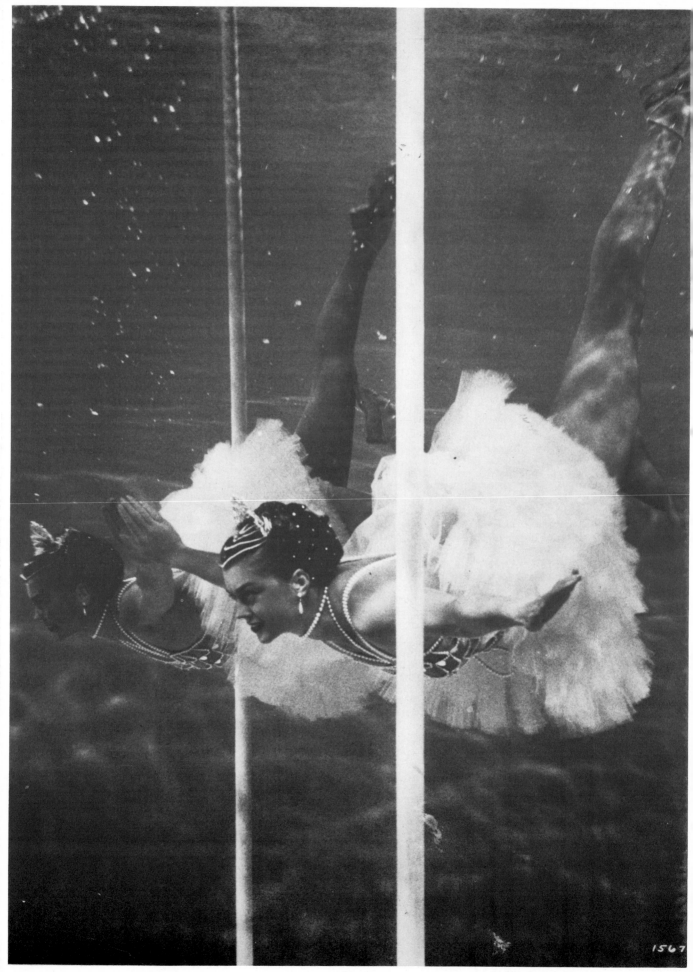

Speed (WB 1930) he plays a humble clerk who pretends to be a millionaire and wins a speed boat race in a vessel owned by his sweetheart's father. In *You Said a Mouthful* (WB 1932) he is mistaken for a champion swimmer. Neither movie could be mistaken for a very good comedy, but the latter contained more laughs. Brown plays an inventor of a 'non-sinkable bathing suit'. The heroine (21-year-old Ginger Rogers) changes the costume for an ordinary one when Joe takes part in a race from Catalina to L.A. He wins by crawling along the ocean bed. Joe E. Brown spent six hours daily for eight days in a studio tank for the shooting. Mervyn LeRoy directed *Top Speed*, a mildly amusing story with a well-handled climactic boat race. Bernice Claire was the girl.

'Wet she was a star.' — 'Only on dry land is she truly out of her depth.' — 'She is a duck in the water but a fish out of it.' These remarks, of course, refer to Esther Williams, 'Hollywood's Mermaid'. She was a champion swimmer at 15 and soon joined Billy Rose's Aquacade before going to Hollywood at 19 where she swam her way through over a dozen bright MGM musicals of the forties and fifties. In *Bathing Beauty* (1944) she was a swimming instructor at a women's college. The picture ended with a spectacular water-ballet set to the 'Blue Danube' with alternate jets of water and flame bursting out of an Olympic-sized pool. In *Million-Dollar Mermaid* (1952 *The One-piece Bathing Suit* — GB) she played Annette Kellerman, the Australian swimming champion who first introduced to the world the one-piece bathing suit. The high spot of the movie was Busby Berkeley's elaborately staged aquatic production number in which Esther (or rather the stunt-girl) dived from a tremendous height into the center of a kaleidoscopic pattern formed by swimmers. Although Esther Williams did most of the swimming, a combination of crawl, breast and backstroke while smiling at the camera, she often had a stand-in (or swim-in) for the more dangerous stunts. She was forever blowing bubbles under water, seemingly having an inexhaustible supply of

Left: Esther Williams in *Million Dollar Mermaid*

air. Script writers were hard put to it to find an excuse to get Esther wet. Most of the time in *Dangerous When Wet* (1953) was taken up by Esther's preparations to swim the English Channel. The best moment was a wet-dream sequence in which Esther swims with Tom and Jerry while trying to avoid an octopus in a beret who gropes her with 6 extra hands while she's attempting her Channel swim.

The water-skiing ballet that ended *Easy to Love* (MGM 1953) was one of Busby Berkeley's last and most spectacular sequences. Filmed on location at Cypress Gardens, Florida, over 30 water skiers are towed in arrow-head formation with Esther Williams at the tip. They jump and slalom around the beautiful amphibian in CinemaScope and Technicolor. Then, seizing a trapeze dangled from a helicopter, she rises to the height of 500 feet, and dives into the pleasure garden lagoon.

Most of Roman Polanski's first feature, *Knife in the Water* (Kanawha Films 1963), takes place on board a weekend sailing sloop. A married couple pick up a young hitchhiker and take him with them on the boat. A game of sexual rivalry ensues, beginning with the husband vaunting himself as a sailor and mocking the clumsiness of the youth. An extremely assured debut by the 28-year-old director.

The celebrated International Grand Prix boat race of Miami is the setting of a trashy melodrama called *Racing Fever* (AA 1964). A speed-boat racer sees his father run down and killed by a hydro-plane piloted by a millionaire playboy. But during the big race, the racer saves the millionaire's life. The villain, however, is shot by his mistress. The son was played by Lee Gunner, the father by Pop Gunner, the mistress by Linda Gunner and the playboy by Gregg Stevenson.

Not much *Fun in Acapulco* (Par. 1964) with Elvis Presley as a singer-cum-lifeguard at a swanky hotel in Mexico's famous holiday resort. The regular lifeguard (Alejandro Rey) gets jealous when Elvis gets involved with social director Ursula Andress. Rey spends his nights diving from the 136 ft. cliff of La Quebrada and he challenges Elvis to do it. However, Elvis is scared of heights since he dropped a

partner from a trapeze in a circus, but after winning a fight with the lifeguard he overcomes his fear and dives from the cliff.

In 1963, with Rock 'n Roll movies a thing of the past and Twist movies on their last swaying legs, a new series of pictures for the youth market hit the screens. The 'Beach Party' movies popularity lasted unbelievably for 4 years. Almost every one of them starred Frankie Avalon and Annette Funicello and involved a group of young surf creeps, usually on Malibu beach, defending their right to continue their mindless activities without interference from 'squares'!

Beach Party (AI 1963) started it all. Robert Cummings studies the sex habits of the 'surfin' and a swingin'' habitués of Malibu including Avalon and Funicello. In *Bikini Beach* (AI 1964) Keenan Wynn attempts to evict surfers from the beach where he wants to build a community for senior citizens. The old people are really swingers and enjoy the pleasures of beach life. Frankie Avalon plays a dual role as a surfer and a British pop star. Funicello, Boris Karloff, Stevie Wonder and Don Rickles are among the flotsam and jetsam. Three Arizona girls arrive at the coast in *Surf Party* (TCF 1964) in search of the brother of one of them. Bobby Vinton is the brother. Frankie Avalon heads a group of surfers who clash with a group of muscle men in *Muscle Beach Party* (AI 1964). Also around are Annette Funicello (who else?), Luciana Paluzzi, Don Rickles, Peter Lorre and Stevie Wonder. Others were *Beach Blanket Bingo* (AI 1965), a mixture of surfing and sky-diving with Avalon, Funicello, Buster Keaton and Don Rickles; *How to Stuff a Wild Bikini* (AI 1965) with Avalon and Funicello, Mickey Rooney, Buster Keaton and Brian Donlevy; *Wild on the Beach* (Lippert Inc. 1965) with Sonny and Cher battling to save a beach house; *The Ghost in the Invisible Bikini* (AI 1966) with Tommy Kirk, Nancy Sinatra, Boris Karloff and Basil Rathbone. Mercifully, the series ended with *The Catalina Caper* (Crown I. 1967) with Tommy Kirk.

Ride the Wild Surf (Col. 1964) was a slightly better class of surf party movie, firstly because it excluded Frankie Avalon and Annette Funicello,

secondly it was set in Hawaii instead of the familiar South Cal. and thirdly because it concentrated more on the surfing than the party. Surfers from all over the world gather at Oahu Island, among them are three American buddies, Fabian, Tab Hunter and Peter Brown. They meet three girls, Shelley Fabares, Susan Hart and Barbara Eden. After the romancing comes the competition. The title is given to the man who stays afloat longest through the biggest waves. The three guys ride the 40 ft. waves against the world's best surfers as the girls watch from the beach. Peter Brown almost drowns and Tab Hunter's surfboard breaks. The sole survivors are Fabian and last year's winner Eskimo (James Mitchum). Their bodies are covered with welts and bruises. Eskimo finally decides to compromise and suggests they ride their last wave together. Fabian refuses and Eskimo quits. Tired but triumphant, Fabian rides the wild surf alone to win the title of 'king of the mountain'. Former actor Don Taylor directed, Jo and Art Napoleon wrote and produced.

California surfer-filmmaker Bruce Brown, produced, directed, wrote, photographed, edited, sound-recorded and narrated *The Endless Summer* (Bruce Brown Films 1966). He took two years to edit this dazzling document of a 3 month, 35,000-mile journey around the world of two Californian surfers (Mike Hynson and Robert August) in search of the 'perfect wave'. They try out the surf in Senegal, Ghana, Nigeria, Australia, New Zealand and Tahiti. On the north shore of Hawaii they ride the 'Pipeline', the Mt Everest of surfdom. In Cape St Francis in S. Africa they enjoy the perfect curl that gives them 'a long, loose ride'. Brown's waterproof camera takes us on the swell, through the 'boomers' and 'over the falls'. The narration is clear, keeping surf-lingo to a minimum, sometimes witty, sometimes repetitious. Bruce Brown loves the word 'ultimate'. 'The ultimate thing in surfing is to be covered up by the wave.' *The Endless Summer* may not be the ultimate surf-movie but it comes pretty close.

Surfari (Don Brown Prod.

Overleaf: Fabian (center) in *Beach Party*

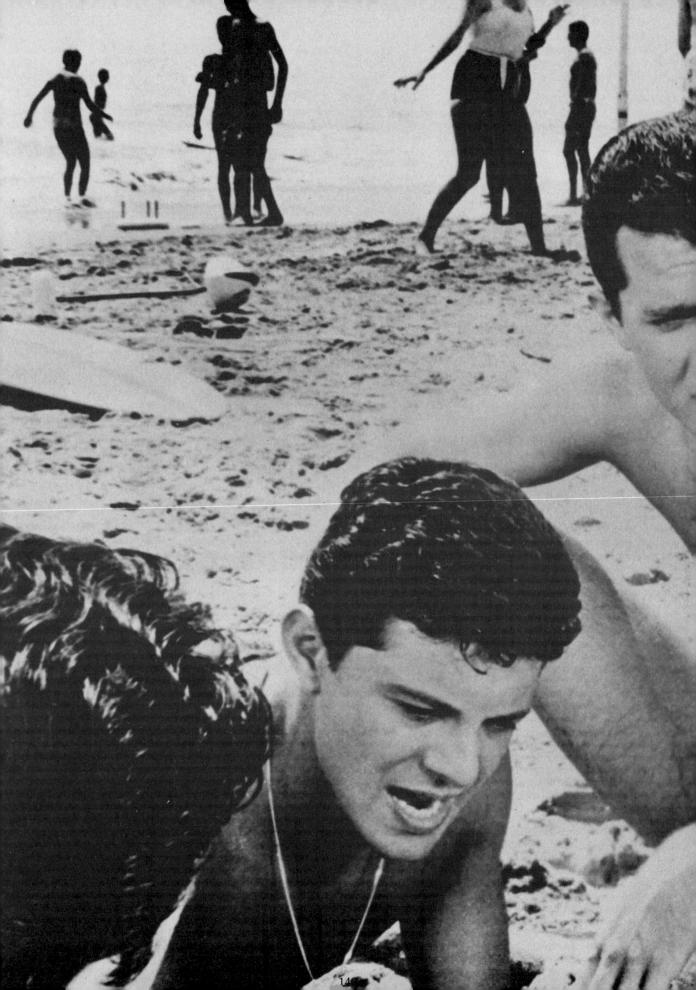

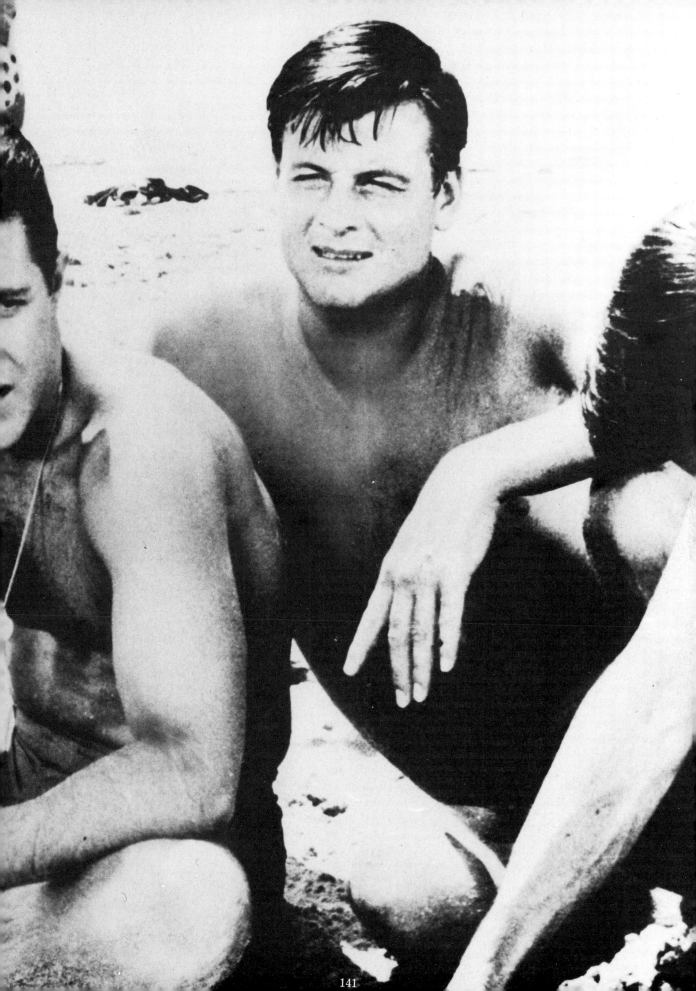

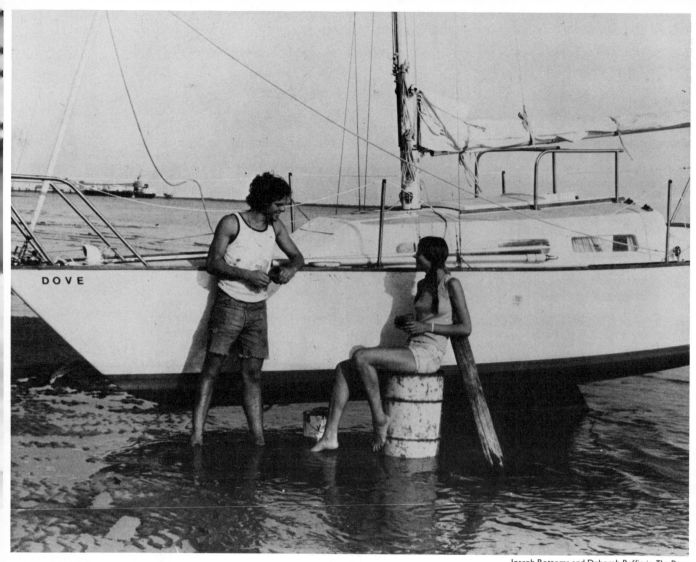

Joseph Bottoms and Deborah Raffin in *The Dove*

1967) covers much the same ocean as *The Endless Summer*. Produced and written by Don Brown, (not to be confused with Bruce Brown of the former film, although they both have appropriate surf-names), it is a record of some spectacular surfing in California, Hawaii and Australia. Unhappily, it is interrupted by beach bum antics, beauty contests, lifeboat drills and skateboarding. The surfing was done by Ricky Grigg, Greg Noll and Mike Bennett. One can enjoy the sun, the sand, the skin and the surf without getting one's feet wet.

Rich boy Elvis Presley wants girls to love him for himself and not for his money, so he changes places with water-ski instructor Will Hutchins in *Clambake* (UA 1967). At a studio-bound Miami beach, he sings songs like 'Hey, hey, hey,' and 'Who needs money?' and instructs golddigger Shelley Fabares in water-skiing. The Orange Bowl International Power Boat Regatta is about to take place and Elvis helps repair a new design boat using a miraculous protective coating called Goop. In the race, playboy Bill Bixby takes the lead in a contest he's won for three successive years. Elvis is second. In a burst of speed, Elvis crosses the line first. He proposes to Fabares who agrees to marry him even before she discovers he's a millionaire. The movie is Goop from start to finish.

Michael Sarrazin, a beach bum in Malibu, tells his girlfriend Jacqueline Bisset that all he wants out of life is the surf and waves. He would like to marry her, but he has to get the beachnik life out of his system. At last, (after 100 mins. of film time) he goes to the beach, makes *The Sweet Ride* (TCF 1968) on his surfboard, then walks away, leaving the board in the sand. He has realized there is more to life than just escapism. He refuses to be a drifter any longer and leaves his tennis hustler friend (Anthony Fransciosa) all alone.

In 1965, 16-year-old Robin Lee Graham left his home port of San Pedro, California on a 23-foot sloop for a 5-year voyage around the world. The name of his sloop and of the film based on his book was *The Dove* (EMI 1974). His voyage took him through the S. Pacific to the Samoan Islands, Fiji, New Guinea and Australia, then around the Cape of Good Hope, up the African coast onto S. America and then back to California. Photographed splendidly on location by Sven Nykvist, directed by Charles Jarrott, produced by Gregory Peck, it stars Joseph Bottoms as Graham. It's a sea-blue movie with most of the footage being of Bottoms. Bottoms weathering a tropical storm, Bottoms in the doldrums, Bottoms swept overboard. There is a cat called Avanga that likes to lick Bottoms but unfortunately the poor creature, who is in danger of stealing the picture, is eaten by sharks. The solo sailing is interrupted in the Fiji Islands by a soppy love story. The teenage mariner meets a young girl (Deborah Raffin), also from California, and they cavort together to the lush musical score of John Barry in what seems like an interminable shampoo commercial.

In surfing mythology, the sport and youth are inextricably linked, a wave being a fountainhead of youth. Rick Carlson (Sam Elliott) is 32 years old and a *Lifeguard* (Par. 1976) on a S. Californian beach. He is highly trained and in good condition, although when he enters a surf competition the gruelling swim and run relay against younger men makes him feel his age. His father tells him to grow up and get a better job. He meets an old high-school friend (Stephen Young) who offers him a job as a car salesman, but Rick turns it down. At a high school reunion, he sees that his contemporaries have all 'gone soft'. Rick likes his job and will remain on the beach until he's too old to do it well. The film, directed by Daniel Petrie, is best when following the daily tasks of the lifeguard (rescue techniques, peace-keeping, handling beach girls etc), but like a Life-saver it has a big hole in the middle. Rick is a likeable, none-too-bright, strapping jock who, although he spends much of the time contemplating his life, doesn't have very much of interest to say. Still, there's always the Pacific in the background. 'I can really get into that ocean,' he says.

In *Jaws* (UI 1975), Robert Shaw was the fishing expert given to long-winded bromides, called in to a one-shark town to get rid of the menace. He appears again in *The Deep* (UI 1977), also based on a Peter Benchley novel, this time as the local treasure-hunting expert in Bermuda. Nick Nolte and Jacqueline Bissett play scuba divers who come across clues to buried treasure. They get involved with voodoo and scuba-diving Haitians looking for buried morphine. Forty per cent of the movie was photographed underwater and the stars did their own diving. Pretty shallow stuff.

For those unfortunate enough not to live on the South Californian coast and to whom 'the perfect wave' is something to do with hair-dressing, *Big Wednesday* (WB 1978) will seem a meandering, mawkish mess of a movie. However, one doesn't have to understand the surf-cult mystique or share the wave fixation of the three leading characters in order to appreciate the splendid surfing sequences photographed by Greg MacGillvray. Jan-Michael Vincent, William Katt and Gary Busey are three surfing freaks trying to come to terms with the social changes that took place in the USA from the early sixties to the mid-seventies. The only things that have meaning and consistency, are the big ones that roll towards the beach at Malibu. Surfing is a way of recapturing their youth or pretending it had never passed. Their tale is told in 4 chapters — 1962, 1965, 1968, and 1974. In the opening chapter, they are teenagers having wild parties and going for weekends in Mexico. Vincent is the most immature, getting involved in brawls and drinking too much, but on a surf-board he is full of grace and is the best surfer of the trio. Katt is more well-behaved. He is the typical All-American boy who will do anything for his buddies. Busey takes nothing seriously except surfing. They sit around a senior surfer called Bear and listen to a sad story in awe. 'The wave was hittin' the cliffs and splashin' 100 feet high — it was like the end of the world,' he says describing the day a surfer disappeared. 'They never found his body. They just found little pieces of his board.' The audience are invited to share their awe. In their twenties, they marry, have a family and are caught in the draft. Only the 'good boy' William Katt goes to Vietnam, while the others pretend to be crippled or insane. On a big Wednesday in 1974, they get together with the best surfers in the country to show they can still master the ocean. In John Milius and Dennis Aaberg's simplistic screenplay, the Vietnam war, the Berkely Protests, the Chicago race riots, Flower Power and the hippie culture are all subservient to the ability to ride the waves. It is an updated 'beach-party' movie, but instead of 'squares' invading their playgrounds, it is the radicals and hippies who foul up 'the scene'. Vincent is furious when he discovers that his favorite hamburger joint now serves organic food. John Milius directed this saga of the surf and 'ultimate' buddy-buddy-buddy movie.

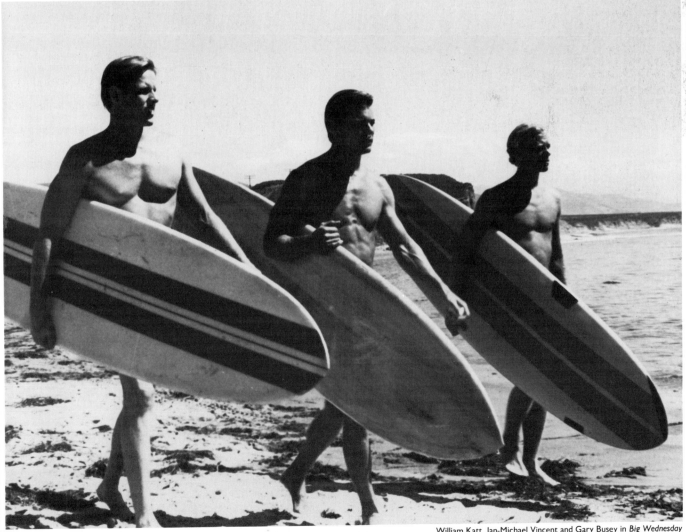

William Katt, Jan-Michael Vincent and Gary Busey in *Big Wednesday*

BALLS AND FALLS, BULLS AND DRAGONS

Basketball is probably the most authentic North American sport, having been invented in 1891 by Dr James Naismith, a PE instructor at the International YMCA Training School in Springfield Mass. It is the only American sport to be practiced all over the world and it has been an Olympic sport since 1936. It is a fast and free-flowing game requiring individual initiative, intelligence and skill rather than brute force. Without the padding and helmets of football and ice hockey, the basketball player is a recognizable human being. Why then has it not received much attention from the arts and the movies in particular? It hasn't the violence of boxing or football, it doesn't have the tradition or mythic quality of baseball, or the reputation for crookedness of the race-track. Basketball only reached its peak of popularity in the late sixties at the same time as the youth culture. Mainly through the presence of black players (they outnumbered whites) it had a freer attitude and was more attractive to the young than the more hidebound football or baseball. It is not surprising that Jack Nicholson, the embodiment of early seventies rebellion, should have chosen basketball as a subject for his first film as director, *Drive He Said*.

Veteran Hollywood director David Butler (an expert purveyor of fluff), started his career with a little thing called *High School Hero* (1927) featuring Nick Stuart and Sally Phipps about the passionate involvement of fathers in their sons' basketball games. Sam Wood also cut his teeth on a campus movie entitled *The Fair Co-ed* (MGM 1927). It's only originality lay in that it concerned a *woman's* college basketball team. Marion Davies, charming and saucy in the title role, falls for the coach (John Mack Brown) and scores in the last seconds with a long throw to basket.

'Basketball . . . is staying in after school in your underwear.'

— Gabriel (MICHAEL MARGOTTA) in
Drive He Said
(Col. 1970)

In order to do his priest buddy (Pat O'Brien) a favor, gangster James Cagney pushes the Dead End Kids onto a basketball court and tries to get them to play according to the rules in *Angels with Dirty Faces* (WB 1938). The only problem is that as a ref Cagney commits more personal fouls than any of the players. Breaking the law automatically spills over into sport. In *Here Come the Coeds* (UI 1945) Abbott and Costello play caretakers of a girls' school. Lou gets involved in a basketball game with the girls. 'I can't dribble,' he says, 'but I can drool.'

It was as disgracefully late as 1950 before blacks were permitted to appear on N.B.A. teams. Previously, the all-black Harlem Globe-Trotters were offering proof, if proof were needed, of the extraordinary ability of black players. Although renowned for their comedy routines, the Globe-Trotters frequently beat pro teams such as the 1949 champions, the Minneapolis Lakers. In the 60's and 70's many of the new black players looked upon them with distaste because of what they considered to be the stereotyping of blacks as entertainers not to be taken seriously as sportsmen. However, The Harlem Globe-Trotters are still the most famous basketball team in the world. Their prestigious prestidigitation occupies much of *The Harlem Globetrotters* (Col. 1951). The Trotters, all of whom seem about 10 feet tall, jump through paper hoops at the start of the game, spin the ball on the fingers and send it up and down their long arms. While clowning around, their uncanny control of the ball enables them to score field goals galore. The simple backstage story that connects the games is of little importance. It tells of the rise to fame of Billy Townsend (Billy Brown) and his quarrel with the team manager Abe Saperstein (Thomas Gomez). 'Goose' Tatum and Marques Haynes stand out among the Trotters and so does the beautiful Dorothy Dandridge. Dane

Clark takes over the role of Abe Saperstein in *Go, Man, Go!* (UA 1954), which also featured the Trotters as themselves. 'It's like having 10 Heifetzes in the same orchestra,' says Saperstein eruditely. The film, skating over the segregation issue, tells the corny story of the team's triumphs despite crooked promoters and lack of sponsorship. Pat Breslin is former beauty queen, Mrs Saperstein and Sidney Poitier appears as Inman Jackson, one of the Trotters. Curiously, it was directed by one of Hollywood's most distinguished cinematographers, James Wong Howe.

23-year-old Jane Fonda made her screen debut in *Tall Story* (WB 1960) and although she was quite pleasing in an irritating role, even a clairvoyant would have had difficulty predicting superstardom. Firstly she is ms-cast as a girl with only marriage on her mind. Secondly, neither Joshua Logan's script (based on a Broadway play based on a novel) gave her much help. Tall girl Fonda enrols at Custer College, the home of one of America's top basketball teams, in search of a tall man to marry. Her quarry is the college's star, Anthony Perkins. (At 28, already a veteran of 10 movies). By applying scientific theory to the game, he is able to score with ease. Fonda becomes cheerleader, attends all the same courses as Perkins and sits next to him at lectures. She soon gets him to propose. Because of his new responsibilities, Perkins accepts a large bribe offered him by crooked gamblers to throw a match against a visiting Russian team. When he fails a midterm ethics exam and becomes ineligible for the team, he tells all. Ray Walston, the professor who failed him, permits him to take an oral exam just before the game. He rushes to the basketball court to find the Russians leading 52-33. Quickly changing, he enters the game and pulls off a dramatic

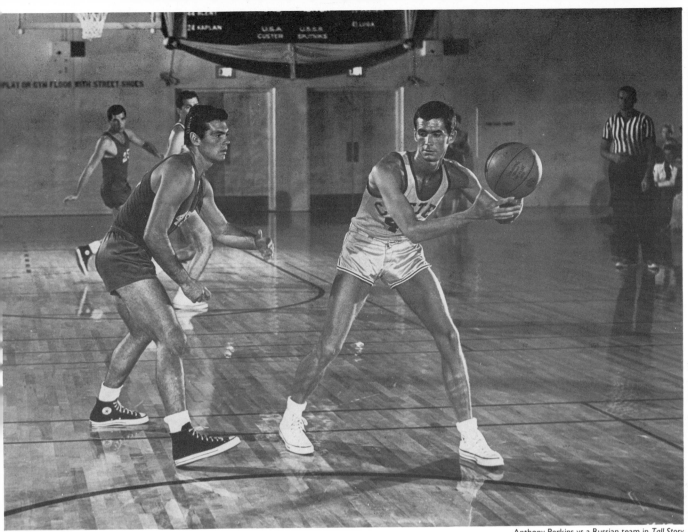

Anthony Perkins vs a Russian team in *Tall Story*

last-minute victory. Perkins gives a credible performance on court, but Custer College can only be found in tired campus comedies such as this.

A campus comedy with far more bounce (in two senses) was *The Absent Minded Professor* (Walt Disney 1961). The professor is Fred MacMurray who invents a substance called Flubber (i.e. flying rubber) which, when put on the soles of the shoes of the college basketball team, permits them to jump high into the air. A game in which 5 small fries leap over the heads of their towering opponents provides some fun.

At the other end of the educational spectrum is *Halls of Anger* (UA 1969). This is a black Blackboard Jungle movie, in which a black English teacher (Calvin Lockhart) overcomes opposition from his deprived and mutinous pupils by his liberal and caring approach. Like many a teleplay, it is well-meaning and reassuring. However, the premise of the film directed by Paul Bogart is an interesting one

which has elements of a social parable. Because of the national integration plan, 600 white students are to be sent to Lafayette High, an all-black ghetto school. Only 60 arrive and they suffer the kind of racism that blacks suffer in a white-dominated society. One of the white students (Jeff Bridges, at 19 in his first important role) tries to get onto the basketball team but meets with considerable resistance from the leader of the militants, J.T. Watson (James Watson). Bridges finds it impossible to play without the others ganging up on him. The teacher, a former basketball star, is challenged by J.T. to a basketball game between the two of them. At the end of a gruelling contest, the older man wins. How easily everything is resolved! If you want your backward students to become interested in reading, then offer them a sexy paperback. If you want to bring the most undisciplined to heel, then get them to paint a mural or challenge their leader to a

basketball contest.

Drive He Said (Col. 1970), Jack Nicholson's first attempt at directing, has a lot in common with his acting persona. It is energetic, nervous, quirky, slightly crazy, chaotic and pretentious. As a director he sinks as many shots as he misses. It's a counter-culture campus comedy-drama which tries too hard to be *the* statement about the schizoid state of American life brought about by the Vietnam war. Nicholson has mischievously drawn long hair, a beard and beads on a portrait of a clean-cut All-American jock. Hector Bloom (William Tepper) is a bonehead basketball player majoring in Greek(!). His roommate Gabriel (Michael Margotta) tries to convince him to join the revolutionary movement. Hector refuses, saying he 'digs the game.' While Hector considers turning pro, Gabriel is 'freaking out' at the draft board. He's been on a 'survival trip' by pill-popping and not sleeping, hoping to avoid the draft. Hector agrees to sign with a pro bas-

ketball team for less money if they lower the price of their 50c hot dogs to 25c and let all the kids under 12 in free. This is his contribution to the revolution. The management refuses and Hector loses interest in the game. The best moments come when Nicholson casts a satirical eye on the rituals of organized sport. The psyching up of the players, the gung-ho, the vacuous post-game interviews, and the coach (brilliantly realized by Bruce Dern) who wants to win at all costs.

Maurice Stokes, a black basketball player with the Cincinnati Royals, was suddenly and mysteriously struck down by a paralysis. He could no longer move his limbs or speak. Jack Twyman, one of the team's white stars, devoted ten years of his life in an attempt to rehabilitate him. In the end Stokes died having recovered his ability to speak. True story that it is, *Maurie* (Ausable Co. 1973) fails to confer a depth, structure and meaning on the material. Director Daniel Mann and writer Douglas Mor-

145

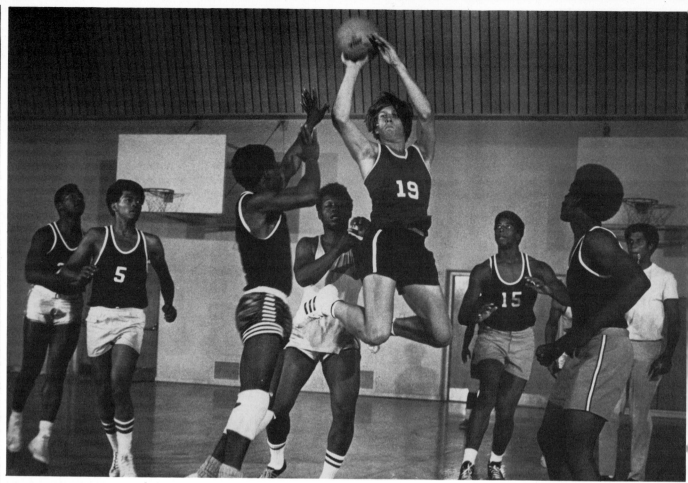

row have turned it into a tear-jerker on the level of *Love Story* — (*Jock Story?*). Although both Bernie Casey as Stokes and Bo Svenson as Twyman give touching performances, their interesting relationship is not explored or their characters developed.

Sentimentality of a more insidious kind pervades *Mixed Company* (UA 1974), produced and directed by Melville Shavelson. Many of Shavelson's films seem to be propaganda for family planning i.e. plan to have a large family. *Room for One More* (1952), *Seven Little Foys* (1956) and *Yours, Mine and Ours* (1968) teach the doctrine of the more the schmaltzier. Joseph Bologna plays the hot-tempered coach of the Phoenix Suns basketball team. He is having trouble with his super-star Walt Johnson (Ron McIlwain) who refuses to give of his best, and with his wife (Barbara Harris) a basket widow who wants another child although they have three children already. Bologna can't oblige, as a recent bout of mumps has left him sterile. So they adopt three orphans despite Bologna's racial prejudices. An 8-year-old Viet-

namese girl, a 4-year-old Hopi Indian and a 10-year-old black boy who is a basketball fanatic. After having problems with the kids and losing his job, Bologna is reinstated and the family is brought together by the wonders of basketball. The whole family assembles misty-eyed in the stands to watch Dad referee. He has learned to love the kids as his own. There is quite a lot of footage of the Phoenix Suns.

One of the best scenes in the Oscar-winning *One Flew Over The Cuckoo's Nest* (UA 1975) had Jack Nicholson organizing a basketball game in the State Mental Institution in order to wake his fellow inmates out of their apathy. By doing so he releases something in the giant Chief Bromden (played by Creek Indian Will Sampson). Nicholson persuades the Indian to stand under the basket, receive a ball and drop it in. The Chief does so as if it's another boring hospital task, but after one or two successes with the ball, his face lights up for the first time. Nicholson opposes him by getting on the shoulders of another patient. The sequence demonstrates the way to the hearts and

minds of the patients, so lacking in the approach of the members of the staff.

One on One (WB 1977) ends with the Paul Williams' song 'Nice guys finish first', reversing Leo Durocher's famous dictum, 'Nice guys finish last.' The cynic will tend towards the latter, the director Lamont Johnson, the writers Robby Benson and Jerry Segal go rather ingenuously for the former. The nice guy is Henry Steele (Robby Benson), a dedicated high school basketball star from a small town in Colorado, who accepts a 4-year athletic scholarship and a new sports car from Western University. He soon finds himself confused by the way the college treats its 'dumb jocks.' At 5ft 10ins he is dwarfed by his teammates and harrassed mentally and physically by the coach (G.D. Spradlin). Steele finds himself keeping the bench warm or being left out on road games. Disenchanted, the innocent freshman (a fresh performance from Benson), turns to the academic side of college and with the help of his part-time tutor (Annette O'Toole) he begins to study and pass exams for the first time in his life. They do

much more together than discuss Moby Dick. The ending is the stuff (and nonsense) that dreams are made of. Henry comes off the bench and scores the winning point in the Big Game, gets top grades, gets his own back on the martinet coach, wins the attractive girl, and emerges from the hypocritical world of 'amateur' basketball with all his ideals intact. As the psychiatry prof. says 'Athletics offers a life of perpetual adolescence.' Despite its soft underside, the dialogue is sharp, the performances accurate and there is the authentic excitement of a ballgame.

Julius Erving, Meadowlark Lemon (of the Harlem Globe-Trotters), Kareem Abdul-Jabbar and a host of NBA players go through their nimble paces in *The Fish That Saved Pittsburgh* (UA 1979), a pretty dumb comedy with a disco beat. A Pittsburgh team is on a losing streak until water-boy James Bond III comes up with the idea of forming a whole team of Pisces (the fish of the title). With the help of astrologist Stockard Channing, they begin to win and land in the championships. The

146

music is by Thom Bell and Gilbert Moses directed. Strictly for Pisces basketball fans from Pittsburgh.

Kareem Abdul-Jabbar (né Lew Alcindor), the 7′ 2″ basketball super-star, turns up again in the amusing Mad spoof, *Airplane* (Par. 1980). He plays the co-pilot Roger. (Everytime the pilot says Roger when communicating with the ground, he answers.) A little boy, stepping out of the conventions of film, recognizes his as the basketball star and begins to criticize his ball playing. He denies that he's Abdul-Jabbar, but when he collapses, he is found to be wearing basketball gear below his flight jacket.

Inside Moves (Goldmark 1981) is, according to the blurb, 'a heart-tugging story of a group of people brought together by hardship, humor, love and the dream of winning.' They are, in fact, a group of misfits and cripples who gather at Max's Bar in L.A., imagining they're in *The Iceman Cometh* or a William Saroyan play. 'It's not just a bar, it's family.' A new arrival is Roary (John Savage), crippled from throwing himself out of a win-dow. 'Look, you get to be a cripple first, then you attempt suicide,' says one of the habitués. Tending the bar is Jerry (David Morse) who has a bad leg but has the potential to be a great basketball player if only he can afford an operation. Jerry manages to have the operation and it's a success. He joins a semi-pro team and has a dazzling season, all the while forgetting his old friends at Max's bar. So nasty has he become that he makes a play for Roary's waitress girl-friend (Diana Searwid). Roary tells Jerry that he may be cured but he's an emotional cripple. Jerry is brought to his senses on the eve of his first game with a pro team. The group from Max's bar hobble to the stadium to see Jerry play because 'his dream is their dream as well.' Valerie Curtin and Barry Levinson's script (based on the Todd Walton novel) has a wry side which counteracts a little of the sweetness. The camera of Laszlo Kovacs seems to be tear-stained and the director Richard Donner unsubtly mixes basket balls with basket cases. Harold Russell, the soldier who lost both hands during World War II, makes his first screen appearance since *The Best Years of Our Lives* (1945). Makek Abdul-Mansour was the basketball advisor, teaching 6′4″ David Morse to look convincing.

Wrestling

'I'm in the business of crazy.'
— The wrestling promoter in
The One and Only (Par. 1978)

All-in wrestling has more in common with the circus than sport. In the movies it is either exploited for its clownishness or its animal side. Pro wrestling is a ready-made morality play with good guys and bad guys often pandering to the racial prejudices of the crowd. Corruption and degradation hang like a pall over the wrestling game in movies such as *Flesh* (MGM 1932), *Night and the City* (TCF 1950) and *Paradise Alley* (UI 1978). No need for stand-ins in wrestling scenes. Any actor can be taught to wrestle; after all every wrestler is taught to act.

Joe E. Brown as a supervisor of a health clinic who gets involved in an all-in wrestling match against a masked oppo-nent, provided a few laughs in *Sit Tight* (WB 1931). Billed as The Tiger Boy, he discovers that behind the mask is an outraged husband who had threatened him with violence. Joe tries every grip in the book against the burly wrestler but to no avail. Eventually he runs for his life around the ring. But this was merely the sub-plot. The sub-standard plot dealt with Winnie Lightner's attempts to train Paul Gregory to become a champion wrestler. Lloyd Bacon directed.

Obviously influenced by German expressionist cinema and the films starring Emil Jannings, *Flesh* (MGM 1932) was an unusual picture from John Ford. Wallace Beery is a Russian waiter at a beer-garden in Germany who also entertains the patrons by taking part in wrestling matches. After he wins the championship of Germany, he is trapped into marriage by a street-walker (Karen Morley) who gets him to take her to America. There he is thrown into a mire of corruption. He is treated brutally by a crooked promoter and his wife takes a lover (Ricardo Cortez). In a fit of jealousy, he kills the lover

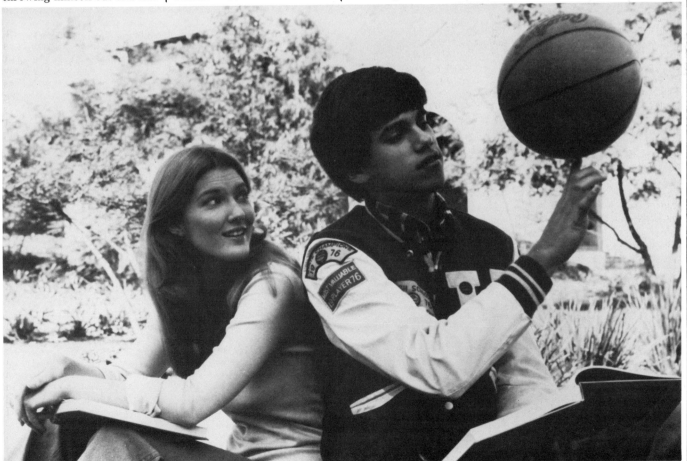

Annette O'Toole and Robby Benson in *One on One*

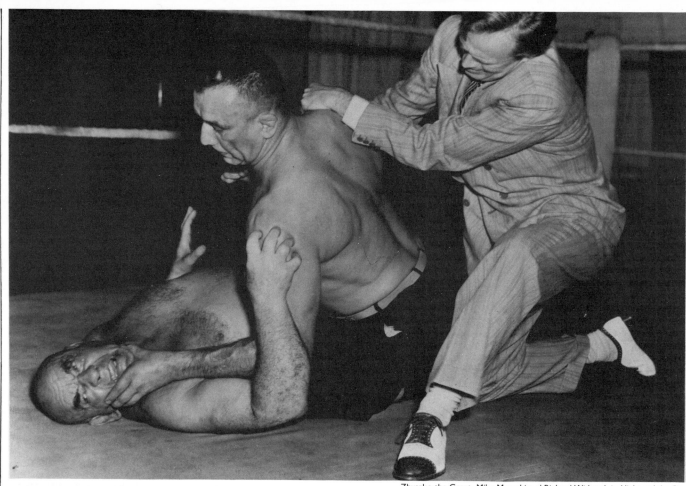

Zbyszko the Great, Mike Mazurki and Richard Widmark in *Night and the City*

and the last shot shows him in prison but with some hope of release. Most of it is mechanical and melodramatic. Beery wallows in pools of sentimentality over the baby he thinks is his own, but manages to carry the film on his ample shoulders. The wrestling bouts are fairly vivid.

'I'll do anything but please don't make me plug wrestling,' says sports columnist James Dunn to a crooked promoter in *The Payoff* (WB 1935). He has become a pawn in the promoter's hands and has to write obsequiously about all-in wrestling instead of satirically. Clair Dodd plays his bitchy wife who starts his downfall. Robert Florey directed this intermittently entertaining comedy-drama.

Humphrey Bogart found himself in the semi-musical, *Swing Your Lady* (WB 1938) as an unsuccessful wrestling promoter who hits on the idea of matching a moronic giant (Nat Pendleton) with an Amazonian lady blacksmith (Louise Fazenda). A little of the hare-brained hill-billy humor goes a long way. Ronald Reagan appeared in a small role. Bogart went on to better things. Ray Enright

directed. In *Straight, Place and Show* (TCF 1938), the Ritz Brothers are thrown into the wrestling ring. Nuff said. Lou Costello is matched against a masked marvel in *Here Come the Coeds* (UI 1945) and gasps to the audience, 'Boy, am I in a mess!' Willard Parker and Lola Albright were in a mess called *Bodyhold* (Col. 1949). Plumber Parker becomes a grappler only to learn that plumbing is a cleaner job. 'In wrestling,' says the shady promoter Ray Roberts, 'the hero has to suffer.' He's not the only one.

The London of seedy night-clubs, spivs, murderers, crooks, touts, squealers and trollops is the background to *Night and the City* (TCF 1950) with hardly a bobby in sight. Americans Richard Widmark and Gene Tierney lead a virtually all English cast in the first film directed by Jules Dassin in Europe after the McCarthy witch-hunt made it impossible for him to work in the States. Widmark plays a hustler touting for custom for the Silver Fox nightclub where his girl-friend (Tierney) works as a singer. His greatest ambition is to promote wrestling matches. In order to do this, he

has to muscle in on the territory of a racketeer (Herbert Lom) who has the monopoly of all-in wrestling in London. Lom's father Gregorius (played touchingly by Zbyszko the Great, Greco-Roman champion of the world in the early 1900's) has brought to London a young wrestler, Nikolas (Ken Richmond), a potential world-beater in the art of true wrestling. Gregorius wants to show up the 'clowns' of the modern all-in style. Widmark tries to match The Strangler (Mike Mazurki) against Nikolas, but The Strangler taunts Gregorius into a brutal fight. Gregorius wins but the strain is too much for his heart and he dies in his son's arms. Crooked deals and double crosses force Widmark on the run. In less than 10 minutes, he runs from Waterloo, on one side of London, to Hammersmith on the other where he hides out. Nobly, he gets Tierney to discover him so she can claim the £1000 reward. The Strangler, living up to his name, kills Widmark and tosses him in the Thames. Although tautly directed, the film is far-fetched, too strong on atmosphere and weak on psy-

chology, but contains some good performances mainly from Googie Withers and portly Francis L. Sullivan as nightclub owners and a back-breaking, bone-crunching wrestling match.

Mr Universe (Eagle Lion 1951) tries its damndest to be funny and satiric about the slick hustlers, phony tactics and gullible spectators of pro-wrestling, but it's difficult to spoof something which is itself a spoof of the real sport. Vincent Edwards (later Ben Casey of TV) is the clean-cut honest young wrestler trying to keep his integrity among Jack Carson, Bert Lahr, Janis Paige and Robert Alda. *The Savage Eye* (Trans-Lux 1960) looks at the more bizarre aspects of life in L.A. including faith-healers, strip-tease joints, beauty parlors and the grotesqueries of all-in wrestlers and the ferocity of the spectators who hurl abuse at them. Directed by Ben Maddow, Joseph Strick and Sidney Meyers, it is a potent semi-documentary of a year in the life of a divorcée (Barbara Baxley). However, the eye is more jaundiced than savage. The depths of humiliation for ex-boxer Anthony

Quinn in *Requiem for a Heavyweight* (Col. 1962) is to dress up in a Red Indian costume and become part of the freak-show that is wrestling, because he cannot box any more or get another job.

'More like a Broadway opening night than a wrestling match,' says the commentator in *The One and Only* (Par. 1978). The link between show business and sport (closest in wrestling) has seldom been dealt with more amusingly. Andy Schmitt (Henry Winkler) dreams of becoming an actor. In fact, from childhood he has never stopped acting. His ambition is to become a Broadway star. Because he doesn't make it, he takes up pro wrestling to support his wife (Kim Darby) and child. Ironically, he is taught wrestling by a midget (Herve Villechaize). He kids himself that it's only temporary until, in the end, entering the ring in pink tights and effeminate hairdo as The Lover, he is told, 'You're a star,' the words he has always wanted to hear. Before hitting on The Lover, he tried various personae. Wearing a German First World War helmet and a swastika on his arm, he goes under the name of Adolph Hitner, the ultimate baddie. The helmet comes in useful for butting his opponents. Winkler plays the sort of character funny on screen but whom one avoids in real life. His non-stop clowning is perfect for the wrestling ring.

Although Sylvester Stallone was born in 1946, he seems to have been influenced by 'every single goddam Warner Brothers epic' of the thirties. No more so than in *Paradise Alley* (UI 1978) which he wrote, directed, starred in and also sings the title song. In order to show how dated it will be, the movie opens with the old Universal logo of an airplane going round the globe. It also derives from boxing movies such as *Golden Boy* (1939) and his own *Rocky* (1976). Stallone believes that 'if at first you succeed then try, try again.' Unlike *Rocky* I, II, III (IV? V? VI?), *Paradise Alley* is about wrestling. It tells of three Carboni brothers, Cosmo (Stallone), a hustler, Lenny (Armand Assante), a cripple, and the youngest Victor (Lee Canalito), a lunkheaded giant. Cosmo and Lenny see a chance of breaking out of the ghetto where they live (New York's Hell's Kitchen) by exploiting the wrestling talents of Victor. Under the name of 'Kid Salami', he is pushed into the ring at the illegal gambling dive of the title. (It's best to ignore any Dantesque analogies). Salami beats fading black wrestler Big Glory (Frank McCrae). It is Xmas day in Hell's Kitchen and Big Glory drowns himself in the river. Being the star, Stallone begins to feel guilty about the whole racket and about the knocks his brother is taking. The brothers quarrel over Victor's future. They decide to put him in the ring one more time for a 1000 dollar purse against Franky, The Thumper (Terry Funk). Paradise Alley is packed to the rafters. For 22 rounds faces are twisted, eyes gouged, throats throttled and fleshy bodies writhe in close-up and slow motion. It ends in chaos with Victor throwing Franky out of the ring. The three brothers embrace and decide to give up wrestling and love each other more. Most of the actors deliver their lines fortissimo in case the audiences can't believe their ears. The corn is as high as Kid Salami's eye which is 6′5″. Lee Canalito, a 255 lbs prizefighter from Houston was making his film debut.

As a pleasant contrast from the monstrousness of all-in wrestling, *Take Down* (Buena Vista 1978) concentrates on high-school wrestling. Edward Herrmann is the English teacher at a small town school who reluctantly becomes coach of the school's team. They need a wrestler in the 185 lbs category and the only one they can find to fill the bill is rebellious student Lorenzo Lamas (son of Fernando Lamas, Argentinian heartthrob of the 50's). Directed by Keith Merrill with a light touch.

All the Marbles (MGM 1981. *California Dolls* — GB) is a noisy, funny, straight-from-the-shoulder, popular entertainment. This tale of female grapplers on the Rocky road to fame, is a simple one. Peter Falk is the manager of a glamorous tag-team called The California Dolls (brunette Vicki Frederick and blonde Laurene Landon) who travel around the halls of small towns until they hit the big time by beating the Toledo Tigers in Reno. The final 20-minute no-

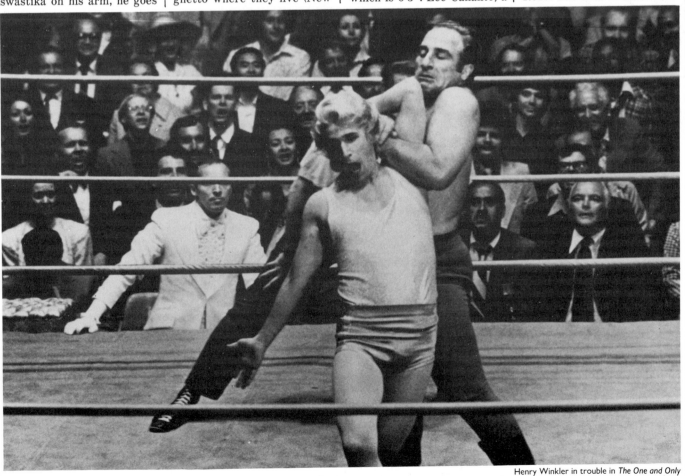

Henry Winkler in trouble in *The One and Only*

holds-barred match is a tour de force with the Dolls pinning their opponents in the last seconds, despite a crooked ref. Subtlety is not director Robert Aldrich's strong point and the brashness of wrestling as a subject suits his extrovert approach. A tenuous attempt is made towards some kind of wider statement. Moving from one smoke-filled town to another, Falk and the girls listen to *Vesti la giubba* from *Pagliacci* 'about a strolling player who goes from town to town entertaining people'. At one moment the Dolls have qualms after being forced to wrestle in mud, but Aldrich never makes it seem freakish nor is he contemptuous of his characters. However, any feminist message contained in the screenplay (by Mel Frohman) is soon banged on the head by the pandering to male sadistic fantasies that the 'sport' implicitly satisfies. There is not much room for soul-searching between the wrestling action which is what it's all about. As a promoter says, 'The customers don't give a damn for class. All they want is tits and ass. If I wanted a class act, I'd get the Bronte sisters.' Excellent are Peter Falk's wise-guy fast-talking manager and the two uncomplicated girls seeming more to enjoy the game than not.

Body Building

'In the mirror now, unmistakably, he existed! The disappointed abandoned youth of a few moments ago was nowhere to be seen. Here was only strong, beautiful muscle, the proof of its existence clear. For what he now beheld was something he had created himself; moreover it *was* himself.'

— Yukio Mishima (*Kyoko's House.*)

The above quote goes some way towards explaining the attraction body-building has for many men (and now women). There is something of the sideshow about the hemetic world of competitive body-building. To the eye accustomed to the average body shape, these Goliaths seem grotesque, twisting their torsos into statuesque poses and rippling and extending their muscles, but if one enters the world as in the documentary *Pumping Iron* (Cinema 5 1977) one's aesthetics can be altered.

One of the best numbers in *Gentlemen Prefer Blondes* (TCF 1953) was Jane Russell singing 'Ain't there anyone here for love?' in a ship's gymnasium to a couple of dozen muscle men. The question in the song is rhetorical as they are plainly more interested in each other. Muscles are a boy's best friend? Former 'Mr Universe' and 'Mr World', Steve Reeves (later to star in Italian spectaculars like *Hercules and the Queen of Sheba* — 1958) was to be seen showing off his musculature in the rather weedy musical, *Athena* (MGM 1954). Louis Calhern and Evelyn Varden, the remarkably athletic septuagenarian grandparents of Jane Powell and Debbie Reynolds, who believe in vegetarianism and numerology, are far from pleased when Jane and Debbie fall for meat-eating weaklings like Edmond Purdom and Vic Damone. How could they when there are so many muscled males to choose from? This health-freak family seem far less cranky today than they did nearly 30 years ago.

With his good looks, gift of the gab and sense of humor, Arnold Schwarzenegger, former Mr World, Mr Olympia and Mr Universe, has done a lot to put a human face onto body building. These qualities are amply demonstrated in *Stay Hungry* (UA 1976) and *Pumping Iron*. In the former, he shows he can act as well. Directed by Bob Rafelson, from the Charles Gains novel, with the participation of the people of Alabama and the International Federation of Body Builders, it has a nice sense of pace and place, even if the tone is uncertain. A mixture between naturalistic drama and a fairy tale (for body builders?), it tells of a young man (Jeff Bridges) from an aristocratic Alabama family who works for a large real estate operation run by a shady businessman (Joe Spinell). Bridges is sent to buy a health club called 'The Olympic Spa', but its owner (R.G. Armstrong) has no intention of selling. In order to persuade him to sell, Bridges joins the club and gets involved in the body building sessions. So engrossed does he become, that he joins forces with the members of the club to oppose the wicked property dealers. Among the people working out in the gym is an Austrian body builder (Schwarzenegger) who is entering for the Mr Universe

contest to be held in Birmingham. While the contest is in progress, Bridges gets into a fight with Armstrong over his girl-friend (Sally Field) and the muscle men come to his rescue. Hundreds of them spill out into the streets in their posing trunks to the amusement and astonishment of the crowds. Losing sight of their mission, they begin to pose and perform. Hercules meets the 'New South'.

Pumping Iron is a documentary by George Butler and Robert Fiore about the Mr Olympia championships held in South Africa in 1976 and the run up to it. It concentrates mainly on six times winner Arnold Schwarzenegger, who talks to camera about his profession. He calls himself a sculptor of his own body. 'You look in the mirror and see you need more deltoids to make symmetry. So you exercise and put more deltoids on. A sculptor will slap stuff on,' he says. The directors of the film try to build up a dramatic confrontation towards the final between the champ and a young giant with hearing difficulties called Lou Ferrigno, but it's obvious that Arnold will beat all comers with aplomb. Lou is trained and spurred on by his father Matty. 'You gotta look as if you're saying "take a look at this hunk of man",' he advises his passive, gloomy son. Matty almost steals the picture from Arnold. In the competition itself, each pose is cheered like at a pop concert and the enthusiasm generates itself from the screen. The humor, warmth and camaraderie of the participants stops certain questions from being raised in the film. What about the dangers of the sport? The narcissism inherent in it? Homosexuality? 'It's like coming when I pump up. I'm coming day and night,' says Schwarzenegger. The sexual implications never go further than that level.

Rollerskating

'The Roller Derby is a sport. Defenestration is also a sport for those who like it.'

— John Lardner.

Charlie Chaplin once played on stage in the Fred Karno troupe in an act called 'Skating' and repeated much of what he had learned in *The Rink* (1916). His extraordinary skill on roller skates was again displayed in

the department store sequence in *Modern Times* (UA 1936). The Marx Brothers also did wonders on roller skates (or at least the wild chase at the end of *The Big Store* (MGM 1941).

The Fireball (TCF 1950) was a hackneyed rags to riches sob story about undersized orphan Mickey Rooney (at his most Rooneyesque) who becomes a pro roller champ with the help of roller-skating teacher Beverly Tyler. Rooney is selfish and conceited but, at the height of his career, he is struck down by polio. His teacher and Father O'Hara from the orphanage (Pat O'Brien giving a good imitation of Pat O'Brien) work with him for two years before he regains the use of his limbs. In the specious ending, Mickey back on roller-skates allows an up-and-coming youngster to win a race, proving that he's really the true winner. Yuk! Tay Garnett wrote and directed. Marilyn Monroe had a small role in it, two years before she became a star.

Two MGM musicals of the 50's featured roller-skating numbers. Donald O'Connor does a spectacular routine in *I Love Melvin* (1953), dancing and singing with wheels on his feet in a bandstand. (Those perceptive enough may see a wire holding him as he whizzes around.) There were no wires holding Gene Kelly as he sings and skates in *It's Always Fair Weather* (1955). Escaping into a roller rink with gangsters on his tail, he forgets to take his skates off when he goes back into the streets. He whirls along the spotless New York sidewalk singing the appropriate, 'I like myself.'

In 1935, Leo Seltzer, the marathon dance impresario, invented the Roller Derby. In the 50's it was a major TV attraction, but in the 60's it began to lose some of its audience. Jerry Seltzer, Leo's son, commissioned *Derby* (Cinerama Releasing 1971), a funny, ironic, exciting and touching portrait of Middle America. Director-cameraman Robert Kaylor's cinema-verité treatment is never snide or superior to the subject. The film intercuts between star skater Charlie O'Connell, captain of the San Francisco Bay Bombers and Mike Snell, a worker at the Dayton Tire and Rubber Co. who dreams of making the big time like Charlie. Snell lives in a cluttered house with his wife, 2 small children and younger brother. By going to roller-derby school, Snell hopes to 'better' himself, to fulfil the American Dream. As he tries to find a way for himself and his family, Charlie O'Connell is thumping his way around the rinks. The symbol is clear.

The symbol in *Kansas City Bombers* (MGM 1972) is a sex symbol in the shape of Raquel Welch. As the independently-minded, gum-chewing, rival-bashing roller-skating star K.C. Carr, Welch is a sight to behold. She is basically a nice girl only in the brutal business for the money to send to her children (Jodie Foster and Stephen Manley). Neither Raquel nor the character she plays seems 'into' the Derby. She is not vulgar or tough enough to be convincing in this fast, loud and violent sport. Helena Kallianiotes is very good as her chief rival, getting loaded from a bottle hidden in a skating boot. A lot of blood, sweat and tears spatter the large screen, but with little effect. Jerrold Freedman directed, shooting real-life Derbies.

The screenplay was adapted from a story by Barry Sandler which he wrote as his Master's thesis at UCLA expecially for Raquel Welch.

In the world of the 21st century where there is no poverty, hunger, war, crime or needs, *Rollerball* (UA 1975) is a game invented to satisfy the populace's lack of excitement. A combination of Roller-Derby, football and motor-cycling, it is the apogee of violence in sport. By foul means or foul, the players score by placing a heavy iron ball through a hole. The team is run with highly technological methods by gray-suited executives who 'dream they were great roller-ballers who had big muscles and could bash someone's face in.' And we, the gray-suited audience are meant to dream the same dream. The film itself, directed glossily by Norman Jewison, wallows in the violence it seems to be condemning. It makes no attempt to distance the blood-thirsty spectators on the screen from those in front of it. James Caan, the embittered hero and top roller-baller, presented as the

moral center, is hardly more individualistic or less sadistic than anyone else in the movie. To study the nature of violence, it is not enough just to depict it. The women in the film find violence a turn-on. A group of party-goers shoot down trees with flame guns, relishing the destruction of beauty. 'A horrible, social spectacle,' comments one of them while enjoying the scene. The same could be said of this kind of film. Caan's friend (John Beck) lies seriously injured in the hospital. 'His heart and lungs are still functioning but his brain has expired,' says the doctor. (How could they tell?) The doctor goes on to speak of the hospital rules. Caan replies, 'No rules in life. Life is a game of Rollerball.' The conclusion is a sad and dangerous one. There is no point in trying to abolish cruelty, crime or to believe in the betterment of mankind, because man is and always will be an ignoble savage. 'Life is a game of Rollerball.' The ultimate game, with no time limit and no substitutions, is played before spectators baying behind the

barriers. Dead bodies are strewn over the track, bikes are aflame, as the lone Caan comes through to win. The dialogue is soft and mindless. The action hard and mindless.

Skateboard (UI 1977) was made to cash in on that short-lived fad of yesterday. It is also another bad *Bad News Bears* spin-off. Allen Garfield plays an unsuccessful gambler who starts a skateboard team. The team ranges from a 10-year-old who seems to have been born on wheels and an 18-year-old who prefers surfing. On the day of the big 20,000 dollar downhill race, their star performer disappears and everything depends on the untried 15-year-old Brad (played by pre-teen heart-throb Leiff Garrett.) Guess who wins? Skateboarding was out of fashion before they learnt to film it imaginatively.

And then came roller-discos which produced such Saturday night headaches as *Rollerboogie* (1979), kids fighting to keep a roller rink open, and *Skatetown USA* (Col. 1979) about a roller disco contest with Scott Baio.

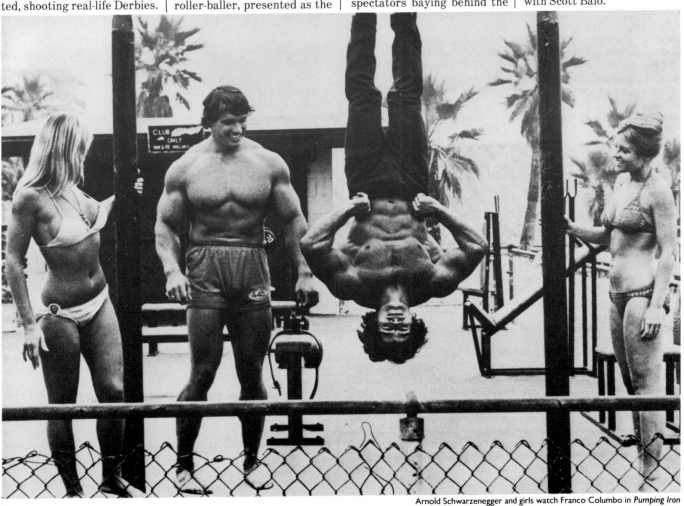

Arnold Schwarzenegger and girls watch Franco Columbo in *Pumping Iron*

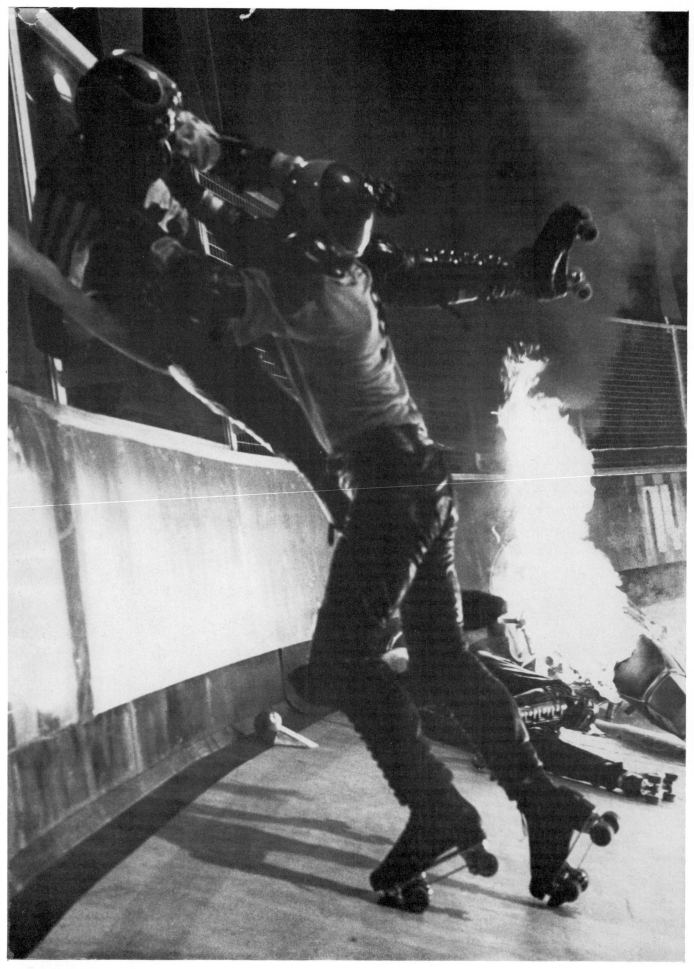

Bullfighting

'The bullfight is not a sport in the Anglo-Saxon sense of word, that is, it is not an equal contest or an attempt at an equal contest between a bull and a man. Rather it is a tragedy; the death of the bull, which is played, more or less well, by the bull and the man involved and in which there is danger for the man but certain death for the animal.'

— Ernest Hemingway *(Death in the Afternoon)*

The tragic story of Rudolph Valentino's rise from peasant boy to the idol of the *corridas* and how he meets his death in the bull-ring is told in *Blood and Sand* (Par. 1922). He has the love of a good girl, (Lila Lee) but is seduced and betrayed by a vamp (Nita Naldi). 'Snake. One minute I love you — the next I hate you,' reads the dialogue title. His sleeked hair, his mascara'd eyes glowing, Valentino is the romantic embodiment of the torero. This opera for silent singers was directed by Fred Niblo.

Eddie Cantor's saucer eyes become Catherine wheels when faced with a bull in *The Kid from Spain* (Goldwyn 1932). In Mexico, Eddie is mistaken for a celebrated matador and has to prove himself a bullfighter. His friend (Robert Young) supplies him with a trained bull who can count up to three and will stop dead when he hears the word 'Popacatepetl', but Eddie can't remember the word and is chased all over the ring. A likeable musical directed by Leo McCarey, numbers staged by Busby Berkeley.

The voluptuous Technicolor photography of Rouben Mamoulian's *Blood and Sand* (TCF 1941), based on Ibanez's book like the 1922 Valentino version, is its chief pleasure. The color richly evokes the atmosphere of the arenas, the swirling capes, the costumes, many sequences being styled after Spanish painters such as Murillo, Goya and Valasquez without seeming arty. The story is ponderous and melodramatic. Tyrone Power marries his childhood sweetheart Linda Darnell, but as he rises to become the top matador, he falls into the clutches of aristocratic siren Rita Hayworth. She saps him financially

Left: James Caan eliminates the last skater against him in *Rollerball*

and physically, and he is mortally gored in the ring. Nazimova is Power's mother and Laird Cregar hams it up as a bullfighting critic of the corridas of Power.

It was rather sad to see 55-year-old Stan Laurel and 53-year-old Oliver Hardy trying to get laughs in *The Bullfighters* (TCF 1945), one of their last movies together. They go to Mexico as private detectives and inevitably Stan is mistaken for a famous Spanish matador and has to substitute in the ring for the real one. The fight itself is stock-footage cut in with Laurel and Hardy running around being chased by a bull.

Esther Williams in *Fiesta*

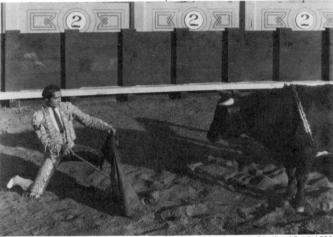
Rudolph Valentino in *Blood and Sand* (1922)

(MGM 1947) strikes a blow for senorita's lib, by proving herself the equal of any male matador. A wealthy retired Mexican bullfighter (Fortunio Bonanova) has a twin son (Ricardo Montalban in his American film debut) and daughter (Fiesta Williams.) He dreams of his son becoming a torero, but Ricardo only wants to compose music. To belie her brother's reputation as a coward, she dons a matador's costume and is triumphant. Directed on location by Richard Thorpe, it was the usual gringo hokum.

It seems than whenever American comedians visit Spain or Mexico they are forced to take part in a bullfight. In *Mexican Hayride* (UI 1948), Bud Abbott and Lou Costello find themselves, naturally, facing a bull before crowds in a bull-ring. It is difficult not to identify with the bull who is trying to hoist them as far away as possible.

As Rouben Mamoulian demonstrated in *Blood and Sand*, the bullfight seemed to

be made for Technicolor. But producer-director Robert Rossen had other ideas when it came to making *The Brave Bulls* (Col. 1951). 'Bullfighting is a grim, realistic business which color would inevitably romanticize. Instead, I've filmed it so raw it jumps out of the screen at you.' Without living up to this 3-D claim, the film does, with the help of James Wong Howe's well-defined black and white photography, manage to be grim and realistic. Mel Ferrer, whose melancholy face is in constant close-up, mumbles about doom and 'the fear that is in my heart.' He is Mexico's leading matador and, after being gored, bulls become his bêtes noires. When

his younger brother (Eugene Iglesias) gets into trouble with a pair of horns, Ferrer overcomes his fear of death and of life. The bulls which lie twitching in their death throes have no such philosophical choice.

Budd Boetticher (the director of many an interesting 'B' Western) had been a bullfighter in his time. He made three movies of the bullring of which *The Bullfighter and the Lady* (Rep 1951) was the first. As expected, the scenes with cape and sword are rich in detail and the 'doubling' is excellently done. Outside the ring (of truth), the story is pure Hollywood bull. An American (Robert Stack) on holiday in Mexico becomes fascinated by bullfighting and persuades the country's leading matador (Gilbert Roland) to teach him. He is saved from death in the ring by Roland who is himself killed. During a benefit performance for the widow (Katy Jurado), the American wins the crowd over to his side with a magnificent display. Joy

Page is the lady of the title. John Wayne produced and his friend John Ford was said to have done much of the editing.

One of the three inter-related stories in *Sombrero* (MGM 1953) tells of a gypsy torero who believes he will only be safe from the bulls while his sister (Cyd Charisse) remains 'pure as an angel'. Hollywood movies set in Mexico like to go in for a kind of ersatz poetic Spanish. She has lived 'all her life in the cities where the bull is killed'. The matador 'flees the black bull of death every Sunday'. As her macho matador brother objects to a love match, Charisse gets an old gypsy women to make an effigy of him. Just as he is about to kill the bull, she puts a pin through the heart of the doll and the bull runs him through. Most of *Sombrero* is pretty old hat.

Unlike Budd Boetticher's first bullfighting picture, *The Magnificent Matador* (TCF 1955. *The Brave and the Beautiful* — GB) had Cinemascope and De Luxe Color. Anthony Quinn is the great Mexican matador with problems. He has been selected to train an 18-year-old boy (Manuel Rojas) to become a fully-fledged matador, but he's very worried for the youngster. Quinn spends a good deal of time praying to Our Lady for guidance. Instead of showing up at the bullring for Rojas' debut, he takes to the hills because 'the fear is eating him'. There he holes up with rich American Maureen O'Hara who suspects he's a coward. (What gives between him and the young matador?) All is soon revealed. Rojas is his illegitimate son. Quinn rushes back, tells the boy (who knew all along) and the following Sunday, father and son go into the ring and slay some bulls together, encouraged by Miss O'Hara. Boetticher said more about dignity and courage in the small-scale Westerns he made with Randolph Scott.

In *The Brave One* (RKO-UI 1956), a brave bull lets itself be hugged and slobbered over by a Mexican kid. The boy loves the bull so much that he goes to see the President of Mexico to ask him to reprieve the animal before it is thrown into the ring again. Kindness to animals is often cruelty to audiences. This sentimental story was directed by Irving Rapper and

Overleaf: Bruce Lee in *The Chinese Connection*

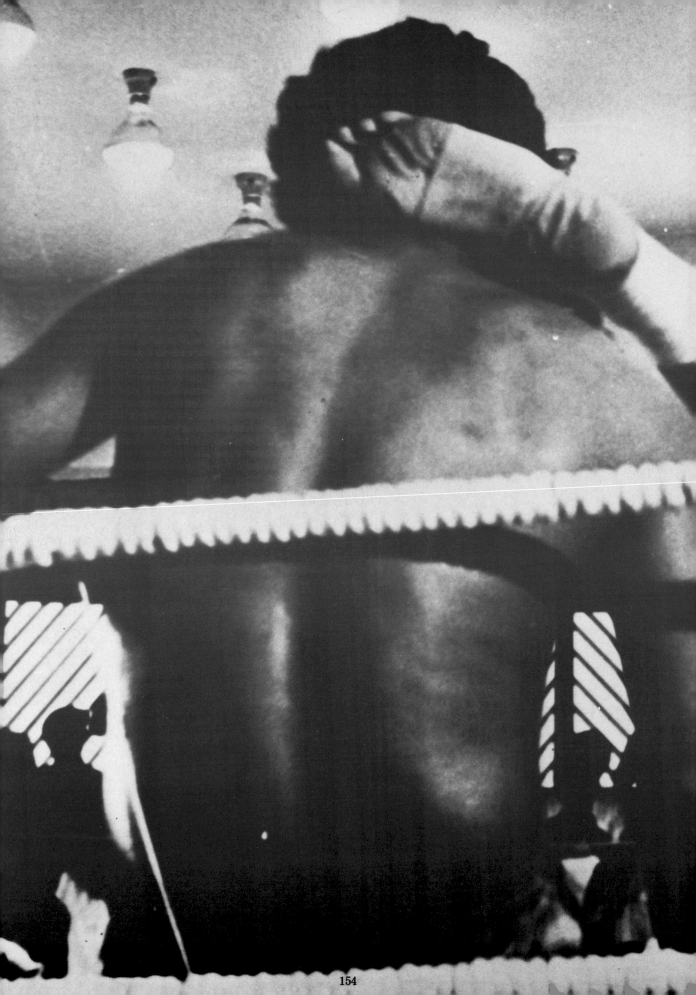

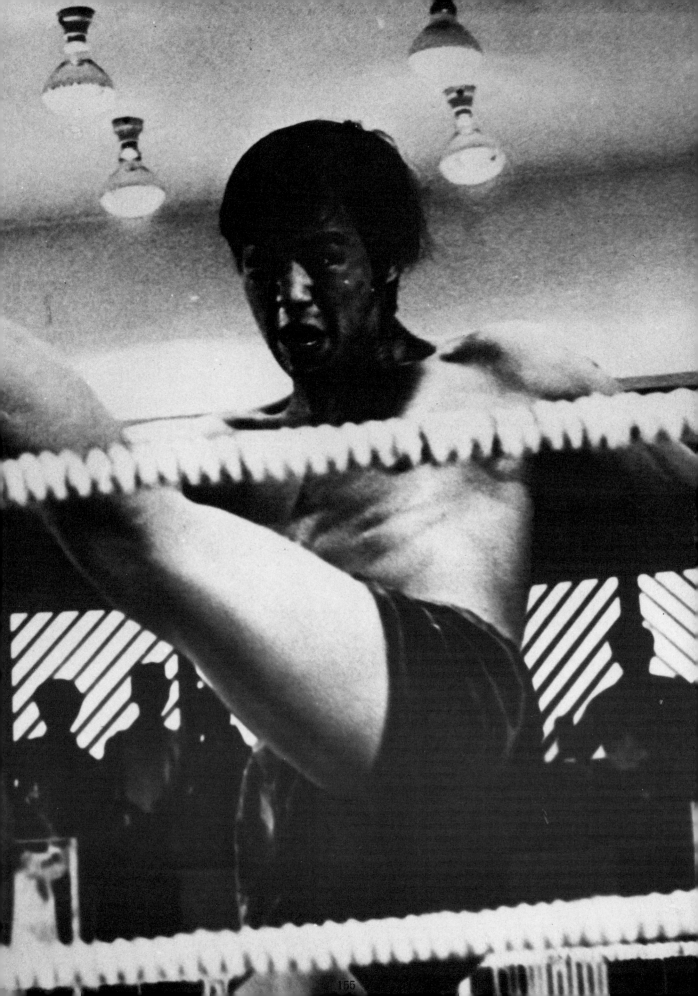

photographed in color and CinemaScope by Jack Cardiff.

Every aspect of the blood-and-sand sport is shown in the documentary, *The Bullfight* (Janus Films 1956) written and directed by Pierre Braunberger. There is footage of bull-fighting before World War I when the picador's horses were unpadded, famous matadors in action, the raising of bulls, the ritual preparations for the corrida and plenty of lingering shots of swords being driven into flesh. There is something almost porno-graphic about the repetitious parade of dying bulls. After all, the spectators at the bull-ring see only three or four die of an afternoon and never in slow-motion.

Cantinflas, the Mexican clown, reenacted his famous burlesque of bullfighting which he had often done in Mexican films, for the Spanish sequence in *Around the World in 80 Days* (Mike Todd Prod. 1956). *The Sun Also Rises* (TCF 1957) seemed 80 days long. Tyrone Power, Ava Gardner, Mel Ferrer, Errol Flynn, Eddie Albert and Juliette Greco as members of the 'lost generation', move from Paris to Pamplona in this sprawling and shallow version of Hemingway's novel. Half of it could have been extracted to make a boring travelogue to accompany the boring main feature. Robert Evans is quite striking as Romero, the young bull-fighter who causes Ava's heart to flutter. It was directed by Henry King and written by Peter Viertel. What they did to Hemingway, the matador did to the bull.

'I wouldn't hurt any animal,' says Tommy Steele in *Tommy the Toreador* (WB Pathe 1960), but he is stranded in Spain and needs money to get back to Blighty so he becomes a tore-ador. He thinks he is to face an old, tame bull, but instead the most ferocious bull in Spain has been substituted. Sid James and Bernard Cribbens play unlikely Spaniards and Tommy sings his hit song, 'Li'l White Bull'. John Paddy Car-stairs directed this pathetic cockney-and-bull story.

The Moment of Truth (AS Films Madrid 1965) is con-sidered by many to be one of the greatest of all bullfighting movies. Made by the Italian director Francesco Rosi, it features one of Spain's most famous matadors, Miguel Mateo Miguelin. Filmed in a semi-documentary style, it unrelentingly shows the slaughtering of the bulls in a sacrificial ceremony to ap-pease a savage god. Between the killings of the death-defying bulls, there is a story of how a peasant boy (Miguelin) from Andalucia comes to Barcelona, becomes a bull-fighter and dies in the ring.

Peter Sellers dies the death in a booboo called *The Bobo* (WB 1967) in which he plays a matador who dreams of becom-ing a singer. Another disaster was *The Caper of the Golden Bulls* (Embassy Pictures 1967) filmed on location in Pamploma during the running of the bulls. A gang plan a bank heist while most of the male population are being pursued from pen to arena. Like the streets the day after, there's a lot of bull-shit on the way. Stephen Boyd, Yvette Mimieux and Walter Slezack were deep in it.

During the making of *The Magnificent Matador*, the great Mexican bullfighter Carlos Arruza was gored, leav-ing his one arm 6″ shorter than the other. Bud Boetticher, who directed the previous movie, made a documentary tracing the career of the bullfighter en-titled simply *Arruza* (Avco-Embassy 1968). Arruza began fighting at the age of 13 and by 1945, in his 20s, he was one of the best in the world, giving his name to the pass called the ar-rucina. This consists of holding the cape between the legs and exposing one's whole body to the charging bull, controlling it with only a fraction of the cape. Narrated by Anthony Quinn, for whom Arruza doubled in *The Magnificent Matador*, it is a fascinating document for affi-cianados.

Kung Fu

'Uhhhhhhhhh!'
— Bruce Lee in *Enter the Dragon* (WB 1973)

Kung Fu or 'chop-socky' movies consist mainly of a series of brilliantly choreo-graphed fights accompanied by shrieks and groans, in which one man or woman faces superior numbers, usually armed with knives or clubs, and defeats them by delivering deadly blows with his or her feet and hands. The plots are simple good versus evil affairs which even the most illiterate spectator could follow. The popularity of Kung Fu movies ('Kung Fu' simply means tech-nique or skill) grew in the early seventies, breaking box-office records all over the world. This trend derived from various sources. The discovery of Zen among the young, the star presence of Bruce Lee and the beastly beauty of his brutal ballets and merely the kicks audiences got out of kicks.

Some selected Kung Fu movies

Five Fingers of Death (Shaw Bros. released by WB 1971. AKA *King Boxer*) belonged to Lo Lieh fighting his way to become Kung Fu champion of all China. At times he has to pit his strength against 20 armed villains. Many of the high leaps were created by off-camera trampolines. *Lady Kung Fu* (Golden Harvest 1971. AKA *Hap Ki Do*) was the name given to Angela Mao, a martial arts expert expelled from Korea for resisting the Japanese oc-cupiers in 1934. She returns to China to set up a school to teach ki do to others. (Hap ki do or Aikido used the attacker's energy against himself.) A neighboring school run by Japanese attacks them. *Billy Jack* (WB 1971) played by Tom Laughlin is a half-breed in search of peace who, with the help of an idealistic school-teacher Delores Taylor (Laughlin's real life wife) fights bigotry in a South-Western town with his integrity and karate chops. Written by Mr and Mrs Laughlin (under aliases) and directed by Tom Laughlin (under the name of T.C. Frank), it became not only big box-office but a cult. It in-spired two sequels, *The Trial of Billy Jack* (1974) and *Billy Jack Goes to Washington* (1977).

Bruce Lee's reputation was based on only 4 films. He ap-peared briefly and effectively in *Marlowe* (1969) in which he smashed up James Garner's of-fice. Garner provokes him to a fatal leap by remarking, 'You're light on your feet — maybe just a little bit gay?'. *Fists of Fury* (Golden Harvest 1971 AKA *The Big Boss*) gave Bruce Lee his first starring role. He plays a country boy who comes to the big city to work in an ice factory. He discovers that it's a front for heroin smuggling and defeats a gang armed with knives, chains and sticks by using his lethal hands and feet. Directed and written by Lo Wei. *The Chinese Connection* (Golden Harvest 1972 AKA *Fist of Fury*) is set in Shanghai in 1938. Bruce Lee plays a member of a martial arts school fighting against Japanese oppression. His 'singing rod of death' is ef-fective against Japanese sword play. Lo Wei wrote and directed again. *Return of the Dragon* (Golden Harvest 1972 AKA *Way of the Dragon*) was written and directed by Bruce Lee himself. Lee comes to Rome from Hong Kong to de-fend a friend's Chinese res-taurant from a gang. There is a fight in the Colosseum bet-ween himself and Chuck Nor-ris (7 times World Karate Champion). Lee introduced an element of intentional comedy missing from previous 'chop-sockies'. *Enter the Dragon* (WB 1973) was Bruce Lee's last completed film before his mys-terious death at the age of 32. At Lee's side in his efforts to break up a gang of white slavers and drug smugglers, were John Saxon (Master of Tai Chi Chuan) and Jim Kelly (Karate Champion). They manage to free hundreds of prisoners from a fortress on a Chinese island over which the evil Han (Shih Kien) holds sway. Directed by Robert Clouse, it was given the Holly-wood treatment and made thousands of dollars for War-ner Bros.

Parallel to the popularity of the Chinese movies were the 'Superspade' movies, part of a trend that included *Blacula* (1972) and *Shaft* (1972). *Cleopatra Jones* (WB 1973) was played by the splendid 6′2″ Tamara Dobson, a black female Government agent on the track of dope peddlars and Shelley Winters in particular. *Black Belt Jones* (WB 1972) cast Jim Kelly, after his suc-cess in *Enter the Dragon*, over-throwing a group of mafiosi who had tried to requisition a karate school building for real-estate purposes. He is helped by Gloria Hendry. *Black Sam-pson* (WB 1974) was the nick-name given to a bartender (Rockne Tarkington) who uses the Japanese art of Kindo to rid his street of dope-peddlars and rescue his kidnapped girl-friend (Connie Strickland). *Cleopatra Jones and the*

Casino of Gold (WB 1975) opposed Tamara Dobson and The Dragon Lady (Stella Stevens) in a tale of espionage and drug smuggling. *Hot Potato* (WB 1976) starred Jim Kelly as a martial arts master rescuing a US senator's daughter from a fiendish warlord in Thailand. Oscar Williams wrote and directed. *Enter the Ninja* (Col. 1981) or enter Franco Nero who goes to Manilla from Japan to protect his buddy (Alex Courtney) from a baddie (Christopher George) and assorted heavies. Nero stabs, chops, kicks and decapitates people all in a good cause. As he says at the end, 'A true Ninja doesn't kill, he eliminates and only for defensive purposes, but there are exceptions.' He winks at the camera in complicity with the audience. Menahem Golan directed. (The Ninja existed in 7th century Japan and used many martial arts techniques for protection against danger.)

Ten Pin Bowling

In Mel Brooks' celebrated comedy *The Producers* (1968), Zero Mostel hopes to make a killing by producing a floperoo. The producers of *Dreamer* (TCF 1979) must have had the same idea. Someone suggested making a movie about ten-pin bowling. And someone else must have approved it. 'I can just visualize it. A story about a guy whose dream comes true when he becomes a pro bowling ace. The climax is this big bowl-off. What will happen in the final frame? Will he get that strike?' Noel Nossek directed. Tim Matheson, Susan Blakely and Jack Warden took part.

Pool

The Hustler (TCF 1961), written, produced and directed by Robert Rossen, contradicts the theory that certain sports are more cinematic than others. The editing and the black and white CinemaScope photography (by Eugene Shuftan), make pool look as exciting as any sport on film. The low light over the table resembles the light over a boxing ring as 'Fast' Eddie Felton (Paul Newman), a pool shark, faces Minnesota Fats (Jackie Gleason) in a straight game. Nobody has beaten Fats for 15 years. The game takes place in Ames Billiard Parlor in New York and lasts 25 hours. 'That fat man moves like a dancer,' says Eddie admiringly as Fats circles the table. Eddie loses and, as the blinds are pulled back from the window and daylight streams in, he collapses from exhaustion. George C. Scott, a professional gambler watching the match, reckons that Eddie had the talent to win but not the character. Eddie has but one ambition — to get enough money together to challenge Fats again. In a bus-station, he meets Sarah (Piper Laurie), a lonely, lame girl. Although very different, they are drawn to each other and Eddie moves into her apartment. Meanwhile he hustles around small-town poolrooms and gets his thumbs broken when he out-hustles a hustler. He is then taken up by George C. Scott who alienates him from Sarah. Feeling she has lost Eddie, Sarah kills herself. Eddie scrapes up the 3000 dollars required for a return with Fats and steps into the poolroom like a gunfighter ready for the showdown. Since Sarah's suicide he has gained character and beats Fats into submission. The last words of the film are of mutual respect. 'Fat man, you shoot a great game of pool.' 'So do you, "Fast" Eddie.' Paul Newman's portrayal is perfection. He manages to suggest arrogance, vulnerability, the seedy and the romantic. All the other parts are taken expertly particularly by Piper Laurie who gives a moving and surprising performance. The poolrooms, bars, hotels, furnished rooms and diners are beautifully caught and Kenyon Hopkin's jazz score adds to the atmosphere. Jake La Motta plays a bartender. There is a moment when Paul Newman becomes lyrical about pool which could apply to any sport. 'When I'm really going, I feel like a jockey must feel. He's sitting on his horse. He's got all that speed and power underneath him. He's coming into the stretch. The pressure's on him and he knows when to let go and how much, 'cos he's got everything working for him. Timing, touch. It's a great feeling when you're right and you know you're right. All of a sudden I've got oil in my arm. Pool cue's part of me. Pool cue's got nerves in it... I feel the roll of those balls. You don't have to look. You just know. You make shots that nobody has ever made before. You play that game the way nobody's ever played it before.'

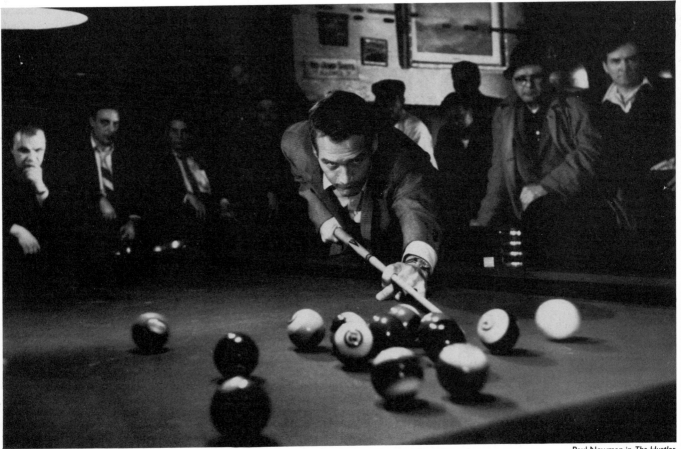

Paul Newman in *The Hustler*

INDEX